Robert L. Cord

Professor of Political Science, Northeastern University

Separation of Church and State:
Historical Fact and Current Fiction

Lambeth Press
New York

ALSO BY ROBERT L. CORD
Protest, Dissent and The Supreme Court
Political Science: An Introduction, with James A. Medeiros and
Walter S. Jones

Copyright © 1982 by Robert L. Cord
All Rights Reserved

Designed and produced by Summer House Press, Cambridge, Massachusetts, and Jean LeGuin.
Jacket design by Kate Winter of Summer House Press and Jean LeGuin.

Library of Congress Cataloging in Publication Data

Cord, Robert L.
    Separation of church and state.

    Bibliography: p.
    Includes index.
    1. Religious liberty—United States—History.
I. Title.
KF4783.C67   342.73'0852   81-20705
ISBN 0-931186-03-x 347.302852   AACR2

Lambeth Press
143 East 37th Street
New York, NY 10016

This book is dedicated to "Mom"—
Evelyn Lewis Cord, and to the
memory of the unique young man
she has always loved.

Contents

Foreword

The First Amendment has become less a safeguard against religion than a religion in itself. A fevered and imaginative exegesis has labored to distill from it an entire way of life; one in which prayer is excluded from public schools and private schools are pressed into marginality.

A familiar way of life, sure enough; but it takes some imagination to suppose that a revenant James Madison would nod his approval to it. There is always the argument that this is what we signed up for when we ratified the Constitution, whether we realized it or not; except that those who argue thus do not welcome any impulse to amend the First Amendment itself. Clearly we face something more than a merely legalistic disposition to deduce inexorable conclusions, however unwelcome, from arbitrary premises. Professor Cord, while maintaining a scholarly equilibrium, understands this, whence the deeper significance of a book that might otherwise go into service merely as historical constitutional revisionism, though that much is certainly important, and that much he has clearly, brilliantly, and definitively accomplished.

The phrase "First Amendment" has acquired an incantatory power wholly independent of its historical provenance, or even its plain language. In liberal rhetoric it represents the center of gravity of the entire Constitution. What we are up against, in both the academy and the judiciary, is a felt disappointment that the American Revolultion was not the French Revolution, and a consequent attempt to Jacobinize the Constitution until religion and its influence are wholly banished from our public life.

Is this what the First Amendment means? Is this what it meant to those who composed and ratified it? The first question is problematical; the second, merely historical. Professor Robert L. Cord, a recognized Constitutional scholar, addresses himself, compellingly, to the second. He shatters the secularist anachronism, then pulverizes the fragments, demolishing beyond recovery the thesis of Professor Leo Pfeffer, adopted by pretty much the last few Supreme Court majorities, that the Framers of the Constitution meant not only to avoid a religious establishment, but virtually to establish unadulterated secularism as our operative national creed.

Professor Cord shows that the Framers intended nothing of the kind. In doing this, he deprives the secularists of their historical pedigree, leaving them exposed as mere ideologues. They may continue to campaign for their predilections; they can no longer affect to be elaborating refined corollaries of our original political compact.

Is it possible that even the enemies of our original tradition find it necessary to believe that the tradition is, at bottom, on their side? Can it be that they would feel their position to be untenable on its own merits, without the patriarchal warranty of the Constitution's Framers? Perhaps. But if so, Professor Cord is dealing them a grievous scholarly blow, demonstrating as he does, through the careful adduction of evidence, that the American polity was at its inception, overwhelmingly and unself-consciously partial to religion, and (of course) especially to the Christian faith.

Professor Cord appeals to the words and deeds of the generation that composed, adopted, and above all implemented the Constitution, there being no better test of meaning and intention than the ingenuous behavior of people who suppose themselves to be executing the mandate they themselves have set down. The generation of the Constitution appointed chaplains to Congress; passed the Northwest Ordinance to foster the spread of religion, among other good things; and tolerated religious establishments within the several states.

But the record of the founding generation is only half the story. The other half is the modern imposition of foreign meanings onto the constitutional texts. Here Professor Cord carefully traces the development of willful misprision, showing, without polemics, the infusion of ideological novelties into judicial interpretation. In the end he establishes, beyond a reasonable doubt, that the Establishment Clause of the First Amendment of Justice Black and his colleagues and successors is no kin to the Establishment Clause that was ratified in 1791, and that they have relied on twisted scholarship (adding a few twists of their own) to make it appear otherwise.

Perhaps the most startling passages in a startling book are those in which Professor Cord shows that the extreme separationists have misconstrued some of the very texts on which they have relied most: principally, James Madison's "Memorial and Remonstrance Against Religious Assessments, 1785," and Jefferson's famous words concerning "a wall of separation between Church and State." We learn, for instance, that Madison, in the very year of his "Memorial and Remonstrance" introduced in the Virginia

Assembly a bill providing for punishing "Sabbath breakers." The hard separationist position can always be saved by simply accusing these men of inconsistency. We learn, too, that in 1803, "President Jefferson asked the Senate to ratify a treaty [with the Kaskaskia Indians—a tribe recently converted to Catholicism] in which one of the conditions was the use of federal money to support a Catholic priest in his priestly duties, and further to provide money to build a church." The facts simply do not accord with the hard separationist position; but they are perfectly consistent with a moderate separationism, under which the state may choose to use sectarian means to accomplish secular ends as long as it refrains from the assumption of ecclesiastical authority or sectarian partisanship. And it is precisely this moderate separationism which, as Professor Cord shows, the First Amendment was universally intended, and taken, to embody. Using this moderate separationist approach embraced by the First Amendment's Framers, Professor Cord convincingly argues that many church-state questions of recent vintage have been erroneously classified as constitutional issues rather than simply public policy questions. Such judicial pre-emption of democratic debate and discussion, he warns, bodes ill for the American political process.

It may be possible to ignore the profound work of Professor Cord. But for those who care to confront the evidence, there can be little doubt that the Establishment Clause of the First Amendment was never intended to be a charter for the totally secularized society. It was, quite simply, a specification of certain limits on Federal authority. The point is that the answers offered by modern secularizers fail to meet the test of the very history they appeal to. Justice William O. Douglas was content to explain away much of that history by averring that the Framers themselves had begun violating the First Amendment before the ink was dry—even such an expedient being preferable to confessing that his generation of jurists was creating an Amendment that had never before existed.

Eric Voegelin has written profoundly of the modern "taboo on theory," which is to say, on the fullest discussion of the whole realm of being, including the being of God. It is ironic that the First Amendment, so often invoked as the bulwark of free discussion, should have been turned into an instrument for excluding consideration of ultimate truths from public education and, more recently, even from public policy deliberations. But that is what has happened, and that is what makes Professor Cord's recovery of historical meaning so urgently pertinent for anyone who cares about the health of the American polity.

William F. Buckley, Jr.

Preface

Separation of Church and State is probably the most distinctive concept that the American constitutional system has contributed to the body of political ideas. In 1791, when the First Amendment's prohibition that "Congress shall make no law respecting an establishment of religion," was added to the United States *Constitution*, no other country had provided so carefully to prevent the combination of the power of religion with the power of the national government.

Today, perhaps as never before in our nation's history, is the meaning of this distinctive American constitutional doctrine hotly debated. Cases involving the constitutionality of prayers or Bible reading in the public schools, tax exemption for church property, Sunday closing laws, and tuition tax credits for parents who send their children to private church schools—to mention just a few—have inevitably found their way to the nation's highest judicial tribunal—the United States Supreme Court.

Although the First Amendment was added to the *Constitution* in 1791, it was not until 1947, in *Everson* v. *Board of Education*, that the Supreme Court comprehensively defined what the constitutional separation of Church and State meant. In 1947, the U.S. Supreme Court ruled essentially that the First Amendment had erected a "high and impregnable" wall between Church and State. The Court's decision cited carefully selected historical instances and documents to justify its broad interpretation of the separation of Church and State required by the *Constitution*. During the third of a century following the *Everson* decision, the Supreme Court has invariably continued to use an historical analysis to support its many decisions in "Church-State" cases. So have the lower courts of the land.

In this book, with the use of mostly primary historical documents, I show conclusively that the United States Supreme Court has erred in its interpretation of the First Amendment. The facts within this study prove beyond reasonable doubt that no "high and impregnable" wall between Church and State was in historical fact erected by the First Amendment nor was one intended by the Framers of that Amendment. Certainly the Framers of the First Amendment believed in separation of Church and State, but, it is clearly evident from my research and analysis in this study that they thought that constitutional separation meant something much different than what the Supreme Court has been saying in most of its Church-State decisions for more than three decades.

The documented public actions of the Framers of the First Amendment, including James Madison, and those of our early Presidents and Congresses indicate that the constitutional doctrine of separation of Church and State to them meant that no national religion was to be instituted by the Federal Government; nor was any religion, religious sect, or religious tradition to be placed in a legally preferred position. It is not surprising then, that the non-discriminatory use by government of religious institutions—such as schools—to accomplish goals within the government's authority was not considered by the Founding Fathers a violation of the *Constitution*. No matter what the Supreme Court, and some prominent constitutional scholars, have written to the contrary, the facts show that Washington, John Adams, Jefferson, Madison and their Congresses, all used, in one way or another, what they viewed as nonpreferential sectarian means to reach secular governmental ends.

While this study establishes that all governmental association with religion is not necessarily a violation of the First Amendment, it should not be interpreted as a brief to support such involvement where it is constitutional. It is not my intent or purpose to comment here on the wisdom or folly of such policy decisions—only their constitutionality. The value judgment as to whether government involvement with religion, where constitutional, is prudent public policy, I leave to the elected representatives of the people, and ultimately to the electorate to whom they are accountable.

Throughout the research and the writing of this book I have incurred many debts. Gratitude is owed to the staff of the Government Documents Section of the Boston Public Library, Widener and Lamont Libraries at Harvard University, and the libraries of Northeastern University. Special thanks is due Frank S.H. Bae, Librarian and Professor of Law, New England School of Law; Ronald E. Swerczek, Archivist, the Diplomatic Branch, and George Perros, Archivist, the Legislative and Natural Resources Branch, of the National Archives, Washington, D.C.; and

Charlene N. Bickford and Constance Bartlett Schulz, Associate Editors, The Documentary History of the First Federal Congress, George Washington University.

Many academic colleagues and friends read parts or all of the manuscript in its various stages providing probing feedback and useful suggestions. Appreciation is especially owed Professors Robert W. Hallgring, Irene A. Nichols, Raymond H. Robinson, Northeastern University, Professor Michael O. Sawyer, The Maxwell School at Syracuse University, and Dr. David Brudnoy. Always I remain indebted to Professors Marguerite J. Fisher and Stuart Gerry Brown.

Three young scholars deserve a unique tribute. At different developmental stages of the project, my junior colleagues Louis J. Rogers, Keith Dubanevich, and Raymond B. Ludwiszewski provided much aid in researching the materials and creativity in discussing the ideas developed herein. They were always a source of inspiration and intellectual fairness. For all of this, to each of them, I am and shall always be grateful.

Lastly, I am indebted to my family and friends for putting up with me during the research and writing phase of the book. None, however, deserves more credit than Richard A. Newman of Lambeth Press, who stimulated my twenty-year latent interest in the American constitutional doctrine of separation of Church and State. To a great degree, this book is as much his as it is mine.

ROBERT L. CORD
BOSTON, MASSACHUSETTS

Separation of Church and State:
Historical Fact and Current Fiction

Chapter One

The Genesis
Of the Establishment
Of Religion Clause

The story of the settlement of the New World in the early seventeenth century provides much of the historical background from which flowed the great guarantees of freedom of religion expressed in the First Amendment. A little more than a century before the first settlement appeared at Jamestown, the unity of the Western Christian world had been destroyed by the inception of the Protestant Reformation. The great nations of western Europe had become internally divided owing to the allegiances of different princes to different Christian codes. Many national schisms were resolved forcefully by the institution of established religions and the suppression of minority sects. Generally the reigning monarch's faith became the established faith of the state. Because of the vast political power held by the German princes or electors, the established religion in each province of the Holy Roman Empire was determined by the ruling elector.

A great many of the early American settlements were formed by dissident religious minorities fleeing from the Protestant establishments of England, Ireland, and Scotland. Paradoxically many Europeans who fled to the New World to escape established religion agreed that Church and State should be combined in their new settlements. With few exceptions, those who fled religious persecution were no more tolerant of religious dissenters than were those from whom they had fled. Thus, established churches became the order of the day in early America.[1]

1. For a general discussion of the early development of religious establishments in the North American Colonies, see Anson Phelps Stokes and Leo Pfeffer, *Church and State in the United States*, rev. ed. in 1 vol. (New York: Harper and Row, 1964), chap. 1, pp. 3–29; and Leo Pfeffer, *Church, State, and Freedom*, rev. ed. (Boston: Beacon Press, 1967), chap. 3, pp. 71–90.

At the outbreak of the American Revolution in 1775, there were established churches in nine of the thirteen colonies.[2] The Anglican Church had been established in Virginia in 1609, in New York's lower counties in 1693, in Maryland in 1702, in South Carolina in 1706, in North Carolina nominally in 1711, and in Georgia in 1758.[3] The Congregational Church was established in Massachusetts, Connecticut, and New Hampshire.[4] By the time that the Constitutional Convention assembled in Philadelphia in the summer of 1787, however, only Georgia, South Carolina, Connecticut, Massachusetts, and New Hampshire had retained their religious establishments.[5] The Anglican Church had been disestablished in Virginia in 1786, and in New York, Maryland, and North Carolina during the Revolutionary War.[6] The elimination of established churches in the several States continued after the ratification of the Federal *Constitution* in 1788 and culminated in the disestablishment of the Congregational Church in Connecticut in 1818,[7] in New Hampshire in 1819,[8] and in Massachusetts in 1833.[9]

For those in the new United States who were concerned about the union of Church and State at the level of the national government the activities of James Madison and Thomas Jefferson in disestablishing the Anglican Church in Virginia provided a useful legacy. Madison's "Memorial and Remonstrance Against Religious Assessments," written in 1785 in opposition to the use of Virginia's public funds to pay teachers of the Christian religion,[10] and Jefferson's "Bill for Establishing Religious Freedom" in

2. Stokes and Pfeffer, *Church and State*, pp. 36–37.

3. Richard B. Morris, ed., *The Encyclopedia of American History*, Bicentennial ed. (New York: Harper and Row, 1976), p. 820.

4. Stokes and Pfeffer, *Church and State*, p. 37.

5. Morris, *The Encyclopedia of American History*, p. 824.

6. Ibid., p. 824; and Samuel Eliot Morison, *The Oxford History of the American People* (New York: Oxford University Press, 1965), p. 293. There is disagreement as to when Maryland, Georgia, and South Carolina disestablished the Anglican Church. Stokes and Pfeffer (p. 37) claim that these States continued their establishments through 1787, while Morison (p. 293) claims

that the Anglican Church was disestablished in "Maryland and the Carolinas" during the war. Morris (p. 820) has the Georgia establishment abolished in 1789, while Stokes and Pfeffer (p. 37) have it ended during the war. These discrepancies may be due to different criteria used to make the judgment as to when disestablishment was accomplished.

7. Morris, *The Encyclopedia of American History*, p. 824.

8. William H. Harris and Judith S. Levey, eds., *The New Columbia Encyclopedia* (New York: Columbia University Press, 1975), p. 1922.

9. Morris, *The Encyclopedia of American History*, p. 824.

10. Saul K. Padover, ed., *The Complete Madison* (New York: Harper and Brothers, 1953), pp. 299–306.

Virginia, proposed in 1779 and enacted in 1786,[11] were immensely important documents to disestablishmentarians who urged the separation of Church and State. Both documents would be invoked more than 150 years later when in 1947 the United States Supreme Court first comprehensively interpreted the "Establishment of Religion" Clause of the First Amendment.[12]

The religious guarantees of the First Amendment to the *U.S. Constitution* provide that: "Congress shall make no law respecting *an establishment of religion* or prohibiting the free exercise thereof;..."[13] The Amendment as written expresses two distinct constraints on the federal state's involvement in religion—one concerns religious establishments and the other the individual's free exercise of religion. The thesis advanced here is that placed in their historical context—with due consideration to the *words and actions* of the initial framers of this Amendment, to the Congress that proposed it to the States, to the States that made it part of the *Constitution*, and to the United States Government bound by it—the two religious prohibitions of the First Amendment were designed to establish a separation of Church and the national State. This separation was to be ensured by denying to Congress the constitutional authority to pass legislation providing for the formal and legal union of any single church, religion, or sect with the Federal Government. Thus the preferential status of one church, religion, or sect—elevating it to an exclusive governmental position of power and favor over all other churches or religious denominations—would be prevented. In addition, this concept of separation of Church and the national State would constitutionally prohibit Congress from interfering with any individual's religious convictions. Consequently the separation of Church and the national State envisioned by the adopters of the First Amendment would leave the matter of religious establishments or disestablishment to the wisdom of the several States.

The words that the First Congress eventually shaped into the First Amendment and its "Establishment" Clause were proposed by James Madison in the House of Representatives on June 8, 1789.[14] Madison—

---

11. Saul K. Padover, ed., *The Complete Jefferson* (Freeport, New York: Books for Libraries Press, 1969), pp. 946–49.

12. *Everson v. Board of Education*, 330 U.S. 1 (1947).

13. This Amendment, passed by Congress on September 25, 1789 and ratified by three-fourths of the States, went into effect December 15, 1791. Emphasis added.

14. *Annals of the Congress of the United States, The Debates and Proceedings in the Congress of the United States*, Vol. I, Compiled from Authentic Materials, By Joseph Gales, Senior (Washington: Gales and Seaton, 1834), p. 434; hereafter referred to as *Annals of the Congress*.

fully aware that several States had ratified the new *Constitution* with the understanding that a series of Constitutional amendments would safeguard certain human rights from encroachment by the national government—called upon the First House of Representatives to act with swiftness tempered by reasonable care. Madison feared that undue delay in proposing that a "Bill of Rights" be added to the recently adopted *Constitution* might lower the credibility of the new central government. Referring to the unenthusiastic constitutional ratification of several States, he told his colleagues in the First House of Representatives that their constituents

> . . . may think we are not sincere in our desire to incorporate such amendments in the Constitution as will secure those rights, which they consider as not sufficiently guarded. The applications for amendments come from a very respectable number of our constituents, and it is certainly proper for Congress to consider the subject, in order to quiet that anxiety which prevails in the public mind. Indeed, I think it would have been of advantage to the Government if it had been practicable to have made some propositions for amendments the first business we entered upon; it would have stifled the voice of complaint, and made friends of many who doubted the merits of the Constitution. Our future measures would then have been more generally agreeably supported; but the justifiable anxiety to put the Government into operation prevented that; it therefore remains for us to take it up as soon as possible. I wish then to commence the consideration at the present moment; I hold it to be my duty to unfold my ideas, and explain myself to the House in some form or other without delay. I only wish to introduce the great work, and, as I said before, I do not expect it will be decided immediately; but if some step is taken in the business, it will give reason to believe that we may come to a final result. This will inspire a reasonable hope in the advocates for amendments, that full justice will be done to the important subject; and I have reason to believe their expectation will not be defeated. . . .[15]

Although several of the State Ratifying Conventions urged the protection of diverse individual rights, amendments guaranteeing freedom of religion were commonly suggested. These suggestions clearly indicated that the States wanted to prevent the establishment of a national religion or the elevation of a particular religious sect to preferred status as well as to prohibit interference by the national government with an individual's freedom of religious belief. For example, the Maryland Ratifying Convention proposed an amendment stating: "That there be *no national religion established by law*; but that all persons be equally entitled to protection in their

15. Ibid., p. 427.

religious liberty."[16] The Virginia Ratifying Convention proposed a "Declaration or Bill of Rights" as amendments to the *Constitution*, of which Article Twenty (adopted on June 27, 1788) stated:

> That religion, or the duty which we owe to our Creator, and the manner of discharging it, can be directed only by reason and conviction, not by force or violence; and therefore all men have an equal, natural, and unalienable right to the free exercise of religion, according to the dictates of conscience, and that *no particular religious sect or society ought to be favored or established, by law, in preference to others.*[17]

The New York Convention similarly declared:

> That the people have an equal, natural, and unalienable right freely and peaceably to exercise their religion, according to the dictates of conscience; and that *no religious sect or society ought to be favored or established by law in preference to others.*[18]

Resolutions passed by the North Carolina and Rhode Island Conventions echoed Virginia's "Bill of Rights."[19]

Madison's original wording of the Establishment of Religion Clause also supports my thesis concerning the separation of Church and the national State: "The Civil rights of none shall be abridged on account of religious belief or worship, *nor shall any national religion be established*, nor shall the full and equal rights of Conscience be in any manner, or on any pretext, infringed."[20] After the lengthy discussion the House essentially referred Madison's religious proposals—and all of the many other prohibitions restricting the national government that he sought to be put into the *Constitution*—to a "Committee of the Whole on the state of the Union."[21] Ultimately on July 21, the House of Representatives voted to establish a Select Committee empowered to consider the subject of Madison's proposed constitutional amendments and to report back to the full House.[22] Madison was appointed one of the Committee's members.[23]

---

16. Jonathan Elliott, *Debates on the Federal Constitution*, Vol. II (Philadelphia: J.B. Lippincott Co., 1901), p. 553. Emphasis added.

17. Ibid., Vol. III, p. 659. Emphasis added.

18. Ibid., Vol. I, p.328. Emphasis added.

19. Ibid., Vol. I, p. 334; Vol. IV, p. 244.

20. *Annals of the Congress*, Vol. I, p. 434. Emphasis added.

21. Ibid., Vol. I, p. 450.

22. Ibid., pp. 664–5.

23. Ibid., p. 665. The other members of the House appointed to the Select Committee were Messrs. Vining, Baldwin, Sherman, Burke, Gilman, Clymer, Benson, Goodhue, Boudinot and Gale.

Interestingly, however, Madison believed that the religion amendment was not really necessary to prevent the Federal Government from establishing a national religion for he considered the national government to be merely one of delegated powers. In his judgment the general government could not legislate in this field since no power to establish a national religion had been delegated to it. Madison expressed this view before the Virginia Convention on June 12, 1788, prior to its ratification of the *Constitution*:

> Fortunately for this Commonwealth, a majority of the people are decidedly against *any exclusive establishment*—I believe it to be so in the other states. *There is not a shadow of right in the general government to intermeddle with religion.* Its least interference with it, would be a most flagrant usurpation. I can appeal to my uniform conduct on this subject, that I have warmly supported religious freedom. . . . The United States abound in such a variety of sects, that it is a strong security against religious persecution, and it is sufficient to authorize a conclusion, that no one sect will ever be able to outnumber or depress the rest.[24]

When one examines the texts of the resolutions offered at the State Ratifying Conventions and the original Madison draft of the Establishment Clause, it becomes obvious, on their face, that they are concerned with preventing the Federal Government from establishing a national religion or raising one religion above the others.

Another concern of the State Ratifying Conventions was to protect freedom of conscience in religious matters. This issue is also evident in Madison's draft resolution submitted to the House. On a motion by Fisher Ames of Massachusetts, the House, acting as a "Committee of the Whole," on August 20, 1789, altered Madison's draft proposal to read: "Congress shall make no law establishing religion, or to prevent the free exercise thereof, or to infringe the rights of conscience."[25] Essentially, the House adopted Ames's versions of the "Establishment" and "Free Exercise" Clauses, which were sent to the Senate where they underwent further revisions.[26]

The Senate version that initially emerged from debate on September 3, 1789, was: "Congress shall make no law establishing one religious sect or society in preference to others, or to infringe on the rights of conscience."[27]

---

24. Padover, *The Complete Madison*, p. 306. Emphasis added.

25. *Annals of the Congress*, Vol. I, p. 766.

26. For an excellent detailed report and analysis of the debates in the House and Senate regarding the Establishment Clause, see Michael J. Malbin, *Religion and Politics, The Intentions of the Authors of the First Amendment* (Washington, D.C.: American Enterprise Institute for Public Policy Research, 1978).

27. Ibid., p. 12.

By the end of the day's deliberation, however, the Senate through further amendments had changed the Clauses to read: "Congress shall make no law establishing religion, or prohibiting the free exercise thereof."[28] After further Senate debate on September 9, 1789, the Senate version which was sent back to the House ultimately read: "Congress shall make no law establishing articles of faith or a mode of worship, or prohibiting the free exercise of religion."[29]

The conference committee for the Bill of Rights included Madison and Roger Sherman of Connecticut, among others from the House, and a contingent from the Senate. The committee reported the "Establishment" and "Free Exercise" Clauses in their current form in the First Amendment: "Congress shall make no law respecting an establishment of religion, or prohibiting the free exercise thereof." This compromise language was accepted by the House on September 24, 1789, and by the Senate the following day.[30]

The words "respecting" and "establishment" are key terms in the Establishment Clause and should therefore be examined further. The word "respecting," which is synonymous with "concerning, regarding, about, anent," indicates that the First Amendment did not prohibit an establishment of religion; rather it prohibited Congress from making any law about, concerning, or regarding an establishment of religion. Since a national religious establishment did not exist at the time of the Amendment, it became unconstitutional to provide one after ratification.

As documented above, Madison took this position before the Virginia Convention on June 12, 1788. Ironically, Roger Sherman of Connecticut, when debating Madison in the House of Representatives, questioned the need for an Establishment of Religion Clause on this same Madison premise. On August 15, 1789, the debate in the House records that "Mr. Sherman thought the Amendment altogether unnecessary, inasmuch as Congress had no authority whatever delegated to them by the Constitution to make *religious establishments*; . . ."[31]

Madison's reply makes clear that some in the States feared that the "Necessary and Proper" Clause of Article I Section 8 might be used to "establish a religion."[32] Without doubt, Madison's retort to Sherman indi-

---

28. Ibid., pp. 12–13.
29. Ibid.
30. Ibid., pp. 13–14.
31. *Annals of the Congress*, Vol. I, p. 730. Emphasis added.
32. U.S. *Constitution*, Art. I Sec. 8. The last paragraph provides the Congress with the power:

To make all laws which shall be necessary and proper for carrying into execution the foregoing powers [all the enumerated powers of the Congress in Article I Section 8], and all other powers vested by this Constitution in the government of the United States, or in any department or officer thereof.

cates that at that time in his career, Madison, the initial proponent of what eventually became the Establishment Clause, took the word "establishment" to mean a governmental religion such as a state church.

> Mr. Madison said, he apprehended the meaning of the words to be, that Congress should *not establish a religion, and enforce the legal observation of it by law*, nor compel men to worship God in any manner contrary to their conscience. Whether the words are necessary or not, he did not mean to say, but they had been required by some of the State Conventions, who seemed to entertain an opinion that under the clause of the Constitution, which gave power to Congress to make all laws necessary and proper to carry into execution the Constitution, and the laws made under it, enabled them to make laws of such a nature as *might infringe the rights of conscience, and establish a national religion; to prevent these effects he presumed the amendment was intended*, and he thought it as well expressed as the nature of the language would admit.[33]

Despite the clarity, that the concern of those who framed the Establishment Clause was addressed to the possible imposition of a *single church or religion* by the Federal Congress, an argument still noted and/or advanced by some scholars is that the European model of a constitutional single established religion *was not* what was feared by the "Fathers" of the First Amendment. This argument has been succintly summarized as follows:

> The phrase "establishment of religion" must be given the meaning that it had in the United States in 1791, rather than its European connotation. In America there was no establishment of a single church, as in England. Four states had never adopted any establishment practices. Three had abolished their establishments during the Revolution. The remaining six states—Massachusetts, New Hampshire, Connecticut, Maryland, South Carolina, and Georgia—changed to comprehensive or "multiple" establishments. That is, aid was provided to all churches in each state on a nonpreferential basis, except that the establishment was limited to churches of the Protestant religion in three states and to those of the Christian religion in the other three states. Since there were almost no Catholics in the first group of states, and very few Jews in any state, this meant that the multiple establishment practices included every religious group with enough members to form a church. It was this nonpreferential assistance to organized churches that constituted "establishment of relig-

33. *Annals of the Congress*, Vol. I, p. 730. Emphasis added.

ion" in 1791, and it was this practice that the Amendment forbade Congress to adopt.[34]

Assuming, but not conceding, the validity of this broad interpretative statement about American religious establishments, this pluralistic view of the concept of established religion cannot, for the following reasons, be reconciled with the historical facts that brought the Establishment Clause into existence.

First, the resolutions of the State Constitutional Ratifying Conventions from Maryland, Virginia, New York, North Carolina, and Rhode Island, understood in their historical context, all urged a constitutional amendment prohibiting *a single national religious establishment.*[35]

Second, in response to these State Ratifying Convention's requests, James Madison introduced his original draft of the Establishment Clause which on its face is clearly designed to foreclose a national religion, *not religions.*

Third, Madison's interpretation given to Roger Sherman during the House's August 15, 1789 debate as to what the House's Select Committee's Report meant (regarding its recommended prohibition "that no religion shall be established by law") indicates clearly that Madison believed Congress was being denied the power to "establish a national religion" *not religions.*[36]

Fourth, the final wording of the religious clauses of the First Amendment—"Congress shall make no law respecting an establishment of religion or prohibiting the free exercise thereof"—shows the intent to prevent a single and not some pluralistic national religious establishment. As Michael J. Malbin has noted:

> Had the framers prohibited "*the* establishment of religion," which would have emphasized the generic word "religion," there might have been some reason for thinking they wanted to prohibit all official preferences of religion over irreligion. But by choosing "an establishment" over "the establishment," they were showing that they wanted to prohibit only those official activities that tended to promote the interests of one or another particular sect.

34. C. Herman Pritchett, *The American Constitution*, 3rd ed. (New York: McGraw-Hill; 1977), p. 401. This pluralistic interpretation of American "established churches" appears to be at odds with Morris, *The Encyclopedia of American History*, and Morison, *The Oxford History of the American People*, both of which indicate, that for the most part, single "establishments" existed in the States which had established churches. See also Pfeffer, *Church, State, and Freedom*, p. 73.

35. See the text at fns. 16–19, supra.

36. See the quote in the text at fn. 33, supra.

Thus, through the choice of "an" over "the," conferees indicated their intent. The First Congress did not expect the Bill of Rights to be inconsistent with the Northwest Ordinance of 1787, which the Congress reenacted in 1789. One key clause in the Ordinance explained why Congress chose to set aside some of the federal lands in the territory for schools: "Religion, morality, and knowledge," the clause read, "being necessary to good government and the happiness of mankind, schools and the means of learning shall forever be encouraged." This clause clearly implies that schools, which were to be built on federal lands with federal assistance, were expected to promote religion as well as morality. In fact, most schools at this time were church-run sectarian schools.[37]

On the basis of the resolutions from the Ratifying Conventions in Maryland, Virginia, New York, North Carolina, and Rhode Island, the original Madison text concerning religious prohibitions placed on national governmental power in the First Amendment, and Madison's own interpretation during debate in the House of Representatives of the prohibitions concerning religion, I conclude that Madison and the other supporters of these prohibitions wished to deny Congress the power to establish a national religion. Congress was to have no power to elevate by law any religion or religious sect to a preferred status, and it was barred from interfering with individual liberty of religious conscience. These limiting principles of the First Amendment are also supported by the early and widely respected scholars of the Federal *Constitution*, Joseph Story and Thomas McIntyre Cooley.[38]

An Associate Justice of the United States Supreme Court from 1811 to his death in 1845 and concurrently a professor at the Harvard Law School from 1829, Story presented in his multivolume work on the *Constitution* an authoritative statement of attitudes toward the religious prohibitions of the First Amendment during the early days of the Republic, when "flesh" was being put on the "skeleton" that was the *Constitution*. Appointed by Madison to the Supreme Court, Justice Story held substantially the same view of the religion clauses of the First Amendment as did the former President when Madison was the Amendment's initial author and champion in the House debates. Story's *Commentaries* saw the First Amendment as prohibitive of a Federal establishment of a national Church or the official preference of a particular religion or religious sect, but not hostile to the encouragement of religion:

37. Malbin, *Religion and Politics*, pp. 14–15.

38. "With Story, he [Cooley] ranks as the most influential commentator on the Constitution." Morris, *The Encyclopedia of American History*, p. 1005.

The real difficulty lies in ascertaining the limits to which government *may rightfully go in fostering and encouraging religion. . . .*[39]

Probably at the time of the adoption of the Constitution, and of the amendment to it now under consideration [First Amendment], the general if not the universal sentiment in America was, that Christianity ought to receive encouragement from the State so far as was not incompatible with the private rights of conscience and the freedom of religious worship. An attempt to level all religions, and to make it a matter of state policy to hold all in utter indifference, would have created universal disapprobation, if not universal indignation.[40]

The real object of the First Amendment was not to countenance, much less to advance, Mahometanism, or Judaism, or infidelity, by prostrating Christianity; *but to exclude all rivalry among Christian sects, and to prevent any national ecclesiastical establishment which should give to a hierarchy the exclusive patronage of the national government. It thus cut off the means of religious persecution (the vice and pest of former ages), and of the subversion of the rights of conscience in matters of religion* which had been trampled upon almost from the days of the Apostles to the present age. . . .[41]

Like Story, Cooley did not consider that the First Amendment, or even state constitutions mandated absolute separation of Church and State. Citing many activities by which the state was aiding religion, Cooley saw no violation of any American constitutional principle as long as the national government treated all religions equally. In *Constitutional Limitations*, first published in 1868, Cooley warned that exclusive aid to a particular religious denomination or sect without doubt is the evil precluded by the principles of the U. S. *Constitution.* Concerning relations between the Federal and State Governments and religion, he wrote:

But while thus careful to establish religious freedom and equality, *the American constitutions contain no provisions which prohibit the authorities from such solemn recognition of a superintending Providence in public transactions and exercises as the general religious sentiment of mankind inspires, and as seems meet in finite and dependent beings.* Whatever may be the shades of religious belief, all must acknowledge the

---

39. Joseph Story, *Commentaries on the Constitution of the United States*, 2nd ed., Vol. II (Boston: Charles C. Little and James Brown, 1851), Sec. 1872, p. 591. Emphasis added.

40. Ibid., Sec. 1874, p. 593.
41. Ibid., Sec. 1877, p. 594. Emphasis added.

fitness of recognizing in important human affairs the superintending care and control of the Great Governor of the Universe, and of acknowledging with thanksgiving His boundless favors, at the same time that we in contrition when visited with the penalties of His broken laws. *No principle of Constitutional law is violated* when thanksgiving or fast days are appointed; when chaplains are designated for the Army and Navy; and when legislative sessions are opened with prayer or the reading of the Scriptures, or when religious teaching is encouraged by exempting houses of religious worship from the taxation for the support of State government. *Undoubtedly the spirit of the Constitution will require, in all these cases, that care be taken to avoid discrimination in favor of any one denomination or sect; but the power to do any of these things will not be unconstitutional, simply because of being susceptible to abuse. . . .*[42]

Finally, that the First Amendment originally left the entire issue of governmental involvement in religion to the States is extremely clear. When ratified in 1788, the *Constitution* contained no prohibition against individual state religious establishments; indeed, some States that ratified the *Constitution* had such religious establishments at the time of ratification, some of which continued to exist even after ratification of the First Amendment until they were ended by the States themselves (as in the case of Massachusetts which finally did so in 1833).

Supporting this view of the constitutional independence of the States in religious matters, President Thomas Jefferson in 1808 noted:

I consider the Government of the United States as interdicted by the Constitution from meddling with religious institutions, their doctrines, discipline or exercises. This results not only from the provision that no law shall be made respecting the establishment, or free exercise, of religion, *but from that also which reserves to the States the powers not delegated to the United States.* Certainly no power to *prescribe any religious exercise, or to assume authority in religious discipline*, has been delegated to the general government. *It must then rest with the State*, as far as it can be in any human authority.[43]

Justice Story's *Commentaries on the Constitution* indicate that he also believed the First Amendment left religious establishments in the hands of the States:

42. Thomas M. Cooley, *Constitutional Limitations* (Boston: Little, Brown and Co., 1868), Chap. XIII, pp. 470–71. Emphasis added.

43. Paul L. Ford, *Life of Jefferson*, Vol. 9 (Cambridge, Mass.: A.W. Elson and Co., 1904), p. 174. Emphasis added.

It was under a solemn consciousness of the dangers from ecclesiastical ambition, the bigotry of spiritual pride, and the intolerance of sects, thus exemplified in our domestic as well as in foreign annals, *that it was deemed advisable to exclude from the national government all power to act upon the subject.* The situation, too, of the different States equally proclaimed the policy as well as the necessity of such an exclusion. In some of the States, Episcopalians constituted the predominant sect; in others, Quakers; and in others again, there was a close numerical rivalry among contending sects. It was impossible that there should not arise perpetual strife and perpetual jealousy on the subject of ecclesiastical ascendency; if the national government were left free to create a religious establishment. The only security was in extirpating the power. But this alone would have been an imperfect security, if it had not been followed up by a declaration of the right of the free exercise of religion, and a prohibition (as we have seen) of all religious tests. *Thus the whole power over the subject of religion is left exclusively to the State governments, to be acted upon according to their own sense of justice and the State Constitutions;* and the Catholic and the Protestant, the Calvinist, the Armenian, the Jew and the Infidel, may sit down at the common table of the national councils without any inquisition into their faith or mode of worship.[44]

From the above documentation, I conclude that, regarding religion, the First Amendment was intended to accomplish three purposes. First, it was intended to prevent the establishment of a national church or religion, or the giving of any religious sect or denomination a preferred status. Second, it was designed to safeguard the right of freedom of conscience in religious beliefs against invasion solely by the national Government. Third, it was so constructed in order to allow the States, unimpeded, to deal with religious establishments and aid to religious institutions as they saw fit. There appears to be no historical evidence that the First Amendment was intended to preclude Federal governmental aid to religion when it was provided on a nondiscriminatory basis. Nor does there appear to be any historical evidence that the First Amendment was intended to provide an *absolute separation or independence* of religion and the national state. The actions of the early Congresses and Presidents, in fact, suggest quite the opposite.

44. Story, *Commentaries on the Constitution*, Sec. 1879, pp. 596–97. Emphasis added. Story relies heavily on *Lloyd's Debates*, which are frequently cited, for these conclusions.

Chapter Two

Resurrecting
Madison and Jefferson

The thesis advanced in chapter one concerning a narrower interpretation of the Establishment of Religion Clause of the First Amendment has been endorsed by a number of distinguished scholars. Besides James Madison, the State ratifiers of the Federal *Constitution*, Justice Joseph Story, and Thomas Cooley in the eighteenth and nineteenth centuries, to that list can be added the names of such noted twentieth-century constitutional scholars as Edward S. Corwin and Alexander Meiklejohn.[1] Corwin's article "The Supreme Court as National School Board," draws attention to J.M. O'Neill's book *Religion and Education Under the Constitution*,[2] which Corwin calls "a devastating assault upon the *McCollum* decision"—a 1948 U.S. Supreme Court decision discussed in detail in chapter five.[3] Indeed the O'Neill book is a devastating assault not only on *McCollum* but also on the broad interpretation given to the prohibition of the Establish-

---

1. The late Edward S. Corwin was McCormick Professor of Jurisprudence, Princeton University, until his retirement in 1946. See his article, "The Supreme Court as National School Board," 14 *Law and Contemporary Problems* 3 (1949). The late Alexander Meiklejohn was most noted in the fields of logic, philosophy, and his writings on the First Amendment, among which were *Free Speech and Its Relation to Self-Government* (New York: Harper and Row, 1948), and "The First Amendment is an Absolute," Philip B. Kurland, ed., *The Supreme Court Review, 1961* (Chicago: University of Chicago Press, 1961), pp. 245–266. See his article, "Educational Cooperation between Church and State," 14 *Law and Contemporary Problems* 61 (1949).

2. (New York: Harper Brothers, 1949). O'Neill's book was more recently reprinted without change, by Da Capo Press in 1972.

3. Corwin, *Law and Contemporary Problems*, p. 14, fn. 44.

ment of Religion Clause by all the opinions in the *Everson* "Bus Case" of 1947[4]—the first case in which the United States Supreme Court advanced a comprehensive interpretation of the Establishment Clause.[5]

The meaning of the Establishment of Religion Clause developed in chapter one has been rejected as a narrow interpretation by the Supreme Court and by many prominent scholars, but none more pre-eminent in writing about the separation of Church and State, than Professor Leo Pfeffer, who has been referred to by the monthly periodical *Church and State* as "the country's leading legal expert on church-state questions. . . ."[6] Instead of embracing what he has referred to as the "narrow" interpretation of the Establishment of Religion Clause, Professor Pfeffer embraces the "broad interpretation" of the Clause agreed to by all the justices of the U.S. Supreme Court in the *Everson* "Bus Case" of 1947.[7]

The "establishment of religion" clause of the First Amendment means at least this: Neither a state nor the Federal Government can set up a church. Neither can pass laws which aid one religion, aid all religions, or prefer one religion over another. Neither can force nor influence a person to go to or to remain away from church against his will or force him to profess a belief or disbelief in any religion. No person can be punished for entertaining or professing religious beliefs or disbeliefs, for church attendance or non-attendance. No tax in any amount, large or small, can be levied to support any religious activities or institutions, whatever they may be called, or whatever form they may adopt to teach or practice religion. Neither a state nor the Federal Government can, openly or secretly, participate in the affairs of any religious organizations or groups and *vice versa*. In the words of Jefferson, the clause against establishment of religion by law was intended to erect "a wall of separation between church and State."[8]

---

4. *Everson v. Bd. of Education*, 330 U.S. 1 (1947).

5. Because it is the precedent case interpreting the Establishment Clause, the major opinions in *Everson* v. *Bd. of Education* will be analyzed in chap. five.

6. *Church and State*, Vol. 30, No. 10 (October 1977), p. 10 (202). It should be noted that Professor Pfeffer has written many books on American Constitutional Law, including *The Liberties of An American* (Boston: Beacon Press, 1956); *This Honorable Court* (Boston: Beacon Press, 1965); with Anson Phelps Stokes, *Church and State in the United States* (New York: Harper and

Row, 1950); *God, Caesar, and The Constitution* (Boston: Beacon Press, 1975); and *Church, State, and Freedom* (Boston: Beacon Press, 1953). Pfeffer has also actively participated in the litigation of more than one half of all the Establishment Clause cases decided by the United States Supreme Court since the *Everson* Case of 1947.

7. Leo Pfeffer, *Church, State, and Freedom*, rev. ed. (Boston: Beacon Press, 1967), p. 149.

8. Ibid., pp. 149–50. See Justice Black's opinion of the Court in *Everson v. Bd. of Education*, 330 U.S. 1, at 15, 16 (1947).

Pfeffer and others who share his interpretation of the Establishment Clause believe that the *intent* of the First Amendment is "not merely to prohibit the establishment of a state church but to preclude *any government aid to religious groups or dogmas*."[9] In addition, Pfeffer argues that government aid to religion, *even on a nonpreferential basis*, violates the Establishment Clause.[10] This view, that Church and State were meant to be *completely* independent and *absolutely* separate, is said to be supported by historical evidence from the careers of Jefferson and Madison and from the events and proposals that led to the formulation of the First Amendment. Approvingly, Pfeffer quotes Justice Frankfurter, "separation means separation, not something less."[11]

Despite some points of agreement, I generally disagree with Pfeffer's basic conclusions about what the Federal *Constitution* dictates in the area of Church-State relations. We disagree, for example, in our interpretations of (a) Madison's and Jefferson's views of the separation of Church and State, (b) the precise constraints of the Establishment Clause, (c) the historical facts that produced the concept of separation of Church and State found in the First Amendment, (d) the ways in which the Legislative and Executive branches of the United States Government have observed that Amendment, (e) the correctness of most of the United States Supreme Court decisions rendered under the Establishment Clause, and (f) most important, while we both recognize that the Establishment Clause of the Federal *Constitution* mandates the principle of separation of Church and State, as indicated in chapter one, we fundamentally disagree as to precisely what that constitutional separation correctly entails.

The Pfeffer school of thought—including its adherents on the United States Supreme Court—relies on historical evidence to prove the validity of its interpretation of the Establishment Clause.[12] If Pfeffer's history is faulty, then his view of the Establishment Clause may not only lack verification, it in fact may run counter to the intent and purpose of that First Amendment Clause.

It is my contention that the historical facts bear out the thesis advanced in the preceding chapter concerning a narrower interpretation of the constitutional principle of separation of Church and State. Consequently I believe that Professor Pfeffer, and those who subscribe to his views, are in error.

---

9. Pfeffer, ibid., p. 149. Emphasis added.

10. Ibid., pp. 150–55.

11. Ibid., p. 150. Frankfurter concurring, *McCollum v. Bd. of Education*, 333 U.S. 203, at 231 (1948).

12. Almost the whole of Pfeffer, *Church, State, and Freedom* substantiates this point, especially chap. 4, "The Principle is Born," pp. 91–127, and chap. 5, "The Meaning of the Principle," pp. 128–80.

Further, I maintain that the public actions of Madison, Jefferson, the Framers of the First Amendment, the early Presidents and the Congresses of the United States examined in this study document that error.

In Search of Mr. Madison

Prior to the passage of Jefferson's "Bill for Establishing Religious Freedom in Virginia," Madison had challenged an effort led by some—most notably Patrick Henry, who became Governor in 1784 and thus was removed from the legislative debate—in the Virginia Legislature to pass "A Bill establishing a provision for Teachers of the *Christian* Religion."[13] Madison attacked the pending bill in his "Memorial and Remonstrance Against Religious Assessments, 1785," with fifteen individually numbered arguments.

There is little dispute that Madison's "Memorial and Remonstrance" is one of the significant documents of American religious liberty. What is very much in dispute is what it means. To supporters of Professor Pfeffer's view the "Memorial" is cited as evidence of Madison's objection to all state aid to religion. On the other hand, as Pfeffer correctly notes, those who disagree with his view of Madison consider the "Memorial" as evidence that Madison was opposed to the Assessment Bill because *it was discriminatory*, and thus placed Christianity in a preferred religious position.[14]

In the "Memorial" Madison attacks the proposed subsidy as a discriminatory religious dole. He argues that if the Commonwealth of Virginia through its legislative power can exclusively subsidize one religion—Christianity—and thereby spread its religious dogma, then might not the legislature subsidize only one Christian sect? Madison makes this point in argument three:

> *Who does not see that the same authority which can establish Christianity, in exclusion of all other Religions, may establish with the same ease any particular sect of Christians, in exclusion of all other Sects?* That the same authority which can force a citizen to contribute three pence only of

---

13. Michael J. Malbin indicates that "Henry was elected governor in November 1784, with Jeffersonian-Madisonian support." *Religion and Politics, The Intentions of the Authors of the First Amendment* (Washington, D.C.: American Enterprise Institute for Public Policy Research, 1978),

pp. 24–25. Whether Jefferson and Madison threw their support to Henry to remove him from the legislative debate is speculative, but the "Assessment Bill" lost its most articulate supporter when Henry became governor.

14. Pfeffer, *Church, State, and Freedom*, pp. 171–72.

his property for the support of any one establishment, may force him to conform to any other establishment in all cases whatsoever?[15]

Not disputing this point Professor Pfeffer claims that of Madison's fifteen arguments, "[o]nly *this one* can be viewed as referring to the exclusive establishment of Christianity; . . ."[16] Pfeffer's evaluation is disproved, however, by Madison's very next argument, number four, which states that "the bill violates that *equality* which ought to be the basis of every law, and which is indispensable. . . ."[17] Madison further emphasizes equality of religious conscience, which the Assessment Bill would violate by placing discriminating burdens on those who do not freely embrace the religion to be exclusively subsidized:

> Whilst we assert for ourselves a freedom to embrace, to profess and to observe the Religion which we believe to be of divine origin, *we cannot deny an equal freedom to those whose minds have not yet yielded to the evidence which has convinced us.* If this freedom be abused, it is an offense against God, not against man: To God, therefore, not to man, must an account of it be rendered. As the Bill violates *equality* by subjecting some to peculiar burdens; so it violates the same principle, by granting to others peculiar exemptions. . . .[18]

In addition to these two arguments, four more in the "Memorial" discuss the dangers of giving any religion a preferred status through the use of public funds and power. Madison's seventh, ninth, eleventh, and twelfth arguments all speak, in some way, to the same intolerance, bigotry, unenlightenment, and persecution that had generally resulted from previous exclusive religious establishments.[19]

Moreover, it is suggested here that several of Madison's other "Memorial" arguments are not generally discussed by those whom Pfeffer calls "narrow" in their interpretation of the Establishment Clause because these points do not seem to be specifically germane to the fight against the passage of the Assessment Bill. Pfeffer himself notes the "emphasis" on "ideological" content in the "Memorial."[20]

Perhaps we should question to what extent the "Memorial and Remon-

---

15. Saul K. Padover, *The Complete Madison* (New York: Harper and Brothers, 1953), p. 301. Emphasis added.

16. Pfeffer, *Church, State, and Freedom*, p. 172. Emphasis added.

17. Padover, *The Complete Madison*, p. 301. Emphasis added.

18. Ibid. Emphasis added.

19. Ibid., pp. 302–4.

20. Pfeffer, *Church, State, and Freedom*, p. 113.

strance" reflects Madison's ideas about Church-State relations four years later when he introduced the clauses on religion in the First House of Representatives? It is suggested here that the "Memorial" has been blown out of proportion in understanding the Church-State views of Madison in 1789.

As Pfeffer attests, the movement to aid teachers of the Christian religion can be traced back definitely to 1779 and perhaps to 1776—the year of the "Declaration of Independence."[21] It is not surprising, then, that many of Madison's arguments in the "Memorial" of 1785 were mainly abstract ideological arguments reflecting the concepts of natural law, natural rights, and the social contract between government and a civil society. These arguments were largely influenced by Locke's writings and were circulated to justify a political revolution in the late 1770s, but they provide few concrete points or little specific language by which to limit feared governmental excesses. Pfeffer illustrates this point well. In his summation of Madison's first two arguments in the "Memorial," Pfeffer distills these arguments as follows:

(1) Religion is wholly exempt from the cognizance of Civil Society, and *in matters of religion no man's right is abridged by the institution of Civil Society, whose authority is necessarily subordinate to the individual's allegiance to the Universal Sovereign.*

(2) Since religion is exempt from the authority of the Society at large, *still less can it be subject to that of the Legislative Body* whose jurisdiction is both derivative and limited.[22]

Although Pfeffer suggests that the "Memorial" stressed among other things "the government's lack of jurisdiction over matters of religion. . . ,"[23] the meaning of "jurisdiction" can be further questioned. Was Madison arguing that government could not justly make any laws about religion, for example, against a religious practice of human sacrifice or polygamy? Could not a court as an "institution of Civil Society" be much less than "subordinate to the individual's allegiance to the Universal Sovereign" and issue an order allowing doctors to give needed blood transfusions to children of Jehovah's Witnesses when parental consent is refused?[24]

Taken literally, most of Madison's "ideological" arguments in the "Memorial" seem more derivative of the call to revolution rather than the proper yardstick against which to measure an appropriate separation between Church and State in *a real society* where both institutions must

21. Ibid., pp. 108–11.
22. Ibid., p. 112. Emphasis added.
23. Ibid., p. 113.

24. Pfeffer himself documents the unreality of his own summation, *Church, State, and Freedom*, pp. 704–5.

coexist. Interestingly the Madison of 1789 understood this as did the other Framers of the First Amendment when they fashioned the constitutional sections dictating the terms of separation between Church and the national State.

In sum, only Madison's arguments against exclusive religious aid—in which he assailed the religious discriminatory Assessment Bill and the evils it was likely to produce—are germane in appraising Madison's attitude about the appropriate relationship between Church and State. His actions in the First Congress are even more useful in understanding Mr. Madison's beliefs about this matter at the time he proposed that prohibitions regarding religious activities by the national government be added to the new *Constitution*.

One of the earliest acts of the First House of Representatives was to elect a chaplain. On Friday, May 1, 1789, "the House proceeded by ballot to the appointment of a Chaplain" and "the Rev. William Linn was elected."[25] James Madison was a member of the Congressional Committee that recommended the Chaplain system.[26] Pfeffer makes note of these facts but offers little explanation as to why his version of Mr. Madison would do this.[27] My understanding of Madison at that time in his career requires no explanation because I, unlike Pfeffer, do not think chaplains in the Congress violate the American principle of separation of Church and State as developed and documented in chapter one. Even though the First Amendment did not become part of the *Constitution* until 1791, if Madison believed in the mammoth concept of separation of Church and State that Pfeffer attributes to him, Madison would probably have objected on principle alone even before the Amendment was proposed or added to the *Constitution*. Instead Madison is not only silent on the record regarding chaplains in Congress, he was a member of the Committee that recommended the Congressional Chaplain system.

Pfeffer does attempt to explain the chaplains in Congress: "When the Continental Congress was replaced by the Congress under the Constitution, the chaplaincy continued as a matter of course,"[28] but in fact the chaplaincy

25. *The Annals of the Congress, The Debates and Proceedings in the Congress of The United States*, Vol. I, Compiled From Authentic Materials by Joseph Gales, Senior (Washington: Gales and Seaton, 1834), p. 242.

26. *Reports of Committees of the House of Representatives*, First Sess. of the Thirty-Third Congress, in three vols. (Washington:

A.O.P. Nicholson, Printer. 1854), Vol. II, House of Representatives Document 124, "Appointment of Chaplains," p. 4. The functions of chaplains in Congress will be discussed further in chap. three.

27. Pfeffer, *Church, State, and Freedom*, pp. 247–48.

28. Ibid., p. 247.

did not merely continue "as a matter of course." That is why a joint House-Senate committee was established, to discuss coordination of the selection of chaplains and the issue of denominations.[29] Further, in 1789, implementing the Committee's recommendation, Congress enacted legislation paying Congressional chaplains an annual salary of $500 out of federal funds.[30] Attempting to bolster his "matter of course" argument Pfeffer argues that since the Constitutional Convention "had neither daily prayers nor a chaplain," if the Federal Congress had succeeded the Convention instead of the Continental Congress, "*it is at least possible*" that the new Congress might have started "without benefit of chaplain or prayer."[31] If the leadership of the new nation and Congress, including Mr. Madison, were as much in favor of absolute separation of Church and State as Pfeffer's books would have us believe, why does Pfeffer discuss this point in terms of possibilities rather than probabilities? It should also be noted that the new Congress certainly did not precede the Constitutional Convention. The lack of prayer at the Constitutional Convention was an outgrowth of the concern of the delegates to the Convention about the public's response to these deliberations rather than a result of adherence to a broad concept of separation of Church and State.

Madison, the "historian" and "notetaker" at the Constitutional Convention, records that on Thursday, June 28, 1787, Dr. Benjamin Franklin, having assessed the "small progress" they had "made after four or five weeks close and continual reasoning with each other" suggested the following remedy in an address to the Convention and its President, George Washington:

> I have lived, Sir, a long time, and the longer I live, the more convincing proofs I see of this truth—*that God Governs in the affairs of men.* And if a sparrow cannot fall to ground without his notice, is it probable that an empire can rise without his aid? We have been assured, Sir, in the sacred writings, that "except the Lord build the House they labor in vain that build it." I firmly believe this; . . .
>
> I therefore beg leave to move—that henceforth prayers imploring the assistance of Heaven, and its blessings on our deliberations, be held in this

---

29. Coordination between the Houses of the Congress was a new problem because unlike the Continental Congress which was unicameral, the U.S. *Constitution* established a bicameral legislature.

30. *Reports of Committees of the House of Representatives*, Document 124, p. 4.

31. Pfeffer, *Church, State, and Freedom*, p. 247. Emphasis added.

Assembly every morning before we proceed to business, and that one or more of the Clergy of this City be requested to officiate in that Service—[32]

After the Franklin motion was seconded, "Hamilton and several others expressed their apprehensions that however proper such a resolution might have been at the beginning of the convention," it might now "lead the public to believe that the embarrassments and dissensions within the Convention, had suggested this measure."[33] Madison's notes indicate that the disagreement over the issue was resolved by adjournment without any vote taken on the issue.[34]

Clearly this record adversely affects Pfeffer's theory on chaplains in the Congress, for it is not unreasonable to conclude from Madison's notes that it was concern about public profile and *not the principle of separation of Church and State* that kept the Constitutional Convention from daily prayers and a chaplain.

Madison was not only a member of the Congressional Committee that recommended and supported the Chaplain system when he was in the First House of Representatives, but also introduced the proposals that would become the Bill of Rights. His first draft of the Establishment Clause read: "The Civil rights of none shall be abridged on account of religious belief or worship, *nor shall any national religion be established*, nor shall the full and equal rights of Conscience be in any manner, or on any pretext, infringed."[35] This version indicates that Madison was concerned not about nondiscriminatory aid to religion but rather about the establishment of a national religion by the Federal Government. In the Madison proposal the word "established" is clearly synonymous with "created," "organized," or "instituted," and this interpretation is substantiated in the subsequent debate in which Madison explained that his proposal was generated, in part, by the resolutions of several of the State Ratifying Constitutional Conventions.[36]

Despite this clarity, Pfeffer argues that it is of little value to examine the early versions of the First Amendment to determine the Congress's intentions because the early versions were altered, and thus were unacceptable to

32. "Debates In The Federal Convention of 1787 As Reported By James Madison," *Documents Illustrative of the Formation of the Union of the American States* (Washington, D.C.: Government Printing Office, 1927), pp. 295–96. Emphasis in the original.

33. Ibid., p. 296.
34. Ibid., p. 297.
35. See text in chap. one at fn. 20. Emphasis added.
36. See the text in chap. one at fns. 15–19.

the legislature.[37] Perhaps this is true. However, here the critical point is not what the Congress intended but what Mr. Madison intended, for he is one of the Framers constantly invoked by Pfeffer as well as by many U.S. Supreme Court Justices and other advocates of the broad, if not absolute, interpretation of the Establishment Clause.

Examining the original draft of Madison's proposed Establishment Clause is also important, *if not crucial*, in understanding Madison's intent, because when Madison submitted his proposal to the First House of Representatives, he had no way of knowing whether it would be amended or adopted *exactly as he wrote it*. Unless it can be seriously argued that Madison introduced a proposal that did not fully prohibit what he thought should be denied to the Federal Government in the area of religion—a proposition too ludicrous to seriously entertain—Madison's first draft of the Establishment Clause should show what he intended in the area of established religion. It is clear on the record. He did not want a national religion or religious coercion and he said so.

If any doubt about Madison's intentions on this matter still persists, Madison's own rebuttal of Roger Sherman on the House floor concerning the interpretation of the amended Establishment Clause carries the same intent.[38] Pfeffer, however, argues that this passage from the House debate is "no freer of ambiguity than the prior versions of the Amendment. . . ."[39] Nonetheless, Madison's final remark to Sherman in the House passage seems telling. After stating that he "apprehended the meaning of the words [of the House's Select Committee's final version of the Establishment Clause] to be, that Congress should not establish a religion, and enforce the legal observance of it by law, . . ." Madison concluded by saying that "he thought it was as well expressed as the nature of language would admit." So do I.

Although Pfeffer notes that "Madison's phrases 'establish a religion' and 'establish a national religion' cannot be assumed to have the limited meaning assigned" by proponents of the narrow interpretation of the Establishment Clause, he does not explain why such meaning cannot be assumed.[40] In fact, no loose assumptions are being made. The historical context of the State Constitutional Ratifying Conventions, the Madison and House documentation, the logic of counter argumentation, and a "reasonable" interpretation of words which are relatively carefully explained should not be confused with mere assumptions.

---

37. Pfeffer, *Church, State, and Freedom*, p. 162.

38. See the text in chap. one at fn. 30.

39. Pfeffer, *Church, State, and Freedom*, p. 163.

40. Ibid., pp. 163–64.

The history of presidential proclamations regarding Thanksgiving, fasting, and prayer—all of which are conceded as religious activities—may shed some further light on Madison's views. Pfeffer is careful to point out that after "a resolution was offered" by one member in the First Congress under the Federal *Constitution* to request the President to issue a proclamation recommending "to the People of the United States a day of Thanksgiving and Prayer, to be observed by acknowledging with grateful hearts the many signal favours of Almighty God," objection was made by another member of Congress because he thought it was a religious matter proscribed from the business of Congress.[41] The entire exchange in the First House of Representatives concerning the proposed "Day of Thanksgiving" is useful in attempting once again an understanding of the attitudes in the First Congress, and that of Mr. Madison, as to the separation of Church and the national State.

On Thursday, September 24, 1789, the *Debates in Congress* show that the First House of Representatives voted by 37-14 to recommend what is now—in its exact wording—the First Amendment to the States for ratification. Voting with Madison for the Amendment was Boudinot of New Jersey and Sherman of Connecticut.[42] Messrs. Burke and Tucker were two of the fourteen votes against.[43] The next day, Friday, September 25, Boudinot, who had voted for the Amendment, proposed the resolution asking President Washington for a Thanksgiving Day Proclamation.[44] What Pfeffer fails to point out is that the House records indicate that Burke and Tucker, both of whom voted *against* the Establishment Clause and the First Amendment, were the House members who objected to the Thanksgiving Day resolution.[45] In fact, the member who Pfeffer quotes opposing the Thanksgiving Day resolution is the same Tucker of South Carolina who voted against the Establishment Clause and the First Amendment. The full record shows that Tucker was not strongly committed to separation of Church and State but that he thought the power to issue such a Proclamation rested with the several States and not with the national State:[46]

DAY OF THANKSGIVING

Mr. Boudinot said, he could not think of letting the session pass over without offering an opportunity to all the citizens of the United States of joining, with one voice, in returning to Almighty God their sincere thanks

41. Ibid., p. 265.
42. *Annals of the Congress*, Vol. I, pp. 947–48.
43. Ibid., p. 948.
44. Ibid., p. 949.
45. Ibid., p. 950.
46. Ibid.

for the many blessings he had poured down upon them. With this view, therefore, he would move the following resolution:

Resolved, That a joint committee of both Houses be directed to wait upon the President of the United States, to request that he would recommend to the people of the United States a day of public thanksgiving and prayer, to be observed by acknowledging, with grateful hearts, the many signal favors of Almighty God, especially by affording them an opportunity peaceably to establish a Constitution of government for their safety and happiness.

Mr. Burke did not like this mimicking of European customs, where they made a mere mockery of thanksgivings. Two parties at war frequently sung *Te Deum* for the same event, though to one it was a victory, and to the other a defeat.

Mr. Boudinot was sorry to hear arguments drawn from the abuse of a good thing against the use of it. He hoped no gentleman would make a serious opposition to a measure both prudent and just.

Mr. Tucker thought the House had no business to interfere in a matter which did not concern them. Why should the President direct the people to do what, perhaps, they have no mind to do? They may not be inclined to return thanks for a Constitution until they have experienced that it promotes their safety and happiness. We do not yet know but they may have reason to be dissatisfied with the effects it has already produced; but whether this be so or not, it is a business with which Congress have nothing to do; it is a religious matter, and, as such, is proscribed to us. *If a day of thanksgiving must take place let it be done by the authority of the several States; they know best what reason their constituents have to be pleased with the establishment of this Constitution.*

Mr. Sherman justified the practice of thanksgiving, on any signal event, not only as a laudable one in itself, but as warranted by a number of precedents in holy writ: for instance, the solemn thanksgivings and rejoicings which took place in the time of Solomon, after the building of the temple, was a case in point. This example, he thought, worthy of Christian imitation on the present occasion; and he would agree with the gentleman who moved the resolution.

Mr. Boudinot quoted further precedents from the practice of the late Congress; and hoped the motion would meet a ready acquiescence.

The question was now put on the resolution, and it was carried in the affirmative; and Messrs. Boudinot, Sherman, and Sylvester were appointed a committee on the part of the House.[47]

It is quite clear from the record that James Madison did not object to the resolution requesting the Thanksgiving Day Proclamation. It is also plain

47. Ibid., pp. 949–50. Emphasis added.

from the day's proceedings that Sherman of Connecticut, who voted for the First Amendment and its Establishment Clause, apparently saw no conflict between his vote for the Amendment and his support for the Thanksgiving Day Proclamation, especially when he rebutted Tucker's objection citing "holy writ." Although Pfeffer notes the objection to the motion regarding a Thanksgiving Day Proclamation, he fails to explain why the same House that approved the Establishment Clause "carried in the affirmative" the motion for the Proclamation. Can it be reasonably doubted that the House members—and apparently Mr. Madison, at least at that time—had a very different view of what the Establishment Clause forbade than does Pfeffer? If they did not, then they proceeded to violate an important principle which, only a day earlier, they had voted to recommend to the States as part of a constitutional amendment.

Madison's "Detached Memoranda"

Despite Madison's membership on the Committee that recommended the Congressional Chaplain system, Pfeffer takes the position that "Madison considered 'the appointment of chaplains to the two Houses of Congress' as an 'establishment' not 'consistent with the Constitution.' "[48] In addition, Pfeffer indicates that although Madison did not object when in the First House of Representatives a resolution was proposed and passed asking Washington to issue a Thanksgiving Day Proclamation,"Presidents Jefferson, Madison, and Jackson all considered presidential proclamations to be violative of the First Amendment."[49] Pfeffer substantiates these conclusions with a document in Madison's handwriting, said to have been written after he left the presidency, and discovered in the family papers of William C. Rives in the spring of 1946.[50] This document—which Madison entitled the "Detached Memoranda"—leaves no doubt as to his views on the constitutionality of chaplains in the Congress at the time that he wrote the "Memoranda,"[51] for in it he condemns the chaplaincy with a much broader interpretation of the Establishment Clause than when he proposed it and defined it in the Congress. In the "Detached Memoranda" Madison argues that the *Constitution* "forbids everything *like* an establishment of a national religion."[52] Of course, that is not what the First Amendment as it is

48. Pfeffer, *Church, State, and Freedom*, p. 170.

49. Ibid.

50. Elizabeth Fleet, ed., "Madison's 'Detached Memoranda,' " *William and Mary Quarterly*, Vol. III (1946), pp. 535–36.

51. Ibid., p. 535.

52. Ibid., p. 558. Emphasis added.

written specifically prohibits; neither does Madison's "Detached Memoranda" say that chaplains in the Congress are an establishment of religion. He says they are like "an establishment of religion." Madison further claims that the Congressional practice violates "equal rights." Here is the pertinent section of the "Memoranda" on chaplains in Congress:

> *Is the appointment of Chaplains to the two Houses of Congress consistent with the Constitution, and with the pure principle of religious freedom?*
>
> *In strictness the answer on both points must be in the negative. The Constitution of the U.S. forbids everything like an establishment of a national religion.* The law appointing Chaplains establishes a religious worship for the national representatives, to be performed by Ministers of religion, elected by a majority of them; and these are to be paid out of the national taxes. Does not this involve the principle of a national establishment, applicable to a provision for a religious worship for the Constituent as well as of the representative Body, approved by the majority, and conducted by Ministers of religion paid by the entire nation.
>
> *The establishment of the chaplainship to Congress is a palpable violation of equal rights, as well as of Constitutional principles:* The tenets of the chaplains elected [by the majority] shut the door of worship agst the members whose creeds & consciences forbid a participation in that of the majority. To say nothing of other sects, this is the case with that of Roman Catholics & Quakers who have always had members in one or both of the Legislative branches. Could a Catholic clergyman ever hope to be appointed a Chaplain? To say that his religious principles are obnoxious or that his sect is small, is to lift the evil at once and exhibit in its naked deformity the doctrine that religious truth is to be tested by numbers, or that the major sects have a right to govern the minor.[53]

As for religious proclamations, when he wrote the "Memoranda" Madison clearly thought they too were unconstitutional. "Religious proclamations by the Executive recommending thanksgiving & fasts," he wrote, "are shoots from the same root. . . ."[54] "Altho' recommendations only, they imply a religious agency, making no part of the trust delegated to political rulers."[55]

Not only does the existence of the "Memoranda" and its views about chaplains and Executive thanksgiving proclamations contradict Madison's earlier thoughts and behavior, but some of his justifications offered in the "Memoranda" are contradictory to other things which he wrote after

53. Ibid. Emphasis added.   55. Ibid.
54. Ibid., p. 560.

leaving the presidency. For example, Madison, who issued at least four "Thanksgiving Day" executive proclamations,[56] tried to justify these actions after he left the White House in a letter to Edward Livingston dated July 10, 1822:

> Whilst I was honored with the Executive Trust I found it necessary on more than one occasion to follow the example of predecessors. But I was always careful to make the Proclamations absolutely indiscriminate, and merely recommendatory; or rather mere *designations* of a day, on which all who thought proper might *unite* in consecrating it to religious purposes, according to their own faith & forms. In this sense, I presume you reserve to the Govt a right to *appoint* particular days for religious worship throughout the State, without any penal sanction *enforcing* the worship.
>
> I know not what may be the way of thinking on this subject in Louisiana. I should suppose the Catholic portion of the people, at least, as a small & even unpopular sect in the U.S., would rally, as they did in Virga when religious liberty was a Legislative topic, to its broadest principle.[57]

In spite of this explanation to Livingston, Madison in the "Detached Memoranda" says that "[an] *advisory* government is a contradiction in terms"[58] and implies that such executive proclamations usually are thought to reflect "the creed of the majority and a single sect, if amounting to a majority."[59] Both of these statements in the "Memoranda" contradict the letter to Livingston which was written five years after Madison left the presidency.

Other aspects of Madison's letter to Livingston and Pfeffer's explanation of Madison's reasons for issuing the proclamations are confusing. Madison states in the Livingston letter, that he found it necessary "to follow the example of [his] predecessors" and to issue the proclamations. But his immediate predecessor, Thomas Jefferson, did not issue Thanksgiving Day Proclamations. Why, then, was it necessary for Madison to issue such proclamations? Were the pressures of the War of 1812 so great that Madison had to abandon his scruples and violate his constitutional oath of office by issuing four proclamations that he believed violated the *Constitution* of the United States? It is also interesting to note that in the letter to Livingston defending his action, while Madison does indicate strongly that

56. The proclamations referred to are those that President Madison issued on July 9, 1812; July 23, 1813; November 16, 1814; and March 4, 1815.

57. Padover, *The Complete Madison*, p. 308. Madison's emphasis.

58. Fleet, "Madison's 'Detached Memoranda,'" p. 560. Emphasis in the original.

59. Ibid., p. 561.

it is best to keep government out of religion and vice versa, he does not say that the proclamations are unconstitutional:

> Notwithstanding the general progress made within the two last centuries in favour of this branch of liberty, & the full establishment of it, in some parts of our Country, there remains in others a strong bias towards the old error, that without some sort of alliance or coalition between Govt & Religion neither can be duly supported. Such indeed is the tendency to such a coalition, and such its corrupting influence on both the parties, that the danger cannot be too carefully guarded agst. And in a Govt of opinion, like ours, the only effectual guard must be found in the soundness and stability of the general opinion on the subject. Every new & successful example therefore of a perfect separation between ecclesiastical and civil matters, is of importance. And I have no doubt that every new example, will succeed, as every past one has done, in shewing [sic] that religion & Govt will both exist in greater purity, the less they are mixed together.
>
> It was the belief of all sects at one time that the establishment of Religion by law, was right & necessary; that the true religion ought to be established in exclusion of every other; and that the only question to be decided was which was the true religion. The example of Holland proved that a toleration of sects, dissenting from the established sect, was safe & even useful. The example of the Colonies, now States, which rejected religious establishments altogether, proved that all Sects might be safely & advantageously put on a footing of equal & entire freedom . . . . We are teaching the world the great truth that Govts do better without Kings & Nobles than with them. The merit will be doubled by the other lesson that Religion flourishes in greater purity, without than with the aid of Govt.[60]

The crucial question, then, is when did Madison first come to believe chaplains in Congress and "Thanksgiving Day" Proclamations were unconstitutional?

My concept of James Madison does not include the incongruous action of fighting for equality of religion and disestablishment in Virginia and then failing to object as a Committee member recommending to Congress a Chaplain system *if he believed it to be unconstitutional* or a basic violation of proper legal Church-State relations. Nor can I conceive of such a Madison not objecting to a proposed "Thanksgiving Day" Proclamation suggested one day after the House passed the First Amendment, which included the Establishment Clause. It is also difficult for me to believe that Madison—Jefferson's closest ally in the Virginia religious battle—would not follow Jefferson's example and instead issue Presidential proclama-

60. Letter to Livingston, Padover, *The Complete Madison*, pp. 308–9.

tions of "Thanksgiving" because they were politically expedient. The historical record of his presidency shows a principled Madison who when confronted with bills from the Congress that he believed violated the principles of separation of Church and State—as he interpreted those principles *when he was President*—Madison not only vetoed the Congressional enactments but he also specified why he did so. The Madison veto of an attempt to incorporate the Episcopal Church in Alexandria, in Washington, D.C., shows a clearly principled Madison on the First Amendment's Establishment Clause.

Veto message, February 21, 1811

To the House of Representatives of the United States:

Having examined and considered the bill entitled "An Act incorporating the Protestant Episcopal Church in the town of Alexandria, in the District of Columbia,"I now return the bill to the House of Representatives, in which it originated, with the following objections:

Because the bill exceeds the rightful authority to which governments are limited by the essential distinction between civil and religious functions, and violates in particular the article of the Constitution of the United States which declares that "*Congress shall make no law respecting a religious establishment.*" [sic] The bill enacts into and establishes by law sundry rules and proceedings relative purely to the organization and polity of the church incorporated, and comprehending even the election and removal of the minister of the same, so that no change could be made therein by the particular society or by the general church of which it is a member, and whose authority it recognizes. *This particular church, therefore, would so far be a religious establishment by law, a legal force and sanction being given to certain articles in its constitution and administration.* Nor can it be considered that the articles thus established are to be taken as the descriptive criteria only of the corporate identity of the society, inasmuch as this identity must depend on other characteristics, as the regulations established are in general unessential and alterable according to the principles and canons by which churches of that denomination govern themselves, and as the injunctions and prohibitions contained in the regulations would be enforced by the penal consequences applicable to a violation of them according to the local law.

Because the bill vests in the said incorporated church an authority to provide for the support of the poor and the education of poor children of the same, an authority which, being altogether superfluous if the provision is to be the result of pious charity, would be a precedent for giving to religious societies as such a legal agency in carrying into effect a public and civil duty.[61]

61. Ibid., p. 307. Emphasis added.

Madison's presidential veto of a Congressional bill reserving land for the use of a Baptist Church displays the same kind of principled public figure.

Veto Message, February 28, 1811

To the House of Representatives of the United States:
Having examined and considered the bill entitled "An act for the relief of Richard Tervin, William Coleman, Edwin Lewis, Samuel Mims, Joseph Wilson, and the Baptist Church at Salem Meeting House, in the Mississippi Territory," I now return the same to the House of Representatives, in which it originated, with the following objection:
Because the bill in reserving a certain parcel of land of the United States for the use of said Baptist Church comprises a principle and precedent for the appropriation of funds of the United States for the use and support of religious societies, *contrary to the article of the Constitution which declares that "Congress shall make no law respecting a religious establishment."* [sic][62]

In appraising what Madison believed was constitutional in matters of Church and State *when he was President*, it should be remembered that a request from Congress, by joint resolution, asking that a Presidential Proclamation be issued concerning a day of "Thanksgiving" and "Prayer" is a legislative act that is not binding on the President. If Congress had by law created a national holiday through appropriate constitutional legislative process—either with the President's concurrence or by overriding his veto—then presidential discretion would not have been involved. But in all of Madison's Thanksgiving Proclamations this was clearly not the case. In short, Madison as President received from Congress joint resolutions requesting the proclamations declaring the days of "Thanksgiving and Prayer" and on four separate occasions issued Presidential Proclamations which were *purely discretionary* executive acts. In no instance was he compelled by law to issue them. If Madison's heart—let alone his principles—had not been in his declaration of the days of "Thanksgiving," then the very texts of his presidential proclamations indict him as a man of little or no scruples on the matter. Consider Madison's Thanksgiving Day Proclamation of March 4, 1815:

By the President of the United States of America.

A Proclamation.

The Senate and House of Representatives of the United States have by a joint resolution signified their desire that a day may be recommended to be observed by the people of the United States *with religious solemnity as*

---

62. Ibid., p. 308. Emphasis added.

a day of thanksgiving and of devout acknowledgements of Almight God for His great goodness manifested in restoring to them the blessing of peace.

No people ought to feel greater obligations *to celebrate the goodness of the Great Disposer of Events* and of the Destiny of Nations than the people of the United States. *His kind providence* originally conducted them to one of the best portions of the dwelling place allotted for the great family of the human race. *He protected and cherished them* under all the difficulties and trials to which they were exposed in their early days. *Under His fostering care* their habits, their sentiments, and their pursuits prepared them for a transition in due time to a state of independence and self-government. In the arduous struggle by which it was attained they were distinguished by multiplied tokens of *His benign interposition.* During the interval which succeeded He reared them into the strength and endowed them with the resources which have enabled them to assert their national rights and to enhance their national character in another arduous conflict, which is now so happily terminated by a peace and reconciliation with those who have been our enemies. *And to the same Divine Author of Every Good and Perfect Gift we are indebted for all those privileges and advantages, religious as well as civil, which are so richly enjoyed in this favored land.*

It is for blessings such as these, and more especially for the restoration of the blessing of peace, that I now recommend that the second Thursday in April next be set apart as a day on which the people of every religious denomination may in their solemn assemblies unite their hearts and their voices in a freewill offering *to their Heavenly Benefactor of their homage of thanksgiving and of their songs of praise.*

Given at the city of Washington on the 4th day of March, A.D. 1815, and of the Independence of the United States the thirty-ninth.

JAMES MADISON[63]

The actions of Madison in the House of Representatives and the White House and some of his private correspondence upon leaving the Presidency, in comparison with the statements in the "Detached Memoranda," suggest that in his discussion of monopolies—the central theme of the "Memoranda"[64]—Madison out of office and as an old man regretted some of his past public actions.

63. James D. Richardson, *A Compilation of the Messages and Papers of the Presidents, 1789–1897*, Vol. I (Washington, D.C.: Bureau of National Literature and Art, 1901), pp. 560–61. Emphasis added. Madison's "Thanksgiving Proclamations" of July 9, 1812; July 23, 1813; and November 16, 1814 are republished in the Addenda and taken from the same source.

64. Fleet, "Madison's 'Detached Memoranda'," see especially the general discussion on "Banks," pp. 548–50, and the section on "Monopolies" of various kinds, including "Ecclesiastical Endowments," beginning on p. 551.

Whereas Pfeffer rests his argument about chaplains in Congress and Thanksgiving Proclamations on one document written in Madison's declining years, I think that Madison should be judged on his behavior, statements, and actions *while he was a public servant in the House and in the Presidency making policy and accountable for it.* An analogous contemporary illustration should make my point. If former President Nixon, reflecting on his tenure as President, in his final years were to publish a book in which he unequivocally wrote that: "Taping conversations, without all parties being aware of the recording, is morally wrong and clearly a flagrant violation of the constitutional right of privacy," then in my judgment, it would be absurd—for any future biographer or analyst evaluating Mr. Nixon as President—to write that: "Richard Nixon believed that surreptitious tapings of conversations in the Oval Office were immoral and unconstitutional." Indeed, the "Detached Memoranda" is appropriately named, for it reflects ideas certainly "detached" from views Madison expounded in the Congress and the White House. While "foolish consistency" may indeed be "the hobgoblin of little minds," the repudiation of one's actions taken when in public power, by an elderly statesman out of power, is hardly a solid base upon which to build a convincing historical argument, much less constitutional law. Obviously the Madison of the "Detached Memoranda" is not the Madison responsible for the First Amendment nor the President who issued Proclamations of days of Thanksgiving and Prayer. One cannot in good conscience and dispassionate scholarship make consistent—the inconsistent.

The Quest for Mr. Jefferson

If there is one of the Founders of the Republic who justly ranks above James Madison in the cause of religious disestablishment, it must be Thomas Jefferson. So proud was Jefferson of the victory disestablishing the Episcopal Church in Virginia that he authorized his "Virginia Statute of Religious Liberty of 1786" to be listed on his tombstone along with two other deeds for which he wanted to be remembered: "Author of the Declaration of American Independence" and "Father of the University of Virginia."[65] No mention is made that he was, among other things, the third President of the United States.

That Mr. Jefferson favored the separation of Church and State is not questioned here, but whether Pfeffer and other scholars of the "broad inter-

65. Saul K. Padover, *The Complete Jefferson* (Freeport, N.Y.: Books for Libraries Press, 1969), p. 1300.

pretation" of the Establishment of Religion Clause read Jefferson correctly as to what he meant and subscribed to as "separation of Church and State" *is very much in dispute here.* As with Madison, it seems clear to me that the interpretation which I ascribe to the religious prohibitions of the Establishment Clause—a view which Pfeffer labels "narrow"—is more consistent with Jefferson's ideas and actions than are those who subscribe to Pfeffer's "broad" interpretive approach.

Professor Pfeffer argues that "[t]hroughout his adult life Jefferson *never swerved* from his devotion to the *principle of complete* independence of religion and government."[66] Either Pfeffer is incorrect, or Jefferson not only "swerved" on several occasions, his public actions did not coincide with his "alleged" principles. A few historically documented incidents should make the point. In disputing the late Professor Edward S. Corwin's interpretation that the Establishment of Religion Clause restricts the federal legislature only inasmuch as it specifically addresses Congress, consequently leaving the President and/or the Federal judiciary unfettered in the area of religious establishments—an argument Corwin advanced defending the constitutionality of sending a presidentially appointed ambassador to the Vatican— Pfeffer countered with a constitutional rebuttal of substantial merit:[67]

> The logic of this argument is predicated on the assumption that but for the First Amendment the Federal government, in its legislative, executive, and judiciary divisions, would have power to act in the area of religion. It follows from this assumption that since the power was taken away only from Congress, it still remains with the President and the Federal courts. *But, as we have seen, the power to deal with religion was never delegated to the Federal government or to any part of it.* Madison used the terms "government" and "general government," not "Congress," in denying "jurisdiction" over religion and the right to "intermeddle" with it. If no branch of the national government has any inherent or delegated power under the Constitution to intermeddle with religion, the fact that the First Amendment expresses a restraint only upon Congressional action may not be construed as an implied grant of power to the President or the judiciary.[68]

From Pfeffer's argument, it would follow that President Jefferson, if Pfeffer's Jefferson is the historical Jefferson, and one house of the Congress, which is expressly addressed by the Establishment Clause, would not and could not constitutionally, in concert, enter into any agreement reflecting less than the "principle of *complete* independence of religion and government." Public documents show, however, that the "unswerving" Jefferson

---

66. Pfeffer, *Church, State, and Freedom*, p. 105. Emphasis added.

67. Ibid., pp. 128–29.

68. Ibid., p. 129. Emphasis added.

offered such a proposal to the United States Senate on October 31, 1803.

In his "Third Annual Message," to the Senate and House of Representatives on October 17, 1803, President Jefferson indicated that the "friendly tribe of Kaskaskia Indians . . . has transferred its country to the United States, reserving only for its members what is sufficient to maintain them in an agricultural way."[69] Following this message on October 31, 1803, Jefferson asked the Senate to advise and consent to the treaty mentioned in this message:[70]

> I now lay before you the treaty mentioned in my general message at the opening of the session as having been concluded with the Kaskaskia Indians for the transfer of their country to us under *certain reservations and conditions.*[71]

Although Pfeffer has commented that "direct grants of money or property to institutions exclusively devoted to worship, *such as churches*, are rare, *and their unconstitutionality is clear*,"[72] President Jefferson asked the Senate to ratify a treaty in which one of the conditions was the use of federal money to support a Catholic priest in his priestly duties, and further to provide money to build a church.[73] The Third Article of the treaty in part provided:

> *And whereas, The greater part of the said tribe have been baptised and received into the Catholic church to which they are much attached, the United States will give annually for seven years one hundred dollars towards the support of a priest of that religion, who will engage to perform for the said tribe the duties of his office and also to instruct as many of their children as possible in the rudiments of literature. And the United States will further give the sum of three hundred dollars to assist the said tribe in the erection of a church.* The stipulations made in this and the preceding article, together with the sum of five hundred and eighty dollars, which is now paid or assured to be paid for the said tribe for the purpose of procuring some necessary articles, and to relieve them from debts which they have heretofore contracted, is considered as a full and ample compensation for the relinquishment made to the United States in the first article.[74]

The Proclamation of the Ratified Treaty was issued on December 23,

69. Richardson, *A Compilation of the Messages*, Vol. I, p. 359.

70. Ibid., p. 363.

71. Ibid. Emphasis added.

72. Pfeffer, *Church, State, and Freedom*, p. 196. Emphasis added.

73. Richard Peters, Esq., ed., *The Public Statutes at Large of the United States of America*, Vol. VII (Boston: Charles C. Little and James Brown, 1848), pp. 78–79.

74. Ibid., p. 79. Emphasis added.

1803,[75] approximately one month after Jefferson laid it before both Houses of Congress "in their legislative capacity" on November 25, 1803, presumably for the appropriation of necessary funds to execute the treaty commitments.[76]

Lest it be argued to the contrary, if Jefferson had thought the "Kaskaskia Priest-Church Treaty Provision" was unconstitutional, he could have followed other alternatives. An unspecified lump sum of money could have been put into the Kaskaskia treaty together with another provision for an annual unspecified stipend with which the Indians could have built their church and paid their priest. Such unspecified sums and annual stipends were not uncommon and were provided for in at least two other Indian treaties made during the Jefferson Administration—one with the Wyandots and other tribes, proclaimed April 24, 1806,[77] and another with the Cherokee nation, proclaimed May 23, 1807.[78]

Furthermore, if Jefferson had had doubts about violating any part of the *Constitution*, including the First Amendment, he certainly must have been aware that under Article VI of the Federal *Constitution*, "all treaties made or which shall be made under the authority of the United States" are listed third as the "Supreme Law of the Land"—the *Constitution* itself having primacy[79]—and that consequently the treaty would be unconstitutional. The conclusion seems inescapable that Pfeffer's version of Jefferson surely would not have used his constitutional prerogatives to submit, sign, request, and spend federal monies for a treaty that hardly reflects "the principle of complete independence of religion and government."

According to Pfeffer, Presidents Jefferson, Madison, and Jackson were opposed to the issuance of "presidential proclamations of thanksgiving to God."[80] I have already discussed Madison's four "Thanksgiving Day" proclamations above, and Andrew Jackson isn't germane to the discussion here. The historical evidence supports Pfeffer's interpretation of Jefferson on this issue, but not as strongly as his book *Church, State, and Freedom* suggests.[81] The joint work by Anson Phelps Stokes and Leo Pfeffer, *Church and State in the United States*, develops the Jefferson attitude on

75. Ibid., p. 78.

76. Richardson, *A Compilation of the Messages*, Vol. I, p. 365.

77. Peters, *Public Statutes at Large*, Vol. VII, "Treaty with the Wyandots, etc.," 1805, Art. IV, p. 88.

78. Ibid., "Treaty with the Cherokees," 1806, Art. II, p. 102.

79. In *Reid v. Covert*, 354 U.S. 1 (1957), although there was no opinion of the Court, the judgment of the Court, announced by Justice Black, indicated that "[N]o agreement with a foreign nation can confer power on the Congress, or any other branch of Government, which is free from the restraints of the Constitution." Id. at 16. On this point it appears his view was not challenged by the other opinions.

80. Pfeffer, *Church, State, and Freedom*, p. 157.

81. Ibid.

executive religious proclamations more thoroughly, however.[82] These authors point out that Washington and Adams issued proclamations of national prayer and that Jefferson broke with this tradition,[83] his reasons being "set forth in a letter to a Presbyterian clergyman in 1808":[84]

I consider the government of the United States as interdicted by the Constitution from intermeddling *with religious institutions, their doctrines, discipline, or exercises. This results not only from the provision that no law shall be made respecting the [sic] establishment or free exercise of religion, but from that also which reserves to the States the powers not delegated to the United States.* Certainly, no power to prescribe any religious exercise, or to assume authority in religious discipline, has been delegated to the General Government. *It must then rest with the States, as far as it can be in any human authority.* But it is only proposed that I should recommend, not prescribe a day of fasting and prayer. That is, that I should indirectly assume to the United States an authority over religious exercises, which the Constitution has directly precluded them from. It must be meant, too, that this recommendation is to carry some authority, and to be sanctioned by some penalty on those who disregard it; not indeed of fine and imprisonment, but of some degree of proscription, perhaps in public opinion. And does the change in the nature of the penalty make the recommendation less a law of conduct for those to whom it is directed? I do not believe it is for the interest of religion to invite the civil magistrate to direct its exercises, its discipline, or its doctrines; nor of the religious societies, that the *General Government* should be invested with the power of effecting any uniformity of time or matter among them. Fasting and prayer are religious exercises; the enjoining them an act of discipline. Every religious society has a right to determine for itself the times for these exercises, and the objects proper for them, according to their own particular tenets; and this right can never be safer than in their own hands, where the Constitution has deposited it.[85]

This letter shows that Jefferson thought the Establishment Clause and the federal division of power between the national government and the States were the constitutional arguments against a national proclamation. Although his personal preference is to keep "the civil magistrate" out of religion, Jefferson also clearly points out that the U.S. *Constitution* does not stop the States from assuming authority in the matters of religion. Thus Jefferson's letter cannot be used as evidence that in 1808 he believed that all

82. Anson Phelps Stokes and Leo Pfeffer, *Church and State in the United States*, rev. ed. in 1 vol. (N.Y.: Harper and Row, 1964), p. 88.

83. Ibid.

84. Ibid.

85. Jefferson's letter as reprinted in Stokes and Pfeffer, *Church and State*, p. 88. Emphasis added.

governmental units—state as well as federal—were to be completely independent of religion under the new constitutional allocation of power.

Although Jefferson's position on the Establishment Clause and Thanksgiving Proclamations is closer to Pfeffer's interpretation of the Clause than mine, it should be noted that of our first four Presidents—who were all close to the adoption of the Federal *Constitution* and the First Amendment, including Madison—Jefferson was the only one who did not issue the Proclamations and expressed his thoughts that they were unconstitutional while in office.

As damaging to Professor Pfeffer's claim, that for Jefferson separation of Church and State meant "complete independence of religion and government," as was the "Catholic church building" treaty with the Kaskaskia Indians in 1803 greater damaging evidence, if that is possible—making the overall Pfeffer interpretation of Jefferson untenable—exists.

On July 27, 1787 the Continental Congress—which had on May 20, 1785, ordained the "Towns Gnadenhutten, Shoenbrun and Salem" with adjoining lands and improvements, "for the sole use of the Christian Indians who were formerly settled there"—had resolved that, among other things, "a quantity of land around and adjoining" be granted each of these towns "amounting in the whole to ten thousand acres, and that the property of the said reserved land be vested" in trust for these Indians with "the Moravian Brethren at Bethlehem in Pennsylvania, or a society of the said Brethren for civilizing the Indians and *promoting Christianity*, . . ."[86] Pursuant to the July 1787 resolution, and, "[o]n a report of a committee consisting of Mr. [Abraham] Clarke, Mr. [Hugh] Williamson and *Mr. [James] Madison* to whom was referred a memorial of John Etwein of Bethlehem, president of *the brethrens society for propagating the Gospel among the Heathen,*"[87] the Continental Congress, on September 3, 1788, ordered that three tracts of land, one adjoining each of the towns, Gnadenhutten, Shoenbrun and Salem on the Muskingum, be conveyed to the Moravian Brethren at Bethlehem in Pennsylvania in trust for the Christian Indians.[88]

In order to facilitate that these lands be used for the good of the Christian Indians, "a society was formed at Bethlehem by the members of the United Brethren, by the title of 'Society of the United Brethren for propagating the Gospel among the Heathen,' which met for the first time September 21, 1787, and was afterwards duly incorporated by the State of Pennsylvania,

---

86. *Journals of the Continental Congress, 1774–1789*, Edited from the Original Records in the Library of Congress by Roscoe R. Hill, Vol. XXXIII, 1787 (Washington, D.C.: United States Government Printing Office, 1936), pp. 429–30. Emphasis added.

87. Ibid., Vol. XXXIV, 1788–1789 (Washington, D.C.: United States Government Printing Office, 1937), p. 485. Emphasis added.

88. Ibid., p. 485–86.

by an act dated February 27, 1788, . . ."[89] Subsequently this newly created evangelical arm of the United Brethren was also incorporated "by the States of New Jersey, Ohio, and New York."[90]

After the adoption of the Federal *Constitution* in 1788 and the addition in 1791 of the First Amendment with its Establishment of Religion Clause, the Fourth Congress in 1796 enacted at least two "Land Statutes." The first, "An Act providing for the *Sale* of the Lands of the United States, in the territory northwest of the river Ohio, and above the mouth of the Kentucky river," was a comprehensive land enactment which became law on May 18, 1796.[91] This act detailed, among other things, the public lands available for sale by the United States Government, modes of payment, and the method of authorization for granting patents (title) to the lands purchased.[92] The second law, approved June 1, 1796 and entitled "An Act regulating *the grants of land* appropriated for Military services and for the Society of the United Brethren, for propagating the Gospel among the Heathen," was distinctly different.[93] Like the preceding Federal statute, this one detailed the lands to be granted; Section Two, however, provided, in part, that "the patents for all lands located under the authority of this act, shall be granted . . . *without requiring any fee therefor.*"[94] Section Five of the law provides that:

> And be it further enacted, That the said surveyor general be, and he is hereby, required to cause to be surveyed there several tracts of land, containing four thousand acres each, at Shoenbrun, Gnadenhutten, and Salem; being the tracts formerly set apart, by an ordinance of Congress of the third of September, one thousand seven hundred and eighty-eight, *for the society of United Brethren for propagating the gospel among the*

---

89. *American State Papers*, Class II, *Indian Affairs*, Volume II, *Documents, Legislative and Executive, of the Congress of the United States*, Selected and Edited, Under the Authority of Congress, by Walter Lowrie, Secretary of the Senate, and Walter S. Franklin, Clerk of the House of Representatives (Washington: Published by Gales and Seaton, 1834), 17th Congress, 2d. Session, Document No. 189, "Progress of the Society of the United Brethren In Propagating the Gospel Among the Indians," p. 374.

90. Ibid.

91. *Public Statutes at Large*, Vol. I, "Acts of the Fourth Congress," Sess. I, Chap. 29, pp. 464–69. Emphasis added.

92. Ibid., Sec. 2–7, pp. 465–68.

93. Ibid., Chap. 46, pp. 490–91.

Emphasis added.

94. Ibid., p. 491. Emphasis added. In *Church, State, and Freedom*, Pfeffer is careful to point out that after the new Federal Congress reenacted the *Northwest Ordinance, Public Statutes at Large*, Vol. I, First Congress, Sess. I, Chap. 8, August 7, 1789, p. 50, "no tracts of land for the support of religion" were granted under the Ordinance after the *Constitution* and the First Amendment were adopted. Pfeffer, *op. cit.*, p. 121. While this may be true, Professor Pfeffer neglects to mention the new Federal statutes under discussion here which clearly document that, after the adoption of both the *Constitution* and the First Amendment, Congress did provide "land for the support of religion."

heathen; and to issue a patent or patents for the said three tracts to the said society, in trust, for the uses and purposes in the said ordinance set forth.[95]

As is evident from its name, this Society was concerned with more than merely controlling and using land set aside, in trust, for the Indians who were already Christians. In addition to exercising their trust in the interest of the Christian Indians living on portions of this land, the Society used some of the resources derived from the cultivation of these lands, and land leases sold to white tenant farmers, to convert souls "from among the neighboring heathen" and to send out missionaries to proselytize.[96]

Due to the unreliability of many white tenant farmers—who incurred debts and then abandoned them and their leased farms—the Society, over a period of years, lost large sums of money. Increased expenses for the Society also resulted from Ohio state land taxes.[97] Because of a continuing growth of indebtedness, the Society asked to be divested of its "trust Estate" in the early 1820s.[98] Shortly thereafter an agreement was reached on August 4, 1823 whereby the Society of the United Brethren, for Propagating the Gospel among the Heathen agreed to "retrocede to the United States the three several tracts of lands . . . which had been patented to the Society by the United States" in consideration of $6,654.25 and several tracts of land on which existed churches, parsonages and graveyards.[99]

Even if this proselytizing arm of the United Brethren was not financially successful—a matter of no consequence here—most significant is the fact that, after the adoption of the Establishment of Religion Clause, the United States Government in effect purchased, with grants of land amounting up to 12,000 acres placed in a controlling trust, the services of a religious evangelical order to settle in western U.S. lands to aid the Christian Indians. This action was tantamount to underwriting the maintenance and spreading of Christianity among the Indians. One is compelled to the conclusion that this Federal law is certainly not a manifestation of the "independence of

95. *Public Statutes at Large*, Vol. I, "Acts of the Fourth Congress," Sess. I, Chap. 46, p. 491. Emphasis added.

96. *American State Papers*, Class II, *Indian Affairs*, Volume II, *Documents, Legislative and Executive, of the Congress of the United States*, 17th Congress, 2d. Session, Document No. 189, "Progress of the Society of United Brethren In Propagating the Gospel Among the Indians," pp. 376–77.

97. Ibid., p. 377. The Society had been led to believe that most of their lands would be tax free. Ohio, becoming a state in 1803, apparently did not tax these lands until 1814. Id.

98. *American State Papers*, Class VIII, *Public Lands*, Volume III, *Documents, Legislative and Executive, of the Congress of the United States, op. cit.*, 17th Congress 2d. Session, Document No. 374, "Application of the United Brethren To Be Divested of the Trust Estate of the Lands Conveyed For the Benefit of Certain Christian Indians," p. 615.

99. Ibid., 18th Congress, 1st Session, Document No. 407, "Lands Reconveyed To The United States By The United Brethren, For Propagating The Gospel Among the Heathen," p. 714.

government and religion." Equally compelling is the conclusion that, if Pfeffer's interpretation of the Establishment Clause is a correct one, this enactment by the Fourth Congress is manifestly unconstitutional as a gross violation of the First Amendment.

Section Four of the 1796 Act also provided that the lands within the boundaries of the Law shall revert to the free disposition of the United States Government—like any other vacant U.S. territory—if not claimed by the services to be rendered under the Act by January 1, 1800.[100] Before this deadline was reached, the Fifth Congress, on March 2, 1799, extended the life and terms of the 1796 Act by repealing its Section Four deadline and instituting a new one, January 1, 1802.[101] The Sixth Congress, on March 1, 1800, made some minor adjustments concerning boundary lines relative to the original 1796 Act but retained the cutoff date of January 1, 1802, set one year earlier by the previous Congress. The Statute's title was also extended and now read: "An Act in addition to an act intituled 'An act regulating the grants of land appropriated for Military services, and for the Society of the United Brethren for propagating the Gospel among the Heathen.' "[102]

The Seventh Congress extended the life of the Statute twice. On April 26, 1802, the new cutoff date was set at January 1, 1803.[103] On March 3, 1803, the Congress passed "An Act to revive and continue in force, an act in addition to an act intituled etc." which was to continue in force until April 1, 1804.[104] Before the April 1, 1804 deadline, however, the Eighth Congress, on March 19, 1804, extended the 1796 Law, as amended, until April 1, 1805. This, the last renewal, had a new statutory name: "An Act granting further time for locating military land warrants, and for other purposes."[105] The "other purposes" were in part the propagating of "the gospel among the heathen."[106] The text of the last "revival" reads:

Chap. XXVI.—An Act granting further time for locating military land warrants, and for other purposes.

Be it enacted by the Senate and House of Representatives of the United States of America in Congress assembled, That the act intituled "An act in

100. *Public Statutes at Large*, Vol. I, "Acts of the Fourth Congress," Sess. I, Chap. 46, p. 491.

101. Ibid., Vol. I, "Acts of the Fifth Congress," Sess. III, Chap. 29, p. 724.

102. Ibid., Vol. II, "Acts of the Sixth Congress," Sess. I, Chap. 13, pp. 14–16.

103. Ibid., Vol. II, "Acts of the Seventh Congress," Sess. I, Chap. 30, pp. 155–56.

104. Ibid., Vol. II, "Acts of the Seventh Congress," "An Act to revive and continue in force, an act in addition to an act intituled 'An Act in addition to an act regulating grants of land appropriated for Military Services and for the Society of the United Brethren for propagating the Gospel among the Heathen,' and for other purposes," Sess. II, Chap. 30, pp. 236–37.

105. Ibid., Vol. II, "Acts of the Eighth Congress," Sess. I, Chap. 26, pp. 271–72.

106. Ibid., p. 271.

addition to an act, intituled An act in addition to an act regulating *the grants of land appropriated for military services, and for the society of the United Brethren for propagating the gospel among the heathen,"* approved the twenty-sixth day of April, eighteen hundred and two, be, and the same *is hereby revived and continued in force,* until the first day of April, one thousand eight hundred and five: Provided, however, that the holders or proprietors of warrants or registered certificates, shall and may locate the same, only on any unlocated parts of the fifty quarter townships, and the fractional quarter townships, which had been reserved for original holders, by virtue of the fifth section of an act, intituled "An act in addition to an act, intituled An act regulating *the grants of land* appropriated for military services, and for *the society of the United Brethren for propagating the gospel among the heathen:"* And provided also, that no holder or proprietor of warrants or registered certificates, shall be permitted to locate the same by virtue of this act, unless the Secretary of War shall have made an endorsement on such warrant or registered certificate, certifying that no warrant has been issued for the same claim to military bounty land, and by virtue of the second section of the act, intituled *"An act to revive and continue in force an act in addition to an act intituled An act in addition to an act regulating the grants of land appropriated for military services, and for the society of the United Brethren for propagating the gospel among the heathen, and for other purposes,"* approved the third day of March, eighteen hundred and three.
Approved, March 19, 1804.[107]

Thomas Jefferson, who was President of the United States during the terms of the Seventh and Eighth Congresses, vetoed not one of the last three extentions of this Act. Like Washington and Adams had done before him, Jefferson signed them into law. Certainly Jefferson, who did not issue Thanksgiving Day Proclamations because he thought that they conflicted with the Establishment Clause's limitations on the Federal Government, would have vetoed these Acts if he had believed that they violated the First Amendment. Pfeffer's suggestion that in "his adult life Jefferson never swerved from his devotion to the principle of complete independence of religion and government" is not borne out by historical evidence.[108] This does not mean that Jefferson violated the First Amendment by signing these Acts of Congress. These historical facts indicate that Jefferson, unlike Pfeffer, *did not see the First Amendment and the Establishment Clause requiring a "complete independence of religion and government."* To conclude otherwise is to virtually force us to imply—if not to state outright— that either Jefferson was not an "adult" when in the White House or that he

---

107. Ibid., pp. 271–72. Emphasis added.
108. Pfeffer, *Church, State, and Freedom*, p. 105.

not only "swerved" from his principles concerning Church and State, in these instances he completely ignored them. Just as a Jefferson without deep convictions about the relationship between government and religion is incompatible with the author of the "Virginia Statute of Religious Liberty," so is Pfeffer's view of Jefferson's principles concerning the relationship between Church and State irreconcilable with Jefferson's treaty provision to build a church and support a priest, as well as signing federal land grants being given in trust to a religious society for the purpose of preaching the Gospel to the Indians. From these instances alone, it seems irrefutable that Professor Pfeffer's Jefferson was not the third President of the United States.

Finding Madison and Jefferson

At the outset of this chapter, I indicated that if my appeals to history match the factual actions of Madison and Jefferson to a greater degree than do Pfeffer's, it should logically follow that his broad view of the Establishment Clause will have to give way to my narrower thesis as to the meaning of that Clause set forth in the preceding chapter. From what has been written above about Madison and Jefferson, it seems clear that my thesis advanced in chapter one presents a more consistent factual picture of both men than does Pfeffer's interpretation.

Madison opposed a national religion and the history of the First Amendment supports that thesis. Both Madison and Jefferson opposed a state church and the "Virginia Bill of Religious Liberty" supports that view. On these two points Pfeffer and I have no quarrel. Madison was opposed to discriminatory aid to any one religion and that is supported by the *germane* sections of his "Memorial and Remonstrance." Madison did not think Thanksgiving Day proclamations violated the Establishment Clause because they neither established a church nor a preferred religion. Moreover, since they were "merely recommendatory"—as he wrote in his letter to Edward Livingston after leaving the Presidency[109]—he also could not have believed his four discretionary executive proclamations violated anyone's freedom of conscience. Finally, Madison apparently did not believe public prayer by a federally paid minister was an act or an appropriation establishing a national religion as indicated by his membership on the Congressional Committee which recommended the Chaplain system. Pfeffer's concept of the First Amendment is so broad that Madison's own statements concerning the First Amendment would be too narrow to support Pfeffer's thesis. And as Pfeffer has written, and I concur, Madison,

109. See text at fn. 57, supra.

"who drafted the First Amendment . . . should have had some idea as to what it meant, . . ."[110]

Concerning Jefferson's view of Thanksgiving Day Proclamations, Pfeffer's interpretation clearly has the edge. As pointed out, however, the Establishment Clause was not Jefferson's only constitutional concern about national Thanksgiving Day Proclamations, as Pfeffer's presentation might have led us to believe. It should be noted that Jefferson was neither at the Constitutional Convention nor in the House of Representatives that framed the First Amendment. The two Presidents who were at the Convention, Washington and Madison, and the President who framed the initial draft of the First Amendment in the House of Representatives, James Madison, issued Thanksgiving Proclamations.

The clearest problems that the Pfeffer interpretation of Jefferson has with the historical facts are: the treaty Jefferson negotiated, signed, and for which he requested money to build a Catholic Church and support priestly duties plus the priest; and Jefferson's support of federal land grant trust laws as inducements to missionaries to aid the Christian Indians and otherwise spread the Gospel. On these historical facts alone the Pfeffer interpretation of Jefferson is untenable. My interpretation of Jefferson and the First Amendment has no problem with these historical occurrences.

Jefferson's treaty and the federal land grant trust laws that he signed neither created a national church nor put any religious sect into a preferred position. In the 1803 treaty with the Kaskaskia Indians, the Catholic Church was funded because priests were working with the Indians, many of whom had become Catholics. Therefore, it made abundant sense to help the Catholic Church in that instance. Clearly, this was not favoritism to the Catholic Church because where it made sense to give aid to the United Brethren in U.S. land grant trusts in Ohio because they were working with the Indians there, Jefferson and the "law-extention" acts followed the same policy. In short, neither sect was favored because of a national religious policy to put any religion or sect into a preferred position. If there is any further question on this point, the documentation in the next chapter should prove conclusive.

On the facts in this chapter and chapter one alone, it should be clear that the traditional interpretation of Madison and Jefferson is historically faulty if not virtually unfounded, despite the fact that it is supported, and to a great degree perpetuated, by prominent and respected scholars such as Professor Leo Pfeffer and others who accept an overbroad, and I must conclude, an invalid view of the prohibitions of the Establishment of Religion Clause.

110.Pfeffer, *God, Caesar, and the Constitution*, p. 160.

Chapter Three

Revelations

"The First Amendment has erected a wall between church and state. That wall must be kept high and impregnable. We could not approve the slightest breach."[1] With those lines of fiction, Mr. Justice Black concluded the first United States Supreme Court opinion that dealt directly with the meaning and the constitutional mandate of the Establishment of Religion Clause of the First Amendment. "Fiction" is a strong term, but a careful analysis of the early history of the Republic, as in chapter two, justifies its use. This chapter presents historical evidence to buttress further the thesis that the First Amendment did not, nor was it intended to, create a "high" and "impregnable" wall between Church and State. Rather, its Framers intended it to serve three other purposes.

First, the religious prohibitions of the Amendment were designed to act as a limitation on the new Federal Congress, constitutionally denying to it the power to establish a national church or religion. This denial of congressional power included the authority to place one religion or religious sect into a preferred state status which generally characterized a religious establishment. Second, the Amendment guaranteed that the right of the individual to exercise freedom of conscience in religious matters was to be safe-guarded against encroachment by the Federal Government. Third, the Amendment was intended to make certain that the relationship between religion and the state would remain under the control of individual States— several of which in 1791 had established state religions.[2]

1. *Everson v. Board of Education,* 330 U.S. 1, 18 (1947).

2. See the discussion in chap. one, at fns. 7–9.

Complete independence of religion and the state or absolute separation of Church and State was not contemplated by the Framers of the First Amendment; such a separation has never existed and does not now exist in any federal or state jurisdiction in the United States despite all that has been written to the contrary.[3] Nor does any substantial evidence suggest that nondiscriminatory or indirect aid to religion or to religious institutions was to come under the ban of the First Amendment.

Leo Pfeffer, whose extensive scholarly accomplishments have already been established in the preceding chapter,[4] has written that "in the minds of the fathers of our Constitution [and the First Amendment], independence of religion and government was the alpha and omega of democracy and freedom."[5] The importance of what was in the minds of the Framers of the First Amendment is an area of total agreement between Professor Pfeffer and myself. Their intent and "mind set" is best revealed by their words and deeds. And although Professor Pfeffer appears to contradict himself by down-playing the importance of the actions of the First Congress elsewhere, indicating that many of its members were also members of the Congress which violated the First Amendment by passage of the "Alien and Sedition Laws" of 1798[6]—a claim which he does not appear to document— he certainly cannot both place significance on the minds of the Framers of the First Amendment when it suits him and withdraw it when it does not.

What the Framers of the First Amendment said and did in the First Congress is crucial if one is to understand the meaning of the First Amendment, which they collectively put into its final form and proposed to the States as a worthy addition to the *Constitution*. This is especially true if one intends to legitimize one's arguments with appeals to historical documentation as Pfeffer does.[7]

On the basis of the historical documentation already presented here it is clearly established that there is no support in the Congressional records that either the First Congress, which framed the First Amendment, or its principle author and sponsor, James Madison, intended that Amendment to create a state of complete independence between religion and government. In fact, the evidence in the public documents goes the other way.

Whatever the Fifth Congress did in 1798 regarding "Sedition" may

3. See fn. 1, Justice Douglas's concurring opinion in *Engel v. Vitale,* 370 U.S. 421, 437, fn. 48 in chap. six, below. Also, the text in chap. six at fns. 44–48, below.

4. See chap. two, fn. 6 and accompanying text.

5. Leo Pfeffer, *Church, State, and Freedom,* rev. ed. (Boston: Beacon Press, 1967), p. 127.

6. Ibid., p. 171.

7. This is especially true in chap. four, "The Principle is Born" and chap. five, "The Meaning of the Principle," Pfeffer, *Church, State, and Freedom,* pp. 91–180.

have, in the opinions of many, violated the First Amendment, however, it was the First House of Representatives—not another Congress nine years later—which proposed the First Amendment one day and the very next day proposed that a presidential proclamation of "Thanksgiving and Prayer" be issued.[8]

Thanksgiving Day Proclamations

When our first President, under the new *Constitution*, received the request of both Houses of Congress concerning a national declaration of a public day of "Thanksgiving and Prayer," George Washington—one of the "Fathers of the *Constitution*" and the President of the Constitutional Convention of 1787, whose members, Professor Pfeffer writes, were convinced that the "independence of religion and government was the alpha and omega of democracy"—issued a "National Thanksgiving Proclamation" without any apparent concern that he might be mixing government and religion.

Consider, for example, the proclamation of 1789 that Washington issued approximately six months after he had assumed the presidency and had sworn to uphold the *Constitution*. That the Congress which recommended the First Amendment be added to the *Constitution* should request, and that the man who had been President of the Constitutional Convention and was now the President of the United States should issue this proclamation, indicates that they had no conviction that such actions violated the desirable degree of separation of Church and State implicitly or explicitly called for by the Federal *Constitution*. Washington's first "National Thanksgiving Proclamation" reads:

PROCLAMATION

A NATIONAL THANKSGIVING

Whereas it is the duty of all nations to acknowledge the providence of Almighty God, to obey His will, to be grateful for His benefits, and humbly to implore His protection and favor; and

Whereas both Houses of Congress have, by their joint committee, requested me "to recommend to the people of the United States a day of

8. See the text in chap. two at fns. 44–47.

public thanksgiving and prayer, to be observed by acknowledging with grateful hearts the many and signal favors of Almighty God, especially by affording them an opportunity peaceably to establish a form of government for their safety and happiness:"

Now, therefore, I do recommend and assign Thursday, the 26th day of November next, to be devoted by people of these States to the service of that great and glorious Being who is the beneficent author of all the good that was, that is, or that will be; that we may then all unite in rendering unto Him our sincere and humble thanks for His kind care and protection of the people of this country previous to their becoming a nation; for the signal and manifold mercies and the favorable interpositions of His providence in the course and conclusion of the late war; for the great degree of tranquility, union, and plenty which we have since enjoyed; for the peaceable and rational manner in which we have been enabled to establish constitutions of government for our safety and happiness, and particularly the national one now lately instituted; for the civil and religious liberty with which we are blessed, and the means we have of acquiring and diffusing useful knowledge; and, in general, for all the great and various favors which He has been pleased to confer upon us.

And also that we may then unite in most humbly *offering our prayers and supplications to the great Lord and Ruler of Nations, and beseech Him to pardon our national and other trangressions*; to enable us all, whether in public or private stations, to perform our several and relative duties properly and punctually; to render our National Government a blessing to all the people by constantly being a Government of wise, just, and constitutional laws, discreetly and faithfully executed and obeyed; to protect and guide all sovereigns and nations (especially such as have shown kindness to us), and to bless them with good governments, peace, and concord; to promote the knowledge and practice of true religion and virtue, and the increase of science among them and us; and, generally, to grant unto all mankind such a degree of temporal prosperity as He alone knows to be best.

Given under my hand, at the city of New York, the 3d day of October, A.D. 1789.

G? WASHINGTON.[9]

Is this the proclamation of a man who thought that the complete independence of government and religion was the essential ingredient of "democracy and freedom"?

The precedent set by the request of the First Congress for a national day

9. James D. Richardson, *A Compilation of the Messages and Papers of the Presidents, 1789–1897*, Vol. I (Washington D.C.: Bureau of National Literature and Art, 1901), p. 64. Emphasis added.

of Thanksgiving and Washington's proclamation of 1789 became a custom during the early life of the new Federal Republic. Of our first Presidents—those closest to the Constitutional Convention and the adoption of the First Amendment—George Washington issued at least two proclamations calling for a day of "public thanksgiving and prayer,"[10] John Adams issued at least two,[11] and James Madison issued at least four.[12] There is no evidence that any of these men believed they were violating the Federal *Constitution*, including the First Amendment and consequently their oath of office, in issuing these proclamations during their presidencies.[13]

Chaplains

The existence of chaplains in the Continental Congress and the First Congress has already been discussed to some degree in chapter two.[14] Further discussion appears in chapter six and redundancy here is unnecessary.[15] In a recent book on Church-State relations under the Federal *Constitution*, Leo Pfeffer wrote that "Caesar was to have no traffic with God or, as Madison phrased it, that there should be 'a separation between religion and government.' "[16] Material in chapter two indicates that Pfeffer's "no traffic" remark is inconsistent with Madison's active role concerning the creation of the Chaplain system in the First House of Representatives and the First Congress.

Pfeffer also wrote that a separation of religion and government—and in the context of the "*no* traffic" remark I interpret Pfeffer to mean an *absolute* "separation between religion and government"—"was the intent of the framers of the *Constitution* [as] evidenced by the fact that during the four months the members of the constitutional convention met in Philadelphia, not once did they engage in prayer."[17] By the same reasoning, the

10. In addition to the one cited in fn. 9, Washington issued another such proclamation on January 1, 1795. Richardson, *A Compilation of the Messages,* Vol. I, pp. 179–80.

11. March 23, 1798, ibid., Vol. I, pp. 268–70, and March 6, 1799, ibid., Vol. I, pp. 284–86.

12. July 9, 1812, ibid., Vol. I, p. 513; July 23, 1813, ibid., Vol. I, pp. 532–33; November 16, 1814, ibid., Vol. I, p. 558; and March 4, 1815, ibid., Vol. I, pp. 560–61.

13. Jefferson thought such proclamations would violate the *Constitution* and did not issue any. See the text in chap. two at fns. 80–85. Madison recanted his proclamations when out of office. See the section in chap. two on the "Detached Memoranda."

14. See the text in chap. two at fns. 25–30.

15. See the text in chap. six at fns. 33—38.

16. Leo Pfeffer, *God, Caesar, and the Constitution* (Boston: Beacon Press, 1975), p. 29.

17. Ibid.

members of the First Congress must have been in favor of a "theocracy" because one of their first official acts was to create a Congressional Chaplain system. Both statements, however, cannot accurately reflect the intentions of the Framers of the *Constitution* or the members of the Congress because they are based on only a single factor.

Furthermore, nowhere in his discussion about the lack of prayer at the Constitutional Convention does Pfeffer mention the request for prayer by Benjamin Franklin, as recorded in Madison's notes on the Convention's happenings, nor does Pfeffer indicate, as do Madison's notes, that the real reason for not bringing in a chaplain once the Convention had been underway was fear that people would think that the Convention's deliberations—which were kept secret while in progress—were fraught with dissension.[18]

The First Congress did more than provide for a Chaplain system of its own—by a law enacted March 3, 1791, it also authorized the President, "by and with the advice and consent of the Senate" to appoint a chaplain for the "Military Establishment of the United States."[19] The compensation for the chaplain was to be "fifty dollars per month, including pay, rations and forage."[20] This statute was superseded by "An Act for making farther and more effectual Provision for the Protection of the Frontiers of the United States," passed by the Second Congress and also providing for a chaplain at the pay of fifty dollars monthly.[21]

The Third Congress further enlarged the U.S. Military Establishment with the passage of "An Act to provide a Naval Armament," on March 27, 1794.[22] This federal law provided for a United States Navy with "one chaplain" who was to be payed "forty dollars per month and two rations per day."[23]

In *Church, State, and Freedom*, Pfeffer indicates that "[c]haplains in the armed forces may be necessary under the constitutional guarantee of freedom of conscience. A soldier drafted into the armed forces and sent to a camp far from his home is deprived of the opportunity to visit his church. To

---

18. See a fuller discussion of the "chaplain issue" in the Constitutional Convention in the text of chap. two, at fns. 31–35.

19. Richard Peters, Esq., ed., *The Public Statutes at Large of the United States of America*, Vol. I (Boston: Charles C. Little and James Brown, 1845), "Acts of the First Congress," Sess. 3, Chap. 28, "An Act for raising and adding another Regiment to the Military Establishment of the United States, and for making farther provision for the protection of the frontiers," Sec. 5, p. 222.

20. Ibid., Sec. 6, p. 223.

21. Ibid., "Acts of the Second Congress," Sess. I, Chap. 9, p. 242.

22. Ibid., "Acts of the Third Congress," Sess. I, Chap. 12, p. 350.

23. Ibid., pp. 350–51.

the extent that such deprivation is necessary to the overriding consideration of national defense, it is constitutional."[24] While I have no quarrel with Pfeffer on this point, it seems to me that if the Framers of the *Constitution* and the First Amendment were so concerned that religion and government should be independent, surely they would have provided facilities in which military personnel could freely exercise their religion but would have left the support of the individual chaplains to the churches involved, in the way that missionaries were supported. Instead, the early Congresses provided the complete support of chaplains—as they did for other military personnel— even though at the time conscription was not the primary means of raising troops.

If the concern for the separation between government and religion had been as great as Pfeffer suggests, the religious needs of military personnel would probably have been met in a way that guaranteed stricter neutrality between religion and government than the early federal statutes regarding military chaplains indicate. The early Congresses did not do this probably because they did not embrace the broad concept of absolute separation of Church and State that is now associated with, and erroneously claimed to be, the correct historical interpretation of the Establishment Clause. This clever attempt at explaining away the contemporary chaplaincy corps does not explain its historical beginnings which had an entirely different setting. Nor does this interpretation of the early chaplaincy statutes explain why millions of tax dollars currently being spent by the Federal Government each year for salaries, veterans' benefits, pensions, clerical garb, clerical equipment, and public chapels—military and otherwise—is constitutional if the broad Pfeffer interpretation of the Establishment Clause is a correct one.[25]

24. Pfeffer, *Church, State, and Freedom,* p. 169.

25. For a comprehensive history of the vast growth of only the United States Army Chaplaincy, see the recently published five-volume work by the Department of the Army: Parker C. Thompson, *The United States Army Chaplaincy: From Its European Antecedents to 1791* (Washington, D.C.: Department of the Army, 1978); Herman A. Norton, *Struggling For Recognition: The U.S. Army Chaplaincy, 1791–1865* (Washington, D.C.: Department of the Army, 1977); Earl F. Stover, *Up From Handymen: The United States Army Chaplaincy, 1865–1920* (Washington, D.C.: Department of the Army, 1977); Robert L. Gushwa, *The Best and Worst of Times: The United States Army Chaplaincy, 1920–1945* (Washington, D.C.: The Department of the Army, 1977); and Rodger R. Venzke, *Confidence in Battle, Inspiration in Peace: The United States Army Chaplaincy, 1945–1975* (Washington, D.C.: Department of the Army, 1977). For the attractive career possibilities including pay allowances, fringe benefits, and retirement programs in the United States Army *only,* see *The Chaplaincy: Maybe It Is for You* (Washington, D.C.: U.S. Government Printing Office, 1978).

On Positioning the First Amendment

Pfeffer's chapter entitled "The Principle is Born," in *Church, State, and Freedom* clearly states his view of the attitude of the "fathers of our Constitution" toward separation of Church and State. His summary in this chapter unequivocally provides us with this information:

> The Bill of Rights, approved by the requisite number of states in 1791, began with a guaranty of religious freedom. The First Amendment reads in full:
>
>> Congress shall make no law respecting an establishment of religion, or prohibiting the free exercise thereof; or abridging the freedom of speech, or of the press; or the right of the people peaceably to assemble and to petition the Government for a redress of grievances.
>
> Other amendments in the Bill of Rights guaranteed the right to keep arms and to be free of compulsory quartering of soldiers in peace, security of person and home against unreasonable searches and seizures, the right to a fair, speedy, and public trial by jury, and prohibitions against deprivation of life, liberty, or property without due process of law, and against cruel and unusual punishments.
>
> What, however, is particularly significant to our study is that the last words of the last article of the Constitution (except for the purely formal article specifying when the Constitution should become effective) prohibit any religious test "as a qualification to any office or public trust under the United States," and the first words of the first article of the Bill of Rights prohibit "any law respecting an establishment of religion." *The significance of this ending and beginning is more than symbolic; it indicates unmistakably that in the minds of the fathers of our Constitution,* independence of religion and government was the alpha and omega of democracy and freedom.[26]

Although I have more serious differences to raise with this interpretation of "the minds of the fathers of our Constitution," it is historically clear that the Framers of the Bill of Rights—including Madison—*did not intend* that what is now the First Amendment should be the first addition to the Federal *Constitution.* I include this rebuttal only because Professor Pfeffer indicates there is not only symbolism in the positioning of the First Amendment but significance as an *unmistakable* guide to the "minds of the fathers of our Constitution."

26. Pfeffer, *Church, State, and Freedom,* chap. four, p. 127. Emphasis added.

When Madison introduced his proposed additions to the *Constitution* on June 8, 1789, he wanted the religious guarantees to be added to Article I, Section 9 of the body of the original *Constitution*.[27] Of course, the religious guarantees do not appear in Article I, Section 9, but that isn't Madison's doing. The point here is that if Madison's suggested positioning for the additional religious guarantees in the *Constitution* had been accepted, Pfeffer would not only be without his symbolism but also without his unmistakable reading of the minds of the "fathers of our Constitution."

Lest it be counterargued that Madison's "positioning" suggestion was rejected by the First Congress because it wanted to do exactly as Pfeffer indicates, it is worth noting that when the additions that became the Bill of Rights were submitted to the States, the current First Amendment was the third proposed congressional amendment.[28] When the first two proposed amendments failed to gain ratification, the third proposed amendment became the first ratified amendment and, as such, became the First Amendment to the *Constitution*. Consequently, unless the members of the First Congress were clairvoyant and knew the first two proposed amendments would not be ratified, they could not have known that the third proposed amendment would become the First Amendment. If it was intended, however, that the First Amendment, being first in the Bill of Rights should serve as a "key" to the minds of the "fathers," as Pfeffer says, why didn't the "fathers" of the Bill of Rights simply put the First Amendment first on the list of the twelve proposed amendments?

So much for "alphas" and "omegas."

Direct Support of Religion By Treaties

More serious is Pfeffer's failure to match his conclusions with the historical facts. Religion and government were not independent when, through the medium of various Indian treaties in the early years of the new Federal Republic, the United States Government spent federal tax dollars directly on religious institutions.

In my discussion of Jefferson and Pfeffer's view of Jefferson in chapter two, a sufficient presentation and analysis was provided to establish the

27. *Annals of the Congress of the United States, The Debates and Proceedings in the Congress of the United States,* Vol. I, Compiled from Authentic Materials, by Joseph Gales, Senior (Washington: Gales and Seaton, 1834), p. 434.

28. See the "Resolution of the First Congress Submitting Twelve Amendments to the Constitution," *Documents on the Formation of the Union of the American States* (Washington, D.C.: Government Printing Office, 1927), pp. 1063–65.

incongruity that would exist if a constitution containing the principle or command of complete independence of religion and government countenanced treaties providing direct aid to religion or religious activities.[29] There, Pfeffer's own logic, his interpretations of Jefferson and of the prohibitions of the Establishment of Religion Clause were turned against him in the discussion of Jefferson's 1803 treaty with the Kaskaskia Indians to provide money to build a church and for other religious needs.[30] However, direct federal monies to support diverse religious activities—through Federal Indian treaties—did not begin nor end with Mr. Jefferson's Administration.

The "allegedly" high and impregnable wall between Church and State of which Justice Black spoke in the 1947 *Everson* Case did not stop President Washington from concluding a treaty with the Oneida, Tuscorora, and Stockbridge Indians, proclaimed on January 21, 1795, whereby the United States paid "one thousand dollars, to be applied in building a convenient church at Oneida," in place of the one which the British burned in the Revolutionary War.[31] Even if it be argued that the end sought by the United States was a constitutional and secular one—that of rewarding its allies in wartime for losses they had suffered—Pfeffer has been careful to point out that to conclude that "government may employ religion as a means *to effect secular ends which are properly within governmental competence* would go far toward making the First Amendment meaningless."[32] If Pfeffer's interpretation is correct, Washington and the Congress in paying the thousand dollars pursuant to the treaty ratified by the Senate acted unconstitutionally just three years after the First Amendment was added to the *Constitution.*

As already discussed in chapter two, if the Pfeffer interpretation of the Establishment Clause is accurate, Thomas Jefferson, by treaty, joined Washington in 1803 by giving hundreds of dollars to the Kaskaskia Indians for religious purposes, to be used on lands which became part of the United States under the terms of that same treaty, and thus helped to further make "the First Amendment meaningless."[33] Indeed, if Pfeffer's Establishment Clause is the valid one, then other rascals in the White House and in the U.S. Senate also helped to make the First Amendment meaningless because they used explicit religious means to reach secular ends through the treaty process.

29. See text in chap. two at fns. 67–79.
30. Ibid.
31. *The Public Statutes at Large,* Vol. VII, "A Treaty Between the United States and the Oneida, Tuscarora, and Stockbridge Indians, dwelling in the Country of the Oneidas," Art. IV, p. 48.
32. Pfeffer, *Church, State, and Freedom,* p. 179. Emphasis added.
33. See fn. 29, supra.

President James Monroe, Madison's former Secretary of State, in a treaty with the Wyandots and other Indian tribes, because of their attachment to the "Catholic religion," granted United States land—by the terms of Article I of that treaty— *"to the rector of the Catholick Church of St. Anne* of Detroit, for the use of said Church, and to the corporation of the college at Detroit, for the use of the said college, to be retained or sold, *as the said rector* and corporation may judge expedient, each, one half of three sections of land, to contain *six hundred and forty acres, . . .*"[34]

Furthermore, President John Quincy Adams, Monroe's former Secretary of State, in a treaty with the Osages and other tribes—proclaimed on December 30, 1825—provided for a "Missionary establishment" on ceded United States land, to teach, civilize, and improve the Indians. Article 10 of the treaty reads as follows:

> It is furthermore agreed on, by and between the parties to these presents, that there shall be reserved two sections of land, to include the Harmony Missionary establishment, and their mill, on the Marias des Cygne; and one section, to include the Missionary establishment, above the Lick on the West side of Grand river, to be disposed of as the President of the United States shall direct, for the benefit of said Missions, and to establish them at the principal villages of the Great and Little Osage Nations, within the limits of the country reserved to them by this Treaty, and to be kept up at said villages, so long as said Missions shall be usefully employed in teaching, civilizing, and improving, the said Indians.[35]

At least two other early American Presidents—Andrew Jackson and his successor Martin Van Buren—joined Thomas Jefferson in committing Federal money to build churches through treaty agreements. Despite the fact that Pfeffer has indicated that "direct grants of money or property to institutions exclusively devoted to worship, such as churches, are rare, and *their unconstitutionality is clear,*"[36] President Andrew Jackson— whom Pfeffer points out did not issue Thanksgiving Day Proclamations because he thought they violated the Establishment of Religion Clause[37]— concluded a treaty with the Kickapoo Indians, proclaimed February 13, 1833, which obligated the United States Government to pay "thirty-seven hundred dollars, for the erection of a mill and a church, . . ."[38] Van Buren's

---

34. *Public Statutes at Large,* "Articles of a Treaty," proclaimed January 4, 1819, Art. 16, p. 166. Emphasis added.

35. Ibid., "Articles of a Treaty," Art. 10, pp. 242–43.

36. Pfeffer, *Church, State, and Freedom,* p. 196. Emphasis added.

37. Ibid., p. 157.

38. *Public Statutes at Large,* "Articles of a Treaty," Art. VI, p. 392.

treaty with the Oneida in 1838 called not only for "the erection of a church," but also for a "parsonage house."[39]

Did all of these early Presidents and Senates of the United States violate the *Constitution* by entering into treaties that disregarded in one manner or another, the First Amendment? Or is Pfeffer's interpretation of the Establishment of Religion Clause too broad? The historical evidence presented here cannot be easily reconciled with the Pfeffer interpretaion of the Establishment Clause of the *Constitution* unless, of course, Professor Pfeffer is prepared to argue that, when the various Congresses passed the Federal appropriation laws necessary to meet these treaty obligations, those Congresses were not making laws "respecting an establishment of religion."

Pfeffer's overbroad explicit and rigid interpretation of the Establishment Clause leaves little room for alternative definitions. If a President of the United States and the U.S. Senate make a treaty to build a church anywhere in the world, let alone on U.S. land, the money that would have to be appropriated by the Congress by law—as Jefferson asked the Congress to do in 1803 for the Kaskaskia Indian church—would have to be, within Pfeffer's interpretation, a "law respecting an establishment of religion!" Did not Jefferson ask Congress "in their legislative capacity" on November 25, 1803,[40] to make a "law respecting an establishment of religion" when he "informed them of the obligations which the United States" undertook in the Kaskaskia treaty—obligations that included money to help build a church and support a priest? The answer must be "Yes" if Pfeffer's version of the Establishment Clause is an accurate one. Consequently, it is again apparent that the historical evidence shows that the "Pfeffer School of Thought" regarding the meaning of the constitutional concept of separation of Church and State is obviously out of harmony with American historical reality.

I would conclude that Washington, Jefferson, Monroe, Quincy Adams, Jackson, Van Buren, and their Senates did not violate the constitutional principle of separation of Church and State. Their actions merely dictate another definition for that doctrine. It is clear that their understanding of the prohibitions concerning religion in the First Amendment, operative on all of the branches of the Federal Government, was different from Professor Pfeffer's. But there is even more historical evidence that this is, in fact, the case. As we shall see, the history of the American Republic supports, still further, the interpretation of the constitutional doctine of separation of Church and State, and the dual religious prohibitions of the First Amend-

39. Ibid., "Articles of a Treaty," proclaimed May 17, 1838, Art. 3, p. 567.

40. Richardson, *A Compilation of the Messages,* Vol. I, p. 365.

ment advanced—not in Pfeffer's writings—but in the first chapter of this work.

"Civilization of the Indians": Federal Money to Support Religious Schools and Religious Teaching

In *Church, State, and Freedom*, Pfeffer notes that after the adoption of the First Amendment, the appropriation of land for religious purposes ceased under the Northwest Ordinance.[41] His discussion of the land granting practice is presented carefully:

> In 1785 a committee of Congress drew up a proposal for the disposition of the western lands which Congress had acquired from the states. The plan proposed that the 16th section of each township should be set aside for the use of public schools, and another section for the support of the ministry, according to the practice of town establishment current in Massachusetts and Connecticut. In the course of committee action the latter proposal was defeated, and evoked the following comment from Madison in a letter to James Monroe:
>> How a regulation so unjust in itself, so foreign to the Authority of Congress, so hurtful to the sale of public land, and smelling so strongly of an antiquated Bigotry, could have received the countenance of a Committee is truly a matter of astonishment.
>
> When, however, the Northwest Ordinance of 1787 was adopted it contained a declaration that
>> Religion, morality and knowledge, being necessary to good government and the happiness of mankind, schools and the means of education shall forever be encouraged.
>
> Moreover, notwithstanding the committee's action in 1785, Congress granted tracts of land for the support of religion, as well as for schools, though it is important to note that *after the Constitution and the First Amendment were adopted no more public land was granted for the support of religion under the Ordinance.*[42]

Even though Congress reenacted the Northwest Ordinance on August 7, 1789,[43] after the ratification of the Federal *Constitution*, the Ordinance had to conform to the provisions of the new *Constitution*.[44] From the way in

---

41. Pfeffer, *Church, State, and Freedom*, p. 121.
42. Ibid., pp. 120–21. Emphasis added.
43. *Public Statutes at Large*, Vol. I,

First Congress, Sess. I, Chap. VIII, "An Act to provide for the Government of the Territory Northwest of the river Ohio," p. 50.
44. Ibid., pp. 51–53.

which Pfeffer presents the question of land grants for religious purposes in the section quoted above, it would appear that no more land was granted for religious purposes after the adoption of the Federal *Constitution* and the First Amendment. That is not historically correct. While no more land may have been granted for religious purposes *"under the Ordinance,"* public land grants, in trust, for religious purposes were bestowed by other Federal laws after the passage of the First Amendment, beginning with the June 1, 1796 law enacted by the Fourth Congress and entitled "An Act regulating *the grants of land* appropriated for Military services and for the Society of the United Brethren, *for propagating the Gospel among the Heathen."*[45] Pfeffer's statement may be technically correct but it is misleading because there is no indication that these laws were considered unconstitutional under the First Amendment, even by President Thomas Jefferson under whose Administration three of them were enacted and which he signed.[46]

Pfeffer uses this same technique in regard to the issue of federal funds to support the teachers and the teaching of religion. With respect to Madison's victory in Virginia against the "Assessment Bill" to pay Christian teachers Pfeffer writes:

> By and large, the American people have been faithful to the unique and radical experiment formalized in the "establishment" and religious liberty provision of the First Amendment. *So conclusive was Madison's victory in the Virginia legislature and in the adoption of the First Amendment, that in the more than a century and a half since the Amendment was adopted Congress has never enacted—nor indeed has been called upon to consider—a bill for the support of teachers of religion.*[47]

Although technically correct, that statement too is historically inaccurate. In fact, under the guise of bringing "Civilization to the Indians," many United States Congresses and Presidents provided hundreds of thousands of dollars of federal money, for more than a century, to support ministers of many religions, missionaries, and religious schools which, I am sure none would dispute, might have taught "just a bit" of religion along with reading, writing, and Western culture. Since Pfeffer's statement is as absolute as the word "never," which he uses, one illustration would disprove his assertion.

In order to illustrate the enormity of his error on this historical point, however, a few of the many official United States reports pertaining to this

---

45. See the text in chap. two, and the fns. at 93–107. Emphasis added.

46. Ibid., see the quote and text at fns. 107–8.

47. Pfeffer, *Church, State, and Freedom,* pp. 165–66. Emphasis added.

matter are reproduced here as documentation of my preceding statements. The following report will help clarify the issue of the expenditure of federal money to support religion, missionary teachers, and church schools in the campaign "to civilize" the Indians. Presented to the House of Representatives of the Seventeenth Congress by a letter of transmittal from President James Monroe, the report includes two parts reproduced here: a letter to Monroe from his Secretary of War in 1822, John C. Calhoun, and a "Statement A" showing the dispersal of funds.

17th Congress. *No. 182* *1st Session.*

CONDITION OF THE SEVERAL INDIAN TRIBES
Communicated to the House of Representatives, February 11, 1822.

To the House of Representatives: Washington, *February* 15, 1822.

In compliance with a resolution of the House of Representatives "requesting the President of the United States to cause to be laid before this House any information which he may have of the condition of the several Indian tribes within the United States, and the progress of the measures hitherto devised and pursued for their civilization," I now transmit a report from the Secretary of War.

JAMES MONROE

Department of War, *February* 8, 1822.

The Secretary of War, to whom was referred the resolution of the House of Representatives "requesting the President of the United States to cause to be laid before this House any information which he may have of the condition of the several Indian tribes within the United States, and the progress of the measures hitherto devised and pursued for their civilization," *has the honor to transmit the enclosed table, (marked A,) containing the number of schools established under the patronage of the Government within the Indian country; the number of scholars at each;* the time of their commencement, where fixed, and by whom established; with remarks on their progress, present condition, &c. By reference to the table, it will appear that there are eleven principal schools, with three subordinate ones, in actual operation; and that three are in a state of preparation; and that the number of scholars at the last return at the principal and subordinate schools amounted to five hundred and eight. On these schools there has been expended $15,827 56, of which $7,447 56 has been on account of buildings, and the balance, $8,380, on account of the expense of tuition. It is made a condition of the subscription on the part of the Government that the schools should be established within the Indian country, and that the system of education, in addition to reading, writing, and arithmetic, should, for the boys, embrace instruction in agriculture and the ordinary mechanic arts, and, for the girls, the common domestic industry of that sex.

It was thought advisable, at the commencement of the system, to proceed with caution, and to enlarge the sphere of operation as experience should indicate the proper measures to be adopted, by which a useless expenditure of public money would be avoided, and the system adopted for the civilization of the Indians have the fairest trial. Experience has thus far justified those which have been adopted; and it is accordingly intended to give this year a greater activity to the funds, of which a much larger portion may be applied to tuition; the necessary buildings at so many points having already been erected.

Whether the system which has been adopted by the Government, if persevered in, will ultimately bring the Indians withing the pale of civilization, can only be determined by time. It has been in operation too short a period to pronounce with certainty on the result. The present generation, which cannot be greatly affected by it, must pass away, and those who have been reared under the present system of education must succeed them, before its effects can be fully tested. As far, however, as civilization may depend on education only, without taking into consideration the force of circumstances, it would seem that there is no insuperable difficulty in effecting the benevolent intention of the Government. It may be affirmed, almost without qualification, that all of the tribes within our settlements and near our borders are even solicitous for the education of their children. With the exception of the Creeks, they have every where freely and cheerfully assented to the establishment of schools, to which, in some instances, they have contributed. The Choctaws, in this respect, have evinced the most liberal spirit, having set aside $6,000 of their annuity in aid of the schools established among them. The reports of the teachers are almost uniformly favorable, both as to the capacity and docility of their youths. Their progress appears to be quite equal to that of white children of the same age, and they appear to be equally susceptible of acquiring habits of industry. At some of the establishments a considerable portion of the supplies are raised by the labor of the scholars and teachers.

With these indications, it would seem that there is little hazard in pronouncing that, with proper and vigorous efforts, they may receive an education equal to that of the laboring portion of our community. Still, however, the interesting inquiry remains to be solved, whether such an education would lead them to that state of morality, civilization, and happiness, to which it is the desire of the Government to bring them; or whether there is not something in their situation which presents insuperable obstacles to such a state? To answer this inquiry, we have but little experience. There is certainly much encouragement to hope for the best, from the fact that the Cherokee nation, which has made the greatest progress in education, has also made the greatest towards this desirable state; but the experience which it affords is yet imperfect. They have adopted some written provisions for their govermnment, to a copy of which, with an extract of a letter from the Rev. Mr. Steiner, a respectable Moravian, who has visited the nation at the interval of twenty years, and states the progress which they have made in that time, and which accompanies this report, (marked B,) I would respectfully refer the House, as furnishing the best testimony of the actual progress which that nation has made towards civilization. The zeal of the Cherokees for improvement, and the progress which they have made, are further evinced from the liberal provision of a school fund, for which the last treaty with them, ratified on the 10th of March, 1819, stipulates; and the fact that there are now established in the nation six schools, (two of which are upon the Lancasterian system,) containing in the aggregate about two hundred and thirty scholars. Notwithstanding these favorable appearances, many obstacles, difficult to be surmounted, will impede the progress of the Indians to a state of complete civilization.

Without adverting to others, the political relation which they bear to us is, of itself, of sufficient magnitude, if not removed, to prevent so desirable a state from being attained. We have always treated them as an independent people; and, however insignificant a tribe may become, and however surrounded by a dense white population, so long as there are any remains, it continues independent of our laws and authority. To tribes thus surrounded, nothing can be conceived more opposed to their happiness and civilization than this state of nominal independence. It has not one of the advantages of real independence, while it has nearly all the disadvantages of a state of complete subjugation. The consequence is inevitable. They lose the lofty spirit and heroic courage of the savage state, without acquiring the virtues which belong to the civilized. Depressed in spirit, and debauched in morals, they dwindle away through a wretched existence, a nuisance to the surrounding country. Unless some system can be devised gradually to change this relation, and with the progress of education to extend over them our laws and authority, it is feared that all efforts to civilize them, whatever flattering appearances they may for a time exhibit, must ultimately fail. Tribe after tribe will sink, with the progress of our settlements and the pressure of our population, into wretchedness and oblivion. Such has been their past history, and such, without this change of political relation, it must probably continue to be. To effect it, many difficulties present themselves. It will require the co-operation of the General Government and the States within which the Indians may reside. With a zealous and enlightened co-operation, it is, however, believed that all difficulties may be surmounted, and this wretched, but in many respects noble race, be ultimately brought within the pale of civilization. Preparatory to so radical a change in our relation towards them, the system of education which has been adopted ought to be put into extensive and active operation. This is the foundation of all other improvements. It ought gradually to be followed with a plain and simple system of laws and government, such as has been adopted by the Cherokees, a proper compression of their settlements, and a division of landed property. By introducing gradually and judiciously these improvements, they will ultimately attain such a state of intelligence, industry, and civilization as to prepare the way for a complete extension of our laws and authority over them.

Before I conclude, I would respectfully refer the House of Representatives, for more full and detailed information in relation to the progress made by the Indians in civilization, to the report of the Rev. Doctor Morse, which was laid before the House in pursuance of a resolution of the 22d January last.

J. C. CALHOUN

To the President of the United States.

A.— *Statement of schools which have been established in the Indian country, showing when commenced, where located, by whom established, and the number of scholars at each.*

When commenced.	Where located.	By whom established.	No. of scholars.
	In the Seneca nation, N. York, on the Buffalo reservation.	*By the Missionary Society of New York.*	45

Remarks. This school appears to have been in existence about eight or nine years, but not of much advantage until lately, for the last two or three years, it has been more prosperous, and is being very useful; the number of scholars is said to be increasing. In addition to reading, writing, and arithmetic, the Indians are instructed in the mechanic arts and the use of agricultural implements. There is, also, at this place a female adult school, consisting of from sixteen to twenty-five, who regularly attend and receive instruction in knitting, sewing, spinning and weaving.*

	In the Tuscarora nation, New York.	*By the Missionary Society of New York.*	45

Remarks. This school appears to have been established about four or five years ago. At times, the number of scholars is said to be greater than that here mentioned. The course of instruction is reading, writing, and arithmetic. A farm is cultivated by the superintendent of the school, which is designed as a model for the Indians.*

---

*These two schools, by an arrangement made early in the year 1821, between the Missionary Society of New York and the United Foreign Missionary Society of New York, were placed under the direction of the latter; since which, measures have been taken to render them more extensively useful.

A.— *Statement of schools which have been established in the Indian country, showing when commenced, where located, by whom established, and the number of scholars at each.* (continued)

When commenced.	Where located.	By whom established.	No. of scholars.
Dec., 1820,	In the Oneida nation, at Oneida Castle, New York.	*By the Hamilton Baptist Missionary Society of New York.*	40

Remarks. This school is on the Lancasterian plan. At the request of the Indians, the society agreed to employ a farmer, carpenter, and a blacksmith, to instruct the children in their respective arts. The school is stated to be progressing in a satisfactory manner, and that the Indians appear desirous to acquire the arts of civilized life.

Dec., 1801,	At Spring Place, in the Cherokee nation.	*By the Society of United Brethren for the Southern States, commonly called Moravians.*	19

Remarks. Between sixty and seventy youths of both sexes have been educated at this school. The number now at it consists of sixteen boys and three girls. They are instructed in reading, writing, arithmetic, and grammar. Between school hours, the boys are employed in agricultural labors, and the girls in sewing, knitting, marking, and various household occupations. One of the girls is stated to have made considerable progress in drawing.

Jan., 1817,	Brainard, in the Cherokee nation.	*By the American Board of Commissioners for Foreign Missions.*	96

Remarks. About two-thirds of the number of scholars males. The school is upon the Lancasterian plan, and appears, from the report of the superintendent, to be progressing with great success. There are several local schools which have grown out of this establishment, in the Cherokee nation, and are under its direction. (See extracts from the report of the superintendent, herewith.)

A.— *Statement of schools which have been established in the Indian country, showing when commenced, where located, by whom established, and the number of scholars at each.* (continued)

When commenced.	Where located.	By whom established.	No. of scholars.
Jan., 1820,	Valley Towns, Cherokee nation.	*By the Baptist Board for Foreign Missions.*	37

Remarks. The number has been as high as sixty. The school is upon the Lancasterian plan. Besides reading, writing, and arithmetic, the boys are instructed in the first principles of husbandry, and the girls in the ordinary domestic arts.

April, 1821,	Tensawattee, on the Hightower river, in the Cherokee nation.	*By the Sarepta Missionary Society, under the patronage of the Baptist Board, &c.*	28

Remarks. The scholars are said to be improving fast, and the school bids fair to be a very useful one.

Aug., 1818,	Elliot, in the Choctaw nation.	*By the American Board of Commissioners for Foreign Missions.*	80

Remarks. Sixty males and twenty females. The extract from the report of the superintendent for 1820, (none having been recieved for 1821,) herewith, will show the prosperity and usefulness of this establishment. The chiefs have shown great liberality in providing for the education of their children, by appropriating in each of the three districts of the nation $2,000 annually, for seventeen years, out of their annuity, for the support of schools, &c.; and the American board has taken measures for the establishment of other schools in the nation, one of which, at Mayhew, is in great forwardness. The school at Elliot is on the Lancasterian plan.

A.— *Statement of schools which have been established in the Indian country, showing when commenced, where located, by whom established, and the number of scholars at each.* (continued)

When commenced.	Where located.	By whom established.	No. of scholars.
Oct., 1820,	Chickasaw nation, near ——,	By the Cumberland Missionary Society.	28

Remarks. Two-thirds of the number, boys. The report states "that the children have been orderly and attentive to their studies, and particularly so to moral and religious instruction; and have volunteered to work a part of their time, and choose rather to take the time from their play than their books."

Oct., 1821,	Chickasaw nation near the agency.	By the Dom. and For. Mis. Soc. of the Synod of S. C. & Geo.	—

Remarks. This school, at the last report, was not in operation, but was expected to be so by last fall. It is conducted upon the Lancasterian plan.

Oct., 1820,	Fort Wayne, Indiana,	By the Baptist Board of Foreign Missions.	50

Remarks. The children at this school are of the Miami tribe, and are taught to read and write. No particular report in relation to the progress of the school has been received.

Oct., 1820,	Osages, on the Arkansas,	By the United Foreign Missionary Society of New York.	—

Remarks. The persons sent out by the society to make this establishment have arrived at their destination, and commenced the erection of the necessary buildings, some of which are completed; but the war which exists between the Osages and Cherokees has prevented the establishment from going into operation.

A.— *Statement of schools which have been established in the Indian country, showing when commenced, where located, by whom established, and the number of scholars at each.* (continued)

When commenced.	Where located.	By whom established.	No. of scholars.
	Osages, in the State of Missouri.	By the United Foreign Missionary Society of New York.	—

Remarks. The persons sent out during the last year by the society to make this establishment have not yet made their report; consequently, cannot state what progress has been made by them.

	Cherokees, on the Arkansas,	By the American Board of Commissioners for Foreign Missions.	—

Remarks. The persons sent out by the American Board of Commissioners, &c. to make this establishment have arrived among the Cherokees, fixed upon a site for it, and commenced the erection of the necessary buildings, some of which are completed; but a school has not yet been opened, in consequence of the war between the Osages and Cherokees.

Remarks. The consent of the Indians to the establishment of the above-mentioned schools in their country has in every instance been first obtained by the society by which they have been respectively made, with the approbation of the Department of War.[48]

48. *American State Papers,* Vol. II, "Indian Affairs Document No. 182" (Washington, D.C.: Gales and Seaton, 1834), pp. 275–77. Emphasis added.

The policy of "Civilizing of the Indians" referred to by President John Quincy Adams in his Fourth Annual Message to Congress on December 2, 1828, can be clearly linked to the Federal program of teaching Christianity.

The attention of Congress is particularly invited *to that part of the report of the Secretary of War* which concerns the existing system of our relations with the Indian tribes. *At the establishment of the Federal Government under the present Constitution of the United States the principle was adopted of considering them as foreign and independent powers and also as proprietors of lands. They were, moreover, considered as savages, whom it was our policy and our duty to use our influence in converting to Christianity and in bringing within the pale of civilization.*

As independent powers, we negotiated with them by treaties; as proprietors, we purchased of them all the lands which we could prevail upon them to sell; as brethren of the human race, rude and ignorant, we *endeavored to bring them to the knowledge of religion and letters.* The ultimate design was to incorporate in our own institutions that portion of them which could be converted to the state of civilization. In the practice of European States, before our Revolution, they had been considered as children to be governed; as tenants at discretion, to be dispossessed as occasion might require; as hunters to be indemnified by trifling concessions for removal from the grounds from which their game was extirpated. In changing the system it would seem as if a full contemplation of the consequences of the change had not been taken. We have been far more successful in the acquisition of their lands than in imparting to them the principles or inspiring them with the spirit of civilization. *But in appropriating to ourselves their hunting grounds we have brought upon ourselves the obligation of providing them with subsistence; and when we have had the rare good fortune of teaching them the arts of civilization and the doctrines of Christianity we have unexpectedly found them forming in the midst of ourselves communities claiming to be independent of ours and rivals of sovereignty within the territories of the members of our Union.* This state of things requires that a remedy should be provided—a remedy which, while it shall do justice to those unfortunate children of nature, may secure to the members of our confederation their rights of sovereignty and of soil. As the outline of a project to that effect, the views presented in the report of the Secretary of War are recommended to the consideration of Congress.[49]

49. Richardson, *A Compilation of the Messages,* Vol. II, pp. 415–16. Emphasis added.

Further evidence of such a link appears in the annual report prepared by the Secretary of War in the Administration of Monroe and Quincy Adams pursuant to an Act of Congress detailing, among other things, the Mission Schools supported, the number of teachers and pupils, and the religious affiliation of the church school. Other verification of federal expenditures to religious schools under the regime of the First Amendment with its Establishment of Religion Clause, which were not thought unconstitutional, appears in the typical report of 1827 reproduced below. The report consists of three parts; a letter and two supporting statements or schedules. Statement "B" is most germane to this discussion.

REPORT FROM THE OFFICE OF INDIAN AFFAIRS.

Department of War,
Office of Indian Affairs,
November 24th, 1827.

Sir:—I had the honor, (in the absence of Col. M'Kenney,) in compliance (in part) with the order of the Department, of the 10th September last, to lay before you, on the 29th ultimo, an estimate of the amount which will be required to be appropriated for the current expenses of the Indian Department for the year 1828, . . . The sum of $181,224, estimated for 1828, is believed to be not a cent more than will be absolutely required for the service of that year. . . . The expense for these objects has been considerable during the present year, and there is no reason to doubt, from present indications, of its being equally so for some years to come.

In further compliance with the order of the 10th September last, I now have the honor to submit the accompanying statements, marked A and B.

Statement A, shows the amount of money disbursed in the Indian Department, under the various heads of appropriation, for the three first quarters of the present year; the amount for which accounts have been rendered; and the amount which remains to be accounted for. The large amount ($309,509 18) which appears to be unaccounted for, arises, in some measure, from the circumstance of the statement showing the amount of remittances to the 30th September, while it only shows the amount of accounts rendered to the 1st of that month, (they *being required to be so rendered annually, by the act of the 6th May, 1822, amendatory of the act of 1802,*) making, of course, a considerable difference, as the remittances made during the month are included in the former, and the disbursements made during the same time emitted in the latter. But the principal reason for this balance is, all the accounts, to the 1st September, had not come in when the statement was prepared. Since then accounts have been received from General Clark, which alone reduce the balance to $221,513 31; and it is believed that when those which yet remain come in, (and they are daily expected,) are received, the balance which remains to be accounted for, will be reduced to a very small amount; probably not more than that which must necessarily result from the difference in the period for which the accounts are rendered, and that which the remittances are made up to. There is, in fact, no reason to doubt, but that the whole will be faithfully accounted for, as soon as all the objects for which the remittances were made are accomplished.

Statement B, shows the number of Indian schools, the number of teachers to each, and the number of pupils. The amount disbursed for the present year, up to the 30th September, on account of these schools, from the annual appropriation of *$10,000 for the civilization of the Indians, is, as will be seen by reference to the statement A, $8,246 84.*

. . . .

All which is respectfully submitted.

To the Hon. James Barbour,
    Secretary of War.

SAM'L. S. HAMILTON.[50]

50. *U.S. Office of Indian Affairs, Annual Reports of the Commissioner of Indian Affairs, 1824–1831,* Vol. I (New York: AMS Press, Inc., 1976), "Report of November 24, 1827." Emphasis added.

[A.]

EXTRACT from the statement of the 2d Auditor, showing the amount of Requisitions issued under the head of appropriation, from the 1st day of January, 1827, to the 30th September; the amount of accounts of the respective agents and disbursing officers, in whose favour said Requisitions were issued, which have been rendered for settlement; and the amount which remains unaccounted for.

	Requisitions issued from 1st Jan. 1827, to 30th Sept.1827.	Amount of acc'ts rendered for settlement.	Amount which remains unaccounted for.
Indian Department	$101,934 25	$101,934 25	
Pay of Indian Agents and Superintendent at St. Louis	40,356 65	25,106 65	$ 15,250 00
Pay of sub-agents	20,461 86	9,386 48	11,075 38
Civilization of Indians	*8,246 84*	*4,400 00*	*3,846 84*
Presents to Indians	14,390 45	14,390 45	
Annuities	227,496 63	159,364 28	68,132 35
Purchase of provisions for Quapaws	2,000 00		2,000 00
Carrying into effect treaties with Osages, Kanzas and Shawnees, per act 20 May, 1826	4,550 00	1,060 37	3,489 63
Running a line dividing Florida from Georgia	3,745 80	3,745 80	
To aid the Creeks in their removal west of the Mississippi, per act 20 May, 1826	29,080 82	2 50	29,078 32
Act for the relief of the Florida Indians	12,750 25	12,750 25	
Treaty with Choctaws and Chickasaws, per act 20 May, 1826	2,445 37	2,445 37	
Treaty with the Creeks of 26 January, 1826, per act of 22 May, 1826	96,472 51	14,081 58	82,390 93

(Continued on page 75.)

EXTRACT A. (continued from page 74.)

	Requisitions issued from 1st Jan. 1827, to 30th Sept.1827.	Amount of acc'ts rendered for settlement.	Amount which remains unaccounted for.
Proceeds of the lands reserved for Choctaw schools under 7th art. of treaty of 18 October, 1820	7,104 40	833 83	6,270 57
Rations to Florida Indians	30,015 96	30,015 96	
Running the line of the land assigned to the Florida Indians	330 56	330 56	
Holding treaties with Cherokees, for a canal to connect with the Highwassee and Conasago	10,000 00		10,000 00
To carry into effect certain Indian treaties, per act 2 March, 1827	147,641 06	69,665 90	77,975 16
Holding treaties with Indians beyond the Mississippi	93 05	93 05	
	$759,116 46	$449,607 28	$309,509 18

RECAPITULATION.

Amount of requisitions issued in the three first quarters of 1827	$759,116 46
Amount of accounts rendered for settlement during said period	449,607 28
	$309,509 18
Amount for which accounts have been rendered by General Clark since the statement, from which the above abstract is taken, was made by the 2d Auditor, to wit,	87,995 87
Leaving the sum to be accounted for	$221,513 31

51

51. Ibid. Emphasis added.

[B.]

STATEMENT showing the number of Indian Schools, where established, by whom, the number of Teachers, &c., the number of Pupils, and the amount annually allowed and paid by the Goverment, with remarks as to their condition, &c.

Number.	Name of Site and Station.	By whom Established.	Number of Teachers.	Number of Pupils.	Amount annually paid by the Government.	Remarks.
1	Spring Place Cherokee Nation, Alabama	United Brethren	7	11	$ 200 00	All the schools which have been reported appear to be in a flourishing condition, and those which have not been reported, it is presumed, are in as good and flourishing a condition as they were last year.
2	Oochgeelogy - do. -	- - do. - -	5	18		
3	Elliot - Choctaw Nation	American Board of Commissioners for Foreign Missions	6	20		
4	Mayhew- - do. - -	- - do. - -	6	54		
5	Bethel- - do. - -	- - do. - -	4	16		
6	Emmaus - - do. - -	- - do. - -	4	25	1,000 00	
7	Goshen - - do. - -	- - do. - -	6	14		
8	Captain Harrison's -do. -	- - do. - -	1	13		
9	Mr. Juzan's - - do. - -	- - do. - -	1	15		
10	Ai-ik-hunna- - do. - -	- - do. - -	3	22		
11	Colonel Folsom's - do. -	- - do. - -	1	70		

(Continued on page 78.)

12	Senecas near Buffalo N.Y.	- - do. - -	8	45	200 00
13	Union - Osages - Arkansas	- - do. - -	6	31	150 00
14	Harmony -do.- Missouri	- - do. - -	27	35	150 00
15	Tuscaroras - - N. York	- - do. - -	-	45	200 00
16	Michilimackinac	- - do. - -	-	50	300 00
17	Ottawas - Miami of the Lake	- - do. - -	21	10	100 00
18	Brainard - Cherokee - East Miss.	- - do. - -	-	-	550 00
19	Carmel - - do. - -	- - do. - -	-	-	50 00
20	Creek Path - - do. - -	- - do. - -	42	84	50 00
21	High Tower - - do. - -	- - do. - -	-	-	50 00
22	Dwight - West Miss.	- - do. - -	15	50	200 00
23	Caiaraugus - Senecas -N.Y.	- - do. - -	9	40	200 00
24	Carey, on the St. Joseph's river among the Potaw-atomies	Baptist General Convention	14	70	300 00
25	Thomas - Grand river Ottawas	- - do. - -	8	20	-
26	Withington - Creek Nation Georgia	- - do. - -	13	25	225 00

STATEMENT B. (continued from page 77.)

Number.	Name of Site and Station.	By whom Established.	Number of Teachers.	Number of Pupils.	Amount annually paid by the Government.	Remarks.
27	Valley-towns - Cherokees East Miss.	- - do. - -	8	50	175 00	*1191 in the schools in the Indian country, and which derive assistance from the appropriation.
28	Tensawattee - do. -	- - do. - -	9	38	175 00	
29	Tonawanda - Senecas N.Y.	- - do. - -	-	30	175 00	
30	Oneida Castle - N.York	Protestant Episcopal Church, N.York	3	30	250 00	100 in the Choctaw Academy.
31	Onedias - - - do. -	Hamilton Baptist Missionary Society	5	35	200 00	1291 total.
32	Wyandots - Near Upper Sandusky, Ohio	Methodist Society	2	69	400 00	
33	Asbury Mission, Creek Nation Georgia	- - do. - -	6	23	100 00	
34	Monroe - Chickasaw Nation	Synod of South Carolina and Georgia	12	24	400 00	
35	Tockshish - - do. -	- - do. - -	4	15	-	
36	Cane Creek -do. -	- - do. - -	6	28	-	

37	Martyn - - do. -	- - do. - -	2	18	
38	Florissant - Missouri -	Society of Jesuits	9	25	400 00
39	Charity Hall - Chickasaw Nation	Cumberland Missionary Board	9	26	250 00
40	Pleasant Point - Quaddy Indians Maine	Society for Propagating the Gospel	1	60	150 00
			-	*1,191	6,600 00
	To which add amount allowed to Bishop Chase, - for education of Indian youths in Ohio —		-	-	200 00
	And also this amount, allowed to Baptist General Convention, for education of Indian youths of promise in N.Y.		-	-	350 00
	Total amount of annual allowances for 1827,		-	-	$7,150 00

NOTE: Under the head of number of teachers, is included all the mission family, including mechanics and laborers. The numbers of teachers in the schools are from one to three. The reports included the whole, without designating.

DEPARTMENT OF WAR,
Office Indian Affairs, November 24th, 1827.
SAM'L. S. HAMILTON[52]

52. Ibid. Emphasis added.

Lest it be argued that this policy violates the narrow interpretation of the Establishment of Religion Clause advanced here, it should be carefully noted that the schools of no single Christian sect were being supported with federal money to the exclusion of others, and thus no particular sect was being elevated to a preferred religious status. Nor does the appropriation of federal monies to Christian schools indicate discriminatory aid to religion, for as Pfeffer himself points out, the number of professed non-Christians were minute in the early years of the Federal Republic.[53]

In his book *Religion and Education Under the Constitution*, J. M. O'Neill discusses this aid to religious education:

> By 1896, Congress was appropriating annually over $500,000 in support of sectarian Indian education carried on by religious organizations. This expenditure of public money appropriated by Act of Congress for over a century following the ratification of the First Amendment constitutes absolute proof that for over a century neither Congress nor the religious leaders interpreted the First Amendment to mean a prohibition of the use of public funds by Congress in aid of religion and religious education.
>
> In 1897, Congress decided upon another policy. They declared by the Act of June 7, 1897 that it should be the settled policy of the government hereafter to make no appropriation whatever for education in any sectarian school. *This was a declaration of policy by Congress . . . . The point is that in declaring this policy, there was no contention that Congress had been committing unconstitutional acts for the last century.*[54]

In light of the thousands of federal tax dollars spent each year for these church schools Pfeffer's claim that since the adoption of the *Constitution* and the First Amendment, Congress never considered a bill or passed "a bill for the support of teachers of religion" is incredible.[55]

Some Conclusions

Chapters two and three have examined several important aspects of the history of the separation of Church and State in the United States and have shown that they do not support Leo Pfeffer's viewpoint in his much respected work *Church, State, and Freedom*[56] and his more recent *God, Caesar, and the Constitution*.[57] Reference has also been made here to the joint work

---

53. Pfeffer, *Church, State, and Freedom*, p. 142.

54. O'Neill, *Religion and Education*, pp. 118–19. Emphasis added.

55. See quote, fn. 47, supra.

56. Pfeffer, *Church, State, and Freedom*, rev. ed. (Boston: Beacon Press, 1967).

57. Pfeffer, *God, Caesar, and the Constitution* (Boston: Beacon Press, 1975).

of Anson Phelps Stokes and Leo Pfeffer, *Church and State in the United States*.[58] What has been the purpose of this critique?

I address Professor Pfeffer's writings because he is the leading exponent of an interpretation of the Establishment of Religion Clause of the First Amendment that I believe to be historically untenable and yet is supported by many scholars, political and legal, and a significant number of federal and state judges in the United States and—more important—some of the Justices of the United States Supreme Court. He has published in the most respected legal journals, political science reviews, and has been the recipient of many awards from important organizations concerned with constitutional law, civil liberties, and individual freedom, including the American Civil Liberties Union to which with pride I subscribe. His arguments and documentation *demand* the scrutiny of anyone who professes an alternative scholarly approach and interpretation of the constitutional doctrine of separation of Church and State. The foundation for the "Pfeffer School of thought" is developed in what I consider the two most important chapters of *Church, State, and Freedom*–chapter four, "The Principle is Born,"[59] and chapter five, "The Meaning of the Principle."[60]

With the documented facts of American history presented here, I believe that I have shown conclusively that the Pfeffer interpretation of the Establishment Clause of the First Amendment is incorrect. The Pfeffer thesis—as largely stated in *Church, State, and Freedom*—is an absolute one that is logically disproven by the mere showing of one exception. Consider the following:

Throughout his adult life Jefferson *never* swerved from his devotion to the principle of *complete* independence of religion and government.[61]

Instances of direct grants of money or property to institutions exclusively devoted to worship, such as churches, are rare, *and their unconstitutionality is clear.*[62]

In summary, therefore, it may be said that under our Constitution, government may seek to achieve *only* secular ends, and in doing so may *employ only secular means.*[63]

The significance of this ending and beginning is more than symbolic; it indicates *unmistakably* that in the minds of the fathers of our Constitution, independence of religion and government was *the alpha and the omega of democracy and freedom.*[64]

58. Pfeffer and Stokes, *Church and State in the United States,* rev. ed. in 1 vol. (New York: Harper and Row, 1964).

59. Pfeffer, *Church, State, and Freedom,* pp. 91–127.

60. Ibid., pp. 128–80.

61. Ibid., p. 105. Emphasis added.

62. Ibid., p. 196. Emphasis added.

63. Ibid., p. 180. Emphasis added.

64. Ibid., p. 127. Emphasis added.

So conclusive with Madison's victory in the Virginia legislature [regarding the defeat of the Assessment Bill to support teachers of the Christian religion] and in the adoption of the First Amendment, that in more than a century and a half since the Amendment was adopted Congress *has never* enacted—nor indeed been called upon to consider—a bill for the support of teachers of religion.[65]

Such statements are so absolute and sweeping that to document any one exception is to prove their incorrectness. In this chapter and the preceding one, however, I have presented, analyzed, and documented *at least one and often more exceptions to every one of these absolute statements so vital to the Pfeffer interpretation.*

Although my documentation is selective, much more exists to corroborate my interpretation, which is, I believe, a more factually supported interpretation of the American constitutional doctrine of separation of Church and State under the First Amendment.

These original documents of American history—reproduced in this book's chapters and its *Addenda*—prove that the sweeping absolute terms used by Pfeffer—or the many adherents of his interpretation of the Establishment of Religion Clause—are factually incorrect and constitute part of the fiction and current mythology embraced by many regarding the religious prohibitions of the Establishment Clause. The documents reproduced here are, in part, the incontrovertible facts for my conclusion regarding the inaccuracy of the Pfeffer thesis. These documents and many others are available in any major library of American government documents to any student or scholar of American history and politics, any United States Senator, Congressman, President, Supreme Court Justice or Clerk, and, most important, to any citizen or student of the American Federal Republic.

As we shall see, the United States Supreme Court—beginning with the first comprehensive Supreme Court case under the Establishment Clause in 1947—has for the most part, either advertently or inadvertently, used the fiction assailed here, to justify and thus attempt to legitimize its constitutional interpretations of the religious prohibitions of the Establishment Clause. *Fiction*—where disinterested scholarly inquiry still freely flourishes—*legitimizes nothing.* Legal fiction only engenders disrespect for the legal institutions that employ it, the judges who invoke it, and the law proclaimed as a consequence of adherence to it. That the opinions of the United States Supreme Court have, for the most part, reflected the Pfeffer thesis and thus an incorrect interpretation of the American constitutional doctrine of separation of Church and State will be adequately shown in the following chapters.

65. Ibid., p. 165–66. Emphasis added.

Chapter Four

Extending the Covenant: The "Establishment" Clause and the Fourteenth Amendment

During the summer of 1787, while the Federal *Constitution* was being written in Philadelphia, Thomas Jefferson was in France as the Ambassador of the United States. Owing to distance, the slowness of travel, and especially the rules of secrecy governing the Convention proceedings, Jefferson was unaware of the substantive debates and compromises that eventually produced a draft proposal of a new constitution, which the Framers hoped would replace the ineffective *Articles of Confederation*.[1]

After the Constitutional Convention, Jefferson, still in Paris, carefully studied the proposed document that had been rushed to him by Franklin, Washington, and Madison.[2] His letter to Madison in December 1787 evaluating the document expressed great concern over the lack of a "bill of rights."[3] After approving many aspects of the proposed constitution,

1. The secrecy rules were adopted by the convention delegates on May 29, 1787, and provided: "That no copy be taken of any entry on the Journal during the sitting of the house, without the leave of the house." "That members only be permitted to inspect the Journal." "That nothing spoken in the house be printed, or otherwise published, or communicated, without leave."

Jonathan Elliot's *Debates on the Federal Constitution*, Vol. I (Philadelphia: J.P. Lippincott Co.; 1901), p. 143.

2. For an interesting and informative account of the Madison-Jefferson roles in the framing of the Bill of Rights see, Adrienne Koch, *Jefferson and Madison, The Great Collaboration* (London: Oxford University Press; 1950); and Robert Allen Rutland, *The Birth of the Bill of Rights 1776–1791* (New York: Collier Books Edition; 1962).

3. Jefferson's letter to James Madison, December 20, 1787, in Adrienne Koch and William Peden, eds., *The Life and Selected Writings of Thomas Jefferson* (New York: The Modern Library; 1944), pp. 436–44.

Jefferson wrote Madison:

> I will now tell you what I do not like. First, the omission of a bill of rights, providing clearly, and without the aid of sophism, for freedom of religion, freedom of the press, protection against standing armies, restriction of monopolies, the eternal and unremitting force of the habeas corpus laws, and trials by jury in all matters of fact triable by the laws of the land, and not by the laws of nations. . . .[4]

After the ratification of the original *Constitution* in 1788,[5] Jefferson "rejoiced" with Madison at its acceptance by nine states, but still argued for the addition of a Bill of Rights.[6] The conditional ratification of the new *Constitution* by several states, pending an added Bill of Rights, was in accord with Jefferson's position.[7] Crucial here, however, is not Madison's proposal of a "Bill of Rights" in the First Congress in 1789 and its enactment in 1791, but the constraints on governmental power that this addition to the fundamental law of the land provided.

Jefferson believed that a Bill of Rights, if added to the Federal *Constitution*, would limit the powers of the Federal Government and the Federal Government only. He drew a clear parallel for Madison in his letter of July 31, 1788: "I hope . . . a bill of rights will be formed to guard the people against the federal government, as they are already guarded against their State governments in most instances."[8] It is ironic that Jefferson's understanding of the delimiting authority of the Bill of Rights was written into American Constitutional Law, seven years after his death, by his former political antagonist, United States Supreme Court Chief Justice John Marshall, in the landmark case of *Barron* v. *Baltimore*.

The Barron Doctrine

In *Barron* v. *Baltimore*, brought before the United States Supreme Court in 1833, Barron sued the City of Baltimore for compensation resulting from what he claimed was a taking of his property for a "public purpose" under

4. Ibid., p. 437.

5. The term "original Federal *Constitution*" as used here refers solely to the original seven articles proposed by the Framers in 1787.

6. Jefferson's letters to Madison, July 31, 1788, Koch and Peden, *The Life and Selected Writings*, pp. 450–52; November 18, 1788, p. 452; March 15, 1789, pp. 462–64.

7. The ratification of the Federal *Constitution* by conventions in Maryland, Virginia, New York, North Carolina, and Rhode Island called for the addition of a bill of rights.

8. Edward Dumbould, ed., *The Political Writings of Thomas Jefferson* (New York: The Liberal Arts Press, Inc.; 1955), p. 142.

the Fifth Amendment.[9] In the paving of its streets, Baltimore had diverted several streams of water that carried large amounts of sand and deposited them around Barron's wharf. Because of these sand deposits, the area surrounding Barron's wharf became so shallow that ocean-going ships were unable to use it for loading and unloading cargo. Assuming the Fifth Amendment of the Federal *Constitution* limited the powers of the States as well as the Federal Government, Barron claimed that the city of Baltimore—a creation of the State of Maryland—owed him "just compensation" under the Amendment because the City's actions had the effect of "taking" the commercial worth of his wharf.[10]

The constitutional issue which this case put before the U.S. Supreme Court for the first time was whether the guarantees of the Bill of Rights were restrictions on the States as well as the Federal Government.[11] Writing the opinion of the Court, Chief Justice John Marshall held that Barron's claim raised no appropriate federal question because the Fifth Amendment was a constitutional restraint on the Federal Government only and the Federal Government was clearly not a party to the suit.

> The Constitution was ordained and established by the people of the United States for themselves, for their own government and not for the government of the individual States. Each State established a constitution for itself and in that constitution provided such limitations and restrictions on the powers of its particular government as its judgment dictated. The people of the United States formed such a government for the United States as they supposed best adapted to their situation, and best calculated to promote their interests. The powers they conferred on this government were to be exercised by itself; and if expressed in general terms, are naturally, and, we think, necessarily applicable to the general government created by the instrument. They are limitations on power granted in the instrument itself; not of distinct governments framed by different persons and for different purposes.
>
> If these propositions be correct, the Fifth Amendment must be understood as restraining the power of the general government, not as applicable to the States.[12]

9. 7 Peters 243 (1833). Part of the historical development of the relationship between the federal Bill of Rights and the States here follows closely my previously published analysis in Robert L. Cord, *Protest, Dissent and the Supreme Court* (Cambridge, Mass.: Winthrop Publishers, Inc.; 1971), pp. 19–29.

10. The relevant section of the Fifth Amend. is: "...nor shall private property be taken for public use, without just compensation."

11. Although the Bill of Rights is popularly identified with the first ten amendments to the U.S. *Constitution*, many Justices of the U.S. Supreme Court and students of American Constitutional law apply this term only to the first eight amendments.

12. 7 Peters 243, at 247, 248.

Marshall's opinion carried the Court's reasoning to the logical conclusion that not only was the Fifth Amendment not applicable to the States but also it inferred that other governmental restraints in the first eight amendments were not applicable to the States by the same reasoning. If the *Barron* decision left unclear the lack of governmental restraints which the Bill of Rights imposed on the State governments, all uncertainty should have been removed after the Supreme Court's decision twelve years later in *Permoli* v. *New Orleans.*[13]

In 1842 New Orleans passed an ordinance imposing a fine on anyone who exposed a corpse in a public place within the municipality. Father Permoli officiated at a funeral in the Roman Catholic Church of Saint Augustine in which the deceased was exposed and blessed in a ceremony prescribed by the Rites of the Roman Catholic Church. Permoli was fined $50. He claimed his actions were protected by the Federal *Constitution* and laws of the United States which prevent the enactment of any law prohibiting the free exercise of religion.

Speaking for the Supreme Court, Mr. Justice Catron applied the *Barron* rationale and held that the religious guarantees of the First Amendment restricted only the actions of the United States Government. In order to have their religious rights protected from State government, citizens of the States would have to look to the State constitutions and laws. Wrote Catron:

> The ordinances complained of must violate the Constitution or laws of the United States, or some authority exercised under them; if they do not we have no power by the 25th section of the Judiciary Act to interfere. *The Constitution makes no provision for protecting the citizens of the respective States in their religious liberties; this is left to the State Constitutions and laws: nor is there any inhibition imposed by the Constitution of the United States. . . .*
>
> In our judgment, the question presented by the record is exclusively of state cognizance, and equally so in the old States and the new ones; and that the writ of error must be dismissed.[14]

The constitutional principles expressed by the Court in the *Barron* and *Permoli* cases are very clear. Reflecting Jefferson's view of the federal Bill of Rights, the Supreme Court had taken the position that the first eight amendments—including the two religious guarantees of the First Amendment—were irrelevant to the exercise of State legislative or judicial power

---

13. 3 Howard 589 (1845). 14. Ibid., at 609, 610. Emphasis added.

and, in fact, were not constitutional limitations on the governmental power of the several States at all.

The "Privileges or Immunities" Clause

The passage of the Fourteenth Amendment to the *Constitution* in 1868 generated new attempts to apply the governmental restrictions of the Bill of Rights to the States. The vehicles that were to "nationalize" the first eight amendments were two clauses of Section One of the Fourteenth Amendment: the "Privileges or Immunities" Clause and the "Due Process" Clause. Both explicitly restrict the governmental power of the several States.[15]

The *Slaughter-House Cases*, requiring the first Supreme Court interpretation of the "Privileges or Immunities" Clause, were decided in 1873.[16] There, the Butcher's Benevolent Association, a group of small independent butchers doing business in New Orleans, challenged the constitutionality of a Louisiana statute that established a monopoly of slaughtering rights in a newly chartered slaughter-house company for twenty-five years. Losing their case in the Louisiana courts, the Butchers asked the U.S. Supreme Court to declare the state law unconstitutional because the monopoly violated the "privileges or immunities" of U.S. citizens engaged in the butchering business. In deciding the case in favor of the Louisiana law, the Supreme Court, by a closely divided vote (5 to 4), so narrowly defined the "Privileges or Immunities" Clause that its potential usefulness in applying any of the restraints of the Bill of Rights against state power was all but completely destroyed.

Speaking for the Court, Mr. Justice Miller explained at length that Section One of the Fourteenth Amendment conferred dual citizenship on Americans; however, different rights derived from the character of the diverse citizenships.[17] Only the rights derived from U.S. citizenship, and not those from state citizenship, were protected from infringement by state law under the Fourteenth Amendment. Said Miller:

---

15. The relevant part of the Fourteenth Amend. is the second sentence in Sec. 1: "No State shall make or enforce any law which shall abridge the privileges or immunities of citizens of the United States; nor shall any State deprive any person of life, liberty, or property, without due process of law; . . ."

16. 16 Wallace 36 (1873).

17. The constitutional provision bestowing dual citizenship in the first sentence of the Fourteenth Amend., Sec. 1 provides: "All persons born or naturalized in the United States, and subject to the jurisdiction thereof, are citizens of the United States and of the State wherein they reside."

The next observation is more important in view of the arguments of counsel in the present case. It is that the distinction between citizenship of the United States and citizenship of a state is clearly recognized and established. Not only may a man be a citizen of the United States without being a citizen of the state, but an important element is necessary to convert the former into the latter. He must reside within the state to make him a citizen of it, but it is only necessary that he should be born or naturalized in the United States to be a citizen of the Union.

It is quite clear, then, that there is a citizenship of the United States and a citizenship of a state, which are distinct from each other and which depend upon different characteristics or circumstances in the individual.

We think this distinction and its explicit recognition in this Amendment of great weight in this argument, because the next paragraph of this same section, which is the one mainly relied on by the plaintiffs in error, speaks only of privileges and immunities of citizens of the United States, and does not speak of those of citizens of the several states. The argument, however, in favor of the plaintiffs, rests wholly on the assumption, that the citizenship is the same and the privileges and immunities guaranteed by the clause are the same. . . .[18]

The Court's opinion, then, rejected the contention that the protection of an individual's civil liberties had been transferred from the protection of the several States to the Federal Government because of the Privileges or Immunities Clause of the Fourteenth Amendment. Miller's opinion continued:

Was it the purpose of the 14th Amendment, by the simple declaration that no state should make or enforce any law which shall abridge the privileges and immunities of citizens of the United States, to transfer the security and protection of all the civil rights which we have mentioned, from the states to the Federal Government? And where it is declared that Congress shall have the power to enforce that article, was it intended to bring within the power of Congress the entire domain of civil rights heretofore belonging exclusively to the states? . . .

We are convinced that no such results were intended by the Congress which proposed these amendments, nor by the legislatures of the states, which ratified them.[19]

In sum, the *Slaughter-House Cases* did not reverse the *Barron* doctrine, but held that the rights protected from federal governmental intrusion by the first eight amendments were still not applicable to the States even

18. 16 Wallace 36, at 73–74.   19. Ibid., at 77–78.

under the Fourteenth Amendment's "Privileges or Immunities" Clause. In addition, the Court majority, while refusing to provide an exhaustive list of the privileges and immunities of U.S. citizenship, did provide some general and some specific statements about those guarantees of national citizenship.

All privileges and immunities which "owed their existence to the Federal government, its national character, its Constitution, or its laws," were derived from national citizenship. To be explicit, the right of participation in the national government, the right to petition the national government, the right to do business with the national government, the right to free access to national seaports, subtreasuries, land-offices, and courts of justice were enumerated.[20] Other rights were also catalogued:

> Another privilege of a citizen of the United States is to demand the care and protection of the Federal government over his life, liberty, and property when on the high seas or within the jurisdiction of a foreign government. Of this there can be no doubt, nor that the right depends upon his character as a citizen of the United States. The right to peaceably assemble and petition for redress of grievances, the privilege of the writ of *habeas corpus*, are rights of the citizen guaranteed by the Federal Constitution. The right to use the navigable waters of the United States, however they may penetrate the territory of the several states, and all rights secured to our citizens by treaties with foreign nations, are dependent upon citizenship of the United States, and not citizenship of a state. One of these privileges is conferred by the very article under consideration. It is that a citizen of the United States can, of his own volition, become a citizen of any state of the Union by a *bona fide* residence therein, with the same rights as other citizens of that state. To these may be added the rights secured by the 13th and 15th articles of Amendment, and by the other clause of the Fourteenth, next to be considered.[21]

The dissenting opinions advanced a significantly different point of view. There it was argued that the immunities designated as those of U.S. citizens protected by the Fourteenth Amendment were rights that "belong to citizens of all free governments." The dissents implied that those rights were identical with the guarantees of the Bill of Rights.[22] This view was sub-

---

20. Ibid., at 79.

21. Ibid., at 79–80.

22. Justice Douglas in his concurring opinion in *Gideon* v. *Wainwright*, 372 U.S. 335 (1963), maintains that Justices Bradley, Swayne, and Field "emphasized that the first eight Amendments granted citizens of the United States certain privileges and immunities that were protected from abridgement by the States by the Fourteenth Amendment." See fn. 1, at 346. The original record seems a bit more ambiguous than Douglas's interpretation.

sequently rejected by the Supreme Court many times, however, and has never been endorsed by an opinion of the Court.[23]

The consistent view of the Supreme Court has been the rejection of the Privileges or Immunities Clause as a way of making the particulars of the Bill of Rights restraints on state authority. Reflecting this view clearly is an opinion of the Court written by Justice Moody in 1908 for a nearly unanimous Court (8 to 1):

> The defendants contend, in the first place, that the exemption from self-incrimination is one of the privileges and immunities of citizens of the United States which the 14th Amendment forbids the states to abridge. It is not argued that the defendants are protected by that part of the 5th Amendment which provides that "no person . . . shall be compelled in any criminal case to be a witness against himself," for it is recognized by counsel that, by a long line of decisions, the first ten Amendments are not operative on the states. *Barron* v. *Balitmore*, 7 Pet. 243; *Spies* v. *Illinois*, 123 U.S. 131; *Brown* v. *New Jersey*, 175 U.S. 172; *Barrington* v. *Missouri*, 205 U.S. 483. But it is argued that this privilege is one of the fundamental rights of national citizenship, placed under national protection by the 14th Amendment, and it is specifically argued that the "privileges and immunities of citizens of the United States," protected against state action by that Amendment, include those fundamental personal rights which were protected against state action by the first eight Amendments; that this was the intention of the framers of the 14th Amendment, and that this part of it would otherwise have little or no meaning and effect. These arguments are not new to this court and the answer to them is found in its decisions. The meaning of the phrase "privileges and immunities of citizens of the United States," as used in the 14th Amendment, came under early consideration in the *Slaughter-House Cases*, 16 Wall. 36.
>
> . . . There can be no doubt, so far as the decision in the *Slaughter-House Cases* has determined the question, that the civil rights sometimes described as fundamental and inalienable, which, before the War Amendments, were enjoyed by state citizenship and protected by state

---

23. In *Walker* v. *Sauvinet*, 92 U.S. 90, at 92 (1876), the Court rejected the claim that the Seventh Amend. embodied a privilege and immunity of U.S. citizenship. "A trial by jury in suits at common law pending in the State courts is not . . . a privilege or immunity of national citizenship, which the States are forbidden by the Fourteenth Amendment to abridge." Similar contentions that particular rights in the first eight amendments restricted state action because they were privileges or immunities of U.S. citizenship were rejected in *Presser* v. *Illinois*, 116 U.S. 252 (1886); *Maxwell* v. *Dow*, 176 U.S. 581 (1900); *Twining* v. *New Jersey*, 211 U.S. 78 (1908); *New York ex rel. Bryant* v. *Zimmerman*, 278 U.S. 63 (1928); and *Palko* v. *Connecticut*, 302 U.S. 319 (1937).

government, were left untouched by this clause of the 14th Amendment. . . .[24]

The refusal by the Supreme Court to interpret the Privileges or Immunities Clause broadly as a way of bringing the first eight amendments under the Fourteenth Amendment, and thereby circumscribing further the governmental powers of the States, remains law today. The failure to broaden federal constitutional restraints on the States through the Fourteenth Amendment did not end with the abortive arguments about the Privileges or Immunities Clause. Collateral attempts to achieve the same goal through the "Due Process" Clause of the Fourteenth Amendment were taking place in the state courts.

The "Due Process" Clause

The "Due Process" Clause in the Fourteenth Amendment is an exact copy of the Fifth Amendment's. Before the Fourteenth Amendment's adoption in 1868, the Fifth Amendment's clause had been generally recognized as a limitation of the U.S. Congress, requiring it to provide the "due process for the enforcement of law; and it was in accordance with this limited appraisal of the clause that the Court disposed of early cases arising thereunder."[25] However, after the Fourteenth Amendment was added to the *Constitution*, attempts were soon made to convert the Due Process Clause into a substantive as well as a procedural restraint on governmental power.

Commenting on this departure from the conventional interpretation which had been given the Clause in the Fifth Amendment, it is not surprising that Justice Miller, speaking for the Court in *Davidson* v. *New Orleans* (1878),[26] expressed some amazement in the Court's opinion, which

---

24. *Twining* v. *New Jersey*, fn.23, *supra*. The lone dissent by the first Justice John Marshall Harlan held to the contrary that "the privileges and immunities mentioned in the original Amendments, and universally regarded as our heritage of liberty from the common law, were thus secured to every citizen of the United States, and placed beyond assault by any government, Federal or state;" by the addition of the Fourteenth Amend. See Harlan's dissenting opinion, 211 U.S. 114.

25. Edward S. Corwin, *The Constitu-*

tion of the United States, rev. and ann. (Washington, D.C.: U.S. Government Printing Office; 1953), pp. 971–73. The only major exception to this early restrictive view of the Fifth Amend. Due Process Clause appears to be *Dred Scott* v. *Sandford*, 19 Howard 393 (1857), where the Court ruled that the "Missouri Compromise" of 1820 deprived persons of their property (slaves) without "due process of law" and was therefore unconstitutional.

26. 96 U.S. 97 (1878).

refused to accept this novel interpretation:

> It is not a little remarkable that while this provision has been in the Constitution of the United States, as a restraint upon the authority of the Federal government, for nearly a century, and while during all that time, the manner in which the powers of that government have been exercised has been watched with jealously, and criticism in all its branches, this special limitation upon its powers has rarely been invoked in the judicial forum or the more enlarged theatre of public discussion. But while it has been part of the Constitution, as a restraint upon the power of the States, only a very few years, the docket of this Court is crowded with cases in which we are asked to hold that State courts and State legislatures have deprived their own citizens of life, liberty, or property without due process of law. There is here abundant evidence that there exists some strange misconception of the scope of this provision as found in the Fourteenth Amendment.[27]

The persistence to include the guarantees of the Bill of Rights in the restrictions that the Due Process Clause of the Fourteenth Amendment placed upon State actions, soon resulted in the landmark case, *Hurtado v. California* (1884).[28] Hurtado was charged with murder before a California County Court by means of an "information."[29] He was subsequently tried in the same court, found guilty, and sentenced to death. His appeals in the California courts to reverse his conviction were rejected and the United States Supreme Court agreed to hear his federal constitutional claim.

Hurtado's lawyers argued that since his indictment for murder was not a result of a presentment by a grand jury, as called for in the Fifth Amendment, his being charged with murder and subsequent trial were unconstitutional. The clear assumption of this argument was that the federal Fifth Amendment indictment process was required in state judicial proceedings and that the Fourteenth Amendment Due Process Clause embodied the protections of the first eight amendments which included the Fifth Amendment indictment procedure.

Rejecting Hurtado's arguments, the U.S. Supreme Court refused, with the same steadfastness (8 to 1) that discarded the arguments concerning the

---

27. Ibid., at 103, 104.

28. 110 U.S. 516 (1884).

29. An "information" is a process of bringing a criminal accusation against a person(s). It differs from an indictment by grand jury in that the prosecutor's case, sufficient to gain the formal public criminal charge necessary for trial, is presented to a competent public officer (usually a judge) instead of a grand jury. The Fifth Amendment guarantees, among other things, that "no person shall be held to answer for a capital or other infamous crime unless on a presentment or indictment of a grand jury, . . ."

Privileges or Immunities Clause, to accept the notion that the Bill of Rights had been made applicable to the States through the Due Process Clause of the Fourteenth Amendment. Speaking for the Court, Justice Matthews advanced a tight logical argument:

The same words are contained in the Fifth Amendment. That article makes specific and express provisions for perpetuating the institution of the grand jury, so far as it relates to prosecutions, for the more aggravated crimes under the laws of the United States. It declares that "no person shall be held to answer for a capital or otherwise infamous crime, unless on a presentment or indictment of a grand jury, except in cases arising in the land or naval forces, or in the militia when in actual service in time of war or public danger; nor shall any person be subject for the same offence to be twice put in jeopardy of life or limb; nor shall he be compelled in any criminal case to be a witness against himself." It then immediately adds: "nor be deprived of life, liberty, or property without due process of law." According to a recognized canon of interpretation, especially applicable to formal and solemn instruments of Constitutional law, we are forbidden to assume, without clear reason to the contrary, that any part of this most important amendment is superfluous. The natural and obvious inference is, that in the sense of the Constitution, "due process of law" was not meant or intended to include, *ex ui termini*, [by the very meaning of the expression used] the institution and procedure of a grand jury in any case. The conclusion is equally irresistible, that when the same phrase was employed in the Fourteenth Amendment to restrain the action of the States, it was used in the same sense and with no greater extent; and that if in the adoption of that Amendment it had been part of its purpose to perpetuate the institution of the grand jury in all the States, it would have embodied, as did the Fifth Amendment, express declarations to that effect. Due process of law in the latter refers to that law of the land, which derives its authority from the legislative powers conferred upon Congress by the Constitution of the United States, exercised within the limits therein prescribed, and interpreted according to the principles of the common law. In the Fourteenth Amendment, by parity of reason, it refers to that law of the land in each State, which derives its authority from the inherent and reserved powers of the States, exerted within the limits of those fundamental principles of liberty and justice which lie at the base of our civil and political institutions, and the greatest security for which resides in the right of the people to make their own laws, and alter them at their own pleasure.[30]

Since the rule that there is no extraneous verbiage in a constitution was generally accepted as a "given" by Constitutional scholars—and today still

30. Ibid., at 534, 535.

is by many—the clear logical extention of the *Hurtado* opinion would have it that none of the particular guarantees of the Bill of Rights could be within the meaning of the Due Process Clause because that Clause itself is in the Bill of Rights and consequently there would be needless redundancy in the first eight amendments.[31]

The *Slaughter-House Cases* and the *Hurtado* Case taken together made it clear that within sixteen years after the ratification of the Fourteenth Amendment, the U.S. Supreme Court had explicitly rejected all attempts to allow the prohibitions and guarantees of the Bill of Rights to be applied to state governmental power. Consequently, the result of *Barron* v. *Baltimore* remained unaffected by the Fourteenth Amendment: the Bill of Rights was still viewed by the Court as imposing restraints on the Federal Government only. Many cases following the precedents of these two landmark decisions—even as late as 1922—indicate that this one-time constitutional controversy had become settled law, but the final words had not yet been written by the United States Supreme Court.[32] Although the *Barron-Hurtado* Cases precluded identification of the Fourteenth Amendment with any of the substantive or procedural rights protected by the Bill of Rights, other substantive rights not specified in the first eight amendments were, by Supreme Court decisions, being written into the Fourteenth Amendment.[33]

Some State legislatures identified with "Progressive Era" politics attempted to curtail corporate abuses by establishing commissions to regulate intrastate rail rates. Several States enacted laws to guarantee reason-

31. For a different view, see Justice Harlan's dissent, 110 U.S. 516, at 538.

32. For an extensive review of the Supreme Court's decisions concerning the historical relationship between the Bill of Rights and the Fourteenth Amendment, see Felix Frankfurter, "Memorandum on 'Incorporation' of the Bill of Rights Into the Due Process Clause of the Fourteenth Amendment," 78 *Harvard Law Review* 746 (1965).

33. Currently due process of law is thought to embrace two classifications of liberties—substantive rights and procedural rights. Although in some instances it is difficult to distinguish between a substantive and a procedural right, generally speaking substantive constitutional rights are those which by their nature tend to limit the legislative goals that constitutional government may legitimately pursue. As with most procedural rights, substantive guarantees in the U.S. *Constitution* are framed in negative terminology. Hence the substantive freedom of religious worship flows from the prohibition on Congress that it "shall make no law respecting an establishment of religion or prohibiting the free exercise thereof; . . ." In contradistinction, procedural rights are those which circumscribe the methodology of constitutional government as it seeks to discharge its executive, legislative, and judicial functions. To illustrate, the conviction of an alleged lawbreaker, obtained by the state without adherence to the trial procedures which limit the state and protect the accused, would be an example of a violation of procedural due process.

able minimal standards for production and conditions of employment.[34] Laissez-faire economic philosophy, dominant in American institutions of power during the late nineteenth and early twentieth centuries, frequently found expression in Supreme Court decisions declaring unconstitutional under the Fourteenth Amendment these state legislative and administrative attempts to regulate private enterprise and property.[35] Decisions supporting such laissez-faire philosophy against state economic regulatory legislation, which became commonplace after the nation moved into the twentieth century, established a category of substantive rights regarded as "liberties" within the meaning of the Fourteenth Amendment's Due Process Clause. Even though those newly declared Fourteenth Amendment economic rights were not guarantees protected by the Bill of Rights, the Court had unequivocally accepted the concept of substantive rights as well as procedural rights in the realm of the constitutional process due each person within the jurisdiction of the several States.

In 1923 the Supreme Court recognized that other substantive rights were protected by the Fourteenth Amendment. Like the "laissez-faire economics" cases, the protected rights in *Meyer* v. *Nebraska*[36] were not ones specifically mentioned in the first eight amendments, so the *Barron-Hurtado* Rule of non-applicability of the Bill of Rights to the States, remained undistrubed. In 1919 the Nebraska state legislature passed a law prohibiting the teaching of any subject in any language other than English in all schools—private as well as public—in the state. The enactment further forbade the teaching of any foreign languages in all Nebraska schools until

34. For a detailed discussion of these developments, see Alfred H. Kelly and Winfred A. Harbison, *The American Constitution—Its Origins and Development*, 5th ed. (New York: W.W. Norton & Co., Inc., 1976), pp. 513–41, and C. Herman Pritchett, *The American Constitution*, 3rd ed. (New York: McGraw-Hill, Inc., 1977), pp. 512–34.

35. In *Chicago, Milwaukee, and St. Paul Ry. Co.* v. *Minnesota*, 134 U.S. 418 (1890), a Minnesota rail rate statute establishing a rail and warehouse commission empowered to reset unreasonable rates was declared unconstitutional because the administrative revision of rates without judicial process was held to be tantamount to the taking of property without due process under the Fourteenth Amendment. In *Allgeyer* v.

Louisiana, 165 U.S. 578 (1897), the Supreme Court held that the "liberty to contract" protected by the due process clause of the Fourteenth Amendment restricted the police power of the state from unreasonably restricting contractual business relationships; in *Lochner* v. *New York*, 198 U.S. 45 (1905), a maximum hour work law was invalidated under the "liberty of contract" theory; and in *Adkins* v. *Children's Hospital*, 261 U.S. 525 (1923), and *Morehead* v. *New York ex rel. Tipaldo*, 298 U.S. 587 (1936), the "liberty to contract" of the Fifth Amendment and Fourteenth Amendment was used respectively to invalidate a minimum wage law in Washington, D.C., and the state of New York.

36. 262 U.S. 390 (1923).

pupils satisfactorily passed the eighth grade. Meyer, who taught in a parochial school, was charged and convicted under this law because he taught Bible stories using as a text a Bible history textbook written in German. Meyer's lawyers attacked the state law as a violation of Meyer's "liberty" to teach under the Fourteenth Amendment.

In the opinion of the Court, Justice McReynolds quickly acknowledged that although the Court had "not attempted to define with exactness the liberty" guaranteed by the Fourteenth Amendment, "some included things have been definitely stated." McReynolds then listed many substantive rights that the Court majority held were definitely protected by the Fourteenth Amendment's Due Process Clause:

> Without doubt, it [the Fourteenth Amendment's protected "liberties"] denotes not merely freedom from bodily restraint but also the right of the individual to contract, to engage in any of the common occupations of life, to acquire useful knowledge, to marry, establish a home and bring up children, to worship God according to the dictates of his own conscience, and generally to enjoy those privileges long recognized at common law as essential to the orderly pursuit of happiness by free men. . . .[37]

Noting that the States have the constitutional power to prescribe curricula for their educational systems, the Court said that power must be used in a manner that is neither arbitrary nor unreasonable. Specifically, McReynolds for the Court identified two new substantive rights as protected "liberties" in the Fourteenth Amendment and argued that these rights required this law be nullified. Meyer "taught this language in school as part of his occupation. *His right thus to teach and the right of parents to engage him so to instruct their children*, we think are within the liberty of the Amendment."[38]

Although the Supreme Court gave substantive meaning—meaning other than procedural rights—to the Due Process Clause in the *Meyer* Case, it in no way indicated that the term "liberty" in the Fourteenth Amendment made applicable to the States any of the specific rights of the Bill of Rights and thus again left the *Barron-Hurtado* decisions intact.

Two years later in *Pierce* v. *Society of Sisters*,[39] McReynolds again speaking for the Court held unconstitutional the Oregon Compulsory Education Act of 1922, which among other things, required every child from the ages of eight to sixteen to attend public schools. The Society of Sisters was an Oregon corporation established in 1880 under the laws of the state with

37. Ibid., at 399, 400.
38. Ibid. Emphasis added.

39. 268 U.S. 510 (1925).

corporate authority to care for orphans, educate and instruct the young, establish and maintain schools, and acquire real and personal property to do so. The Society ran independent primary schools, high schools, junior colleges, and orphanages. In its primary schools the subjects taught followed the curriculum of the Oregon public schools; however, religious courses reflecting the moral principles and religious tenets of the Roman Catholic Church were also required. Using the Fourteenth Amendment precedent set in *Meyer*, the Court's opinion declared that it was "plain that the Compulsory Education Act of 1922 unreasonably interferes with *the liberty of parents and guardians to direct the upbringing and education* of children under their control."[40]

It should be carefully noted that the Court's opinion in no way attempted to link the religious protections of the First Amendment with the Fourteenth Amendment's Due Process Clause. That same year, however, the U.S. Supreme Court took the first step in overturning the *Barron-Hurtado* standard and started a metamorphic constitutional process that has not yet been brought to a conclusion. The precedent-shattering case that swept away more than fifty years of U.S. Supreme Court denials of a relationship between the specific guarantees of the Bill of Rights and the Due Process Clause of the Fourteenth Amendment was *Gitlow* v. *New York*.[41]

Nationalizing The "Establishment" Clause

Benjamin Gitlow was tried and convicted in the Supreme Court of New York for the statutory crime of criminal anarchy. Gitlow had published and circulated, unlawfully, pamphlets advocating the forceful and violent overthrow of the system of government in the United States. The judgment of the Supreme Court of New York was affirmed by the Appellate Division and the New York State Court of Appeals. Gitlow claimed that he had been denied freedom of speech and of the press without "due process of law." He claimed that these freedoms guaranteed by the First Amendment were restraints on state legislation because of the Fourteenth Amendment's Due Process Clause. Assuming Gitlow's interpretation for statutory analysis, the Court said:

> For present purposes we may and do assume that freedom of speech and of the press—which are protected by the First Amendment from abridgement by Congress—are among the fundamental personal rights

40. Ibid., at 534, 535. Emphasis added.   41. 268 U.S. 652 (1925).

and "liberties" protected by the Due Process Clause of the Fourteenth Amendment from impairment by the states.[42]

Six years later, the "assumption" of the majority in *Gitlow* became an accepted canon of law in the realm of the Fourteenth Amendment. Wrote Chief Justice Hughes in 1931: "It is no longer open to doubt that the liberty of the press and of speech is within the liberty safeguarded by the due process clause of the Fourteenth Amendment from invasion by state action. . . ."[43]

In 1937 the Supreme Court added another First Amendment right to the growing list of "liberties" protected from the power of the several States by the Fourteenth Amendment: "Freedom of speech and of the press are fundamental rights which are safeguarded by the due process clause of the Fourteenth Amendment of the Federal Constitution. . . . *The right of peaceable assembly* is a right cognate to those of free speech and free press and is equally fundamental."[44]

However, most important for our consideration were the two religious guarantees of the First Amendment which the Court held to be within the purview of the Fourteenth Amendment's Due Process Clause. In the Court's opinion in *Cantwell* v. *Connecticut*, Justice Roberts declared:

> We hold that that statute, as construed and applied to the appellants deprives them of their liberty without due process of law in contravention of the Fourteenth Amendment. The fundamental concept of liberty embodied in that Amendment embraces the liberties guaranteed by the First Amendment. *The First Amendment declares that Congress shall make no law respecting an establishment of religion or prohibiting the free exercise thereof. The Fourteenth Amendment has rendered the legislatures of the States as incompetent as Congress to enact such laws.* The Constitutional inhibition of legislation on the subject of religion has a double aspect. On the one hand, it forestalls compulsion by law of the acceptance of any creed of the practice of any form of worship. Freedom of conscience and freedom to adhere to such religious organization or form of worship as the individual may choose cannot be restricted by law. On the other hand, it safeguards the free exercise of the chosen form of religion. Thus the Amendment embraces two concepts—freedom to believe and freedom to act. The first is absolute but, in the nature of things, the second cannot be.[45]

42. Ibid., at 666.

43. *Near* v. *Minnesota*, 283 U.S. 697, at 707 (1931).

44. *De Jonge* v. *Oregon*, 299 U.S. 353, at 364 (1937). Emphasis added.

45. 310 U.S. 296, at 303–304 (1940). Emphasis added.

Even though *Cantwell* in 1940 spoke clearly about the limitations on the state legislatures regarding the First Amendment's "Establishment of Religion" Clause, the Establishment Clause itself did not come before the the U.S. Supreme Court until 1947, in the landmark case of *Everson* v. *Board of Education.*[46] In *Everson*, a narrowly divided Supreme Court (5 to 4) agreed unanimously on at least one point: that the Establishment of Religion Clause of the First Amendment—a restraint on the U.S. Congress—was now, through the Fourteenth Amendment's Due Process Clause, a similar restraint on state legislative power.[47]

From the 1940s through to its present decisions, the United States Supreme Court has held that many more of the specific guarantees of the first eight amendments are applicable to the States through the Fourteenth Amendment.[48] Whether the "liberties" found in the Bill of Rights and made applicable to the States through the Fourteenth Amendment are as potent in limiting the power of state government as are the rights in the first eight amendments in limiting the Federal Government, was the subject of a lengthy judicial controversy during the tenure of the Roosevelt, Vinson, and Warren Courts, and recently with the Burger Court.[49] Since *Everson*, however, in all of the Fourteenth Amendment Establishment Clause cases, no opinion of the U.S. Supreme Court has held that the constitutional religious restraints on the States have been less than on the United States Government.

The legal evolution traced in this chapter substantiates that the Establishment Clause now through the Fourteenth Amendment places the same legislative restraints on the States as it does directly through the First Amendment on the Congress. While the First Amendment provides that "Congress shall make no law respecting an establishment of religion," the Fourteenth Amendment is seen by the United States Supreme Court as providing that the State legislatures shall also "make no law respecting an establishment of religion."

---

46. 330 U.S. 1 (1947).

47. Ibid., at 8.

48. For a complete review of all of the Bill of Rights guarantees which have been made applicable to the States under the Fourteenth Amendment, see Robert L. Cord, "The Nationalization of the Bill of Rights" republished in Peter W. Lewis and Kenneth D. Peoples, *The Supreme Court and the Criminal Process* (Philadelphia: W.B. Saunders Co.; 1978), pp. 58–63.

49. For a detailed and thorough evalua-

tion of this entire controversy, see Robert L. Cord, "Neo-Incorporation: The Burger Court and the Due Process Clause of the Fourteenth Amendment," 44 *Fordham Law Review* 215 (1975); Charles Fairman, "Does the Fourteenth Amendment Incorporate the Bill of Rights? The Original Understanding," 2 *Stanford Law Review* 5 (1949); and Justice Hugo Black's dissenting opinion in *Adamson* v. *California*, 332 U.S. 46, at 92–123 (1947).

Chapter Five

The Absolute-Separation-of-Church-and-State Litany

Beginnings

Prior to the *Everson* Case in 1947 only two decisions by the United States Supreme Court could be interpreted as concerned primarily with the meaning of the phrase "an establishment of religion."[1] In the first case, *Bradfield* v. *Roberts,*[2] a unanimous Court upheld a federal appropriations act that had set aside a sum of money for the construction of buildings on privately owned hospital grounds in the District of Columbia. Pursuant to this appropriations act, the Commissioners of the District of Columbia and the Surgeon General of the United States entered into an agreement with Providence Hospital, which was incorporated by the U.S. Congress to operate a hospital in the City of Washington. Joseph Bradfield, a taxpayer, a citizen of the United States, and a resident of Washington, D.C., brought

1. *Everson* v. *Board of Education,* 330 U.S. 1 (1947). In a case decided on February 3, 1890, *Davis* v. *Beason,* 133 U.S. 333, a brief definition was given to the religious prohibitions of the First Amendment in the Court's *obiter dicta.* Justice Field, who delivered the opinion of the Court, while clearly stating that the *only* inquiry before the U.S. Supreme Court on appeal in the case was one of jurisdiction of the trial court, id. at 341; nevertheless wrote that the First Amendment was in part "intended. . . to prohibit legislation for the support of any religious tenets, or the modes of worship of any sect." Id. at 342. Field's own definition of the sole issue before the Supreme Court alluded to earlier hardly makes his statement about the First Amendment a convincing rationale for defining the case as an "Establishment Clause" case. The fact that Justice Field's statement is out of harmony with American historical fact as developed in the preceding chapters of this book is also irrelevant here.

2. 175 U.S. 291 (1899).

suit for an injunction to enjoin performance of the agreement, claiming that since the members of the hospital corporation were the Sisters of Charity—a monastic order or sisterhood of the Roman Catholic Church—the appropriations law allowed Congress to provide money "to a religious society, thereby violating the constitutional provision which forbids Congress from passing any law respecting an establishment of religion."[3]

Noting that "nothing is said about religion or about the religious faith of the incorporators" in the act of incorporation and that Bradfield had made no allegation that the hospital's work was confined to members of the Catholic Church, nor that the management of the hospital had violated even "in the smallest degree" its corporate charter,[4] the U.S. Supreme Court—apparently unanimous in its decision—held that the case was simply one of "*a secular corporation being managed by people who hold to the doctrines of the Roman Catholic Church*, but who nevertheless are managing the corporation according to the law under which it exists."[5] Interestingly, in rejecting Bradfield's charge of unconstitutionality, the Supreme Court held that a hospital run by a religious order was to be viewed as a secular corporation as long as it performed its purposes as stated in the articles of incorporation despite the "alleged 'sectarian character of the hospital'."[6] Not challenged before the High Court—nor disputed by it—was that Congress had the authority to incorporate hospitals pursuant to the general police power, which it exercises only in federally governed property such as in the District of Columbia.[7] Inasmuch as the Supreme Court did not view the appropriations act as a congressional action "respecting an establishment of religion," Justice Peckham, who delivered the opinion of the Court, avoided defining the meaning of that constitutional prohibition.

The second case, *Reuben Quick Bear* v. *Leupp*,[8] decided in 1908, on the other hand does not clearly involve the "Establishment of Religion" Clause. In this case the Commissioner of Indian Affairs had contracted with the Bureau of Catholic Missions, a private corporation sectarian in character, for the education of certain members of the Sioux tribe and had allocated funds in his control for payment to the Bureau. Funds in the Com-

---

3. Ibid., at 295.
4. Ibid., at 297–98.
5. Ibid., at 298–99. Emphasis added.
6. Ibid., at 299.
7. In *Lockner* v. *New York*, 198 U.S. 45 (1905), Justice Peckham's opinion for the Court defined the legal concept of police power with perhaps the greatest clarity the Supreme Court has officially given this elusive, but most important, assignment of inherent governmental power. Wrote Peckham:

"There are, however, certain powers, existing in the sovereignty of each State in the Union, somewhat vaguely termed police powers, the exact description and limitation of which have not been attempted by the courts. Those powers, broadly stated and without, at present, any attempt at a more specific limitation relate to the safety, health, morals and general welfare of the public." Id., at 53.

8. 210 U.S. 50 (1908).

missioner's control were of two kinds: (1) trust funds, which were moneys appropriated by Congress in one lump sum in 1889 in payment for certain land cessions and the income which was used for Indian education;[9] and (2) treaty funds, which were moneys appropriated annually by Congress in fulfillment of treaty obligations arising out of other land cessions.[10]

Reuben Quick Bear, and other members of the Sioux Tribe of Indians, brought suit for themselves and all other members of the Tribe to enjoin Commissioner Francis E. Leupp from using Indian funds to execute the contract with the Catholic Missions. "The validity of the contract for $27,000 [was] attacked on the ground that all contracts for sectarian education among the Indians [were] forbidden by certain provisos contained in the Indian appropriation acts of 1895, 1896, 1897, 1898, and 1899."[11] Thus, Chief Justice Fuller's opinion as to the facts of the case indicates that the contract with the Bureau of Catholic Missions was not assailed as a violation of the Establishment Clause of the First Amendment. Consequently, in the opinion of the Court, Fuller saw no need to define the limitations imposed on the Federal Government by the Establishment Clause since no contention was raised—according to the U.S. Supreme Court—that the First Amendment was violated by the contract with the Bureau of Catholic Missions.

Ultimately the Chief Justice, writing for an apparently unanimous Court,[12] indicated that the "payments under the contract were to be made from the 'Sioux trust fund' and the 'Sioux treaty fund,'" both sums of which were within "the discretion of the Commissioner of Indian Affairs" to disperse for the benefit of the Indian Tribe,[13] and thus were not monies appropriated under the recent Congressional statutes prohibiting as new national policy—not constitutional command—Indian education by sectarian schools.

The "Child-Benefit" Theory and State Police Power

Before discussing the *Everson* Case, we should mention *Cochran* v. *Louisiana*,[14] decided in 1930 by a unanimous Court. This case bears only incidentally on the constitutional problem of *Everson*, but it is an important precedent case because the U.S. Supreme Court subscribed to the "Child-Benefit" theory that was later used to justify the majority position in the *Everson* Case.

---

9. Ibid., at 80–81.
10. Ibid., at 80.
11. Ibid., at 77–78.
12. No concurring or dissenting opinions

are recorded. Ibid., at 82.
13. 210 U.S. 50, at 82 (1908).
14. 281 U.S. 370 (1930).

Emmett Cochran, a taxpayer and citizen of Louisiana and a patron of the public school system, brought suit for an injunction to stop the Louisiana State Board of Education from spending funds to buy books for children attending parochial school. The books were to be purchased pursuant to the Louisiana statute that authorized and directed the Louisiana State Board of Education to provide all "school books for school children free of cost to such children," not including those attending colleges or universities.[15] Cochran claimed that tax money used to buy books for private school students—including students who went to parochial schools—would constitute "a taking of private property for a private purpose" in violation of the Due Process Clause of the Fourteenth Amendment.[16] The private purpose would be aid to private schools—religious and secular—which were not part of the public educational system.[17]

Chief Justice Hughes, who delivered the opinion of the Court, quoted extensively from the opinion of the Supreme Court of Louisiana, which sustained the State statute.[18] The rationale of the "Child-Benefit" theory is captured in the Louisiana Supreme Court's wording:

> One may scan the acts in vain to ascertain where any money is appropriated for the purchase of school books for the use of any church, private, sectarian or even public school. The appropriations were made for the specific purpose of purchasing school books for the use of the school children of the state, free of cost to them. *It was for their benefit and the resulting benefit to the state that the appropriations were made.* True, these children attend some school, public or private, the latter, sectarian or nonsectarian, and that the books are to be furnished them for their use, free of cost, whichever they attend. *The schools, however, are not the beneficiaries of these appropriations. They obtain nothing from them, nor are they relieved of a single obligation because of them. The school children and the state alone are the beneficiaries. . . .* [19]

Stressing that under Louisiana law "the same books that are furnished for children attending public schools shall be furnished children attending private schools," Hughes argued that "none [could be] adapted to religious instruction."[20] It is important to note that at the end of the Court's opinion, the Chief Justice developed the relationship between the state's general police power—which includes the authority and the goal to provide for the public's education—and the "Child-Benefit" theory as a constitutional

15. Ibid., at 374.
16. Ibid.
17. Ibid.
18. 168 La. at 1020; 67 A.L.R. 1183; 123 So. 655.
19. 281 U.S. 370, at 374–75. Emphasis added.
20. Ibid., at 375.

method for reaching that end. Concluded Hughes: "[W]e cannot doubt that the taxing power of the State is exerted for a public purpose. The legislation does not segregate private schools or their pupils, as its beneficiaries or attempt to interfere with any matters of exclusively private concern. Its interest is education, broadly; its method comprehensive. Individual interests are aided only as the common interest is safeguarded." [21]

As noted above, the concept of "police power," although somewhat elusive, is considered to be a power "inherent" in governmental sovereignty and generally embraces those powers necessary to protect the "safety, health, morals and general welfare of the public." [22] In the area of domestic legislation governing the residents of the States of the Union, it is settled constitutional law that the States exercise the "police power," not the Federal Government, which is a government of enumerated powers and implied powers that are reasonably derived from the national government's enumerated powers. [23]

Rejecting an argument before the U.S. Supreme Court, by counsel for the United States Government, to the effect that the national government has powers unspecified in the *Constitution* which flowed from "the doctrine of sovereign and inherent power," Justice Brewer, in an opinion of the Court in 1907, wrote that, "The proposition that there are legislative powers affecting the nation as a whole which belong to, although not expressed in the grants of powers, *is in direct conflict with the doctrine that this is a government* [the Federal Government] *of enumerated powers.*" [24] Consequently, it is clear that the governments of the States—under our

21. Ibid.

22. See fn. 7, supra.

23. *McCulloch* v. *Maryland*, 17 U.S. 316 (1819).

24. *Kansas* v. *Colorado*, 206 U.S. 46 (1907). Emphasis added. Although the Supreme Court has resisted the notion that the Federal Government has no "inherent" power in domestic affairs, its rulings in foreign affairs appear to embrace the contrary view. See Justice Sutherland's opinion of the Court in *United States* v. *Curtiss-Wright Corporation*, 299 U.S. 304 (1936).

It should be noted that without deviating from the principle that the "police power" is reserved to the States, the Supreme Court has sanctioned, especially in recent years, the use by the Federal Government of its enumerated powers to seek goals that are clearly within the general realm of the "po-

lice power." Thus the Court has upheld as constitutional Congress's use of its power to regulate "commerce among the several States" to enact federal laws: prohibiting the traffic of lottery tickets across state lines, *Champion* v. *Ames*, 188 U.S. 321 (1903); limiting prostitution, *Hoke* v. *United States*, 227 U.S. 308 (1913); banning adulterated foods, *Hipolite Egg Co.* v. *United States*, 220 U.S. 45 (1911); outlawing car theft, *Brooks* v. *U.S.*, 267 U.S. 432 (1925); creating the right of collective bargaining, *N.L.R.B.* v. *Jones and Laughlin Steel Corp.*, 301 U.S. 1 (1937); providing fair labor standards, *U.S.* v. *Darby Lumber Co.*, 312 U.S. 100 (1941); and outlawing racial segregation in almost all business establishments in the United States, *Katzenbach* v. *Morgan*, 384 U.S. 641 (1966).

present Constitutional division of authority between the Federal and State governments—deal most frequently with legislation making illegal what is considered undesirable social behaviour or crime and with legislation thought to foster the beneficial needs of the community.

In accordance with their constitutional responsibility—under the police power to provide for the morals, the health, and the public's general welfare—the States of the Union have passed compulsory education laws generally requiring children to attend primary and secondary schools which meet the States' educational requirements. These laws no doubt reflect the conviction etched in stone on Boston's Public Library: "The Commonwealth requires the Education of the People as the safeguard of order and Liberty."

As chapter four pointed out, under the U.S. Supreme Court's decision in *Pierce* v. *Society of Sisters*, parents as legal guardians may constitutionally meet their responsibilities under state compulsory education attendance laws by sending their children to private schools—sectarian and non-sectarian—that are accredited, usually by the State's Board of Education.[25] Inasmuch as this is a constitutional right, private school authorities and parents who send their children to private schools—which include sectarian schools—have argued that state monies available for a variety of educationally related programs should be available to all of a state's children, irrespective of the school they attend to meet the state's compulsory education requirements. When this argument was advanced and sustained by the U.S. Supreme Court in regard to non-sectarian textbooks in Louisiana's schools in the *Cochran* Case of 1930, the two religious prohibitions of the First Amendment had not yet been made applicable to the States under *Cantwell* v. *Connecticut* decided in 1940.[26] In the "Parochial School Bus Transportation" Case of 1947—*Everson* v. *The Board of Education*[27]— the constitutional circumstances were different in that the U.S. Supreme Court, by its previous decision in *Cantwell*, had committed itself to the concept that no state legislature—or the Congress of the United States— could make a law "respecting an establishment of religion."

In sum, it is accurate to say that prior to the *Everson* "Bus Transportation" Case, the U.S. Supreme Court cases that involved the Establishment of Religion Clause were minute in number and none were of any significant value in determining just what legislation that Clause constitutionally prohibited.

---

25. See the text in chap. four, at fns. 39 and 40.

26. 310 U.S. 296.

27. 330 U.S. 1.

Everson *v.* Board of Education: *"The Parochial School Bus Transportation" Case*

Everson v. Board of Education[28] is the single most important American constitutional law case in the realm of the Establishment of Religion Clause. There, for the first time—over a century and a half after the Clause was added to the *Constitution*—the U.S. Supreme Court set forth a comprehensive interpretation of the *minimal* prohibitions that the Court said were required by the phrase: "Congress shall make no law respecting an establishment of religion, . . ."[29] In the opinion of the Court, Mr. Justice Black advanced the following definition:

> The "establishment of religion" clause of the First Amendment means *at least* this: Neither a state nor the Federal Government can set up a church. Neither can pass laws which aid one religion, *aid all religions*, or prefer one religion over another. Neither can force nor influence a person to go to or to remain away from church against his will or force him to profess a belief or disbelief in any religion. No person can be punished for entertaining or professing religious belief or disbelief, for church attendance or non-attendance. *No tax in any amount, large or small, can be levied to support any religious activities or institutions, whatever they may be called, or whatever form they may adopt to teach or practice religion. Neither a state nor the Federal Government can, openly or secretly, participate in the affairs of any religious organizations or groups and vice versa.* In the words of Jefferson, the clause against establishment of religion *was intended to erect a "wall of separation between church and State.* . . ."[30]

Although the case was decided on a 5–4 split decision, there is no indication that any of the nine justices did not subscribe to Justice Black's *minimal* definition. On this crucial point—what the Establishment Clause "means [in the] least"—the Supreme Court was unanimous.[31]

The facts of the case are relatively simple. In 1941, the New Jersey Legislature passed a state statute authorizing the "local school districts to make rules and contracts for the transportation of children to and from

---

28. Ibid.

29. United States *Constitution*, Amendment I.

30. 330 U.S. 1, at 15–16. Emphasis added.

31. Almost the entire *Everson* Case is reproduced in the *Addenda*.

school."[32] Pursuant to this law, the Board of Education of the Township of Ewing, New Jersey, passed a resolution authorizing reimbursement to parents for money spent sending their children to public or Catholic parochial schools "on regular busses operated by the public transportation system."[33]

Everson, in his capacity as a taxpayer in the school district, challenged the constitutionality of both the school board resolution and the state law in the New Jersey courts as violative of the New Jersey and Federal *Constitutions*, claiming that: first, the State was using public funds for a private purpose, thus depriving him of his property without due process of law; and second, the State "statute and the [school board] resolution forced inhabitants to pay taxes to help support and maintain schools which are dedicated to, and which regularly teach, the Catholic Faith,"[34] thus violating the Establishment Clause of the First Amendment made applicable to the States by the Due Process Clause of the Fourteenth Amendment.

Losing, on appeal, in New Jersey's highest court, which held that neither the New Jersey nor the Federal *Constitution* was violated,[35] Everson pursued the First/Fourteenth Amendment questions to the United States Supreme Court.

Everson's first contention was quickly dismissed by all the justices of the Court, who using almost the same settled legal rationale they had in the *Cochran* "Textbook" Case held that a tax may be constitutionally levied against people who do not themselves receive any direct benefit from the tax.[36]

The majority opinion next turned to a constitutional argument which, upon the record of the case, had apparently not been made by Everson's attorneys in their challenge of the School Board's resolution. Inasmuch as the resolution provided reimbursement for travel money for only public and Catholic parochial school students, was this not discriminatory aid against students who were attending other private educational institutions in the school district?[37] If so, did that not amount to an "unequal protection of the

---

32. 330 U.S. 1, at 3. In part, the New Jersey statute provided that: "Whenever in any district there are children living remote from any schoolhouse, the board of education of the district may make rules and contracts for the transportation of such children to and from school, including the transportation of school children to and from schools other than a public school, except such school as is operated for profit in whole or in part." Id., at 3, fn. 1.

33. Ibid., at 3.

34. Ibid., at 5.

35. 133 N.J.L. 350.

36. See the text at fns. 18–21, supra.

37. 330 U.S. 1, at 4–5.

law" under Section 1 of the Fourteenth Amendment?[38] Since neither the State's law nor the School Board's resolution was challenged on that ground, Justice Black noted that: "Striking down a state law is not a matter of such light moment that it should be done by a federal court on a postulate neither charged nor proved, but which rests on nothing but a possibility."[39]

With these relatively minor legal points settled, the *Everson* majority opinion turned to the precedent issue: What governmental action did the Establishment Clause preclude? After reviewing the history of some of the horrors of religious establishments and the struggle for religious liberty in the American colonies—especially in Virginia[40]—Justice Black reached the heart of the major constitutional issue. It is at this point in the opinion of the Court that the *minimal* prohibitions on religious activity by government, presented above,[41] are carefully enunciated. Many of these prohibitions equated with the Establishment Clause are verifiable by primary historical documents. Regrettably, more are fiction completely at odds with the thesis advanced in chapter one as to the meaning of the Establishment Clause but, more important, completely out of harmony with the clear testimony of the primary historical documents and recorded events of American history. This statement is a serious one and thus demands scholarly verification and analysis not simply my assertion.

"The 'establishment of religion' clause of the First Amendment means at least this:" wrote Black, "Neither a state nor the Federal Government can set up a church."[42] With this part of Justice Black's interpretation, I have no quarrel. It conforms closely to the original draft of the Establishment Clause that Madison introduced in the House of Representatives on June 8, 1789.[43] In addition, it is easily reconciled with Madison's reply to Sherman during the House debate on August 15, 1789, as to the meaning of the House's Select Committee's final wording of the amended Establishment Clause.[44] Since the prohibition by Congress of a national religion had been extended to the States—as explained in chapter four—by the Fourteenth Amendment, Justice Black's point on this matter is entirely supportable and in complete harmony with the thesis of this book.

38. In part, Sect. 1 of the Fourteenth Amendment provides that: "No state shall . . . deny to any person within its jurisdiction the equal protection of the law." The Ewing School Board, as a creature of the State of New Jersey, would be bound by that constitutional prohibition.

39. 330 U.S. 1, at 4, fn. 2.

40. 330 U.S. 1, at 8–15.

41. See Black's opinion in the text at fn. 30, supra.

42. 330 U.S. 1, at 15.

43. See the text at fn. 20 and fn. 20 in chap. one.

44. See the text at fns. 31–33 and the footnoted sources 31–33 in chap. one.

Justice Black's interpretation of the Establishment Clause begins to stray from American historical reality in the next sentence of his definition: "Neither [a State nor the Federal Government] can pass laws which aid one religion, *aid all religions*, or prefer one religion over another."[45] With the exception of "aid[ing] all religions," these words also agree with the thesis advanced in chapter one and the historical documentation I presented in chapters one, two, and three. There is no historical evidence to suggest, however, that the Establishment Clause in any way constitutionally precludes *non-discriminatory* governmental aid to religion. In fact, the converse is confirmed historically.

How can the hundreds of thousands of federal dollars given to missionaries of many Christian faiths to support their mission schools in christianizing the Indians—a practice that was continuous since the First Amendment was added to the *Constitution* and curtailed as late as the end of the nineteenth century—be reconciled with Justice Black's pronouncement? Did all of our early Presidents and Congresses violate the Establishment Clause and the First Amendment for over a century? Or could it be that Justice Black is wrong?

American history, shows that on a non-discriminatory basis the Catholic Church and many Protestant denominations—including church schools—were directly aided by federal money through treaty obligations, federal legislation, and even, in some cases, control of large grants of land to help propagate the Gospel among the Indians.[46]

The next two lengthy sentences of Justice Black's interpretation of the Establishment Clause and that of the Court's majority are supported by the historical record and the goals sought by those who framed and ratified what is now the First Amendment. With Black—under the Establishment Clause—I believe that:

Neither [a state nor the Federal Government] can force nor influence a person to go to or to remain away from church[47] against his will or force him to profess a belief or disbelief in any religion. No person can be punished for entertaining or professing religious belief or disbelief, for church attendance or non-attendance.[48]

---

45. 330 U.S. 1, at 15. Emphasis added.
46. See the text at fns. 86–108 in chap. two.
47. On this point I note one clear exception. Until a recent policy change, cadets at national military academies were required to attend their own religious worship services. In those instances the Federal Government, through the regulations of the academies, could easily be charged with forcing or influencing persons to attend church. It should be mentioned that this required attendance policy was in force when Justice Black wrote his *Everson* opinion.
48. 330 U.S. 1, at 15–16.

However, the remaining sentences of Justice Black's interpretation of the prohibitions required by the Establishment Clause, limiting federal and state involvement with religion, ignore American historical fact and run counter to many policies pursued by the U.S. Government from its inception to the present time. The majority opinion by Black continues:

> No tax in any amount, large or small, can be *levied* to support any *religious activities* or institutions, whatever they may be called, or whatever form they adopt to teach or practice religion. Neither a state nor the Federal Government can, openly or secretly, participate in the affairs of any religious organizations or groups or vice versa.[49]

If Justice Black meant to restrict his definition concerning the use of tax money to support the religious activities mentioned, to tax money specifically "levied" for those purposes, his definition of the Establishment Clause does not restrict either the States or the Federal Government from aiding religious activities because neither government today levies taxes that are specifically designed to support or aid religion. Given the strong tone of government non-involvement of the entire Black definition, it must logically follow that Justice Black was interpreting the Establishment Clause to mean that no tax money may be used to support religious activities or institutions.

Inasmuch as I believe that Justice Black, and the rest of the Court, meant the latter interpretation to be the Establishment Clause requirements, either they are wrong or the people who framed the First Amendment, our early Presidents, and our early Congresses, did not know what the First Amendment's Establishment Clause meant. Although this is a ridiculous choice forced upon us by the Black interpretation alone, the entire Supreme Court—dissenters as well as those who comprised the opinion of the Court—make matters worse by appealing to early American history as the only basis and substantiation for their decision. As mentioned before, the historical record of the American Republic makes this interpretation of the First Amendment's religious guarantees untenable.

Did not the prayers of Congressional Chaplains in the First Congress, which formed the Establishment Clause, constitute "religious activities"? Were their salaries not paid from tax revenues? Are not these same activities, performed in the U.S. Congress by clergymen today, irreconcilable with the Court's interpretation? How can the clear and direct financial aid to missionaries and the U.S. treaties to build churches be reconciled with the *Everson* definition? The clearest answer is that much, if not most, of

---

49. Ibid., at 16. Emphasis added.

Black's *Everson* interpretation of the Establishment Clause and the reality of American governmental involvement in religious practices from the earliest days of the Federal Republic are mutually exclusive.

Jefferson's Danbury Baptist Letter

In *Everson*, Justice Black sums up his interpretation of the Establishment Clause with a quotation from a famous letter written by Jefferson in 1802. Black's definition concludes: "In the words of Jefferson, the clause against establishment was intended to erect a 'wall of separation between church and State.' "[50] As Leo Pfeffer ably points out, there has been much dispute among scholars of the Establishment Clause as to whether the term "separation of Church and State" should even be used because it does not appear in the text of the original *Constitution* or any of its amendments.[51] Pfeffer counters that many terms not specifically found in the *Constitution* have been accepted by constitutional scholars and students to describe principles universally accepted as constitutionally recognized.[52] His point is well illustrated: "the right to a fair trial is generally accepted to be a constitutional principle; yet the term 'fair trial' is not found in the Constitution."[53]

Like Pfeffer, I consider the term "separation of Church and State" to be a useful one in the extensive dialogue concerning what the Establishment of Religion Clause constitutionally precludes government from doing. Consequently, I have no apprehension about the term itself, however, I do have a very decided quarrel with the way the term has been used, as illustrated in the Black opinion of the Court in *Everson*.[54] The phrase, "a wall of separation between church and State," which Justice Black used in the *Everson* Case, is a quotation in part from a letter that President Jefferson sent the Danbury Connecticut Baptist Association on January 1, 1802. The entire paragraph containing this phrase reads:

> Believing with you that religion is a matter which lies solely between man and his God, that he owes account to none other for his faith or his worship, that the legislative powers of government reach actions only, and not opinions, I contemplate with sovereign reverence that act of the whole

---

50. Ibid.

51. For a more complete discussion of this dispute, see Leo Pfeffer, *Church, State, and Freedom*, rev. ed. (Boston: Beacon Press, 1967), pp. 131–33.

52. Ibid., p. 133.

53. Ibid.

54. 330 U.S. 1, at 16.

American People which declared that their legislature should "make no law respecting an establishment of religion, or prohibiting the free exercise thereof," *thus building a wall of separation between church and State.* Adhering to this expression of the supreme will of the nation on behalf of the rights of conscience, I shall see with sincere satisfaction the progress of those sentiments which tend to restore to man all his natural rights, convinced he has no natural right in opposition to his social duties.[55]

This passage of Jefferson's letter to the Danbury Baptists refers to "that act of the whole American People." Surely he is discussing in it the ratification of the First Amendment by the representatives of the people in their legislatures. Jefferson says that this act by the "whole American People" declared that "their legislature" should make no law, and so forth. He recognizes the First Amendment as a restriction on the Congress or the legislature of the "whole American People," but in those days government authority over all matters that the Supreme Court discussed in the *Everson* Case (that is, religious affairs, education, relation of religion to education, public support of either, safety and health provisions) rested with the States. Except for the power to establish a national religion or to provide national restrictions on religious freedom, authority over all the other matters was exclusively the responsibility of the individual states and Jefferson knew that the First Amendment did not curb their actions in any way.[56] He also knew that it did not create a "wall of separation" in any state jurisdictions. By this phrase Jefferson could only have meant that the "wall of separation" was erected "between church and State" in regard to possible federal action such as a law establishing a national religion or prohibiting the free exercise of worship. In Jefferson's time, Congress had no other power in religious matters to curb. Therefore, to leave the impression that Jefferson's "separation" statement was a universal one concerning the whole of the federal and state political system is extremely misleading.

More important, what would Jefferson's "wall" be separating in terms of Church and the federal State? His actions as President, which are important guidelines to his thinking about this "separation," indicate clearly that Jefferson certainly was not an advocate of the "absolute separation of Church and [the federal] State." If he had been, he would not have made a treaty with the Kaskaskia Indians in 1803—a year after the Danbury Baptist letter—pledging federal money to build them a Roman Catholic Church

---

55. Saul K. Padover, *The Complete Jefferson* (Freeport, N.Y.: Books for Libraries Press, 1943), pp. 518–19.

56. See Jefferson's letter of 1808, in the text of chap. two, at fn. 85, which clearly shows that he understood the First Amendment as in no way placing limitations on the State governments in regard to religion.

and to support their priest.[57] Nor would he have asked the Congress to appropriate the monies to meet the treaty's obligations as he did on November 25, 1803.[58] Unlike Justice Black, Jefferson apparently saw no conflict in asking the Senate to advise and consent to the Kaskaskia Indian Treaty and asking Congress for the funds to implement it and the prohibition that "Congress shall make no law respecting an establishment of religion, . . ." An *absolute* "wall of separation between church and the [federal] State" must not have been Jefferson's view—as indicated by his actions in the Kaskaskia matter *after* the Danbury Baptist letter—or else he was a rascal, violating the First Amendment and his oath of office. If Jefferson's concept of separation of Church and State can be reconciled with these actions of his Presidency, it should certainly follow that he would not believe that this constitutional doctrine would be seriously impaired or violated by the refunding of bus transportation costs to parents who send their children to parochial schools.

Justice Black's "Judicial" History in Everson

Not only is Justice Black's definition of the minimal requirements of the Establishment Clause out of harmony with American historical reality, in the *Everson* opinion his interpretation of previous U.S. Supreme Court decisions is misleading and, for the most part, irrelevant in defining the Clause.

Immediately prior to his definition of the Establishment Clause, Black's *Everson* opinion leads one to believe that the U.S. Supreme Court had already addressed Itself several times to the meaning of *both* religious guarantees of the First Amendment. Wrote Black for the Court in 1947:

> The meaning and scope of the First Amendment, *preventing establishment of religion* or prohibiting the free exercise thereof, in the light of its history and the evils it was designed forever to suppress, *have been several times elaborated by the decisions of this Court prior to the application of the First Amendment to the states by the Fourteenth.*[21] The broad meaning given the Amendment by these earlier cases has been accepted by this Court in its decisions concerning an individual's religious freedom rendered since the Fourteenth Amendment was interpreted to make the prohibitions of the First applicable to state action abridging religious freedom.[59]

57. See the text and the fns. 70–79, in chap. two.

58. Ibid.

59. 330 U.S. 1, at 14–15. Emphasis added.

Justice Black provides us with footnote "21" to substantiate his assertion that the Court had several times elaborated on the meaning of the Establishment Clause. Five U.S. Supreme Court cases are cited to document his claim:

^{21}*Terret* v. *Taylor,* 9 Cranch 43; *Watson* v. *Jones,* 13 Wall. 679; *Davis* v. *Beason,* 133 U.S. 333; *Cf. Reynolds* v. *United States, supra,* 162 [98 U.S. 145 (1879)]; *Reuben Quick Bear* v. *Leupp,* 210 U.S. 50.[60]

The fact is that the U.S. Supreme Court—while addressing itself in several cases to the "free exercise of religion" guarantee—*did not* before 1947 address itself elaborately or in any other significant way to the "meaning and scope" of the First Amendment's prohibition on Congressional power "preventing an establishment of religion."

In *Terrett* v. *Taylor,*[61] a case decided in 1815, the opinion of the Court by Justice Story dealt mainly with a struggle over ownership of church property that belonged to a particular Episcopal Church that was part of the Established Church of Virginia prior to the Revolution. While the land ownership struggle in the case was complex, both parties to the suit recognized that "the Episcopal Church no longer retained its character as an exclusive religious establishment" with "superiority over other religious sects,"[62] which indicates that the "Establishment Issue" was not a significant factor in the case. Furthermore the opinion of the Court does not provide any definition of a religious establishment that would support Justice Black's definition in *Everson* over the definition advanced in this book. In fact, the terms used by Justice Story to describe the status of the Episcopal Church when it was established in Virginia—as even the few quotes above indicate—support my view of what was seen as some of the characteristics of a religious establishment in 1815, characteristics that both Justice Black and I would consider to be a violation of the Establishment Clause.[63] These characteristics of "an establishment of religion" in *Terrett* v. *Taylor,*[64] however, are not germane to the *Everson* Case and do not support those parts of Justice Black's overbroad interpretation of the Establishment Clause that I dispute. Apart from reviewing some of the characteristics of the disestablished Virginia Episcopal Church—a religious establishment that no longer existed when the First Amendment was added to the *Constitution* in 1791—the *Terrett* Case is not an Establishment Clause case but a disputed property case, as the Supreme Court's

60. Ibid., at 15, fn. 21.
61. 9 Cranch 43 (1815).
62. Ibid., at 49.

63. Ibid., at 50–52.
64. *Terrett* v. *Taylor,* 9 Cranch 43 (1815).

ruling in Justice Story's opinion clearly indicates: "On the whole, the majority of the court are of the opinion that the *land in controversy* belongs to the Episcopal Church of Alexandria, and has not been divested by the revolution, or any act of the legislature passed since that period; . . ."[65]

Similarly, *Watson* v. *Jones*[66] is a church property case that grew out of a "schism in a church." Justice Miller specifically says so in the opinion of the Court: "The pleadings in the present suit show conclusively a different state of facts, different issues, and a different relief sought. *This is a case of a division or schism in a church. It is a question as to which of two bodies shall be recognized as the Third or Walnut Street Presbyterian Church. . . .*"[67]

Although the Court's opinion does discuss the two religious protections of the First Amendment in *Watson*, even in that part of the opinion most of the discussion concerns the protection that the *Constitution's* First Amendment provides for freedom of religious belief:

> In this country the full and free right to entertain any religious belief, to practice any religious principle, and to teach any religious doctrine which does not violate the laws of morality and property, and which does not infringe personal rights, is conceded to all. *The law knows no heresy, and is committed to the support of no dogma, the establishment of no sect.* The right to organize voluntary religious associations to assist in the expression and dissemination of any religious doctrine, and to create tribunals for the decision of controverted questions of faith within the association, and for the ecclesiastical government of all the individual members, congregations, and officers within the general association, is unquestioned.[68]

It should be carefully noted that the sentence which does discuss the substance of the Establishment Clause can hardly be said to support those sections of the Court's expansive definition of the Clause disputed earlier in this chapter.[69] Under the Establishment Clause, the law cannot embrace one religion or sect, making its beliefs "dogma" and their violations "heresy." That understanding—which I think is the substantive meaning of the emphasized sentence in the immediate above quote from *Watson*—is in complete harmony with the interpretation of the Establishment Clause advanced here.

My critique of invoking *Davis* v. *Beason*[70] as an Establishment Clause

---

65. Ibid., at 55. Emphasis added.
66. 13 Wall. 679 (1872).
67. Ibid., at 717. Emphasis added.

68. Ibid., at 728–29. Emphasis added.
69. See the text at fns. 42–54, supra.
70. 133 U.S. 333 (1890).

case of any real significance has already been discussed elsewhere in this chapter,[71] therefore let us turn our attention to the fourth case Justice Black appeals to as having "elaborated" the meaning of the Establishment Clause—*Reynolds* v. *United States*.[72]

The *Reynolds* Case involved, among other things, the Mormon religion's practice of bigamy. The nature of the charge that the judge gave to the jury concerned the fact that Reynolds was married to more than one living woman at the same time.[73] Inasmuch as Reynolds maintained that the criminal bigamy statute that Congress enacted for federal territories[74] was unconstitutional because it interferred with his "free exercise of religion," the U.S. Supreme Court discussed extensively the First Amendment's religious protections.

The part of Chief Justice Morrison Waite's opinion of the Court concerned with the Establishment Clause discussed in the most superficial terms the background of religious establishments in the colonies; invoked Madison's "Memorial and Remonstrance," Jefferson's "Virginia Bill of Religious Liberty," and Madison's leadership in the House of Representatives advocating religious freedom; and finally culminated with an extensive quote from Jefferson's letter to the Danbury Connecticut Baptist Association.[75] In sum, there is nothing in Waite's opinion of the Court that adds any substance to the historical argument in defense of the broad interpretation of the Establishment Clause that has not been already refuted or explained with primary historical documents. It is important to note that notwithstanding the comments of Chief Justice Waite in the case, *Reynolds* v. *United States* is in essence a "Freedom of Religious Exercise" case and not an Establishment Clause case. The Court's opinion makes this extremely clear in holding that the freedom to act on one's religious beliefs is not absolute and can—and in some cases must—be appropriately tempered by the needs of the society.[76] Following is part of Waite's argument on this matter:

---

71. See fn. 1, supra.

72. 98 U.S. 145 (1879).

73. Ibid., at 161–62. The Statute which Reynolds was charged with violating stated in part: "Every person having a husband or wife living, who marries another, whether married or single, in a Territory, or other place over which the United States have exclusive jurisdiction, is guilty of bigamy, and shall be punished by a fine of not more than $500, and by imprisonment for a term of not more than five years." Id. at 146.

74. Prior to becoming States, territories belonging to the United States come within the complete legislative discretionary powers of the U.S. Congress. See the U.S. *Constitution*, Article IV, Sect. 3.

75. 98 U.S. 145 at 162–64.

76. Ibid., at 166.

So here, as a law of the organization of society under the exclusive dominion of the United States, it is provided that plural marriages shall not be allowed. Can a man excuse his practices to the contrary because of his religious belief? To permit this would be to make the professed doctrines of religious belief superior to the law of the land, and in effect to permit every citizen to become a law unto himself. Government could exist only in name under such circumstances.[77]

One cannot help but muse that if the "free exercise" of religion—which is expressed in as absolute terms as the prohibition on laws "respecting an establishment of religion"—might constitutionally yield to a societal institution such as monogamy, then why, by the same logic should other societal needs, which might be considered vital, not justify a less than absolute ban on laws "respecting an establishment of religion?"

The last case that Justice Black's *Everson* opinion cites as elaborating the "meaning and scope of the First Amendment['s] preventing an establishment of religion" is *Reuben Quick Bear* v. *Leupp*.[78] This case has been more than adequately discussed here[79] and it is extremely clear that nowhere in that case does the U.S. Supreme Court assign any interpretation to the Establishment of Religion Clause.

What should also be clear is that all the previous Supreme Court decisions—which Justice Black cites in the opinion of the Court at footnote 21—provide no precedent of any significance for determining the "meaning and scope" of the First Amendment's Establishment Clause. While it may be conventional and desirable legal practice to cite previous judicial decisions in order to legitimize one's interpretation of a section of the U.S. *Constitution* from the U.S. Supreme Court's bench, cases cited which bear little, if any, significant relevance—and in some instances which may be totally irrelevant—do not serve well either to substantiate the High Court's interpretation or to engender respect for its legal research and scholarship.

Justice Black's Madison and Jefferson in Everson

Incredible as it may seem, if one were to read only the Court's opinion in the *Everson* Case, it would not be improbable that one might come to the conclusion that Madison and Jefferson fought the battle for religious freedom in Virginia, wrote a few letters on the subject, and then retired from the issue of defining the proper relationship between Church and State.

77. Ibid., at 166–67.   79. See the text at fns. 8–13, supra.
78. 210 U.S. 50 (1908).

Although Justice Black's opinion discusses Madison's "Memorial and Remonstrance" against the levy to support teachers of the Christian religion and Jefferson's "Virginia Bill for Religious Liberty"—both of which comprised part of the movement for the disestablishment of the Episcopal Church in Virginia in 1785–1786[80]—it is astonishing that virtually nothing is said about the history of the First Amendment. Justice Black's Madison resembles Professor Pfeffer's Madison. No mention is made of his membership on the committee which recommended the Chaplain system in the First Congress nor of the wording of the original draft of his Establishment Clause, nor his interpretation of the House's Select Committee's final draft of the religion clauses, nor the texts of his Thanksgiving Day Proclamations as President. In short, by carefully selecting his history, Justice Black misrepresents Madison by omitting significant materials discussed in chapter two.[81]

The same technique is used to portray Jefferson. Nothing is mentioned about lands granted, in trust, to a sectarian society dedicated to propagating "the gospel among the Heathen" extended during the Jefferson Administration nor the Kaskaskia Indian Treaty of 1803. Apparently only the Madison and Jefferson of 1785 and 1786 in Virginia were important to the U.S. Supreme Court's quest to understand and interpret the First Amendment of 1791.[82]

Equally unbelievable is that the *Everson* opinion is devoid of any attempt to explore the actions and debates of the First Congress which proposed to the States what would become the First Amendment. The Supreme Court's weak historical "analysis" in this most important precedent case interpreting the Establishment Clause, could easily lead one to believe that Madison, who had only one vote in the House of Representatives, and Jefferson, who was at the time Secretary of State and played no part in the constitutional amending process, were the only ones responsible for adding the Establishment Clause to the *Constitution*. Justice Black and the opinion of the Court completely ignore the constitutional fact of law that is documented in Article V—the amending process—of the *Constitution*. It was the two-thirds affirmative votes of both Houses of Congress and three-fourths of the State legislatures that added the Establishment of

---

80. 330 U.S. 1, at 11–14.

81. Justice Black is careful to note the existence of the "Detached Memorandum." 330 U.S. 1, at 12, fn. 12.

82. It is in a slightly perverted sense amusing that the only two historical documents which the Supreme Court attached as an "Appendix" to the *Everson* Case were Madison's "Memorial and Remonstrance Against Religious Assessments (1785)," 333 U.S. 1, at 63, and "A Bill Establishing A Provision for Teachers of the Christian Religion [in Virginia]," id., at 72.

Religion Clause to the *Constitution*, not merely the efforts of Madison and Jefferson. However, this fact notwithstanding, the First Congress and the State legislatures are not mentioned in the U.S. Supreme Court's opinion in this crucial case.

The "Child-Benefit" Theory and the Everson Case

When I first read *Everson* v. *The Board of Education* as an undergraduate student, until I reached the seventeenth page of the eighteen page opinion of the Court, I was certain that the Court intended to strike down both the School Board Resolution and the New Jersey Statute as unconstitutional violations of the First Amendment's Establishment Clause, which had been made applicable to the States by the Due Process Clause of the Fourteenth Amendment.[83]

Suddenly I was confronted with Justice Black's last paragraph in the Court's opinion: "The First Amendment has erected a wall between church and State. That wall must be kept high and impregnable. *We could not approve the slightest breach. New Jersey has not breached it here.*"[84] Justice Jackson in dissent amusingly expressed the shock I, too, experienced:

> [T]he undertones of the opinion, advocating complete and uncompromising separation of Church from State, seem utterly discordant with its conclusion yielding support to their commingling in educational matters. The case which irresistibly comes to mind as the most fitting precedent is that of Julia who, according to Byron's reports, "whispering 'I will ne'er consent,' consented."[85]

What had happened in the closing paragraphs of the Court's opinion? How could Justice Black and the Court majority justify the refund of transportation money for children who were traveling to Catholic parochial schools instead of public schools? The answer was to be found in the Court's use of the Child-Benefit theory discussed above.[86]

Simply put, the *Everson* majority saw the New Jersey law as a valid exercise of the State's police power. The Establishment Clause of the First Amendment, in the opinion of the Court, did not prohibit "New Jersey from

---

83. The legal-historical development that made the Establishment Clause applicable to the States is discussed in chap. four.

84. 330 U.S. 1, at 18. Emphasis added.

85. Jackson dissenting, 330 U.S. 1, at 19.

86. See the text at fns. 14–27, supra.

spending tax-raised funds to pay the bus fares of parochial school pupils as *a part of a general program under which it pays the fares of pupils attending public and other schools.*"[87]

Not denying that helping to transport children to parochial schools may help the church schools, Black argued that many expenditures of public funds under the police power of the State incidentally aid church schools, but it was not the purpose of the First Amendment to discriminate against citizens who elected to send their children to parochial schools pursuant to the constitutionally declared right in the *Pierce* Case.[88] The core of the majority's opinion—and the Child-Benefit theory—is that the State's intent was not to foster religion or to aid church schools. The State sought to protect children going to school. Its intent was clearly within the police power and consequently any incidental aid to church schools was not relevant. That a State's responsible discharge of its police power must incidentally aid parochial schools in a complex modern society seemed to Black obvious as he concluded his argument:

> It is undoubtedly true that children are helped to get to church schools. There is even a possibility that some of the children might not be sent to the church schools if the parents were compelled to pay their children's bus fares out of their own pockets when transportation to a public school would have been paid for by the State. The same possibility exists where the state requires a local transit company to provide reduced fares to school children including those attending parochial schools, or where a municipally owned transportation system undertakes to carry all school children free of charge. Moreover, state-paid policemen, detailed to protect children going to and from church schools from the very real hazards of traffic, would serve much the same purpose and accomplish much the same result as state provisions intended to guarantee free transportation of a kind which the state deems to be best for the school children's welfare. And parents might refuse to risk their children to the serious danger of traffic accidents going to and from parochial schools, the approaches to which were not protected by policemen. Similarly, parents might be reluctant to permit their children to attend schools which the state had cut off from such general government services as ordinary police and fire protection, connections for sewage disposal, public highways and sidewalks. Of course, cutting off church schools from these services, so separate and so indisputably marked off from the religious function, would make it far more difficult for the schools to operate. But such is obviously

---

87. 330 U.S. 1, at 17. Emphasis added.   88. See the text at fns. 39–40 in chap. four.

not the purpose of the First Amendment. That Amendment requires the state to be a neutral in its relations with groups of religious believers and non-believers; it does not require the state to be their adversary. State power is no more to be used so as to handicap religions than it is to favor them.

This Court has said that parents may, in the discharge of their duty under state compulsory education laws, send their children to a religious rather than a public school if the school meets the secular educational requirements which the state has power to impose. See *Pierce* v. *Society of Sisters,* 268 U.S. 510. It appears that these parochial schools meet New Jersey's requirements. *The State contributes no money to the schools. It does not support them. Its legislation, as applied, does no more than provide a general program to help parents get their children, regardless of their religion, safely and expeditiously to and from accredited schools.*[89]

The acceptance of the Child-Benefit theory in the *Everson* Case—after the Supreme Court held the Establishment of Religion Clause was applicable to the States—would prove to have far reaching effects in other "church-school aid" cases in the coming decades.

Justice Rutledge's Dissent in Everson

The most agreed upon dissent in the *Everson* 5–4 split decision was authored by Justice Wiley Rutledge.[90] With regret Justice William O. Douglas, who did not join the Rutledge dissent in *Everson*, retrospectively — in *Engel* v. *Vitale,*[91] the "New York State Prayer" Case, which will be discussed in chapter six—expressed the view that he thought it contained "durable First Amendment philosophy."[92] With all due respect to Justice Douglas, the Rutledge dissent in *Everson* is virtually reckless in its disregard of the indisputable facts of American history regarding the Establishment Clause of the First Amendment. As with the majority opinion by Justice Black, Justice Rutledge quotes at large Madison's "Memorial and Remonstrance" and discusses at length the history of Virginia's disestablishment struggle.[93]

---

89. 330 U.S. 1, at 17–18. Emphasis added.

90. Rutledge's dissent was joined by Justices Frankfurter, Jackson, and Burton. 330 U.S. 1, at 28. Justice Jackson also wrote a dissenting opinion joined only by Justice Frankfurter. Id., at 18.

91. 370 U.S. 421 (1962).

92. Ibid., Douglas concurring at 443.

93. Rutledge dissenting, 330 U.S. 1, at 31–40.

Referring to Madison, Justice Rutledge commences his argument against the Ewing, "New Jersey Bus Transportation Rebate" law by interpreting the First Amendment so broadly that *any* aid—direct, indirect, or incidental—to *any* religious institution would violate the First Amendment.

> *Not simply an established church, but any law respecting an establishment of religion is forbidden. The Amendment was broadly but not loosely phrased. It is the compact and exact summation of its author's views formed during his long struggle for religious freedom.* In Madison's own words characterizing Jefferson's Bill for Establishing Religious Freedom, the guaranty he put in our national charter, like the bill he piloted through the Virginia Assembly, was "a Model of technical precision, and perspicuous brevity." Madison could not have confused "church" and "religion," or "an established church" and "an establishment of religion."[94]

It is interesting to note that Rutledge quotes Madison—in the above excerpt from his opinion—characterizing Jefferson's Bill for Establishing Religious Freedom in Virginia in order to suggest Madison's interpertation of the Establishment Clause. Isn't it preferable to quote Madison in the House of Representatives' debate on the meaning of the Establishment Clause to determine Madison's interpretation of the Establishment Clause? On the House floor, Madison said that the House's Select Committee's final draft of the Establishment Clause meant that "Congress should not establish a religion and enforce legal observation of it by law, . . ."[95]

More sweeping assertions, undocumented by Justice Rutledge, are in his dissent. Consider this Rutledge interpretation:

> The Amendment's purpose was not to strike merely at the official establishment of a single sect, creed or religion, outlawing only a formal relation such as had prevailed in England and some of the colonies. Necessarily it was to uproot all such relationships. But the object was broader than separating church and state in this narrow sense. *It was to create a complete and permanent separation of the spheres of religious activity and civil authority by comprehensively forbidding every form of public aid or support for religion. . . .*[96]

Justice Rutledge not only ignores the fact that Madison was responding to many concerns from the individual State Ratifying Conventions about the

---

94. Ibid., at 31. Emphasis added.
95. See Madison's entire statement at

the text in chap. one, fns. 32–33.
96. Ibid., at 31–32. Emphasis added.

possibility of Congress creating a national religion,[97] he also ignores Madison's own original wording of the Amendment and his emphasis as to what was the "Amendment's purpose." Madison was clearly responding to the resolutions of the State Ratifying Conventions and said as much on June 8, 1789, when he introduced the words that would eventually be fashioned into the First Amendment.[98] It is most difficult to reconcile what Justice Rutledge has written—at footnote 96 above—with Madison's original draft that "[t]he civil rights of none shall be abridged on account of religious belief or worship, *nor shall any national religion be established,* nor shall the full and equal rights of Conscience be in any manner, or on any pretext, infringed."[99] Where in Madison's draft, or even in the First Amendment itself is the "forbidding [of] every form of public aid or support for religion"?

Further, in light of the federal division of power, Justice Rutledge's interpretation of one of the Amendment's purposes—"to create a complete and permanent separation of the spheres of religious activity and civil authority by comprehensively forbidding every form of public aid and support for religion"—is absurd. Madison certainly knew that the proposed amendments to the new *Constitution* would place no limitiations on the political power of the States. Consequently Madison knew that the Amendment, even if adopted, would neither disestablish the remaining state established churches nor prevent a state at that time from establishing a church or religion. As this was the case in 1791, how could Justice Rutledge believe that the Amendment, once adopted, would forbid "every form of *public aid or support for religion*" unless Rutledge believed aid from a State government is not public aid or support for religion? Irrespective of this point, if Madison thought the First Amendment was designed to do what Rutledge claims in *Everson*, how could Madison expect the States with religious establishments to ratify such an amendment? When these historical factors are weighed against the Rutledge claims, as the intended prohibitions of the Establishment Clause, this absolutist argument becomes preposterous. Justice Rutledge's logic in his *Everson* dissenting opinion is no better. "Religion," Justice Rutledge argues, "appears only once in the Amendment."

> *But the word governs two prohibitions and governs them alike.* It does not have two meanings, one narrow to forbid "an establishment" and another, much broader, for securing "the free exercise thereof." "Thereof" brings

97. See the text and quotes in chap. one, fns. 15–20.

98. *Annals of the Congress,* Vol. I, p. 434.

99. Ibid. Emphasis added.

down "religion" with its entire and exact content, no more and no less, from the first into the second guaranty, so that Congress and now the states are as broadly restricted concerning the one as they are regarding the other.

No one would claim today that the Amendment is constricted, in "prohibiting the free exercise" of religion, to securing the free exercise of some formal or creedal observance, of one sect or of many. It secures all forms of religious expression, creedal, sectarian or nonsectarian, wherever and however taking place, *except conduct which trenches upon the like freedoms of others or clearly and presently endangers the community's good order and security....*[100]

As I have emphasized, Justice Rutledge concedes that the "free exercise of religion" is not absolute when it collides in some way with what the community considers necessary to "good order and security." Certainly, the "Free Exercise of Religion" Clause did not render federal antipolygamy statutes unconstitutional.[101] Noting that "[p]olygamy has always been odious among the northern and western nations of Europe," Chief Justice Waite held in the opinion of the Court in *Reynolds* v. *United States*,[102] that "it is impossible to believe that the constitutional guaranty of religious freedom was intended to prohibit legislation in respect to this most important feature of social life."[103] Given Justice Rutledge's own argument above concerning the equal vitality of the two religious prohibitions in the First Amendment, how can he logically maintain that the Establishment Clause provides for an absolute ban on governmental action while the Free Exercise Clause does not?

As with the majority opinion, the Rutledge dissent constantly falls back on the "Memorial and Remonstrance" written by Madison in 1785, so much so that Rutledge tells us that "the Remonstrance is at once the most concise and most accurate statement of the views of the First Amendment's author [Madison] concerning what is 'an establishment of religion.' "[104] Madison was not, however, the only author of the First Amendment or its religious prohibitions.[105] Had he been, the term "an establishment of religion"—which was not in his original proposal to the House on June 8, 1789—would not even appear in the First Amendment. Justice Rutledge notwithstanding, the "Remonstrance" written in 1785 is hardly a better guide to what Madison thought was meant by a religious establishment than

---

100. 330 U.S. 1, at 32. Emphasis added.
101. See the text at fns. 72–76, supra.
102. 98 U.S. 145 (1878).
103. Ibid., at 164–65.

104. 330 U.S. 1, at 37.
105. See the text in chap. one at fns. 20–30.

Madison's own reply given to Roger Sherman on August 15, 1789, in the House of Representatives when Sherman asked Madison why the Amendment was necessary.[106]

Proceeding as if Madison's "Memorial and Remonstrance" was the First Amendment, Justice Rutledge's dissent presses his point that for Madison any governmental aid to religion was inherently wrong.[107] Completely ignoring the discriminatory nature of the aid that characterized the Virginia Assessment Bill in that it would provide funds for teachers of the Christian religion only,[108] Justice Rutledge develops his argument thus:

> With Jefferson, Madison believed that to tolerate any fragment of establishment would be by so much to perpetuate restraint upon that freedom. Hence he sought to tear out the institution not partially but root and branch, and to bar its return forever.
>
> In no phase was he more unrelentingly absolute than in opposing state support or aid by taxation. Not even "three pence" contribution was thus to be exacted from any citizen for such a purpose. Remonstrance, Par. 3. Tithes had been the lifeblood of establishment before and after other compulsions disappeared. *Madison and his coworkers made no exceptions or abridgments to the complete separation they created. Their objection was not to small tithes. It was to any tithes whatsoever....*[109]

The Rutledge dissent continues with this inexplicable passage:

> In view of this history no further proof is needed that the Amendment forbids any appropriation, large or small, from public funds to aid or support any and all religious exercises. But if more were called for, the debates in the First Congress and this Court's consistent expressions, whenever it has touched on the matter directly, supply it.[110]

What makes this passage so incredible is that neither Justice Rutledge's dissenting opinion nor its footnotes—either vaguely or precisely—indicate which debates in the First Congress prove that the First Amendment *"forbids any appropriation, large or small, from public funds to aid or support any and all religious exercises."*[111] Was it the debate addressing the selection of a chaplain for the Houses of Congress?[112] Perhaps it was the debate

---

106. See the text at fn. 95, supra.

107. 330 U.S. 1, at 40–41.

108. See the text in chap. two at fns. 13–20 where the "Memorial and Remonstrance" is discussed.

109. 330 U.S. 1, at 40–41. Emphasis added.

110. Ibid., at 41.

111. Ibid. Emphasis added.

112. See the text and the fns. in chap. two at fns. 25–27.

concerning the payment of a salary of $500 to congressional chaplains, which came out of public funds, pursuant to a plan recommended by a Congressional Committee on the appointment of chaplains of which James Madison was a member?[113] Or might it have been the debate in the First Congress that led to the adoption of the federal law passed March 3, 1791, providing for payment of a chaplain for the Army?[114] Certainly Justice Rutledge was not thinking of the Acts of the Second and Third Congresses that enlarged the chaplaincy corps even to the extent of funding, with federal tax money, a chaplain for the Navy.[115] Justice Rutledge, with a statement by mere affirmation, contrary to historical public documents, fails to document this statement that is crucial to his version of the Madison of 1789, the First Congress, and the meaning of the Establishment of Religion Clause. The actions of the First Congress, however, prove that much more than "three pence" of public funds were spent to directly support religious exercises in the Congress alone.

Also perplexing is Justice Rutledge's contention that "this Court's consistent expressions whenever it has touched on this matter *directly*" support the historical view that the First Amendment forbids the use of public funds for any and all religious exercises when, at the outset of his opinion, he writes that "[this] case forces us to determine squarely for *the first time* what was 'an establishment of religion' in the First Amendment's conception; . . ."[116] If this is the first significant Establishment Clause case—as it is—how could the Supreme Court's past decisions bolster the Rutledge interpretation? The fact of the matter is that the U.S. Supreme Court did not touch on the matter of comprehensively interpreting the Establishment Clause directly until *Everson* in 1947.

Although Rutledge's footnotes fail to cite one piece of legislation in the First Congress to indicate his "absolute separation" position was the one Congress supported,[117] he does cite some previous U.S. Supreme Court decisions to bolster his claim that the past principal decisions by the U.S. Supreme Court regarding the Establishment Clause "confirm the [First] Amendment's broad prohibition."[118] Rutledge's footnote 35 allegedly provides his supporting evidence:

> [35] The decision most closely touching the question, where it was squarely raised, is *Quick Bear* v. *Leupp*, 210 U.S. 50. The Court distinguished sharply between appropriations from public funds for the sup-

---

113. See the text and the fn. in chap. two at fn. 30.

114. See chap. three, fn. 19.

115. See chap. three, the fns. and text at

fns. 20–23.

116. 330 U.S. 1, at 29.

117. See the quote at fn. 110, supra.

118. 330 U.S. 1, at 43, fn. 35.

port of religious education and appropriations from funds held in trust by the Government essentially as trustee for private individuals, Indian wards, as beneficial owners. The ruling was that the latter could be disbursed to private, religious schools at the designation of those patrons for paying the cost of their education. *But it was stated also that such a use of public moneys would violate both the First Amendment* and the specific statutory declaration involved, namely, that "it is hereby declared to be the settled policy of the Government to hereafter make no appropriation whatever for education in any sectarian school." 210 U.S. at 79. Cf. *Ponce* v. *Roman Catholic Apostolic Church*, 210 U.S. 296, 322. . . .[119]

While page 79 of *Reuben Quick Bear* v. *Leupp* does correctly quote the new congressional policy of the U.S. Appropriation Act of 1896[120] regarding the education of the Indians, there is no reference at page 79 that such expenditures would violate the First Amendment as Justice Rutledge claims. Furthermore, Justice Rutledge's dissent neglects to point out that the U.S. Indian Appropriations Act of 1896 in no way indicates that previous use of federal monies appropriated for the support of Indian schools violated the First Amendment. This is no small omission.

The U.S. Appropriations Act of 1896 under the section "Support of Schools" clearly "declared" a "settled" change of "*policy* of the Government to *hereafter* make no appropriation whatever for education [of the Indians] in any sectarian school. . . ,"[121] provided that nonsectarian schools were available.

Most significantly, Justice Rutledge's opinion fails to point out that a public policy change had been made by the Federal Congress regarding appropriations for Indian education. This change in legislative policy was the result of a political decision not a constitutional command. No court was declaring the use of these federal funds or the use of additional federal monies earmarked as "Indian trust funds," which grew out of federal treaties, and which supported church schools for over a century under the regime of the First Amendment, unconstitutional. Why not? If the Establishment Clause is as absolute as Justice Rutledge's opinion would have us believe, could Congress, each year, even pursuant to Indian treaties made under the process and authority of the U.S. *Constitution*, support church schools without violating the First Amendment?

Lest it be counterargued that the money belonged to the Indians pur-

---

119. Ibid. Emphasis added.

120. *The Statutes At Large of the United States of America*, Vol. XXIX (Washington, D.C.: Government Printing Office, 1897), Fifty-Fourth Congress, Sess. I, Chap. 398, 1896, "Support of Schools," p. 345.

121. Ibid.

suant to the treaties, it ought to be asked: "Can the Senate and the President violate the First Amendment by treaty although the President and the entire Congress by passage of national legislation may not?" It should not go unnoticed that these "Indian Funds" were controlled by the United States Government acting through the Commissioner and the Bureau of Indian Affairs. Presumably these people were employees and agents of the United States Government. As such, were their actions not subject to the authority of the *Constitution* of the United States and its First Amendment? Are they to be viewed as free agents to enter into sectarian school contracts if Rutledge's Establishment prohibition is the correct historical interpretation?

Some answers to these questions are provided in the footnotes of the *Reuben Quick Bear* Case that Justice Rutledge does not cite in his *Everson* dissent. Justice Rutledge does not mention, for example, that the footnotes in the *Reuben Quick Bear* Case indicate that "Catholic mission schools were erected at the cost of charitable Catholics" and with the approval of the United States Government and, that to aid these schools under an "Act of 1819, ten thousand dollars was appropriated for the purpose of extending financial help" to those engaged in these enterprises to help educate and civilize the Indians through the work of religious organizations.[122] Neither does Justice Rutledge mention the *Quick Bear* footnote indicating that in "1820, twenty-one schools conducted by *different religious societies* were given $11,838 by the United States Government and from that date until 1870 the principal educational work in relation to the Indians was under the auspices of these bodies" with financial aid by the national Government.[123] Nor does he cite the fact that "[i]n 1870, an act of Congress was passed appropriating one hundred thousand dollars ($100,000) for the support of Indian Schools among Indian tribes" which did not have treaty stipulations for educational purposes and "that these appropriations continued until 1876."[124]

In sum, Justice Rutledge can hardly cite *Reuben Quick Bear* v. *Leupp* to sustain a thesis that federal monies were not used to support religious schools and institutions in the nineteenth century when the footnotes of the case and the opinion of the Court by Chief Justice Fuller indicate that these funds were used in great quantity for over a century after the ratification of the First Amendment and its Establishment Clause.

Rather than recognizing the historical fact that during the early years of 1824–1831 alone, the *Annual Reports of the Commissioner of Indian*

---

122. 210 U.S. 50, at 57–64, fn. 12.
123. 210 U.S. 50, at 64–66, fn. 12. Emphasis added.
124. Ibid.

Affairs document that the U.S. Government supported church schools run by the Society of the United Brethren, the American Board of Foreign Missions, the Baptist General Convention, the Hamilton Baptist Missionary Society, the Cumberland Missionary Board, the Synod of South Carolina and Georgia, the United Foreign Missionary Society, the Methodist Episcopal Church, the Western Missionary Society, the Catholic Bishop of New Orleans, the Society for Propagating the Gospel among the Indians, the Society of Jesuits, the Protestant Episcopal Church of New York, the Methodist Society and the Presbyterian Society for Propagating the Gospel,[125] Justice Rutledge's dissent with broad and largely undocumented statements rewrites American history as if a complete and absolute separation of Church and State had been desired and secured by the Framers of the First Amendment—an absolute separation that has been reflected by the public governmental actions throughout the history of the Republic.

Ignoring all the historical evidence to the contrary, Justice Rutledge concludes his dissent as though a century and a half of absolute separation of Church and State was now being shattered by the Court majority's opinion:

> Two great drives are constantly in motion to abridge, in the name of education, the complete division of religion and civil authority which our forefathers made. One is to introduce religious education and observances into the public schools. The other, to obtain public funds for the aid and support of various private religious schools... *In my opinion both avenues were closed by the Constitution. Neither should be opened by this Court.* The matter is not one of quantity, to be measured by the amount of money expended. *Now as in Madison's day it is one of principle, to keep separate the separate spheres as the First Amendment drew them*; to prevent the first experiment upon our liberties; and to keep the question from becoming entangled in corrosive precedents. We should not be less strict to keep strong and untarnished the one side of the shield of religious freedom than we have been of the other.[126]

If Justice Douglas is correct and the Rutledge dissent in *Everson* is ever to become "durable First Amendment philosophy," it will not be because his dissent reflects the history of the Republic or the demonstrated intentions of the Amendment's Framers. It could only become so because, like Justice Douglas, ultimately the members of the United States Supreme

---

125. *Annual Reports of the Commissioner of Indian Affairs*, 1824–1831, Vol. I (New York: A.M.S. Press, Inc., 1976).
126. 330 U.S. 1, at 63.

Court will have made a political value judgment. But under the American Constitutional System, political value judgments about public policy are consigned to the political branches of government. They have no legitimate place in the courts of the land.

The "Released Time Case"—McCollum v. Board of Education

One year later, in *McCollum* v. *Board of Education of Champaign, Illinois*,[127] the Supreme Court for the first time held that an action by a local school board was unconstitutional under the Establishment of Religion Clause as made applicable to the States by the Due Process Clause of the Fourteenth Amendment. The 5–4 split decision of the *Everson* Case gave way to a nearly unanimous vote (8–1) on the issue of constitutionality,[128] as almost every member of the nation's highest court embraced the distorted "separation of Church and State" history put forth in the *Everson* opinions of Justices Black and Rutledge the previous year.

The *McCollum* Case was distinctly different from the *Everson* "Bus Transportation" Case in that *no monetary expenditures* of budgetary significance could be traced to the actions involving the Champaign Board of Education and any sectarian educational institutions or parents who sent their children to them. The facts of the case were relatively uncomplicated. In 1940, members of the Jewish, Roman Catholic, and some Protestant denominations formed a "voluntary association called the Champaign Council on Religious education."[129] This Council asked the Board of Education to allow "public school pupils in grades four to nine inclusive" to be permitted to attend weekly religious instruction, on a voluntary basis, without having to leave the *public school premises*.[130]

Pursuant to its authority under Illinois law,[131] the Champaign Board of Education instituted a "released time" program whereby students, whose parents gave permission to attend religious instruction classes, could do so as a substitute "for secular education provided under the [State's] compulsory education law" for not more than forty-five minutes a week.[132]

---

127. 333 U.S. 203 (1948).

128. Not all eight justices joined the opinion of the Court by Justice Black even though there was only one vote to sustain the constitutionality of the "Released Time" program. Justices Frankfurter and Jackson wrote concurring opinions as to the disposition of the case but did not join Chief Justice Vinson and Justices Douglas, Rutledge, Burton, and Murphy, who subscribed to the opinion of the Court.

129. 333 U.S. 203, at 207.

130. Ibid.

131. *Ill. Revised Statutes*, Chap. 122, Sec. 123 and Sec. 301 (1943).

132. 333 U.S. 203, at 205.

Students who did not attend religious instruction classes were not released from their secular educational obligations. The Council employed teachers of the Protestant, Roman Catholic, and Jewish faiths "*at no expense* to the [public] school authorities, but the instructors were subject to the approval and supervision of the superintendent of schools."[133] These teachers were permitted to provide religious instruction in the public school rooms designated for them weekly.

Mrs. Vashti McCollum, mother of a Champaign school boy, a taxpayer in the Champaign school district, and a taxpayer in the State of Illinois, challenged the constitutionality of the "released time" program in the Illinois courts as a violation of the First Amendment and Fourteenth Amendment.[134] Specifically, Mrs. McCollum asked the Illinois courts to order the Board of Education to: "adopt and enforce rules and regulations prohibiting all instruction in and teaching of religious education in all public schools in Champaign School District Number 71, . . . and in all public school houses and buildings in said district when occupied by public schools."[135] Losing in the Illinois courts, she carried her appeal to the United States Supreme Court before which the case was argued on December 8, 1947.

In his opinion of the Court, handed down four months later, Justice Black reiterated the sweeping prohibitions that he attributed to the Establishment Clause in the "Bus Transportation" Case.[136] In reversing the Illinois courts and finding the "released time" program unconstitutional, the Court's opinion speaks to basically two points which it holds cannot be reconciled with the concept of separation of Church and State: "Here not only are the State's tax-supported public school buildings used for the dissemination of religious doctrines. The State also affords sectarian groups an invaluable aid in that it helps to provide pupils for their religious classes through use of the State's compulsory public school machinery. This is not separation of Church and State."[137] The majority's opinion cites *Everson* many times but gives no new historical or other justification as to why the Establishment Clause should be at odds with either of these two propositions. Substantial documentation indicates, however, that the two actions given in the majority's opinion in *McCollum*, to nullify the Board of Education's "released time" program, were not viewed historically as violations of separation of Church and State.

Justice Black states in *McCollum* that the "released time" program is:

---

133. Ibid., at 209. Emphasis added.
134. Ibid., at 205.
135. Ibid.
136. Ibid., at 211. He also makes clear

that the entire *Everson* Court subscribed to that interpretation even though the Court vote was a 5–4 split decision. Id., at 211.
137. Ibid., at 212.

"beyond all question a utilization of the tax-established and tax-supported public school system to aid religious groups to spread their faith. *And it falls squarely under the ban of the First Amendment* (made applicable to the States by the Fourteenth) as we interpreted it in *Everson* v. *Board of Education*, 330 U.S. 1."[138] Apparently, Thomas Jefferson did not realize that the use of "tax-established and tax-supported public schools to aid religious groups" violated the principles of the First Amendment.

Jefferson, whom the majority and minority opinions in the *Everson* "Bus Transportation" Case correctly cited as one of the foremost advocates of separation of Church and State in the early years of the Republic, in his Regulations for the University of Virginia, which has always been supported wholly from public funds, advocated close cooperation between the University and sectarian schools adjacent to it. Further, Jefferson's regulations make clear that if any student of an adjacent religious school attended "any school of the University [of Virginia]," they should be accorded all the same "rights and privileges" as the University's students. Here are the relevant sections of Jefferson's Regulations regarding these matters:

> Should the religious sects of this State, or any of them, *according to the invitation held out to them*, establish within, or adjacent to, the precincts of the University, schools for instruction in the religion of their sect, the *students of the University will be free, and expected to attend religious worship at the establishment of their respective sects*, in the morning, and in time to meet their school in the University at its stated hour.
>
> The students of such religious school, if they attend any school of the University, *shall be considered as students of the University, subject to the same regulations, and entitled to the same rights and privileges.*[139]

Could it be that Justice Black and his brethren on the High Court in 1948 knew better than Thomas Jefferson—whom they invoke as their source of historical support—what came "squarely under the ban [of the principles] of the First Amendment?" Perhaps an even more supportive statement by Jefferson regarding the aiding of religious schools with public funds is that of October 7, 1822.[140]

Subscribing to the opinion that religious doctrines were important to the world of ideas, Jefferson supported a proposal that would attempt to simul-

---

138. Ibid., at 210. Emphasis added.
139. "Regulations," October 4, 1824. See Padover, *The Complete Jefferson*, pp.

1110–11. Emphasis added.
140. Ibid., pp. 957–58.

taneously commingle religious ideas and religious school students and the University's students and facilities, while still emphasizing the independence of the different educational institutions. Jefferson's prescription could hardly have passed the constitutional standards invented by the United States Supreme Court in 1947 and 1948 as to the meaning of "separation of Church and State."

Here is Jefferson's solution to the difficult problems posed by the creation of a public university that must in some way address itself to the ideas found in religious opinion:

October 7, 1822

In the same report of the commissioners of 1818 it was stated by them that "in conformity with the principles of constitution, which place all sects of religion on an equal footing, with the jealousies of the different sects in guarding that equality from encroachment or surprise, and with the sentiments of the legislature in freedom of religion, manifested on former occasions, *they had not proposed that any professorship of divinity should be established in the University*; that provision, however, was made for giving instruction in the Hebrew, Greek and Latin languages, the depositories of the originals, and of the earliest and most respected authorities of the faith of every sect, and for courses of ethical lectures, developing those moral obligations in which all sects agree. That, proceeding thus far, without offence to the constitution, they had left, at this point, to every sect to take into their own hands the office of further instruction in the peculiar tenet of each."

It was not, however, to be understood that instruction in religious opinion and duties was meant to be precluded by the public authorities, as indifferent to the interests of society. On the contrary, the relations which exist between man and his Maker, and the duties resulting from those relations, are the most interesting and important to every human being, and the most incumbent on his study and investigation. The want of instruction in the various creeds of religious faith existing among our citizens presents, therefore, a chasm in a general institution of the useful sciences. But it was thought that this want, and the entrustment to each society of instruction in its own doctrine, were evils of less danger than a permission to the public authorities to dictate modes or principles of religious instruction, or than opportunities furnished them by giving countenance or ascendancy to any one sect over another. *A remedy, however, has been suggested of promising aspect, which, while it excludes the public authorities from the domain of religious freedom, will give to the sectarian schools of divinity the full benefit the public provisions made for instruction in the other branches of science.* These branches are equally necessary to the divine as to the other professional or civil characters, to enable them to fulfill the duties of their calling with understanding and usefulness. *It has, therefore, been in contemplation, and suggested by some pious individuals, who perceive the advantages of associating other studies with those of religion, to establish their religious schools on the confines of the University, so as to give to their students ready and convenient access and attendance on the scientific lectures of the University*; and to maintain, by that means, those destined for the religious professions on as high a standing of science, and of personal weight and respectability, as may be obtained by others from the benefits of the University. *Such establishments would offer the further and greater advantage of enabling the students of the University to attend religious exercises with the professor of their particular sect, either in the rooms of the building still to be erected, and destined to that purpose under impartial regulations, as proposed in the same report of the commissioners, or in the lecturing room of such professor.* To such propositions the Visitors are disposed to lend a willing ear, and would think it their duty to give every encouragement, by assuring to those who might choose such a location for their schools, *that the regulations of the University should be so modified and accommodated as to give every facility of access and attendance to their students, with such regulated use also as may be permitted to the other students, of the library which may hereafter be acquired, either by public or private munificence. But always understanding that these schools shall be independent of the University and of each other.* Such an arrangement would complete the circle of the useful sciences embraced by this institution, and would fill the chasm now existing, on principles which *would leave inviolate the constitutional freedom of religion*, the most inalienable and sacred of all human rights, over which the people and authorities of this state, individually and publicly, have ever manifested the most watchful jealousy: and could this jealousy be now alarmed, in the opinion of the legislature, by what is here suggested, the idea will be relinquished on any surmise of disapprobation which they might think proper to express.[141]

Is there much doubt that even though Jefferson is careful to point out that these religious schools and the University shall be independent of each other, the proposal offered would be assailed by the Supreme Court today as close cooperation between religious education and tax-supported facilities, which once again "falls squarely under the ban of the First Amendment?"

141. Ibid., Emphasis added.

If indeed Thomas Jefferson was urging regulations for the governance of the publicly funded University of Virginia that was inconsistent with the letter or spirit of the separation of Church and State required by the First Amendment—unlike Justice Black and the *McCollum* Court—Jefferson must not have known what the principles of the Establishment Clause prohibitions required. When the *McCollum* majority opinion is compared with these sections of Jefferson's Regulations for the University, Justice Black's conclusions are untenable.

Jefferson, who authored the first bill for religious equality in Virginia, certainly was not ignorant of the principles of the First Amendment regarding separation of Church and State. For Jefferson, Madison, and the other leaders who subscribed to the separation of Church and State, the First Amendment was designed to make separate for all time national control over a national church by precluding the national government from passing any law in regard to a national religious establishment. Separation of Church and State to Jefferson meant religious disestablishment or the prevention of a religious establishment. From what he wrote in the "Regulations" and the October 7, 1822 statement, it can certainly be seen that for Jefferson "separation of Church and State" did not mean that tax-supported facilities could not be used to help attain sectarian purposes.

As already mentioned, the *McCollum* majority gave as a second reason for invalidating the "released time" program the argument that the State affords religious groups aid in providing them pupils by compelling students to come to school and then releasing them from this secular educational requirement weekly if they attend religious instruction instead.[142] However, Jefferson in his "Regulations" wrote that those University of Virginia students who have a religious school of their sect adjacent to the University "will be free and *expected to attend religious worship at the establishment of their respective sects, . . .*"[143] This supplying of students for religious instruction "is not separation of Church and State," according to Justice Black.[144] Either Justice Black is wrong or Thomas Jefferson did not believe in "separation of Church and State."[145]

---

142. See the quote in the text at fn. 137, supra.

143. See the quote in the text at fn. 139, supra. Emphasis added.

144. See the quote in the text at fn. 137, supra.

145. Stokes and Pfeffer, advocates of an absolute separation of Church and State, have indicated, despite what seems to be a clear requirement in the University's rules, that no compulsion to attend existed. Not only do they fail to provide adequate documentation for that interpretation of Jefferson's rules, they also fail to explain why Jefferson —who in their view was an absolutist in separation of Church and State—would

Commenting on Jefferson's Regulations for the University of Virginia, Justice Reed, the only *McCollum* dissenter, discusses just this point in his dissenting opinion:

> Thus the "wall of separation between Church and State" that Mr. Jefferson built at the University which he founded did not exclude religious education from the school. The difference between the generality of his statements on the separation of Church and State and the specificity of his conclusions on education are considerable. A rule of law should not be drawn from a figure of speech.[146]

Mr. Justice Black ignores another consideration with this line of argument. Inasmuch as the U.S. Supreme Court has held that parents may send their children to parochial schools to meet the requirements of state compulsory education laws,[147] the States have, through their compulsory school machinery, provided religious schools with students ever since parochial schools had their inception. Education in parochial schools has never been successfully challenged as unconstitutional because of this aid to religion from the compulsory school laws.

Before ending the discussion of Justice Black's opinion of the Court in the *McCollum* Case, two more comments about Jefferson's view as to the relationship between Church and State, in the field of education, seem pertinent.

In a letter to his nephew, Peter Carr on September 7, 1814, Jefferson advanced a comprehensive plan for an educational system that he had pledged to draft some time earlier.[148] Jefferson wrote that he had "long entertained the hope that this, *our native State, would take up the subject of education, and make an establishment,* either with or without incorporation, into that of William and Mary, where every branch of science, deemed useful at this day, should be taught in its highest degree."[149] Five years later, in 1819, the University of Virginia was founded as a state establishment supported by public funds.

Under the Jefferson plan the state establishment would include at its

---

even include this admonition regarding religious worship in the regulations of a public university in the first place. See Anson Phelps Stokes and Leo Pfeffer, *Church and State in the United States*, rev. ed. in 1 vol. (N.Y.: Harper and Row, 1964), p. 54.

146. 333 U.S. 203, at 247.

147. *Pierce* v. *Society of Sisters*, 268 U.S. 510 (1925).

148. Padover, *The Complete Jefferson*, p. 1064.

149. Ibid. Emphasis added.

highest educational level "Professional Schools."[150] "In these professional schools," wrote Jefferson, "each science is to be taught in the highest degree it has yet attained."[151] The "3d Department" Jefferson recommended was a professional school of "*Theology* and Ecclesiastical History; Law, Municipal and Foreign."[152] While it might be argued that "Ecclesiastical History" should be included as an area of intellectual study, it is difficult to harmonize Thomas Jefferson advocating the establishment of a state professional school of "Theology" with the "Pfeffer-Rutledge" doctrine of absolute separation of Church and State.

Somewhat amusing to me—but perhaps not to those who claim Jefferson believed in an absolute independence of the state and religion—is an amendment to the student "Regulations" for the University of Virginia that Jefferson wrote on October 5, 1825.[153] The regulation to be amended was written by Jefferson on October 4, 1824[154] and reads:

> Habits of expense, of *dissoluteness, dissipation*, or of playing at games of chance, being obstructive to the acquisition of science by the student himself and injurious by example to others, shall be subject in the first instance to admonition and reproof to the offender, and to communication and warning to the parent or guardian, and, *if not satisfactorily corrected, to a refusal of further continuance at the University.*[155]

In his amendment, Jefferson urged that after the word "dissipation," in the above regulation, the words "of profane swearing" should be inserted.[156] Why "profane" swearing, which has the character of derision of that which is held "sacred or holy," should be an act, which if not discontinued, would lead to expulsion from a public university could be of such serious consequence to a man supposedly committed to an absolute separation of religion and the state is extremely hard to understand. In these instances, as in the others documented above, Thomas Jefferson displayed a markedly dif-

---

150. Jefferson's plan was so comprehensive that it also encompassed provisions for "Elementary Grades in the 'Ward Schools' and 'General Grade' schools." Ibid., pp. 1065–66, 1068.

151. Ibid., pp. 1067–68.

152. Ibid., p. 1068.

153. Ibid., p. 1115.

154. Padover, *The Complete Jefferson*, p. 1106.

155. Ibid., p. 1109. Emphasis added.

156. Ibid., p. 1115. The unabridged *Random House Dictionary of the English Language* (New York: Random House, 1969), p. 1148, has the following listing for "profane": "adj. 1. characterized by irreverence or contempt for God or sacred principles or things; irreligious." The less preferred definitions offer little support to any idea that the word "profane" is not usually taken to mean "irreverence."

ferent perception of separation of Church and State than the broad interpretation that the "absolute separationists" on the U.S. Supreme Court and off have urged in his name.

The single dissenter in the *McCollum* "Released Time" Case, Justice Stanley Reed, cited several historical primary sources attempting to justify his claim that Madison and Jefferson never intended the kind of absolute separation of Church and State embraced by the rest of the Court.[157] Pointing to the incongruity of the Court's holding and the then-current practices at the nation's military academies which are directly under the authority of the Congress and the First Amendment, Justice Reed wrote:

> In the United States Naval Academy and the United States Military Academy, schools wholly supported and completely controlled by the federal government, there are a number of religious activities. Chaplains are attached to both schools. Attendance at church services on Sunday *is compulsory* at both the Military and Naval Academies. At West Point the Protestant services are held in the Cadet Chapel, the Catholic in the Catholic Chapel, and the Jewish in the Old Cadet Chapel; at Annapolis only Protestant services are held on the reservation, midshipmen of other religious persuasions attend the churches of the city of Annapolis. These facts indicate that both schools since their earliest beginnings have maintained *and enforced* a pattern of participation in formal worship.[158]

These religious practices were not even voluntary, as was the case in the "Released Time" program. Thus, it is difficult to understand how the eight other Justices in *McCollum* could reconcile these activities at the U.S. service academies with their concept of an absolute and "impregnable wall" of separation of Church and State.

Perhaps too easily missed in the Reed dissent is the extremely important distinction made between an unwise law and an unconstitutional law. Indeed, governmental bodies may use their constitutionally conferred powers to make foolish public policy. Laws reflecting outright stupidity are not necessarily unconstitutional even though that is frequently how they are attacked. Calling attention to the distinction between a public policy decision which may be unconstitutional and one which may be unwise, Justice Reed virtually lectured the majority:

---

157. See Justice Reed's fns. 8–14, 333 U.S. 203, at 245–47.

158. Ibid., at 254–55. Emphasis added.

As indicated above these practices, as a matter of policy, have been discontinued in recent years.

With the general statements in the opinions concerning the constitutional requirement that the nation and the states, by virtue of the First and Fourteenth Amendments, may "make no law respecting an establishment of religion," I am in agreement. But, in the light of the meaning given to those words by the precedents, customs, and practices which I have detailed above, I cannot agree with the Court's conclusion that when pupils compelled by law to go to school for secular education are released from school so as to attend the religious classes, churches are unconstitutionally aided. *Whatever may be the wisdom of the arrangement as to the use of the school buildings made with the Champaign Council of Religious Education, it is clear to me that past practice shows such cooperation is not forbidden by the First Amendment. When actual church services have always been permitted on government property, the mere use of the school buildings by a non-sectarian group for religious education ought not to be condemned as an establishment of religion.* For a non-sectarian organization to give the type of instruction here offered cannot be said to violate our rule as to the establishment of religion by the state. The prohibition of enactments respecting the establishment of religion do not bar every friendly gesture between church and state. It is not an absolute prohibition against every conceivable situation where the two may work together, any more than the other provisions of the First Amendment—free speech, free press—are absolutes.[159]

Reed's dissent fell on deaf ears. So intent was the *McCollum* majority on upholding the sweeping prohibitions attributed to the Establishment of Religion Clause in the *Everson* "Bus Fare Reimbursement" Case a year earlier, that without any explanation at all Justice Black's opinion rejected the Champaign Board's argument by simply mere affirmation:

They [Champaign School Board] argue that historically the First Amendment was intended to forbid only government preference of one religion over another, not an impartial governmental assistance of all religions. In addition they ask that we distinguish or overrule our holding in the *Everson* Case that the Fourteenth Amendment made the "establishment of religion" clause of the First Amendment applicable as a prohibition against the States. *After giving full consideration to the arguments presented we are unable to accept either of these contentions.*[160]

The majority opinion provides not one reason why "these contentions" are unacceptable. There is no attempt to show historically that nondiscrimina-

159. Ibid., at 255–56. Emphasis added.
160. Black's opinion of the Court, at 211. Emphasis added.

tory cooperation with religion is unconstitutional. The only explanation offered by any of the eight prevailing justices that differed from the sloppy history of the *Everson* Case came from Justice Jackson, who concurred in the result of the case but apparently did not join the opinion of the Court.[161]

In a spark of refreshing candor, Justice Jackson, in his concurring opinion, wrote: "*It is idle to pretend that this task is one to which we can find in the Constitution one word* to help us as judges to decide where the secular ends and the sectarian begins in education. Nor can we find guidance in any other legal source. It is a matter on which we can find no law *but our own prepossessions....*"[162] If this is indeed the case, then one cannot help wondering why the U.S. Supreme Court overruled an elected public policy making body in the name of a silent *Constitution*. A predetermined and undocumented commitment by the Supreme Court, on a purely public policy question, which does not clearly fall under the ban of the *Constitution*, can in the long run only serve to weaken the notion that courts are, or at least attempt to be, somewhat above partisan politics.

Concluding Reflections on Everson *and* McCollum

The actions of all the justices in the *Everson* "Bus Transportation" Case and the *McCollum* "Released Time" Case clearly indicate that not one of them interpreted the prohibitions of the Establishment Clause as its framers intended. Even Justice Reed in *McCollum* did not disassociate himself from the broad interpretation given the First Amendment in the *Everson* decision.

The Rutledge dissent in *Everson* and to a lesser degree the Black opinions of the Court in both *Everson* and *McCollum* are built upon the theory that Jefferson, Madison, and the other framers of religious liberty in the United States conceived of the First Amendment religious injunctions as creating two absolutely distinct and separate spheres of activity, one being religion and the other the state. That this theory is sheer fiction and is not compatible with American historical fact is more than adequately documented by the historical data presented and discussed in chapters one, two, three, and here. Nothing in these cases is said about federal monies used to build churches, support church schools, U.S. land trusts to a society dedicated to spreading the "Gospel among the Heathen," nor prayers in our public buildings, to mention just a few omissions.

161. 333 U.S. 203, at 232.
162. Ibid., at 237–38. Emphasis added.

Further, the decisions in *Everson* and *McCollum* hang their "historical arguments" essentially on only four historical documents: the Madison "Remonstrance" and the Jefferson "Bill for Religious Liberty," both of which predate the *Constitution* and the First Amendment; the Jefferson "Danbury Baptist" letter; and Madison's "Detached Memoranda," written sometime after he left public office. The Court's use of carefully selected documents and glaring omissions, together with frequently misleading versions and citations of early U.S. Supreme Court decisions, are obvious as one reads carefully through the chapters mentioned above.

Neither the U.S. Supreme Court in these two cases nor the scholarship of the "absolute separationists," whom they in part rely on, present any credible counter historical evidence as to what I believe is the correct interpretation of the Establishment Clause. Instead the actions of Madison, Jefferson, the First Congress and the preceding and succeeding Presidents and Congresses support the thesis that the First Amendment's two religious guarantees were intended to prevent the U.S. Congress from establishing a national religion or church and from putting one religion or religious sect on a preferred plane. In addition, the Amendment prohibited the Federal Government from interfering with any individual's freedom of religious ideas. Subsequently, as historically developed in chapter four, these religious prohibitions on national governmental action were made applicable to the States through the U.S. Supreme Court's interpretation of the content of the "Due Process" Clause of the Fourteenth Amendment. Consequently, when correctly viewed, the public policies reviewed in *Everson* and *McCollum* are *not unconstitutional* under the First and Fourteenth Amendments. Neither the refunding of bus fare to parents who send their children to parochial schools, nor a "released time" program such as the one authorized in Champaign, Illinois, were state actions "respecting an establishment of religion" or creating a religious establishment within the proper understanding of the Establishment of Religion Clause.

Inasmuch as historical arguments were the only justifications offered by the High Court in *Everson* and *McCollum*, and given that American historical fact does not adequately support the Court's conclusions, the constitutional theories regarding Church and State resulting from the *Everson-McCollum* decisions rest on nothing more than what Justice Jackson honestly described as the Court's "own prepossessions." For me, this form of judicial decison making is incompatible with the rule of law. That grand concept relies on a more dispassionate form of judicial decision making, based on an absence of judicial predilections, especially in historical research, if history is invoked as dictating the Court's conclusions about the constitutionality of a political act.

The tremendous damage that the erroneous history and decisions of the *Everson-McCollum* Cases have wrought on the legitimate interaction between religion and community is clearly evident since their status as the precedent setting cases interpreting the Establishment Clause is constantly invoked by federal and state courts on all jurisdictional levels in cases dealing with the American constitutional doctrine of separation of Church and State.

Chapter Six

Judicial Last Rites For State-Run Religious Practices

More than a decade after the *McCollum* Released Time Case was addressed three cases were decided by the United States Supreme Court that had notably different characteristics from either *Everson* or *McCollum*.[1] In *Everson* and *McCollum*, the Court spoke to the issue of whether or not various incidental state aids to church-affilated institutions constituted an "Establishment of Religion" in violation of the First and Fourteenth Amendments. However, in *Engel* v. *Vitale*,[2] *Abington* v. *Schempp*,[3] and its companion case *Murray* v. *Curlett*,[4] the focus of the Supreme Court's inquiry into claimed violations of the Establishment Clause was significantly different. In these three cases a governmental employee had either devised and/or conducted what were generally acknowledged to be religious activities in the public schools as required by state law. As Justice William O. Douglas was to comment in his concurring opinion in the *Engel* Case, the constitutional questions raised by these three cases were extremely narrow ones: Do the States overstep constitutional bounds when they finance and/or conduct religious exercises?[5]

In the "Public School Prayer Case," *Engel* v. *Vitale*,[6] the State Board

---

1. Several other cases involving the Establishment Clause as applied to the States via the Fourteenth Amendment were decided by the Court during this period of time. Those relevant to this study will be discussed in chap. seven.

2. 370 U.S. 421 (1962).

3. 374 U.S. 203 (1963).

4. Ibid.

5. Justice Douglas's actual wording was: "The question presented by this case is therefore an extremely narrow one. It is whether New York oversteps the [constitutional] bounds when it finances a religious exercise." 370 U.S. 421, at 439.

6. 370 U.S. 421 (1962).

of Regents, an agency established by the Constitution of the State of New York with broad authority over the State's public school system,[7] authored a nondenominational prayer which was to be recited at the beginning of every public school day. The public school teachers were to lead their classes in reciting the prayer, "Almighty God, we acknowledge our dependence upon Thee, and we beg Thy blessings upon us, our parents, our teachers and our country."[8] State officials justified the prayer ceremony as a desirable part of a child's moral and spiritual training.[9]

Subsequently, the Board of Education in New Hyde Park, New York, instructed all the public school principals to have the prayer recited every school day.[10] After the New Hyde Park Board's action, several parents brought suit to stop the recitation of the prayer, claiming that it was "contrary to the beliefs, religions, or religious practices of both themselves and their children."[11] More important, the parents asked the New York Court to declare unconstitutional both the School Board's order that the prayer be said in class and any New York State legislation or other state action regarding the prayer as a violation of the Establishment of Religion Clause contrary to the Fourteenth Amendment's application of that prohibition to the States.[12] After the lower New York courts sustained the use of the prayer, the New York State Court of Appeals concurred in a split decision that the public school prayer was not unconstitutional.[13] Subsequently, the United States Supreme Court accepted the case,[14] which was argued before it in April 1962.

In 1963, two other cases reached the Supreme Court that were not unlike the New York Regents Prayer Case. *Abington* v. *Schempp*, a Pennsylvania case, and *Murray* v. *Curlett*, a Baltimore, Maryland case, were argued together before the U.S. Supreme Court on February 27 and 28, 1963, because they essentially raised the same Establishment Clause questions: Were the practices of starting each public school day by requiring a public school employee to read sections of the "Holy Bible" and/or lead students in the recitation of the "Lord's Prayer" constitutional?[15]

The facts of *Abington* and *Murray* are very similar. In *Abington*, a Pennsylvania law required that "At least ten verses from the Holy Bible shall be read, without comment, at the opening of each public school on

7. Ibid., at 422, 423, fn. 1.
8. Ibid., at 422.
9. Ibid., at 423.
10. Ibid.
11. Ibid.
12. Ibid.
13. N.Y. 2d. 174.
14. 368 U.S. 924.

15. The full names of these cases are: *School District of Abington Township et al. v. Edward Lewis Schempp et al.*, 374 U.S. 203 (1963); and *William J. Murray III et al. v. John N. Curlett, President, et al., of the Board of School Commissioners of Baltimore City*, 374 U.S. 203 (1963).

each school day."[16] The Statute also provided that "Any child shall be excused from such Bible reading, upon the written request of his parent or guardian."[17] Edward Schempp, a father of three children in the Abington School District, brought suit to stop the enforcement of the Statute and further to enjoin the recitation of the "Lord's Prayer," which was also taking place in some schools, arguing that his and his children's rights under the Fourteenth Amendment were being violated by what he considered to be unconstitutional practices.

In the newer Abington schools, the reading of the Bible and the recitation of the "Lord's Prayer" were broadcast into each classroom through the intercommunications system. In schools without intercom systems, Justice Tom Clark, who delivered the opinion of the Court, wrote that "It appears from the record . . . Bible reading and the recitation of the 'Lord's Prayer' were conducted by the home-room teacher,[18] who chose the text of the verses and read them herself or had students read them in rotation or by volunteers."[19] The Bibles used were the *King James*, the *Douay*, the *Revised Standard Versions*, and the *Jewish Holy Scriptures*.

In the *Murray* Case public schools were opened each day in Baltimore by "reading without comment, of a chapter of the Holy Bible and/or the use of the Lord's Prayer."[20] Mrs. Madalyn Murray and her son William, who were admitted atheists, challenged the morning school exercise on the same constitutional grounds as in the *Schempp* Case.

The *Schempp* Case was heard in Federal District Court and an injunction against the morning religious exercises was granted on the constitutional grounds of violation of the Establishment Clause.[21] The School District appealed to the U.S. Supreme Court and the Court accepted the case.[22] Dissimilarly, the *Murray* Case went through the Maryland Court system which sustained the constitutionality of the state statute and the practices pursuant to it in the Maryland Public Schools.[23] Like *Schempp*, the U.S. Supreme Court put the *Murray* Case on its docket.[24]

Before exploring the opinions written in these three cases, we should

16. 24 *Pa. Stat.*, Sec. 15–1516, as amended, *Public Law* 1928 (Supp. 1960) December 17, 1959. Emphasis added.

17. Ibid.

18. The statute as amended did not penalize a teacher refusing to perform the exercises. See Justice Clark's fn. 2 at 374 U.S. 203, 208. Emphasis added.

19. 374 U.S. 203, at 207–208.

20. These opening exercises were established by the Baltimore Board of School Commissioners in 1905 pursuant to Art. 77, Sec. 202 of the *Annotated Code of Maryland*. Emphasis added.

21. 201 F. Supp. 815.

22. 371 U.S. 807.

23. 228 Md. 239. Although the Maryland Court of Appeals sustained the opening school practices, the seven voting justices split 4–3 over the issue.

24. 371 U.S. 809.

note that no formal, informal, or authorized coercion and no punishment in any form was to be attached to a child's refusal to take part in these exercises. Thus these three "Religious Ceremony" cases are crucially dissimilar to the two "Flag Salute" cases of the early 1940s.

In the first Flag Salute case, *Minersville School District* v. *Gobitis*,[25] two children, who were Jehovah's Witnesses, were expelled from their public schools for refusing to salute the flag and recite the "Pledge of Allegiance" required at that time by a Pennsylvania law as a daily school exercise. The children refused to participate because their religion interprets the flag salute ceremony as a violation of the Ten Commandments.[26] Inasmuch as Jehovah's Witnesses regard the Bible as the Word of God, they thought it a sin to take part.

The Gobitis children could not go back to school without conforming to the flag-salute ceremony. Shortly after their expulsion, their parents were charged with violation of Pennsylvania's compulsory school attendance law. Ultimately the U.S. Supreme Court, speaking through Justice Felix Frankfurter, decided the religious issue that was carefully noted in the opinion of the Court:

> We must decide whether the requirement of participation in such a ceremony, exacted from a child who refuses upon *sincere* religious grounds, infringes without due process of law the liberty guaranteed by the Fourteenth Amendment. . . .
>
> In the judicial enforcement of religious freedom we are concerned with a historic concept. . . . The religious liberty which the Constitution protects has never excluded legislation of general scope *not directed against* doctrinal loyalties of particular sects. Judicial nullification of legislation cannot be justified by attributing to the framers of the Bill of Rights views for which there is no historic warrant. Conscientious scruples have not, in the course of the long struggle for religious toleration, relieved the individual from obedience to a general law *not aimed at the promotion or restriction of religious beliefs.* . . .[27]

In this case, the Court clearly took the view that as long as the state was pursuing a valid constitutional goal through its legislation, religious beliefs

---

25. 310 U.S. 586 (1940).

26. The two specific commandments in the King James version of the *Old Testament, Exodus*, 20: 4–5, which seemed most in question, read:

Thou shalt not make unto thee any graven image, or any likeness of any-

thing that is in heaven above, or that is in the earth beneath, or that is in the water under the earth:

Thou shalt not bow down thy-self to them, nor serve them: . . .

27. 310 U.S. 586, at 592, 594. Emphasis added.

that the state had *no aim or intent* in violating would have to give way, despite the First and Fourteenth Amendment religious guarantees—neither of which is absolute.

The coercive nature of the flag-salute ceremony, however, soon brought about its downfall. Especially repugnant to the Supreme Court's new majority in the second "Flag Salute" case—*West Virginia Board of Education* v. *Barnette*[28]—was forcing people to say what they did not believe by the invocation of the power of the State. Within three years the Supreme Court overruled its decision in *Gobitis* with careful and precise sentences, written by Justice Jackson speaking for the Court:

> If there is any fixed star in our constitutional constellation, it is that no official, high or petty, can prescribe what shall be orthodox in politics, nationalism, religion, or other matters of opinion *or force citizens to confess by word or act their faith therein.* If there are any circumstances which permit an exception, they do not now occur to us.[29]

Certainly, the lack of coercion is a practice that clearly differentiates the Prayer and Bible Reading cases from the Flag Salute cases inasmuch as the power of the State was not being used to compel either the recitation of the New York State Regent's Prayer, the "Lord's Prayer," or even the presence of the students during these school-administered ceremonies.[30] Indeed, the absence of coercion concerning these activities may be seen as crucial because it further narrows our attention to the single constitutional question alluded to earlier: May the state—where no coercion exists and with the willingness of the students who choose to participate—constitutionally conduct an admitted religious worship service?

The United States Supreme Court, on June 25, 1962, in part answered that question. Justice Hugo Black, speaking for the Court in *Engel* v. *Vitale*, declared that government-sponsored prayer in the public schools is unconstitutional: "We think that by using its public school system to encourage recitation of the regents' prayer, the State of New York has adopted a practice *wholly inconsistent* with the Establishment Clause."[31]

The Supreme Court's opinion by Justice Black in the "New York Regents' Prayer" Case ostensibly presents an historical argument to justify the decision that the Prayer is unconstitutional under the Establishment

28. 319 U.S. 624 (1943).

29. Ibid., at 642. Emphasis added.

30. The absence of coercion in the New York Regent's "Prayer Case" is mentioned in the Supreme Court's opinion delivered by Justice Black, 370 U.S. 421, at 423, fn. 2, and at 430. The irrelevance of coercion to the Court majority in this case is also discussed in Arthur E. Sutherland, Jr., "Establishment According to Engel," 76 *Harvard Law Review* 25 (1962), at 26.

31. 370 U.S. 421, at 424. Emphasis added.

Clause. The opinion is based on carefully selected historical statements, many of which are irrelevant to the adoption of the Establishment Clause. Further, historically relevant actions and records that clearly indicate that prayer sponsored by government was not considered a violation of the First Amendment's prohibition concerning an establishment of religion were nowhere discussed or explained away in the Black opinion. The following comparison between Justice Black's opinion for the Court in the Prayer Case and what the Framers of the First Amendment believed—as attested to by their *public actions in their official capacity* under the new *Constitution*—should clarify the issue and document the criticisms here of the Supreme Court's opinion.

As in the *Everson* Case, Black's American historical appeal from primary documents is taken almost entirely from James Madison's "Memorial and Remonstrance Against Religious Assessments," which reflected Madison's strong beliefs that an attempt by some in the Virginia legislature to enact "A Bill Establishing a Provision for Teachers of the Christian Religion" was unwise and undesirable for the Commonwealth of Virginia.[32] The discriminatory religious aid, had that bill been passed, has already been discussed in chapter two. As has already been noted, such aid would have given the Christian religion a special status, reflecting the hallmark of established religions on the European continent. If that had been the situation in the Regent's Prayer Case, then the facts would have been significantly different. But that was not the circumstance in the Regent's Prayer Case. No religion was put into a preferred status by the innocuous prayer written by the New York State Board of Regents.

Extremely significant is the fact that the Supreme Court's opinion relies solely on Madison's "Remonstrance," written in 1785. What specifically has that to do with the First Amendment proposed by the First Congress in 1789 and ratified by the constitutional requisite number of States in 1791? Why does the Court's opinion not look to the First Congress, of which Mr. Madison was an important member of the House of Representatives, to discern what it thought was an "Establishment of Religion," since that Congress submitted the Establishment of Religion Clause to the States, hoping it would become part of the new *Constitution*? The primary records of the sessions of the First Congress strongly indicate what that Congress believed about government-sponsored prayer and its relationship to the First Amendment.

More than a decade before the N.Y. Regent's Prayer Case, J.M. O'Neill wrote: "The First Congress demonstrated by specific actions deliberately taken that their conception of the first clause of the First Amendment [the

32. Ibid., at 431, fns. 13, 14; at 432, fns. 15, 16; at 436, fn. 22.

Establishment of Religion Clause] was not at all what the current judges of the Supreme Court say it was."[33] The actions of the First Congress certainly bear him out in regard to government-sponsored prayer. Even the actions of James Madison, as a member of the First House of Representatives in 1789, run counter to Justice Black's opinion of the Court in the Prayer Case.

During the First Congress, Madison was a member of the Congressional Committee that recommended that Congressional Chaplains be elected.[34] Accepting that recommendation, the House of Representatives, in its early days on May 1, 1789, "proceeded by ballot to the appointment of a chaplain to Congress on this part of the House. Upon examining the ballots it appeared," the proceedings of the First Congress go on to say, "that the Rev. William Linn was elected."[35] Can it be intelligently claimed that—irrespective of what he was paid—Rev. William Linn did not become an agent or instrument of the very House of Representatives that would submit the Establishment of Religion Clause to the States for ratification? Can it validly be pretended that the Rev. Linn's prayers as Chaplain to the First House of Representatives were not government-authorized public prayer? Does it not seem even a greater violation of the Establishment of Religion Clause, under the Supreme Court's opinion in 1962, that the House authorized a *minister* as a governmental agent to invoke a prayer rather than merely a lay person as in the Regent's Prayer Case? And when Rev. Linn composed his prayers in performance of his office, was he as an agent of the House of Representatives any less an agent of the state than the New York State Regents were when they wrote the prayer declared unconstitutional under the First and Fourteenth Amendments?[36]

Also contrary to the Black interpretation of the Establishment Clause is the fact that the First Senate, after it had concurred by a two-thirds vote to add what became the First Amendment to the Federal *Constitution,*

33. J.M. O'Neill, *Religion and Education Under the Constitution* (New York: Harpers, 1949), reprinted without change by Da Capo Press, 1972, p. 110.

34. *Reports of Committees of the House of Representatives*, First Sess. of the Thirty-Third Congress, in three vols., (Washington: A.O.P. Nicholson, Printer. 1854), Vol. II, House of Representatives Document 124, "Appointment of Chaplains," p. 4. Along with Madison the House chose Boudinot, Bland, Tucker, and Sherman. "The result of their consultation was a recommendation to appoint two chaplains of different denominations—one by the Senate and one by the House—to interchange weekly." Id.

35. *The Debates and Proceedings in the Congress of the United States*, Vol. I, Compiled From Authentic Materials by Joseph Gales, Senior (Washington: Gales and Seaton, 1834), p. 242.

36. The technicality that the House did not agree to the text of what became the First Amendment until September 24, 1789, which was after Rev. Linn's selection, or that the First Amendment did not become part of the *Constitution*, binding Congress in these matters, until 1791 does not alter the principle discussed here or in the Prayer Case because the Chaplain system remained in effect after ratification of the Amendment.

resolved, on Thursday, January 7, 1790, concerning a chaplain for the U.S. Senate, ". . . that the Right Reverend Doctor Samuel Provost be appointed for the present session, on the part of the Senate."[37] Needless to say, it hardly supports Justice Black's opinion in the Prayer Case that the Senate chose the Reverend Provost after receiving a message from the House of Representatives, which by this date had also endorsed the Establishment of Religion Clause, stating "that they have resolved that two Chaplains, of different denominations, be appointed to Congress for the present session, one by each House, who shall interchange weekly."[38]

It is noteworthy that after the First House of Representatives endorsed the proposed amendment which was to become the First Amendment[39] (the Senate had already agreed by a vote of 37–14) the next day (Friday, September 25, 1789), the House by resolution agreed to send several of its members along with several Senate members as a joint committee to ask the President of the United States "to recommend to the people of the United States a day of public Thanksgiving and prayer, to be observed by acknowledging, with grateful hearts, the many signal favors of Almighty God. . . ."[40] The behavior of the First Congress is important to note carefully because, unlike Justice Black's historical argument and citations in the Supreme Court's Regent's Prayer opinion, we must recognize the constitutional process by which the Establishment Clause found its way into the U.S. *Constitution.* Influential and important as Mr. Madison may have been, it was the members of the First Congress who authored what eventually became the First Amendment. Certainly Madison submitted the first draft of the proposed amendment, as discussed in an earlier chapter, but, under the constitutional amending process, it took at least two-thirds of the First House of Representatives and two-thirds of the First Senate to propose the Amendment to the States. In addition, three-quarters of the States were required to ratify the Amendment to place the Establishment of Religion Clause into the United States *Constitution.*[41] Essential as Mr. Madison was, his views and actions alone did not make the First Amendment part of the Supreme Law of the Land. Nevertheless, as has been shown in the analysis of Madison's public actions, as a member of the First Congress and subsequently as President, his public performance was, for

---

37. *Debates and Proceedings in the Congress,* Vol. I, p. 968.

38. Ibid.

39. The First Congress submitted twelve proposed amendments to the new *Constitution.* The third amendment which it proposed became the First Amendment to the *Constitution* because the first two proposed amendments were never ratified by the requisite number of States. For the full text of the

"Resolution of the First Congress Submitting Twelve Amendments to the *Constitution,*" see *Documents on the Formation of the Union of the American States* (Washington: Government Printing Office, 1927), pp. 1063–65.

40. *Debates and Proceedings in the Congress,* Vol. I, pp. 949–50.

41. U.S. *Constitution,* Article V.

the most part, consistent with the interpretation of the Establishment Clause and the meaning of separation of Church and State that has been advanced here.

Justice Black's opinion of the Court in the Prayer Case also invokes the much-respected name of Thomas Jefferson in support of his historical analysis. Referring to Jefferson's and Madison's campaign to disestablish the Anglican (later Episcopal) Church in Virginia, Black wrote:

> In 1785–1786, those opposed to the established Church, led by James Madison and Thomas Jefferson, who, though themselves not members of any of these dissenting religious groups, opposed all religious establishments by law on grounds of principle, obtained the enactment of the famous "Virginia Bill for Religious Liberty" by which all religious groups were placed on an equal footing so far as the state was concerned.[42]

That Jefferson was embattled to disestablish a state church in Virginia follows the thesis advanced here about the true meaning and intention of the Establishment Clause. Had the Establishment Clause, as interpreted here, been part of the Virginia *Constitution* in 1785–1786, the preferred position of the Anglican Church would have been unconstitutional under Virginia's *Constitution* because the Commonwealth of Virginia would be endorsing a particular church.

Oddly, Thomas Jefferson took other actions that are more relevant to the facts of the Prayer Case but that are not mentioned in the Black opinion. Writing the "Regulations" of the University of Virginia, a public university funded with public money, Thomas Jefferson specified:

> Should the religious sects of this State, or any of them, according to the invitation held out to them, establish within, or adjacent to, the precincts of the University, schools for instruction in the religion of their sect, the Students of the University will be free, *and expected to attend religious worship at the establishment of their respective sects*, in the morning, and in time to meet their school in the University at its stated hour.[43]

Apparently Jefferson would not have been content with an innocuous prayer being said each morning in a public classroom, a prayer from which students could excuse themselves. His rules for the University of Virginia expect students to fulfill the public University's regulations of attending worship services each morning should their religion have an establishment geographically close to the University. Following Justice Black's position

---

42. 370 U.S. 421, at 428.

43. "The University of Virginia, Regulations," October 4, 1824. See Saul K. Padover, *The Complete Jefferson* (New York: Books for Libraries Press, 1943), p. 1110. Emphasis added.

in the Prayer Case, such a requirement or expectation on the part of a state university would almost certainly be declared unconstitutional today, irrespective of its coercive or noncoercive feature. Perhaps the U.S. Supreme Court might once more invoke Mr. Jefferson's name to bolster its "historical" justification for such a decision.

As indicated previously, for Justice Douglas, who wrote a concurring opinion[44] in the New York Regents Prayer Case, the constitutional issue was an "extremely narrow one." "It is whether New York oversteps the bounds [of the Establishment Clause] when it finances a religious exercise."[45] The Douglas opinion is very candid about the "many aids" that governments at all levels in the United States have given various religious institutions since the beginning of the Republic, a fact that clearly flies in the face of the Rutledge-Pfeffer claims of absolute separation of Church and State.[46] For Douglas, they are all unconstitutional: "The point for decision is whether the Government can constitutionally finance a religious exercise. Our system at the federal and state levels is presently honeycombed with such financing.[1] Nevertheless, I think it is an unconstitutional undertaking whatever form it takes."[47]

Douglas's footnote 1 is a list, which he carefully indicates is not exhaustive, of many of these "unconstitutional undertakings."[48] Incredibly this

---

44. 370 U.S. 421, at 437.
45. Ibid., at 439.
46. Ibid., at 437.
47. Ibid.
48. "There are many 'aids' to religion in this country at all levels of government. *To mention but a few at the federal level, one might begin by observing that the very First Congress which wrote the First Amendment provided for chaplains in both Houses and in the armed services.* There is compulsory chapel at the service academies, and religious services are held in federal hospitals and prisons. The President issues religious proclamations. The Bible is used for the administration of oaths. N.Y.A. and W.P.A. funds were available to parochial schools during the depression. Veterans receiving money under the 'G.I.' Bill of 1944 could attend denominational schools, to which payments were made directly by the government. During World War II, federal money was contributed to denominational schools for the training of nurses. The benefits of the National School Lunch Act are available to students in private as well as public schools.

The Hospital Survey and Construction Act of 1946 specifically made money available to non-public hospitals. The slogan 'In God We Trust' is used by the Treasury Department, and Congress recently added God to the pledge of allegiance. There is Bible-reading in the schools of the District of Columbia, and religious instruction is given in the District's National Training School for Boys. Religious organizations are exempt from the federal income tax and are granted postal privileges. Up to defined limits—15 per cent of the adjusted gross income of individuals and 5 per cent of the net income of corporations—contributions to religious organizations are deductible for federal income tax purposes. There are no limits to the deductibility of gifts and bequests to religious institutions made under the federal gift and estate tax laws. This list of federal 'aids' could easily be expanded, and of course there is a long list in each state." Ibid., at 438, fn. 1. Emphasis added. In addition, Douglas's fns. 2–5, 370 U.S. 421, at 439–42, are filled with examples that he considers unconstitutional governmental religious aids.

lengthy footnote implies that the First Congress which wrote the First Amendment violated it. Is it not more likely that those who framed the Establishment Clause in the First Amendment had a different interpretation of its governmental prohibitions than does Douglas? That the Framers of the First Amendment would disagree with Douglas is clear from his own statements on the face of his concurring opinion. As to which view of the First Amendment should carry greater weight in our constitutional system—Douglas's or the views of the members of the First Congress who wrote and voted out the Amendment by a two-thirds majority in each House—is equally clear.

The candor reflected in the Douglas Prayer Opinion even reaches the point of indicating the prayer is not truly an establishment of religion in the historic meaning of those words.[49] If this fact is conceded by Justice Douglas, as the record shows, one is left to question what constitutional justification there is for Douglas's assent to the opinion that the Regents' Prayer is invalid under the Establishment of Religion Clause as made applicable to the States by the Fourteenth Amendment.[50]

The lone dissenter in the New York Regents Prayer Case was Justice Potter Stewart.[51] Stewart's dissent centered in part on the thesis advanced here, that a major purpose of the First Amendment was to prevent the establishment of a national church or a religion officially sanctioned by the government. Focusing on Justice Black's statement in the Court's opinion that the "Establishment Clause . . . is violated by the enactment of laws which establish an *official religion* . . . ,"[52] Stewart countered that he "cannot see how an 'official religion' is established by letting those who want to say a prayer say it."[53]

Rejecting the Court's arguments which invoked the horrors of national establishments and official religions of earlier centuries in Europe as not germane, Stewart cited the differing American system which from the beginning of the Federal Republic in 1789 reflects the religious commitments of a people who have not been zealots in punishing disbelievers.[54] Then speaking directly to the issue of government-sanctioned prayer,

49. ". . . I cannot say that to authorize this prayer is to establish a religion in the strictly historic meaning of those words." Douglas, concurring, 370 U.S. 421, at 442.

50. It is interesting to note that in his concuring opinion Justice Douglas expressed regret about the decison in the *Everson* Bus case. 370 U.S. 421, at 443. Douglas joined Black's opinion of the Court in the 5–4 split decision in *Everson*. If he had joined Rutledge's dissenting opinion, which in his concurring opinion in the Prayer case he stated

"is durable First Amendment philosophy," *Everson* would have been decided against the reimbursement of parents' bus fares for parochial school children.

51. 370 U.S. 421, at 444. Neither Justice Frankfurter nor Justice White took part in the decision of this case. Id., at 436.

52. 370 U.S. 421, at 430. Emphasis added.

53. Ibid., at 445.

54. Ibid., at 445–46.

Stewart begins his rebuttal by reminding his brothers on the Court of its own "religious" practices and those of the other coordinate branches of the U.S. Government—none of which, in his view, either violates the Establishment Clause or creates an official religion:

> At the opening of each day's Session of this Court we stand, while one of our officials invokes the protection of God. Since the days of John Marshall our Crier has said, "God save the United States and this Honorable Court." Both the Senate and the House of Representatives open their daily Sessions with prayer. Each of our Presidents, from George Washington to John F. Kennedy, has upon assuming his Office asked the protection and help of God.
>
> The Court today says that the state and federal governments are without constitutional power to prescribe any particular form of words to be recited by any group of the American people on any subject touching religion. The third stanza of "The Star-Spangled Banner," made our National Anthem by Act of Congress in 1931, contains these verses:
>
> > "Blest with victory and peace, may the heav'n rescued land
> > Praise the Pow'r that hath made and preserved us a nation!
> > Then conquer we must, when our cause it is just,
> > And this be our motto 'In God is our Trust.' "[55]
>
> I do not believe that this Court, or the Congress, or the President by the actions and practices I have mentioned established an "official religion" in violation of the Constitution. And I do not believe the State of New York has done so in this case.[56]

It should be re-emphasized that the central thesis of this analysis of the twofold religious prohibitions on the legislative power of the Congress placed in the First Amendment by the First Congress consisted of constitutionally foreclosing: first, the establishment of a national church or official religion; second, the national government's elevation of one religious sect into a preferred status which had been an important characteristic of European establishments; third, encroachment by the Federal Congress on individual freedom of conscience in religious matters; and fourth, the interference in the relationship between religion and the several States which was at that time in the hands of the individual state governments.

Because of the disestablishment of the last state church in 1833 and the application of the First Amendment to the States through the Fourteenth Amendment, discussed in chapter four, the first three religious prohibitions

55. Ibid., at 446–49.   56. Ibid., at 450.

sought by the First Amendment's framers currently operate against all the governmental units in the United States. Using these three criteria to determine whether the First Amendment has been violated, the decision of the United States Supreme Court in the N.Y. Regents' Prayer Case— *Engel v. Vitale*—must be adjudged an erroneous one. Can the writing of a prayer by the New York State Board of Regents be seriously equated with creating a state church or an official religion? Does a single prayer constitute a religion or a church, or an acorn a tree? Can a prayer so innocuous that it merely mentions the phrase "Almighty God" place a particular religion in a preferred governmental status? Finally, can the lack of governmental coercion—and beyond that a statutory admonition against it—meet the requirements of governmental encroachment on the individual's freedom of religious conscience?

The answers to these questions indicate how ludicrous the Court's opinion in the Prayer Case really is. Perhaps more important than the majority's decision in the Prayer Case, however, are the substance and methodology used by the Court to justify its opinion. The historical substance has already been addressed here and found wanting, but the methodology is also disturbing.

In what appears to be a response to anticipated questions raised by Justice Stewart in dissent, Justice Black for the Court merely declares:

> There is of course nothing in the decision reached here that is inconsistent with the fact that school children and others are officially encouraged to express love for our country by reciting historical documents such as the Declaration of Independence which contain references to the Deity or by singing officially espoused anthems which include the composer's professions of faith in a Supreme Being, or with the fact that there are many manifestations in our public life of belief in God. Such patriotic or ceremonial occasions bear no true resemblance to the unquestioned religious exercise that the State of New York has sponsored in this instance.[57]

Why not? Justice Stewart, in reply, put it directly. He expressed his inability to understand how the Court could without any supporting argument dismiss the religious ceremonies in the Congress, at presidential inaugurals, and before the Supreme Court itself as bearing "no true resemblance to the unquestioned religious exercise that the State of New York has sponsored in this instance." Justice Stewart asked, ". . . [I]s the Court suggesting that the Constitution permits judges and Congressmen and Presidents to join in prayer, but prohibits school children from doing so?"[58]

Courts write opinions to be used, studied, and/or cited in other courts, or

---

57. Ibid., at 436, fn. 21.   58. Ibid., at 450, fn. 9.

to serve in any capacity as intelligent guidelines in a legal system such as ours that is based heavily on precedents decided in the past and employed in present and future cases. Without intending to minimize the power behind the Supreme Court's rulings,[59] the conclusion of any court must follow from a reasoned argument. The holdings of the United States Supreme Court, over the long run, tend to stand or fall more on their rationale rather than the considerable power of the Court. In short, the Court's written opinion must present a credible and convincing argument for the Court's decision *in order to legitimize that decision*. To present no reasonable argument, or to present a fallacious argument as justification for a Supreme Court decision, is to invite scorn for the Court, undermine its role as referee of the American Constitutional and political system, and smacks of the exercise of raw power, which is antithetical to constitutional government itself.

The "Lord's Prayer" and Bible Reading Cases— Abington *v.* Schempp *and* Murray *v.* Curlett

Stated simply, as with the "Regent's Prayer" Case, the basic constitutional question in these two cases was: May the state—where no coercion exists and with the willingness of the students who choose to participate—constitutionally conduct an admitted religious worship service? My conclusions in the Prayer Case, discussed above, indicate that consistent with the First Amendment all religious worship services or acts performed by agents who act for either the Federal Government or the States *are not necessarily* unconstitutional if the Establishment Clause is properly interpreted.

The thesis advanced in chapter one indicates that the Framers of the First Amendment, in part, wanted to prohibit Congress from establishing a national religion or putting one religion or religious sect in a preferred status.[60] It is important to remember that James Madison's initial speech to the First House of Representatives concerning amendments to the *Constitution*, protecting individual rights not mentioned in the recently adopted new "Supreme Law of the Land," on June 8, 1789, reminded the House that several of the State Ratifying Conventions were concerned about these omissions.[61]

Clearly the Virginia Ratifying Convention and the New York Convention were concerned not only about the lack of a constitutional prohibition forbidding a national religion but also with preventing the favoring of any

---

59. In *Cooper* v. *Aaron*, 358 U.S. 1 (1958), the U.S. Supreme Court held that in effect its interpretations of the *Constitution* are the supreme law of the land.

60. See my conclusions as to the correct interpretation of the Establishment of Religion Clause in chap. one, pp. 5, 15.

61. See the text and quotations at chap. one, fns. 14 and 15.

"religious sect or society."[62] On this point the words of the North Carolina Convention's proposed "Declaration of Rights," Section 20, reads: ". . . and that no particular religious sect or society ought to be favored or established by law in preference to others."[63] This exact phrase also appears in Rhode Island's instrument of ratification.[64]

Following these expressions of concern from some of the ratifying States, I think it is historically clear that the First Amendment was intended not only to preclude the establishment of a national religion but also to prohibit Congress from giving any special significance to any one religion or sect. Inasmuch as these prohibitions were extended to limit the state governments from taking any similar actions through the Due Process Clause of the Fourteenth Amendment, as explained in chapter four, today no state legislature or any other agent of the several States may establish a state religion or assign preferred status to any one religion or religious sect. To do so would clearly violate the correct doctrine of separation of Church and State under the regime of the First and Fourteenth Amendments.

Supportive of this interpretation of the concept of separation of Church and State is the record of public funds that were paid to religious schools for over a century before Congress, through a change in public policy, cut off U.S. appropriations to sectarian institutions.[65] Reflecting the religious reality of the early days of the Republic, Leo Pfeffer indicates in *Church, State, and Freedom* that the "number of professed non-Christians" was minute.[66] Consequently, because of this Christian universality, federal funds to aid Christian-affiliated schools were, in those days, not unconsitutional unless the Federal Government discriminated against some Christian denominations or sects and thus put one version of the Christian faith in a preferred status contrary to the First Amendment. That this was not the case is well substantiated by the documents cited in chapter three,[67] those reproduced in the *Addendum*, and the listing of many diverse Christian church schools mentioned in the preceding chapter.[68] As already discussed elsewhere, this nondiscriminatory financial aid to religion was not assailed as unconstitutional under the First Amendment and not thought to be so until Justice Black's declaration interpreting the minimal prohibitions of the Establishment Clause in the *Everson* "Bus Transportation" Case.[69]

---

62. See the quotations in chap. one at fns. 17 and 18.

63. Jonathan Elliot, *Debates on the Federal Constitution*, Vol. IV (Philadelphia: J.B. Lippincott Co., 1901), p. 244.

64. Ibid., Vol. I, p. 334.

65. See the text at chap. five, fns. 121–24.

66. Leo Pfeffer, *Church, State, and*

Freedom, rev. ed. (Boston: Beacon Press, 1967), pp. 141–42.

67. See the chart of religious schools aided with federal money in the text of chap. three, at fn. 52.

68. See the text in chap. five at fn. 125.

69. 330 U.S. 1, at 15–16. For a full discussion of the *Everson* Case, see chap. five.

Further evidence that this pattern of federal nondiscriminatory aid to sectarian schools was not considered a violation of the First Amendment was the introduction of several proposed constitutional amendments during the latter part of the nineteenth century to make this aid unconstitutional—the most notable of which was the "Blaine Amendment" of 1876.[70] Although none of these attempts to amend the *Constitution* were successful, these very efforts serve to reenforce the fact that the Establishment of Religion Clause was not seen as broadly in 1876 as it was by the *Everson* Court in 1947.

The religious diversity of the population of the United States was much different in 1963—the year *Murray* v. *Curlett* was decided—than in the early days of the Republic. That diversity continues, and its magnitude is a unique characteristic of contemporary American society. Consequently, the "professed non-Christians" in the United States today are not only no longer minute but are instead sizeable in number.

The "Lord's Prayer" is distinctively a Christian prayer, the most commonly used recitation of which is found in the *New Testament* Gospel attributed to Matthew.[71] As such, any enactment by either the Federal Government, the governments of the States of the Union, or any political body which exercises the constitutional prerogatives of the States delegated to them by the State legislatures—such as the City of Baltimore and its

70. The 1876 Blaine Amendment, when it passed the House of Representatives (it failed to get the two-thirds Senate endorsement and was thus never sent to the States for ratification) read as follows:

No state shall make any law respecting an establishment of religion or prohibiting the free exercise thereof; and no religious test shall ever be required as a qualification to any office or public trust under any state. No public property, and no public revenue of, nor any loan of credit by or under the authority of the United States or any state, territory, District, or municipal corporation, shall be appropriated to, or made or used for, the support of any school, educational, or other institution, under the control of any religious or anti-religious sect, organization or denomination, or wherein the particular creed or tenets of any religious or anti-religious sect, organization, or denomination shall be taught. And no such particular creed or tenets shall be read or taught in any school or institution supported in whole or in part by such revenue or loan of credit; and no such appropriation or loan of credit shall be made to any religious or anti-religious sect, organization or denomination, or to promote its interests or tenets. This article shall not be construed to prohibit the reading of the Bible in any school or institution; and it shall not have the effect to impair rights of property already invested. . . . House Resolution 1, 44th Congress, 1st Session (1876).

Many subsequent proposed amendments, having the same purpose as the Blaine Amendment, have been defeated in Congress. Between 1870 and 1888 eleven different amendments introduced in the Houses of Congress attempted to reduce the powers of the States in domestic concerns as religion and education. See Herman V. Ames, *Proposed Amendments to the Constitution, 1789–1889* (Washington, D.C.: Government Printing Office, 1897).

71. Matthew 6: 9–13.

school board—that would make recitation of this specific prayer school policy would be unconstitutional. Irrespective of the lack of coercion, no agency of government has any legitimate authority whatsoever to violate the *Constitution* of the United States. In *Murray* v. *Curlett* the fact that the Baltimore Board of Education authorized a purely Christian prayer to be said in the public schools[72] placed the Christian faith in a preferred status, which is banned by the First and Fourteenth Amendments.

In a constitutional democratic state there can be no actions that deviate from the basic or supreme law of the land—which the Federal *Constitution* is in the United States. In my view of the Establishment Clause, to elevate any one religion or religious sect to a superior status in the United States, even where there may be near unanimity of desire to do so, cannot be constitutionally accomplished if the First Amendment remains unchanged. Short of constitutional amendment, the recitation of any prayer that is exclusively identified with a "particular religion or religious sect" is constitutionally foreclosed by a correct historical interpretation of the American doctrine of separation of Church and State.

Unhappily, the opinion of the Court by Justice Clark did not use this narrow interpretation of the Establishment Clause as the basis for the disposition of the case.[73] Instead, the Court majority invoked the rationale of the *Everson* Case and the *McCollum* Case together with a rehash of twenty years of decisions, almost all of which were based on the erroneous "history" that characterized those two precedent cases. *Everson* and *McCollum* are relied on so extensively that almost no early primary historical source is invoked by Justice Clark, with the exception of Madison's "Remonstrance" of 1785.[74]

The only redeeming feature that I see in the Court's opinion is Justice Clark's use of data from the Bureau of Census to establish that as of 1963, "83 separate religious bodies each with memberships of over 50,000" existed in the United States.[75] These data alone, as employed above, should have been the basis for the Court's opinion and disposition of the case. In place of a relatively simple decision based on the fact that the recitation of the "Lord's Prayer" constitutes placing Christianity in a preferred status and thus violates the First Amendment, the Court cites previous cases built on faulty history to create yet another decision that will be used in future

---

72. 374 U.S. 203, at 211.

73. There was reference in the opinion of the Court to testimony by Dr. Solomon Grayzel to the effect that differences existed between the Jewish Holy Scriptures and the Christian Holy Bible, 374 U.S. 203, at 209, but these statements were not the specific basis for the Court's ruling.

74. The Court's opinion makes reference to Madison and the "Remonstrance," 374 U.S. 203, at 213.

75. 374 U.S. 203, at 214.

Establishment Clause cases to yield more of the same.[76] The practice authorized in *Abington* and *Murray*, of reading Bible verses without comment, is, in my judgment, unconstitutional for the same reason.

In testimony before the trial court, Dr. Solomon Grayzel testified that "portions of the *New Testament* were offensive to Jewish tradition and that, from the standpoint of the Jewish faith, the concept of Jesus Christ as the Son of God was 'practically blasphemous.' "[77] While such concepts, common to all Christian sects in the early days of the First Amendment, would not be viewed as putting any particular religious sect in a preferred status, the existence today of many professed "non-Christians" would bring the reading of the *New Testament* under the ban of the historic interpretation of the Establishment Clause for the same reasons detailed above concerning the "Lord's Prayer." But the unconstitutionality of the practice of Bible reading goes much further than the reading of the "Lord's Prayer," or what some might view as "offensive" portions of the *New Testament*.

In both of these cases writings considered "sacred" by the Christian and/or Judeo-Christian religious traditions were the only religious writings authorized by law to be read.[78] Neither the *Book of Mormon*, the interpretive writings of Mary Baker Eddy, the *Koran*, *The Analects of Confucius*, nor other writings, considered as revered works by many who live in the United States, were included for reading in these public school worship services. Inasmuch as the Establishment Clause precludes placing any religion or religious sect in a preferred status by governmental action, the changed religious nature of the population of the United States has in effect enlarged the ban of the Establishment Clause even though the interpretation remains constant.

Unlike the innocuous prayer in the *Engel* Case, specific writings, which are identified exclusively with particular religions and religious sects, are in these cases embraced by the state and referred to as "holy" writings. As has been documented, one of the historic prohibitions of the Establishment Clause is the assignment of an exclusive or preferred status to any religion. The exclusivity of such an assignment to the writings of the Judeo-Christian

---

76. An example of the "faulty history" from *Everson* perpetuated by Justice Clark's opinion of the Court in the *Abington* and *Murray* companion cases is his reference at 374 U.S. 216 to Justice Jackson's dissent in *Everson*, 330 U.S. 1, at 18. Clark quotes Jackson's dissent regarding the importance of the placement of the Establishment Clause by the Framers: "This freedom was first in the Bill of Rights because it was first in the forefather's minds; . . . Id. 330 U.S. 1, at 26." That the Establishment Clause accidentally appears first in the Bill of Rights rather than having been placed there by some significant design in "the forefathers' minds" is clearly shown in chap. three at the text and quotations at fns. 26–28 entitled, "On Positioning the First Amendment."

77. 374 U.S. 203, at 209.

78. Ibid., at 205, 207, and 211.

religions in these cases violated this ban of the First and Fourteenth Amendments.

The religious prohibitions of the Establishment Clause do not depend on the composition of the public school audience or even necessarily on the intent of the legislature. The First and Fourteenth Amendments preclude any agent of the Federal or State Government from establishing any sectarian practice that in effect elevates any particular religion or religious sect to a preferred status either as an "end" or as a "means." This is not to say, as Leo Pfeffer has written, that the means of government must always be secular.[79] All sectarian means that might be used by government to reach a valid end committed to it by the *Constitution do not necessarily* violate the Establishment Clause. Jefferson's Kaskaskia Indian Treaty of 1803 which, among other things, committed the United States to build a Roman Catholic Church, is an example of a sectarian means used to reach a secular end.

Jefferson's treaty was designed to increase the territory of the United States, to "civilize the Indians," and, probably through the teaching of Christianity to the Indians, to make less dangerous the settlements on the western fringe of the United States. Protection of American settlers was certainly a federal constitutional governmental goal or end. Using religion, in part, to reach that end did not violate the First Amendment because neither Jefferson's administration, nor administrations that preceded or succeeded his, used Roman Catholicism as the *exclusive sectarian means* by which to accomplish their secular constitutional goals. Had that been the case, the sectarian means would have been unconstitutional because of the exclusive use of one Christian sect that would have created for it a preferred status in violation of the Establishment Clause.[80]

In a religiously *homogeneous* society, governmental legislation that in some way uses, touches, or benefits religion may be by definition nondiscriminatory. That seemed to be the case in the United States when Christianity in its many varieties was used by the Federal Government in the eighteenth and much of the nineteenth centuries as a means of accomplishing secular goals. In twentieth century America that is no longer the case. The religious pluralism that now exists in the United States has as a consequence made the historic prohibitions of the Establishment Clause more delimiting of governmental actions. Today, because of the present *religious diversity* in the nation, public-sponsored activities that were nondiscriminatory in the past can no longer be reconciled with the First and Fourteenth Amendments' ban against placing any purely sectarian activity identified with one religious tradition into a preferred position.

79. Pfeffer, *Church, State, and Freedom*, p. 180.

80. See the discussion in chap. two under the section entitled: "Finding Madison and Jefferson."

Chapter Seven

The "Gospel" According to the Warren and Burger Courts

The Legacy

"We are a religious people whose institutions presuppose a Supreme Being."[1] With that description of the American public, Justice William O. Douglas, writing the opinion of the United States Supreme Court in *Zorach* v. *Clauson*[2]—the second "Released Time" Case—upheld as constitutional a New York State law that allowed students to be absent from public school for "religious observance *and education*" under "rules that the New York State Commissioner of Education shall establish."[3] The *Zorach* decision came just four years after the nearly unanimous (8–1) U.S. Supreme Court decision in the *McCollum* Case which held that the Champaign, Illinois "released time" program was unconstitutional.[4] Although the New York program and the Champaign, Illinois, program were significantly different, the badly split Court (6–3) decision contained three stinging dissents.

Under the New York State law and the Regulations of the Commissioner of Education, the New York City Board of Education established a program whereby students attending the City's public schools could be released from classes once a week to attend religious instruction at their respective religious places of worship upon written request by their parents. Rule Three of the Board's regulations specifically provided that: "The

1. *Zorach* v. *Clauson*, 343 U.S. 306, at 313.
2. 343 U.S. 306 (1952).
3. Ibid., at 308, fn. 1. Emphasis added.
4. Ibid.

religious organizations and parents will assume full responsibility for attendance at the religious schools and will explain any failures to attend on the weekly attendance reports"[5] which presumably were sent from the religious organizations to the public schools.

Mrs. Tessim Zorach and Mrs. Esta Gluck, both taxpayers and residents of New York City whose children attended its public schools, attacked the state law and the City's released time program as unconstitutional with arguments that Justice Douglas summarized as follows:

> Their argument, stated elaborately in various ways, reduces itself to this: the weight and influence of the school is put behind a program for religious instruction; public school teachers police it, keeping tab on students who are released; the classroom activities come to a halt while the students who are released for religious instruction are on leave; the school is a crutch on which the churches are leaning for support in their religious training; without the cooperation of the schools this "released time" program, like the one in the the McCollum Case, would be futile and ineffective. . . .[6]

The Court's opinion addressed these arguments and drew a careful distinction between New York's "released time" program and the one declared unconstitutional only four years earlier in *McCollum*. Douglas pointed out there was no coercion to attend religious instruction[7] and "no religious exercise or instruction is brought to the classrooms of the public schools."[8] The difference between the Champaign released time program and New York's was significant, Douglas maintained, and in the process of differentiating the two programs he declared that the Establishment Clause does not require "hostility to religion":

> In the McCollum Case the classrooms were used for religious instruction and the force of the public school was used to promote that instruction. Here, as we have said, the public schools do no more than accommodate their schedules to a program of outside religious instruction. We follow the McCollum Case. But we cannot expand it to cover the present released time program unless separation of Church and State means that public institutions can make no adjustments of their schedules to accommodate the religious needs of the people. We cannot read into the Bill of Rights such a philosophy of hostility to religion.[9]

5. Ibid.
6. Ibid., at 309–10.
7. Ibid., at 311.

8. Ibid.
9. Ibid., at 315.

Extremely significant in the Court's opinion is Douglas's attempt to have his constitutional cake and eat it, too. While maintaining that the First Amendment's religious prohibitions are absolute, he clearly had to reconcile this constitutional interpretation with our "institutions presupposing a Supreme Being." Douglas's opinion for the Court finesses this apparent contradiction with an interesting proposition, much of which he repudiated ten years later in his concurring opinion in the "New York Regent's Prayer" Case discussed in the preceding chapter.[10] Douglas's solution is clever; although the First Amendment's religious prohibitions are absolute, they are not all inclusive. The Court's opinion by Douglas carefully makes the point:

> There is much talk of the separation of Church and State in the history of the Bill of Rights and in the decisions clustering around the First Amendment. . . . There cannot be the slightest doubt that the First Amendment reflects the philosophy that the Church and State should be separated. And so far as interference with the "free exercise" of religion and "establishment" of religion are concerned, the separation must be complete and unequivocal. *The First Amendment within the scope of its coverage permits no exception; the prohibition is absolute. The First Amendment, however, does not say that in every and all respects there shall be a separation of Church and State.* Rather, it studiously defines the manner, the specific ways, in which there shall be no concert or union or dependency one on the other. That is the common sense of the matter. Otherwise, the state and religion would be aliens to each other—hostile, suspicious, and even unfriendly. Churches could not be required to pay even property taxes. Municipalities would not be permitted to render police or fire protection to religious groups. Policemen who helped parishioners into their places of worship would violate the Constitution. Prayers in our legislative halls; the appeals to the Almighty in the messages of the Chief Executive; the proclamations making Thanksgiving Day a holiday; "so help me God" in our courtroom oaths—these and all other references to the Almighty that run through our laws, our public rituals, our ceremonies would be flouting the First Amendment. A fastidious atheist or agnostic could even object to the supplication with which the Court opens each session: "God save the United States and this Honorable Court."
>
> We would have to press the concept of separation of Church and State to these extremes to condemn the present law on constitutional grounds . . . .[11]

10. See the text and fns. in chap. six at fns. 44–50.

11. 343 U.S. 306, at 312–13. Emphasis added.

What makes this passage of the majority's opinion so important is the Court's acceptance of the proposition that in fact there has never been nor now exists a complete separation of Church and State. While Justice Douglas, a decade later, will indeed "press the concept of the separation of Church and State" to the extreme and claim that it is virtually all inclusive, the rest of the U.S. Supreme Court must struggle to determine in which "respects" the First Amendment does not require separation of Church and State.

Perhaps the most distressing part of the Court's opinion—in the New York Released Time Case—to adherents of the broad interpretation of the Establishment Clause was the emergence of a clearly enunciated principle of cooperation between government and religion that was not seen as banned by the First and Fourteenth Amendments. Wrote Douglas for the Court in 1952:

> *We are a religious people whose institutions presuppose a Supreme Being.* We guarantee the freedom to worship as one chooses. We make room for as wide a variety of beliefs and creeds as the spiritual needs of man deem necessary. We sponsor an attitude on the part of government that shows no partiality to any one group and that lets each flourish according to the zeal of its adherents and the appeal of its dogma. *When the state encourages religious instruction or cooperates with religious authorities by adjusting the schedule of public events to sectarian needs, it follows the best of our traditions. For it then respects the religious nature of our people and accomodates the public service to their spiritual needs.* To hold that it may not would be to find in the Constitution a requirement that the government show a callous indifference to religious groups. That would be preferring those who believe in no religion over those who do believe. Government may not finance religious groups nor undertake religious instruction nor blend secular and sectarian education nor use secular institutions to force one or some religion on any person. *But we find no constitutional requirement which makes it necessary for government to be hostile to religion* and to throw its weight against efforts to widen the effective scope of religious influence. The government must be neutral when it comes to competition between sects. It may not thrust any sect on any person. It may not make a religious observance compulsory. It may not coerce anyone to attend church, to observe a religious holiday, or to take religious instruction. *But it can close its doors or suspend its operations as to those who want to repair to their religious sanctuary for worship or instruction.* No more than that is undertaken here.[12]

___

12. Ibid., at 313–14. Emphasis added.

The Douglas opinion for the Court in *Zorach* also embraces an idea that runs through many court cases and that is constantly confused. The six-man majority opinion makes clear that the Court is not endorsing the New York program as a wise educational institution or even as one that is good for harmony in the vastly diverse New York City community. The Court stresses that those value judgments are political considerations that are not relevant to the constitutional issue. Carefully it is pointed out that inquiry into the merits of a law is not the same as inquiry into its constitutionality. Value judgments as to whether a prospective bill will be a wise law are to be made in the political, not the judicial, process. A state legislature, may, through the medium of legislation make policies that seem foolish to many, but foolish laws are not necessarily unconstitutional laws. Inasmuch as the two are often equated, the Court in *Zorach* speaks to that issue:

> *The briefs and arguments are replete with data bearing on the merits of this type of "released time" program.* Views pro and con are expressed, based on practical experience with these programs and with their implications. We do not stop to summarize these materials nor to burden the opinion with an analysis of them. *For they involve considerations not germane to the narrow constitutional issue presented.* Those matters are of no concern here, since our problem reduces itself to whether New York by this system has either prohibited the "free exercise" of religion or has made a law "respecting an establishment of religion" within the meaning of the First Amendment.[13]

It is certainly clear that the Court in *Zorach* does not confuse legislative motives or legislative wisdom with the issue of whether or not a governmental enactment violates some section of the *Constitution. That inquiry is the only germane judicial question in the Establishment Clause cases.*

The three dissenters, Justices Black, Frankfurter, and Jackson each wrote separate opinions.[14] Justice Frankfurter's dissent speaks mainly to two points. His first objection to the released time program is that sectarian education is being substituted for secular education with the cooperation of the City. Frankfurter's second concern involved what he perceived to be the failure of the Court majority to deal correctly with the issue of coercion that Mrs. Zorach attempted to raise in the New York Appellate courts. Douglas's opinion for the Court indicated that coercion was not involved in any way with the administration of the program.[15] Douglas does mention

13. Ibid., at 310. Emphasis added. The six-man majority in *Zorach* reiterate this point in the Douglas opinion, id., at p. 314.

14. In addition to writing his dissent, Justice Frankfurter also appears to have subscribed to Justice Jackson's dissent.

15. 343 U.S. 306, at 311 and fn. 6 of the opinion of the Court.

that in the New York State Court of Appeals a new trial was denied Mrs. Zorach even though she contended that she wasn't given a proper opportunity "to prove that the system [had] in fact [been] administered in a coercive manner."[16] Douglas "put aside that claim of coercion" because on appeal she apparently had not properly raised the "claim in the manner required by state practice."[17]

Here is Justice Frankfurter dissenting on these terms:

> The pith of the case is that formalized religious instruction is substituted for other school activity which those who do not participate in the released-time program are compelled to attend. The school system is very much in operation during this kind of released time. If its doors are closed, they are closed upon those students who do not attend the religious instruction in order to keep them within the school. That is the very thing which raises the constitutional issue. It is not met by disregarding it. Failure to discuss this issue does not take it out of the case.
>
> Again, the Court relies upon the absence from the record of evidence of coercion in the operation of the system. "If in fact coercion were used," according to the Court, "if it were established that any one or more teachers were using their office to persuade or force students to take the religious instruction, a wholly different case would be presented." Thus, "coercion" in the abstract is acknowledged to be fatal. But the Court disregards the fact that as the case comes to us, there could be no proof of coercion, for the appellants were not allowed to make proof of it. . . .[18]

Frankfurter leaves to Justice Jackson—whose opinion he apparently joined—the frontal attack on the issue raised in *McCollum*, that the City was virtually rounding up customers for the religious education program. With sarcasm Jackson spoke to this issue:

> The greater effectiveness of this system over voluntary attendance after school hours is due to the truant officer who, if the youngster fails to go to the Church school, dogs him back to the public schoolroom. Here schooling is more or less suspended during the "released time" so the nonreligious attendants will not forge ahead of the churchgoing absentees. But it serves as a temporary jail for a pupil who will not go to Church. It takes more subtlety of mind than I possess to deny that this is governmental constraint in support of religion. It is as unconstitutional, in my view, when exerted by indirection as when exercised forthrightly.[19]

16. Ibid., at 311, fn. 7.

17. Ibid.

18. Ibid., at 321.

19. Ibid., at 324.

But Jackson saved his most stinging broadside for the final paragraph of his dissent. Comparing *McCollum* and the New York released time program, Justice Jackson used not only sarcasm but a good lacing of mockery in evaluating the totality of the Court's opinion:

> A number of Justices just short of a majority of the majority that promulgates today's passionate dialectics joined in answering them in Illinois ex rel. Mc Collum v. Board of Education, 333 US 203. . . . The distinction attempted between that case and this is trivial, almost to the point of cynicism, magnifying its nonessential details and disparaging compulsion which was the underlying reason for invalidity. A reading of the Court's opinion in that case along with its opinion in this case will show such difference of overtones and undertones as to make clear that the McCollum Case has passed like a storm in a teacup. The wall which the Court was professing to erect between Church and State has become even more warped and twisted than I expected. *Today's judgment will be more interesting to students of psychology and of the judicial processes than to students of constitutional law.* [20]

Justice Black, who wrote the Court's opinion for an eight-man majority in the *McCollum* "Champaign Released Time" Case, now found himself in dissent. Quoting from his opinion in *McCollum*, Black mentioned that two factors made that program unconstitutional: the use of public school rooms for religious instruction and "the use of the State's compulsory public school machinery."[21] Inasmuch as the New York City program only remedied one of those constitutional infirmities, Black held that the remaining constitutional violation must legally doom the program. In the following passage from his dissent, Justice Black went so far as to label the New York City released time program a "combination of Church and State."

> Here the sole question is whether New York can use its compulsory education laws to help religious sects get attendants presumably too unenthusiastic to go unless moved to do so by the pressure of this state machinery. That this is the plan, purpose, design and consequence of the New York program cannot be denied. The state thus makes religious sects beneficiaries of its power to compel children to attend secular schools. Any use of such coercive power by the state to help or hinder some religious sects or to prefer all religious sects over nonbelievers or vice versa is just what I think the First Amendment forbids. In considering whether a state has entered this forbidden field the question is not whether

---

20. Ibid., at 325. Emphasis added.   21. Ibid., at 316.

it has entered too far but whether it has entered at all. New York is manipulating its compulsory education laws to help religious sects get pupils. This is not separation but combination of Church and State.[22]

What is difficult to understand about all of the dissents in *Zorach* and in the eight-man majority opinion in the *McCollum* "Released Time" Case is that so much is made of the fact that the state is "allegedly" using its compulsory school attendance laws to aid or provide students for sectarian education as if this were a new legal phenomenon. If indeed this use of state power is a "combination of Church and State," as Justice Black proclaims in *Zorach*, why did he not call for the overruling of *Pierce v. Society of Sisters*[23] when he wrote his nearly unanimous opinion in *McCollum*?[24]

In the *Pierce* Case, in what appears to be a unanimous decision written by Justice James McReynolds, the U.S. Supreme Court declared unconstitutional the section of the Oregon Compulsory Education Act of 1922 which would have required that all chldren between the ages of eight and sixteen years old be sent "to a public school."[25]

While the Supreme Court in *Pierce* raises "no question concerning the power of the State reasonably to regulate all schools, to inspect, supervise and examine them, their teachers and pupils," and, among other things, "*to require that all children of proper age attend some school,...*"[26] and describes the Society of Sisters as an "Oregon corporation organized in 1880," which runs primary schools where many children between the ages of eight and sixteen are "taught the subjects usually pursued in Oregon public schools,"[27] the Court finds nothing unconstitutional about the fact that "[s]ystematic religious instruction and moral training according to the tenets of the Roman Catholic Church are also regularly provided."[28] On the contrary, the irony of the *Pierce* Case is that the Court holds unconstitutional the state of Oregon's attempt, by use of its compulsory education power, to put these children into a public educational system.

If state compulsory school attendance laws that allow for released time once a week for no more than an hour for sectarian education amount to a "combination of Church and State," how can the allowance of the systematic teaching of religion within parochial schools be constitutionally tolerated as satisfying the state's compulsory school attendance statutes? Lest it be argued that the *Pierce* Case was decided in 1925 before the

22. Ibid., at 318.
23. 268 U.S. 510 (1925).
24. As discussed in chap. five, only Justice Reed dissented in the *McCollum* Case.

25. 268 U.S. 510, at 530.
26. Ibid., at 534. Emphasis added.
27. Ibid., at 531–32.
28. Ibid.

Establishment Clause of the First Amendment was made applicable to the States through the Fourteenth Amendment, as recently as 1966—long after the Establishment Clause was applied to the States—Justice Douglas writing an opinion for the Court specifically held that: "While a State may not segregate public schools so as to exclude one or more religious groups, *those sects may maintain their own parochial educational systems.*"[29] *Pierce* v. *Society of Sisters* was cited by Douglas as the legal authority for his statement.[30] In addition, one cannot help wondering how parochial schools can be constitutionally accepted as educational surrogates for the public schools within the state's compulsory educational attendance laws but not be constitutionally eligible for other direct aid from the state without violating the Establishment Clause.

Those who argue for an absolute separation of Church and State have maintained that parochial schools are indeed being aided, if not directly, then indirectly. The legal mechanism to aid these sectarian primary and secondary schools indirectly was accepted as constitutional by Justice Black when, speaking for the Court in the *Everson* "Bus Transportation" Case, he sanctioned the "Child-Benefit" theory. Although this judicial concept was touched on in chapter five, a more detailed examination is appropriate here.[31]

Contrary to the dicta in the *Everson*[32] and *McCollum* Cases,[33] historical examination reveals that neither the First nor Fourteenth Amendments erected a wall between religion and the State governments. Today, as before *Cantwell* v. *Connecticut*[34] and *Everson*, State legislatures are still convened with prayer; Sunday blue laws remain in effect; official documents are, for the most part, still dated "in the year of our Lord;" and some religious holidays remain governmentally declared legal holidays. Irrespective of the foregoing, the closest cooperation between religion and the States continues to be in the area of education. Despite the fact that almost every State constitution has some clause prohibiting the use of public funds for the support of sectarian institutions[35] and the fact that the Establishment Clause of the First Amendment has been made applicable to the States through the Fourteenth Amendment,[36] public aid is usually provided to sectarian (and other private) schools in some form or another, not as an appropriation to the institution, but as a State measure—under its

29. *Evans* v. *Newton*, 382 U.S. 296, at 300. Emphasis added.
30. Ibid.
31. See the text in chap. five at fns. 14–26 and 86–89.
32. 330 U.S. 1 (1947).
33. 333 U.S. 203 (1948).
34. 310 U.S. 296 (1940).
35. 50 *Yale Law Journal* 917 (1941).
36. See the text in chap. four at fns. 45–47.

police power—designed to benefit the children who attend those schools. This type of legislation has usually been challenged on two grounds: first, that it violates either or both of the federal or state constitutional provisions prohibiting public funds from being used for sectarian purposes, and second, that it appropriates public tax moneys for private purposes. In applying either federal or state constitutional prohibitions against aid to sectarian institutions, State courts have often attempted to distinguish between "direct" and "indirect" aid to sectarian schools. What is considered "direct" aid has been held—virtually without exception—to be constitutionally invalid by State courts.

Perhaps the best, albeit not precise, definition of what constitutes "direct" as opposed to "indirect" governmental aid to sectarian schools was provided, before either the *Cantwell* or *Everson* Cases were decided by the U.S. Supreme Court, in a New York State Case—*Judd* v. *Board of Education*, decided in 1938.[37] In *Judd*, the New York State Court of Appeals, invalidating a state law providing bus transportation for parochial school students as a violation of the New York State *Constitution*, attempted to define the distinction between "direct" and "indirect" governmental aid to sectarian institutions as follows. Aid provided "directly," the New York Court said, would be:

> ... that furnished in a direct line, both literally and figuratively, to the school itself, unmistakably earmarked, and without circumlocution or ambiguity. Aid furnished "indirectly" clearly embraces any contribution, to whomsoever made, circuitously, collaterally, disguised, or otherwise not in a straight, open and direct course for the open and avowed aid of the school, that may be to the benefit of the institution or promotional of its interests and purposes.[38]

Even though the *Judd* Case decided that "indirect" aid to sectarian schools was also unconstitutional, other States did not interpret their constitutions in that way.[39] The judicial doctrine used by State courts to sustain "indirect" State aid against state constitutional attack—and eventually federal constitutional arguments—on the grounds that such legislation is a valid exercise of the States' police power to provide for the health, safety,

---

37. 118 A.L.R. 789 (1938).

38. Ibid., at 796.

39. Subsequent to the decision in the *Judd* Case, the New York State Constitution was amended in 1938 to allow for the transportation of private school students—who included students attending parochial schools—as an exception to the general prohibition against the use of public funds for sectarian purposes. See Article IX, Sec. 4 of the New York State Constitution as amended in 1938.

and welfare of its children has been commonly referred to as the "Child-Benefit" theory.[40]

In the twentieth century, state cases involving aid to sectarian schools initially grew out of the consolidation of small school districts that gave rise to the need for transporting school children sometimes as far as ten to fifteen miles from their homes. At first, transportation was provided only for students of the free common public schools, no doubt on the basis of the following philosophy:

> While education is compulsory in this State between certain ages, the State has no desire to and could not if it so wished to compel children to attend the free public common schools when their parents desire to send them to parochial schools (*Pierce* v. *Society of Sisters*, 268 U.S. 510), but their attendance upon the parochial school or private school is a matter of choice and the cost thereof not a matter of public concern.[41]

Irrespective of this point of view, eventually some state school districts made transportation provisions for students attending private secular and sectarian institutions. Before the *Everson* "Bus Transportation" Case came to the U.S. Supreme Court, at least nineteen states and one territory (Hawaii not being a state at the time) had either a constitutional and/or statutory provision for some type of transportation aid for parochial school students.[42] As a consequence, it came as no surprise that the first Establishment Clause case under the Fourteenth Amendment should involve a state practice of providing aid to sectarian school children for bus transportation. Similarly, it was not surprising that the "Child-Benefit" arguments used successfully in several state cases[43] would be invoked before the U.S. Supreme Court in the *Everson* Case of 1947.

Proponents of the Child-Benefit theory argue that a state or a federal legislative enactment that has a constitutionally lawful immediate end should not be judicially declared unconstitutional if incidental and/or "indirect" benefits happen to accrue to private institutions.[44] Perhaps the

40. See fn. 31, supra.

41. *Judd* v. *Board of Education*, 118 A.L.R. 789, at 795.

42. California, Colorado, Connecticut, Hawaii, Illinois, Indiana, Kentucky, Louisiana, Maryland, Massachusetts, Michigan, New Hampshire, New Jersey, New Mexico, New York, Ohio, Oregon, Rhode Island, Washington, and Wyoming all had such provisions.

43. Among these state cases are *Board of Education of Baltimore County* v. *Wheat*, 199 A. 628 (1938); *Adams* v. *Saint Mary's County*, 26 A. 2nd 377 (1942); *Nichols* v. *Henry*, 168 A.L.R. 1385 (1945); *Bowker* v. *Baker*, 167 P. 2nd 256 (1946); and *Everson* v. *Board of Education of Ewing, New Jersey*, 44 A. 2nd 333 (1945).

44. *Bowker* v. *Baker*, 167 P. 2nd 256, at 261.

most succinct but comprehensive argument advanced by adherents of the Child-Benefit theory is the following excerpt from the opinion of the California District Court of Appeals in *Bowker* v. *Baker*:

> When we consider the complexities of our modern life we realize that many expenditures of public money give indirect and incidental benefit to denominational schools and institutions of higher learning. Sidewalks, streets, roads, highways, sewers, are furnished for the use of all citizens regardless of religious belief. No one has yet challenged the right of any law abiding citizen to travel to a school over a highway built with public funds because of his religious beliefs or because he is attending a denominational institution, yet to paraphrase the expression used in Judd v. Board of Education, 118 A.L.R. 789, without roads over which pupils could reach the school there would be no school. Police and fire departments give the same protection to denominational institutions that they give to privately owned property and their expenses are paid from public funds.[45]

Adopting this mode of thinking in the state cases prior to *Everson* in 1947, advocates of transportation legislation recognized that attendance at a parochial school might be increased slightly as a result of such legislation but they argued that this benefit to the school is an unintentional by-product of a valid state action and should not render the act invalid. "There is no benefit to the [parochial] schools, except, perhaps as one may receive an accidental benefit in the sense that some parents might place their children in religious schools when they anticipate transportation provision, though they might hesitate to do so if the children were compelled to make their own way."[46] The primary purposes of the legislation, they consistently maintained, are to provide a safe means of getting children to and from school, thus insuring their attendance for the amount of time prescribed by the state educational code.[47]

Finally, adherents of the Child-Benefit theory contended that a line distinguishing between aid to the student and aid to the school was too tenuous to be drawn with clarity. Given that the state constitutionally has the right, under its police power, to provide for the health, welfare, and safety of its children, and by so doing through bus transportation to parochial school students, they reasoned that if incidental assistance is given the school that aid is not sufficient to have the legislation declared invalid. To attempt to aid the students must always result in aiding, in some manner, the school they attend.

45. Ibid., at 262.
46. *Judd* v. *Board of Education*, 118

A.L.R. 789, dissenting opinion at 801.
47. Ibid., at 800.

Prior to *Everson* opponents of the Child-Benefit theory had their days in court, too. In many state courts of finality, state laws or school board provisions allowing bus transportation for sectarian school children were struck down as violative of state constitutional prohibitions against aiding sectarian schools with public funds.[48] Whether aid to such schools was termed "direct" or "indirect," absolute separationists argued that any aid to church affiliated schools was unconstitutional, the police power of the state notwithstanding. The *Judd* majority opinion in the New York State Court of Appeals concisely made the case against the Child-Benefit theory:

> It is claimed that the statute [allowing bus transportation for parochial school students in New York State] may be sustained as a valid exercise by the Legislature of the police power of the State. This argument overlooks the consideration that even the police power must be exercised in harmony with the restrictions imposed in the fundamental law. . . . No authority has been called to our attention nor has one been found in any jurisdiction to the effect that a statute purporting to be enacted in the exercise of the police power of the State may be held valid if repugnant to any Constitutional provision or restriction.[49]

Attacking the Child-Benefit theory at its basic assumption, complete separationists argued that once it is assumed that aid to the parochial school is aid to the child or aid to education, there exists no logical reason to withhold full support from the school. "It is true that this use of public money and property aids the child, but it is no less true that practically every proper expenditure for school purposes aids the child."[50] In fact, the argument carried to its logical conclusion could, they reasoned, sustain against the various state constitutional attacks any piece of state legislation providing health services, tuition, books, athletic equipment, fuel, electrical power, or even the building of the sectarian school itself. Could not all these aids be seen as aid to the children who attended these schools? In sum, they argued that the alleged "indirect" aids to sectarian schools were legislative attempts to do indirectly that which the various state constitutional pro-

---

48. Among these cases are *Wisconsin ex rel. Van Straten* v. *Milquet*, 192 N.W. 392 (1923); *Delaware ex rel. Traub et al.* v. *Brown et al.*, 172 A. 835 (1934); *Judd et al.* v. *Board of Education of Union Free School District No. 2, Hemstead, Nassau County*, 118 A.L.R. 789 (1938); an Oklahoma Case, *Gurney et al.* v. *Ferguson et al.*, 122 P. 2nd 1002 (1941); a Kentucky case, *Sherrard* v. *Jefferson County Board of Education*, 171 S.W. 2nd 963 (1942)—this decision was reversed in *Nichols* v. *Henry*, supra (1945); and a Washington State case, *Mitchell* v. *Consolidated State District*, 146 A.L.R. 612 (1943).

49. *Judd* v. *Board of Education*, supra, at 798.

50. *Gurney* v. *Ferguson*, supra, at 1003.

hibitions against using public funds for parochial schools forbade the state governments from doing directly.[51]

As a result of the *Pierce* Case, the *Zorach* "Neutrality Principle between Church and State," and the embracing of the Child-Benefit theory in the *Everson* "Bus Transportation" Case, the Warren and Burger Courts inherited a legacy that certainly was not one of absolute legal or constitutional separation of Church and State. The question of where aid to sectarian schools is sanctioned by the Federal *Constitution* and where it is not is part of this confused inheritance. Where legislation or cooperation by the State governments is neither aid nor hostility but neutrality toward religion or sectarian schools, and where aid to children attending those sectarian schools ends and "alleged constitutionally forbidden" aid to parochial schools begins are also part of this uncertain legal bequest. It has been left to the Warren and Burger Courts to develop the criteria with which to determine when "alleged" aid to religion—and religious schools in particular— has been in keeping with the Federal *Constitution* and when it has not.

Developing such criteria has demanded virtually a case-by-case review by the United States Supreme Court of almost every claim pressed in the state and lower federal courts that the Establishment of Religion Clause of the First and Fourteenth Amendments has been violated. The result of this confused legacy has produced a practice that has proved not only counterproductive but that has nearly negated the underlying principles of an appellate court system. Almost each case and/or "alleged" governmental aid to religion has had to be treated as virtually a new question each time the U.S. Supreme Court issued the discretionary writ of certiorari thereby taking jurisdiction of an Establishment Clause case from either a state or federal court.[52]

In fact, this needless burden, for the most part, had fallen on the Warren Court and now on the Burger Court because of the difficulty of developing sufficiently clear criteria to be applied by courts of original jurisdiction or intermediate appellate courts so that they might be able to dispose finally of

---

51. *Borden* v. *Louisiana*, 123 So. 655 (1945).

52. As noted in the text, the "writ of certiorari" is a discretionary one which, when issued by a higher court to a lower one, brings the case within the jurisdiction or authority of the higher tribunal. The United States Supreme Court issues this writ under what is known as the "rule of four." Simply put, this rule requires that four justices on the U.S. Supreme Court be in favor of issuing the writ to a lower court before the Supreme Court can take control of a case decided in a lower court for review. Today most cases decided by the United States Supreme Court come from either a lower federal court or the highest state court through the issuance of this writ.

these Establishment Clause questions. Instead of relatively clear guidelines for lower courts to apply, the Warren-Burger Courts have, in most instances, made worse the confusion concerning the constitutional prohibitions of the Establishment Clause, basically because a majority of the Justices have refused to apply the constitutional principle of separation of Church and State as the Framers of the First Amendment intended it and as historically authenticated here in chapters one, two, three, and five.

The more significant Establishment Clause cases during the period of the Warren and Burger Courts will now be reviewed briefly in order to: (1) provide an overview of the kind of "sectarian aids" that have been legislated and constitutionally challenged before the United States Supreme Court in recent years; (2) provide an examination of the judicial criteria and tests that the High Court has attempted to develop and employ recently in this sensitive area of constitutional litigation; and (3) show the failure, for the most part, of the Warren and Burger Courts to provide relatively clear guidelines defining the constitutional prohibitions of the Establishment Clause.

The Warren and Burger Court Cases

The Establishment Clause cases reaching the United States Supreme Court during the years of the Warren and Burger Courts appear to fit into two general classifications. The first class of cases are those in which it is alleged that either religion in general, or individual religions or religious sects in particular, are aided unconstitutionally by some specific governmental action. Supreme Court decisions dealing with the constitutionality of "Sunday Closing Laws," a state anti-evolution statute, and the tax exemption status of organized religion comprise the cases of this kind.

The second group of cases is more numerous, encompassing the Supreme Court decisions dealing with alleged unconstitutional practices by the State and/or the Federal Government to support, in some way, the commingling of religion and education. This second class of cases includes such varied specific issues as whether or not, consistent with the Establishment Clause, federal governmental funds can be provided as twenty-year loans for the construction of non-sectarian facilities at church-affiliated institutions of higher education; and the constitutionality of a state law providing textbooks for secular subjects to students attending primary or secondary parochial schools.

An overview of the Establishment Clause cases in which religion itself is allegedly aided during the years of the Warren and Burger Courts is my beginning point.[53]

The "Aid to Religion" Cases

In 1961 the Warren Court dealt decisively with the issue of whether or not "Sunday Closing Laws," which were passed pursuant to the general power of state governments to protect "the health, safety, recreation and general well-being of [its] citizens," were unconstitutional as violative of the Establishment of Religion Clause.[54]

Chief Justice Earl Warren writing the opinion of the Court in *McGowan* v. *Maryland*[55] and a companion case—*Two Guys from Harrison-Allentown* v. *McGinley*[56]—held that the Maryland and Pennsylvania "Closing Laws" were not designed to aid religion but were passed, in fact, "to set aside a day of rest and recreation" and as such were not violative of the First Amendment.[57]

The most comprehensive of the High Court's opinions on "Sunday Closing" or "Blue Laws" was rendered in the *McGowan* Case. There the U.S. Supreme Court summarized the basic argument advanced by the opponents of these state enactments as follows:

> The essence of appellants' "establishment" argument is that Sunday is the Sabbath day of the predominant Christian sects; that the purpose of the enforced stoppage of labor on that day is to facilitate and encourage church attendance; that the purpose of setting Sunday as a day of universal rest is to induce people with no religion or people with marginal religious beliefs to join the predominant sects; that the purpose of the atmosphere of tranquility created by Sunday closing is to aid the conduct of church services and religious observance of the sacred day....[58]

Conceding that "Sunday Closing Laws" did indeed, at their inception in

---

53. Recent U.S. Supreme Court cases that have already been discussed in previous chapters will not be reviewed here.

54. *McGowan* v. *Maryland*, 366 U.S. 420 (1961), at 444–45. "Blue Laws" had their origin in America in the Puritan New England Colonies. Traditionally they made illegal certain practices such as drinking, dancing, or working on Sunday—which was considered to be the "Lord's Day." Today,

"Blue Laws" or "Sunday Closing Laws" exist throughout most of the United States but are generally confined to prohibiting Sunday work and commercial retailing not considered essential to the immediate well-being of the community.

55. 366 U.S. 420 (1961).

56. 366 U.S. 582 (1961).

57. 366 U.S. 420, at 449.

58. Ibid., at 431.

England and in the Colonies, have a religious purpose,[59] the Chief Justice's opinion pointed out that "despite the strongly religious origin of these laws, beginning before the eighteenth century, *nonreligious* arguments for Sunday closing began to be heard more distinctly and the statutes began to lose some of their totally religious flavor."[60] Warren traced the gradual secularization of these laws through the history of the Colonies and the early days of the U.S. Republic to a U.S. Supreme Court decision at the end of the nineteenth century. Quoting Justice Stephen J. Field in 1885, the Chief Justice established the more contemporary secular basis for these "Blue Laws":

> "Laws setting aside Sunday as a day of rest are upheld, not from any right of the government to legislate for the promotion of religious observances, but from its right to protect all persons from the physical and moral debasement which comes from uninterrupted labor. Such laws have always been deemed beneficent and merciful laws, especially to the poor and dependent, to the laborers in our factories and workshops and in the heated rooms of our cities; and their validity has been sustained by the highest courts of the States."[61]

Indicating that even Madison and Jefferson did not consider "Sunday labor prohibitions" inconsistent with their struggle for religious liberty in Virginia,[62] the opinion of the Court in *McGowan* concluded that "Sunday Blue Laws" today are constitutional legislative acts designed by the States to achieve a secular state end—a uniform day of rest. Declaring them unconstitutional simply because the state chooses Sunday as the rest day which conveniences Christians would, Warren wrote, be hostile to the public welfare rather than safeguarding the separation of Church and State:

> In light of the evolution of our Sunday Closing Laws through the centuries, and of their more or less recent emphasis upon secular considerations, it is not difficult to discern that as presently written and administered, most of them, at least, are of a secular rather than of a religious character, and that presently they bear no relationship to establishment of religion as those words are used in the Constitution of the United States.
>
> Throughout this century and longer, both the federal and state governments have oriented their activities very largely toward improvement of the health, safety, recreation and general well-being of our citizens. Numerous laws affecting public health, safety factors in industry, laws

59. Ibid., at 431–33.
60. Ibid., at 433–34. Emphasis added.
61. Mr. Justice Field's opinion in *Soon* *Hing* v. *Crowley*, 113 U.S. 703 (1885) at 710 as quoted by Warren at 366 U.S. 436.
62. 366 U.S. 437–40.

affecting hours and conditions of labor of women and children, weekend diversion at parks and beaches, and cultural activities of various kinds, now point the way toward the good life for all. Sunday Closing Laws, like those before us, have become part and parcel of this great governmental concern wholly apart from their original purposes or connotations. The present purpose and effect of most of them is to provide a uniform day of rest for all citizens; the fact that this day is Sunday, a day of particular significance for the dominant Christian sects, does not bar the State from achieving its secular goals. To say that the States cannot prescribe Sunday as a day of rest for these purposes solely because centuries ago such laws had their genesis in religion would give a constitutional interpretation of hostility to the public welfare rather than one of mere separation of church and State.[63]

It should be carefully noted that the Court's opinion in *McGowan* also made clear that "Sunday legislation" could be struck down as a violation of the Establishment Clause if it could be demonstrated that the legislation's purpose "is to use the State's coercive power to aid religion."[64]

An aid to religion in violation of the *Constitution* is exactly what the lone dissenter—Justice William O. Douglas—saw in the "Sunday Closing Laws."[65] Writing one opinion to serve as his dissent in all of the "Blue Law" Cases,[66] Douglas indicated that this type of legislation violated not only the Establishment Clause of the First Amendment but the "Free Exercise" Clause as well. Douglas counterargued:

The State can, of course, require one day of rest a week: one day when every shop or factory is closed. Quite a few States make that requirement. Then the "day of rest" becomes purely and simply a health measure. But the Sunday laws operate differently. They force minorities to obey the majority's religious feelings of what is due and proper for a Christian community; they provide a coercive spur to the "weaker brethren," to those who are indifferent to the claims of a Sabbath through apathy or scruple. Can there be any doubt that Christians, now aligned vigorously in favor of these laws, would be as strongly opposed if they were prosecuted

63. Ibid., at 444–45.

64. Ibid., at 453.

65. In *McGowan* and *Two Guys* the voting alignment on the Court seems to be identical. Justices Black, Brennan, Clark, Stewart, and Whittaker appear to have joined the opinion of the Court by Chief Justice Warren. Justice Frankfurter wrote a lengthy opinion that appears to concur in the result of the disposition of the cases only. Justice Harlan joined the Frankfurter concurring opinion. Only Justice Douglas wrote a dissent.

66. In all, the U.S. Supreme Court decided four "Sunday Closing" Cases on the same day, May 29, 1961. Douglas's dissent in *McGowan* applied to all of these cases.

under a Moslem law that forbade them from engaging in secular activities on days that violated Moslem scruples?

There is an "establishment" of religion in the constitutional sense if any practice of any religious group has the sanction of law behind it. There is an interference with the "free exercise" of religion if what in conscience one can do or omit doing is required because of the religious scruples of the community. Hence I would declare each of those laws unconstitutional as applied to the complaining parties, whether or not they are members of a sect which observes as its Sabbath a day other than Sunday.[67]

In addition to *McGowan* and *Two-Guys*, the Supreme Court disposed of two more "Sunday Closing" cases the same day. Unlike the first two cases, there was no opinion of the Court in the second two cases—*Braunfeld* v. *Brown*[68] and *Gallagher* v. *Crown Kosher Super Market*[69]—because Justices Brennan and Stewart, who both had joined the Warren opinions of the Court in *McGowan* and *Two-Guys*, dissented in part in *Braunfeld* and *Gallagher*, and thus left an insufficient number of Justices agreeing on one opinion to make it "the opinion of the Court."[70]

In *McGowan* the Court had upheld the constitutionality of Maryland's "Sunday Closing" statute as not violative of the Establishment of Religion Clause. Similarly in *Two-Guys*, the Court upheld Pennsylvania's law as not repugnant to the Establishment Clause. In *Braunfeld* and *Gallagher*, however, Justices Brennan and Stewart, while still agreeing with Warren's view that "Sunday Closing Laws" did not constitute an establishment of religion, dissented in part because Braunfeld and the owners of Crown Kosher Super Market—all members of the Orthodox Jewish faith—had in their judgment been denied their First Amendment free exercise of religion.[71]

In sum then, only one member of the United States Supreme Court in any of the four "Sunday Closing Law" cases was of the opinion that those state statutes violated the Establishment Clause of the First Amendment which, since the *Everson* Case in 1947, was equally restrictive of State power because of the Due Process Clause of the Fourteenth Amendment. That one dissenter on the Establishment Clause issue was, as noted above, Mr. Justice Douglas.[72] A survey of these four "Sunday Closing Law" cases

---

67. 366 U.S. 420, at 576–77.
68. 366 U.S. 599 (1961).
69. 366 U.S. 617 (1961).
70. When all nine justices of the U.S. Supreme Court participate and vote in a case—as happened in the four "Sunday Closing" Cases—at least five justices must

agree on all parts of one written opinion for it to become "the opinion of the Court."
71. See Brennan's separate opinion in *Braunfeld* at 366 U.S. 610 and Stewart's dissent at 366 U.S. 616. Also see Brennan and Stewart's dissent at 366 U.S. 631.
72. See fn. 66, supra.

indicates that all other eight justices of the Warren Court in 1961 saw no violation of the Establishment Clause if the State was pursuing a valid legislative goal, that is, the setting aside of a common day of community rest, which incidentally "happened" to fall on what most Christian sects consider the "Lord's Day." To this overwhelming majority of the U.S. Supreme Court, it would appear that legislative intent to violate the Establishment Clause was a necessary requisite in having "Sunday Closing Laws" adjudged unconstitutional under the First and Fourteenth Amendments. Even the accommodation of religion by the State's careful choice of Sunday as the common day of rest was in the *McGowan* opinion of the Court not considered an Establishment of Religion.[73]

Epperson v. *Arkansas*[74] raised a different Establishment Clause question challenged before the Warren Court as unconstitutional. In 1928 the State of Arkansas enacted a law prohibiting in its public schools and institutions of higher education the teaching of the theory that man evolved from a lower order of life. In addition, this "anti-evolution" statute—a product of the "fundamentalist" Christian religious movement of the 1920s during which the famous Scopes "Monkey Trial" was held under a similar Tennessee law—made illegal the use of any textbook that taught the theory in any state-supported educational facility in Arkansas.[75] Susan Epperson, a tenth-grade biology teacher at Little Rock's Central High School, brought suit in an Arkansas Court to have the statute declared void because the

73. See the quote from *McGowan* in the text at fn. 63, supra.

74. 393 U.S. 97 (1968).

75. Initated Act No. 1, Ark. Acts for 1929; Ark. Stat. Ann. 1947, paragraphs 80–1627, 80–1628. The text of the law is as follows:

80–1627.—"Doctrine of ascent or descent of man from lower order of animals prohibited.—It shall be unlawful for any teacher or other instructor in any University, College, Normal, Public School, or other institution of the State, which is supported in whole or in part from public funds derived by State and local taxation to teach the theory or doctrine that mankind ascended or descended from a lower order of animals and also it shall be unlawful for any teacher, textbook commission, or other authority exercising the power to select textbooks for above mentioned educational institutions to adopt or use in any such institutions a textbook that teaches the doctrine or theory that mankind descended or ascended from a lower order of animals."

80–1628.—"Teaching doctrine or adopting textbooks mentioning doctrine—Penalties—Positions to be vacated.—Any teacher or other instructor or textbook commissioner who is found guilty of violation of this act by teaching the theory or doctrine mentioned in section 1 hereof, or by using, or adopting any such textbooks in any such educational institution shall be guilty of a misdemeanor and upon conviction shall be fined not exceeding five hundred dollars [$500.00]; and upon conviction shall vacate the position thus held in any educational institutions of the character above mentioned or any commission of which he may be a member." 393 U.S. 97, fn. 3, at 99.

biology textbook she was assigned to use contained a chapter on evolution, and she feared criminal prosecution in addition to loss of her job under the terms of the law.

The Arkansas Chancery Court held that the "anti-evolution" statute violated freedom of speech as protected by the First and Fourteenth Amendments.[76] The State appealed to the Supreme Court of Arkansas, which reversed the lower court and held that the "anti-evolution" law was not unconstitutional as it was "a valid exercise of the state's power to specify the curriculum in its public schools."[77]

Ignoring as the basis for its ruling the free speech issue and other constitutional questions raised in the Arkansas courts, the U.S. Supreme Court, in an opinion written by Mr. Justice Fortas, declared that "the law must be stricken because of its conflict with the constitutional prohibition of state laws respecting an establishment of religion or prohibiting the free exercise thereof."[78] The "overriding fact" for the High Court was that the Arkansas law proscribed a particular segment of knowledge "for the sole reason" that it conflicted "with a particular religious doctrine; . . . a particular interpretation of the Book of *Genesis* by a particular religious group."[79]

Invoking the Establishment Clause interpretation of the *Everson* and *McCollum* Cases and the neutrality principle of *Zorach* v. *Clauson*, the U.S. Supreme Court's opinion continued:

> Government in our democracy, state and national, must be neutral in matters of religious theory, doctrine, and practice. It may not be hostile to any religion or to the advocacy of no-religion; and it may not aid, foster, or promote one religion or religious theory against another or even against the militant opposite. The First Amendment mandates governmental neutrality between religion and religion, and between religion and nonreligion.[80]

> Arkansas' law cannot be defended as an act of religious neutrality. Arkansas did not seek to excise from the curricula of its schools and universities all discussion of the origin of man. The law's effort was confined to an attempt to blot out a particular theory because of its supposed conflict with the biblical account, literally read. Plainly, the law is contrary to the mandate of the First, and in violation of the Fourteenth, Amendment to the Constitution.[81]

Even though not all members of the High Court subscribed to the entire

76. 393 U.S. 97, at 100.
77. 242 Ark. 922, 416 S.W. 2d 322 (1967).
78. 393 U.S. 97, at 103.

79. Ibid.
80. Ibid., at 103–04.
81. Ibid., at 109.

opinion of the Court, it appears that no less than seven members of the Warren Court saw the law as violating the Establishment Clause.[82]

In terms of pure economics, perhaps the single most important case involving state financial aid to religion was *Walz* v. *Tax Commission of the City of New York*,[83] decided by the U.S. Supreme Court in 1970. The opinion of the Court, authored by the new Chief Justice, Warren E. Burger, addressed itself to the long-standing privilege of tax-exempt status that houses of worship generally enjoy in the United States.[84] In this "Tax-Exemption" Case, Frederick Walz, who owned real estate in New York City, went into the New York courts seeking to stop the New York Tax Commission from granting tax exemptions "to religious organizations for religious properties used solely for religious worship."[85] A provision of the State's Constitution and an implementing New York State law qualified these properties for "real property tax" exemption.[86]

Chief Justice Burger summarized Walz's constitutional argument as follows:

> The essence of appellant's [Walz's] contention was that the New York State Tax Commission's grant of an exemption to church property indirectly requires the appellant [Walz] to make a contribution to religious bodies and thereby violates provisions prohibiting establishment of religion under the First Amendment which under the Fourteenth Amendment is binding on the States.[87]

Answering Walz's contention, the Court's opinion relies heavily on history. Indicating that tax-exemption for churches goes back to pre-Revolutionary colonial times, Burger found it "significant that Congress, from its earliest days has viewed the religion clauses of the Constitution as

---

82. Justices Black, Brennan, Marshall, White, and Chief Justice Warren apparently joined Justice Fortas's opinion to make it the opinion of the Court. In addition, Justice Harlan's separate concurring opinion indicates that he only joined in that part of the Court's opinion that held "the Arkansas statute constitutes an 'establishment of religion' forbidden to the States by the Fourteenth Amendment." 393 U.S. 97, at 115. In separate concurring opinions Justices Black and Stewart indicated that they would hold the statute void because of vagueness. Id. at 114, and id. at 116.

83. 397 U.S. 664 (1970).

84. Chief Justice Earl Warren, appointed by President Eisenhower in 1953, resigned in 1969 and was replaced by Burger that same year. The new Chief Justice was President Nixon's first appointment to the Supreme Court. When the *Walz* Case was decided, only eight justices took part owing to the resignation of Justice Abe Fortas in May 1969, and the failure of the U.S. Senate to confirm President Nixon's first two nominees for the Fortas seat.

85. 397 U.S. 664, at 666.

86. Ibid. For the relevant section of the law, see fn. 1, at 667.

87. Ibid., at 667.

authorizing statutory real estate tax exemptions to religious bodies."[88] "In 1802," Burger noted, "the 7th Congress enacted a taxing statute for the County of Alexandria, adopting the 1800 Virginia statutory pattern which provided tax exemptions for churches."[89] The Chief Justice could also have noted, but did not, that Thomas Jefferson, then President of the United States, did not veto this federal law on the assumption that it was or created "an establishment of religion" forbidden by the First Amendment. In fact, Jefferson signed it.

The rationale for this type of tax exemption, which today includes all fifty States as well as the Federal Government, is not, Burger maintained, intended aid to religion but instead provides governmental assistance to all institutions offering social welfare services or "good works." Wrote Burger for the Court:

> The legislative purpose of a property tax exemption is neither the advancement not the inhibition of religion; it is neither sponsorship nor hostility. New York, in common with the other States, has determined that certain entities that exist in a harmonious relationship to the community at large, and that foster its "moral or mental improvement," should not be inhibited in their activities by property taxation or the hazard of loss of those properties for nonpayment of taxes. It has not singled out one particular church or religious group or even churches as such; rather, it has granted exemption to all houses of religious worship within a broad class of property owned by non-profit, quasi-public corporations which include hospitals, libraries, playgrounds, scientific, professional, historical and patriotic groups. The State has an affirmative policy that considers these groups as beneficial and stabilizing influences in community life and finds this classification useful, desirable, and in the public interest. . . .[90]

As mentioned in earlier chapters, the U.S. Supreme Court's reliance on historical documentation to justify its interpretation of the First Amendment in Establishment Clause cases is virtually complete. In keeping with previous Establishment Clause cases, a final appeal to U.S. history as the verifying agent "disclosing" the intent and meaning of this First Amendment Clause closes the Court's opinion in *Walz*:

> It appears that at least up to 1885 this Court, reflecting more than a century of our history and uninterrupted practice, accepted without discussion the proposition that federal or state grants of tax exemption to

88. Ibid., at 677.
89. Ibid.

90. Ibid., at 672–73.

churches were not a violation of the Religious Clauses of the First Amendment. As to the New York statute, we now confirm that view.[91]

Justice Brennan's separate concurring opinion is also filled with historical evidence, as emphasis, that religious tax-exemption is not inconsistent with the American constitutional concept of separation of Church and State.[92] Not only did Brennan proclaim "that the tax exemptions *were not* among the evils which the Framers and Ratifiers of the Establishment Clause sought to avoid,"[93] he invoked the names and political activities of both Jefferson and Madison as conclusive proof that this interpretation is correct historically and consequently valid today:

> Thomas Jefferson was President when tax exemption was first given Washington churches, and James Madison sat in sessions of the Virginia General Assembly which voted exemptions for churches in that Commonwealth. I have found no record of their personal views on the respective acts. The absence of such a record is itself significant. *It is unlikely that two men so concerned with the separation of church and state would have remained silent had they thought the exemptions established religion.* And if they had not either approved the exemptions, or been mild in their opposition, it is probable that their views would be known to us today. Both Jefferson and Madison wrote prolifically about issues they felt important, and their opinions were well known to contemporary chroniclers. . . .[94]

> The exemptions have continued uninterrupted to the present day. They are in force in all 50 States. No judicial decision, state or federal, has ever held that they violate the Establishment Clause. . . .[95]

Justice Brennan's reliance on an historical argument led him to analyze the clear disparity between Madison's public activities in the Virginia General Assembly and the House of Representatives, and Madison's "Detached Memoranda."[96] In a lengthy footnote to his opinion Brennan, in my judgment, correctly dismisses the "Memoranda" as being of little value in determining what the "Framers and the Ratifiers of the Bill of Rights" meant to prohibit the Federal Government from doing in the realm of religion.[97]

---

91. Ibid., at 680.

92. Ibid., at 680–86. It is not clear from the record as to whether Justice Brennan also joined in the opinion of the Court.

93. Ibid., at 682.

94. Ibid., at 684–85. Emphasis added.

95. Ibid., at 685.

96. See the discussion of Madison's "Detached Memoranda" in chap. two.

97. "In an essay written after he had left the presidency, Madison did argue against tax exemptions for churches, the incorporation of ecclesiastical bodies with the power of acquiring and holding property in perpetuity,

Justice Harlan's separate concurring opinion, which unequivocally stated that "New York's constitutional provision, as implemented by its real property law, does not offend the Establishment Clause,"[98] left Justice Douglas as the Court's sole dissenter.[99]

Viewing property tax exemption of a church as a government subsidy of religion,[100] Douglas's judgment was that such an act by a state violates the Establishment Clause of the First and Fourteenth Amendments. It bears noting that in his dissent, Douglas uses a technique in dealing with historical evidence which is usually characteristic of the Court's majority opinions in Establishment Clause cases. In my judgment, the U.S. Supreme Court in general—and in this case, Justice Douglas in particular—uses historical documents on an extremely selective basis. Historical documents that support the Court's conclusions are invariably invoked. Those that do not, generally go unmentioned or are inadequately explained away.

In this case, specifically, Justice Douglas's opinion first carefully warns against the use of history: "[i]f history be our guide, then tax exemption of Church property in this country is indeed highly suspect, as it arose in the early days when the church was an agency of the state."[101] Then, after quoting Justice Rutledge's interpretation of Madison's *Memorial and Remonstrance* in the *Everson* "Bus Transportation" Case, Douglas accuses the Court majority of trying to avoid Rutledge's "historic argument as to the meaning of 'establishment' and 'free exercise' by relying on the long practice of the States in granting the subsidies challenged here."[102] What does this mean? Does Douglas mean that by looking at a 200 year historical practice of tax exemption for churches the Supreme Court is ignoring "history"? Or perhaps Douglas, who warns the Court about using history in this case in the first place, means that the Court is not focusing on the one

---

the right of the houses of Congress to choose chaplains who are paid out of public funds, the provision of chaplains in the army and navy, and presidential proclamations of days of thanksgiving or prayer—though he admitted proclaiming several such days at congressional request. See Fleet, Detached [sic] Memoranda, 3 William & Mary Quarterly 534, 555–562 (1946). These arguments were advanced long after the passage of the Virginia exemption discussed in the text, supra, and even longer after the adoption of the Establishment Clause. They represent at most an extreme view of church-state relations, which Madison himself may have reached only late in life. He certainly expressed no such understanding of Establishment during the debates on the First Amendment. See 1 Annals of Congress 434, 730–731, 755. And even if he privately held these views at that time, there is no evidence that they were shared by others among the Framers and Ratifiers of the Bill of Rights." Brennan, 397 U.S. 664, at 684–85, fn. 5.

98. Ibid., at 694.
99. Ibid., at 700.
100. Ibid., at 704.
101. Ibid., at 703.
102. Ibid., at 706.

selective historical document that allegedly makes his point?[103] Whatever is meant by the Douglas dissent, it serves as a good example of the selective uses of history by those who argue that the Establishment Clause requires an absolute separation of Church and State whether they be on the U.S. Supreme Court or not.

Perhaps the "historical arguments" ambiguity of the *Walz* Case is somewhat balanced by what the case did clearly establish. Of the eight members who participated, only Justice Douglas believed that property tax exemption for houses of worship was a violation of the constitutional concept of separation of Church and State.[104]

Some conclusions regarding these cases involving "alleged" aid to religion seem appropriate before examining the "aid to religious education" cases. Using what I believe has been shown in earlier chapters to be the correct reading of the Establishment Clause's doctrine of separation of Church and State, I do not think that any of these practices—Sunday Closing Laws, anti-evolution statutes, or property tax exemption for "houses of worship"—constitute the establishment of a national or state church either of which would be a direct and clear violation of the First and/or Fourteenth Amendment. However, the constitutional question becomes more difficult when one asks whether these practices have put any religion or religious sect into a state-created preferred position—which I have shown the Establishment Clause was also intended to constitutionally prohibit.

The homogeneous religious nature of the American Colonies and the early States of the Union precluded the elevation of Christianity into a preferred position because of its virtual universality at that time. As noted earlier, even Leo Pfeffer in *Church, State, and Freedom* refers to the "number of professed non-Christians" at that time as being minute.[105] Sunday Blue Laws, consequently, could not possibly have had the religious discriminatory impact that they do today in as religiously diverse a nation as the United States. This is not to say that the state with its vast police power may not legislate a "day of rest" for reasons of health. Indeed, the States of the Union may mandate that each person, for reasons of health and their own welfare, observe at least one day of rest each week. And beyond that,

---

103. See my discussion of Justice Rutledge's *Everson* dissent in chap. five.

104. The seven other justices who did not hold to the Douglas position were Chief Justice Burger and Justices Black, Brennan, Harlan, Stewart, White, and Marshall.

105. Leo Pfeffer, *Church, State, and Freedom*, rev. ed. (Boston: Beacon Press, 1967), pp. 141–42.

inasmuch as the state was seeking a valid secular end, it might not even be inconsistent with the Establishment Clause if the state should designate Sunday as *a recommended day* of rest. Such a recommendation would merely parallel somewhat the religious profile of most of its people. But what the state cannot constitutionally command is that persons who do not observe Sunday, but some other day as their "Sabbath," take a day of rest on Sunday—irrespective of their religious wishes—without elevating the predominating Christian sects[106] into a preferred religious position.

The argument that it would be difficult for a state to enforce a non-uniform day of rest, raised in Chief Justice Warren's opinion, has already been answered by the U.S. Supreme Court in regard to the exercise of another power that the *Constitution* reserved to the States, that of education. In the "Little Rock, Arkansas" Desegregation Case of 1958, a unanimously signed opinion of the Court made quite clear that although "the responsibility for public education is primarily the concern of the States, . . . it is equally true that such responsibilities, *like all other state activity*, must be exercised consistently with federal constitutional requirements as they apply to state action."[107] If the Establishment Clause of the U.S. *Constitution*, which does apply to state action under the Fourteenth Amendment, is to be respected in a religiously pluralistic society, the state may not legislate a "day of rest"—required of all persons—which accommodates only one religion without thereby elevating that religion to a preferred legal status. Inasmuch as Sunday Closing Laws do not provide for religious diversity, they are, in my judgment, violations of the concept of separation of Church and State required by the First and Fourteenth Amendments.

A most repugnant offshoot of the religious establishment of Sunday Closing Laws ought not to be overlooked here. As a result of these laws, in the *Braunfeld* and the *Crown Kosher Market* Cases both businessmen were discriminated against by placing on them a burden of being forced to close their stores the entire weekend merely because their Orthodox Jewish faith prohibited them from working on Saturday, their "Sabbath." Had these businessmen been of the religious faith in which Sunday was the "day of rest," they would not have clashed with state authority. This is one of the odious incidentals that characterized established religions in Europe, accepted legal discrimination against individuals whose religious faith was

---

106. Some Christians such as the Seventh Day Adventists observe Saturday as their "Sabbath."

107. *Cooper* v. *Aaron*, 358 U.S. 1 (1958), at 19. Emphasis added.

not that of the state's establishment.[108] There is no place for this kind of religious discrimination in the United States if the principles of the Establishment Clause are to be respected.

Unlike the complexities arising from the existence of Sunday Closing Laws or any closing laws that might provide preferential treatment of a particular religion or religions, the cases dealing with an "anti-evolution" teaching policy and church property tax exemption are relatively uncomplicated when measured against an historically correct interpretation of the American constitutional doctrine of separation of Church and State.

The Arkansas "Anti-Evolution" Law struck down as unconstitutional in the *Epperson* Case clearly was intended and had the effect of putting the religious interpretation of "fundamentalist Christianity" as to the origin of man into a religiously preferred status. As such, the law was unconstitutional as it was out of harmony with what the Establishment Clause was historically intended to—and still does—preclude.

Finally, property tax exemption for houses of worship, available on a discriminatory religious basis, in no way elevates any particular religion or religious sect into a preferred position and therefore no more violates the Establishment Clause today than such exemptions did when they were legislatively provided by the "Framers and Ratifiers of the First Amendment" in the eighteenth century.

The "Aid to Education" Cases

As noted earlier, the Warren and Burger Courts have decided many cases in which the basic constitutional issue addressed was whether the Establishment of Religion Clause of the First—and by application to the States—or Fourteenth Amendment was violated by some type of federal or state assistance to either church-affiliated schools and/or the students who attend them. The first such case to be fully examined by the Warren Court was from New York State and involved loans of textbooks to children in private

---

108. The fact that Sunday Closing Laws may adversely affect economically those whose religion requires another "day of rest" or "Sabbath" and thus, as applied to them, may also violate their "free exercise of religion" does constitute another interesting and important constitutional question. Although I think these laws are unconstitutional for the additional reason that in certain instances—such as the *Braunfeld* and the *Crown Kosher Market* Cases—they also violate the Free Exercise Clause, that constitutional issue is not pursued here because it is not completely germane to this study of the Establishment Clause.

schools, including parochial schools—*Board of Education of Central School District* v. *James E. Allen, Jr., Commissioner of Education of New York.*[109]

In two respects, the *Bd. of Education* v. *Allen* "Textbook" Case clearly differed from the "Louisiana Textbook" Case, *Cochran* v. *Louisiana,* (see chapter five).[110] First, when *Cochran* was decided in 1930, the religion clauses of the First Amendment had not yet been made applicable to the States. Consequently, the *Cochran* Case, unlike *Bd. of Education* v. *Allen,* was not an Establishment Clause case.[111] Second, in the Louisiana Case the textbooks furnished to the children of private sectarian or non-sectarian schools were to be—according to Chief Justice Hughes's reading of the state statutes—"the same books that are furnished children attending public schools. ..."[112]

In contrast, the New York State Law allowed textbooks to be loaned to private school children if those books were either designated for use in any public school or "approved by any boards of education, trustees or other school authorities."[113] This particular section of the relevant New York Education Law[114] would allow private parochial school teachers to have the State buy textbooks selected by the parochial schools and then loaned to their students, as long as the books were approved by the appropriate public educational authority. Unlike the Louisiana Case, the textbooks provided by New York for parochial or sectarian school children could be different from those being used by the State's public school students if the proper public educational authorities consented.

The opinion of the United States Supreme Court, authored by Justice Byron White,[115] followed the rationale and conclusion of the *Everson* "Bus Transportation" Case. Noting that *Everson* had held that the Establishment Clause applied to the States,[116] White pointed out that the Court had,

---

109. 392 U.S. 236 (1968).

110. 281 U.S. 370 (1930). The *Cochran* Case is discussed in chap. five, under "The 'Child-Benefit' Theory and State Police Power."

111. Not until *Cantwell* v. *Connecticut* in 1940 and the *Everson* Case in 1947 was it settled that the Establishment Clause applied to the States through the "Due Process Clause" of the Fourteenth Amendment. See chap. four, text at fn. 44 to the end of the chapter.

112. 281 U.S. 370, at 375.

113. 392 U.S. 236, at 239–40, fn. 3.

114. New York Education Law, Sec. 701 (1967 Supplement), Subsection 3.

115. White was joined by Justices Harlan, Brennan, Stewart, Marshall, and Chief Justice Warren. Justice Harlan also wrote a separate concurring opinion. 392 U.S. 236, at 249.

116. 392 U.S. 236, at 241–42.

in 1963,[117] "fashioned a test" to distinguish between "forbidden involvements of the State with religion and those contacts which the Establishment Clause permits." The test inquired as to "the purpose and primary effect of the enactment" challenged as violative of the Establishment Clause. "That is to say," wrote White, "that to [have the statute] withstand the strictures of the Establishment Clause there must be a *secular legislative purpose and a primary effect that neither advances nor inhibits religion.*"[118] This, of course, is little more than a general abstraction of which the "Child-Benefit" theory is the one specific illustration most relevant in sectarian school/student aid cases.

Corroborating this judgment, the Court's opinion next invoked the specifics of the *Everson* "Transportation" Case with the modification that here the parochial school children, not the sectarian schools, were being benefited by public-funded books instead of public-funded transportation. "The law merely makes available *to all children the benefits* of a general program to lend school books free of charge."[119] White's opinion continued: "[b]ooks are furnished at the request of the pupil and ownership remains, *at least technically*, in the State. Thus no funds or books are furnished to parochial schools, and *the financial benefit is to parents and children, not to schools.*"[120] Justice Black in dissent indicated that even though the Court's majority and the New York State Court of Appeals "purported" to follow his 1947 *Everson* opinion for the Court, he believed "upholding a State's power to pay bus or streetcar fares for school children cannot provide support for the validity of a state law using tax-raised funds to buy school books for a religious school."[121]

The longest dissenting opinion in the *Allen* Case was written by Justice Douglas.[122] The main thrust of the Douglas dissent was that local school boards will generally approve the books requested by the parochial schools for purchase and use in their secular classes and if that indeed be the case, Douglas asked: "Can there be the slightest doubt that the head of the parochial school will select the book or books that best promote its sectarian creed?"[123] If the school board resists rubber stamping the parochial school

---

117. White's reference was to the Court's opinion in the "Bible Reading and Lord's Prayer" Case—*Abington* v. *Schempp*, 374 U.S. 203 (1963)—written by Justice Clark. See the discussion of the *Abington* Case in chap. six.

118. 392 U.S. 236, at 243. Emphasis added.

119. Ibid. Emphasis added.

120. Ibid., at 244. Emphasis added.

121. Ibid., at 252.

122. Justices Black, Douglas, and Fortas each wrote a separate dissenting opinion.

123. 392 U.S. 236, at 256.

textbook requests, Douglas predicted a political battle to put the independent school board "under church domination and control."[124]

Turning to Justice White's use of the *Everson* Case, Douglas, who voted for the transportation funds for parochial students in *Everson*, countered with his own version of what primarily benefits a child and what benefits a church-affiliated private school:

> Whatever may be said of *Everson*, there is nothing ideological about a bus. There is nothing ideological about a school lunch, nor a public nurse, nor a scholarship. The constitutionality of such public aid to students in parochial schools turns on considerations not present in this textbook case. The textbook goes to the very heart of education in a parochial school. It is the chief, although not solitary, instrumentality for propagating a particular religious creed or faith. How can we possibly approve such state aid to a religion?[125]

Clearly it was not as easy for the dissenting judges to see the "primary effect" of this "secular" law as advancing education rather than religion.[126]

In 1973 the Burger Supreme Court[127] decided a more recent suit, a Mississippi case, which involved the lending of state-owned books to private religiously affiliated schools *segregated on the basis of race*. Speaking for seven members of the Court in *Norwood* v. *Harrison*,[128] Chief Justice Burger held that such a textbook-lending program by the state is unconstitutional. The Court reasoned that lending textbooks "is not legally

---

124. Ibid.

125. Ibid., at 257.

126. In his dissent Justice Fortas wrote: "This statute calls for furnishing special, separate, and particular books, specially, separately, and particularly chosen by religious sects or their representatives for use in their sectarian schools. This is the infirmity, in my opinion. This is the feature that makes it impossible, in my view, to reach any conclusion other than this statute is an unconstitutional use of public funds to support an establishment of religion." 392 U.S. 236, at 271.

127. The term "Burger Court" is used here to describe the U.S. Supreme Court after Justice Lewis F. Powell, Jr., replaces Justice Hugo Black and Justice William H.

Rehnquist replaces Justice John Marshall Harlan. Both Justices Powell and Rehnquist were confirmed by the U.S. Senate in December 1971 and began participating in the Court's work in 1972. Initially, the membership of the Burger Court, as the term is used here, included Chief Justice Burger and Associate Justices Douglas, Brennan, Stewart, White, Marshall, Blackmun, Powell, and Rehnquist. Justice Douglas was replaced by Justice John Paul Stevens in 1975.

128. 415 U.S. 455 (1973). Justices Stewart, White, Marshall, Blackmun, Powell, and Rehnquist joined Burger's opinion of the Court. Justices Douglas and Brennan concurred in the result without filing a separate opinion. Id., at 735.

distinguishable" from other forms of state assistance, and since racial discrimination was barred by the *Constitution* in state operated schools, it could not be promoted by a State through "private persons."[129] The Establishment Clause issue was discussed in the Court's opinion but was not the dispositive factor.

At the end of the 1960's not only did the "Child-Benefit" theory metamorphose into the larger and more general "Secular Purpose and Primary Effect" test, as noted above in the discussion of the *Allen* "Textbook" Case, but in the *Walz* "Tax Exemption" Case (1970), the Court introduced a new criterion, "excessive government entanglement with religion,"[130] which it would use as an additional guide in determining whether any given governmental program attacked in court as a violation of the doctrine of separation of Church and State, was unconsitutional under the Establishment Clause. Consequently, throughout the Establishment Clause cases in the early 1970's, most of the members of the U.S. Supreme Court have their opinions sprinkled with these terms—"secular purpose and primary effect of the legislation" and "excessive government entanglement with religion"—used as constitutional criteria and tests against which challenged programs are to be measured. The Court's success or lack thereof in communicating to state courts, lower federal courts, and even some of its own members what these terms specifically mean in a given case leaves much to be desired. Consider the Court's following decisions.

In 1971 the U.S. Supreme Court decided four companion Establishment Clause cases, three of which (*Lemon* v. *Kurtzman, Early* v. *DiCenso*, and *Robinson* v. *DiCenso*[131]) were handled in one opinion of the Court and the fourth (*Tilton* v. *Richardson*[132]) decided by a plurality opinion because at least five justices could not reach agreement on one opinion.

In the *Lemon* Case— referred to by the Justices after 1973 as "*Lemon I*" because a case involving the same litigants came twice to the United States Supreme Court on appeal, involving different issues[133]—Chief Justice Burger, writing the opinion of the Court, set forth the newly combined criteria that would be used to decide Establishment Clause cases in the early 1970's:

> Every analysis in this area [Church and State cases] must begin with consideration of the cumulative criteria developed by the Court over many

---

129. 415 U.S. 455, at 463–65. In 1975 another case involving more aid than just textbooks—*Meek* v. *Pittenger*, 421 U.S. 349—came before the High Court. It will be discussed below.

130. 397 U.S. 664, at 674.
131. 403 U.S. 602 (1971).
132. 403 U.S. 672 (1971).
133. 411 U.S. 192 (1973).

years. Three such tests may be gleaned from our cases. First, the statute must have a secular legislative purpose; second, its principal or primary effect must be one that neither advances nor inhibits religion, Board of Education v. Allen, 392 U.S. 236, 243 (1968); finally, the statute must not foster "an excessive government entanglement with religion." Walz, 397 U.S. 664, 668 (1970).[134]

Thereafter, Burger's Court opinion held that a Rhode Island Law that would have allowed up to a 15 percent supplement from public funds for parochial school teachers' salaries and a Pennsylvania Statute allowing direct reimbursements to parochial schools for "secular educational services"—which included supplemental funds for teachers' salaries, textbooks, and instructional materials— were unconstitutional because "the statutes in each State involve[d] excessive entanglement between government and religion."[135] This decision by the Court was rendered in spite of the fact that the Court held that the legislative purposes of the acts were not intended to advance religion but were intended "to enhance the quality of secular education in all schools covered by the compulsory attendance laws."[136]

Failing any part of the threefold test seemed to be enough to hold the state laws unconstitutional. This became apparent when Chief Justice Burger noted that the Court need not decide whether the principal or primary effect of the programs offended the Religion Clauses because excessive government entanglement with religion was sufficient for the Court to constitutionally doom the laws.[137] It should be noted that that vague value judgment, without clear standards provided by the Court majority as to where "excessive entanglement" begins and ends, was enough to void legislation that the Court, in its opinion, conceded had a secular purpose constitutionally within the police power of the state.

In his *Lemon* opinion, Chief Justice Burger remarked that "the language of the Religion Clauses of the First Amendment is at best opaque, particularly when compared with other portions of the Amendment."[138] In *Tilton* v. *Richardson*,[139] decided the same day as *Lemon*, the opaqueness

134. 403 U.S. 602, at 612–13. Burger's opinion for the Court was joined by Justices Black, Douglas, Harlan, Stewart, and Blackmun. Justice Douglas also wrote a concurring opinion in which Justices Black and Marshall joined. Justice Brennan wrote a concurring opinion not joining the Burger opinion of the Court. Justice White con-

curred in the *Lemon* Case but dissented in *Early* and *Robinson*.
135. Ibid., at 613–14.
136. Ibid., at 613.
137. Ibid., at 613–14.
138. Ibid., at 612.
139. 403 U.S. 672 (1971).

of the First Amendment's "Religion Clauses" became excessively "murky" for the Court as it grappled with the constitutionality of sections of the federal Higher Education Facilities Act of 1963 which, among other things, authorized construction grants to colleges and universities, including church-related institutions.

As noted above, there was no opinion of the Court in *Tilton* inasmuch as five of the nine justices could not agree on all points of one opinion. Chief Justice Burger joined by Justices John Marshall Harlan, Potter Stewart, and Harry Blackmun thought there would not be "excessive government entanglement" with the church-affiliated institutions of higher education as the Federal Government inspected minimally to see that the facilities built with government assistance would be used only for secular purposes.[140] Justice White concurred separately and thus the law was saved.[141]

Justice Douglas, joined by Justices Hugo Black and Thurgood Marshall, dissented, invoking the same selective, and consequently distorted, history characteristic of the absolute separationist position. Citing Madison's "Remonstrance" as if it was the only document regarding religion Madison subscribed to in public life, Douglas ended his dissent:

> It is almost unbelievable that we have made the radical departure from Madison's Remonstrance memorialized in today's decision.
>
> I dissent not because of any lack of respect for parochial schools but out of a feeling of despair that the respect which through history has been accorded the First Amendment is this day lost.
>
> It should be remembered that in this case we deal with federal grants and with the command that "Congress shall make no law respecting an establishment of religion or prohibiting the free exercise thereof." The million-dollar grants sustained today put Madison's miserable "three pence" to shame. But he even thought, as I do, that even a small amount coming out of the pocket of taxpayers and going into the coffers of a church was not in keeping with our constitutional ideal.[142]

Subsequently, in *Hunt* v. *McNair*,[143] the Court, speaking through Justice Lewis Powell, decided that a South Carolina Statute aiding colleges, including church-affiliated institutions, by the issuance of revenue bonds for construction of facilities, expressly not to be used for sectarian purposes,

---

140. Ibid., at 688.

141. A 20-year limit on the prohibition of nonsecular use of facilities constructed with the assistance of federal funds—provided for in the Act—was struck down as unconstitutional. Ibid., at 689.

142. Ibid., at 696–97.

143. 413 U.S. 734 (1973).

constituted a law: which did not have as its primary effect the advancing of religion; which did have a valid public purpose, the aiding of the students attending institutions of higher education in the state; and which did not constitute excessive government entanglement with religion.[144]

Another Establishment Clause case decided on the same day as *Hunt—Committee for Public Education and Religious Liberty* v. *Nyquist, Commissioner of Education*[145]—began to show somewhat the divergence of the Court's personnel as they used their criteria to decide Establishment Clause cases in the 1970's. In the *Nyquist* Case, the U.S. Supreme Court held that several additions to New York State's Education and Tax laws were unconstitutional under the Establishment Clause because their "effect" would subsidize and advance the religious mission of the sectarian schools. The New York Law provided: (a) direct money grants to nonpublic schools for "maintenance and repair" of facilities and equipment to ensure the students' "health, safety, and welfare;" (b) a partial tuition reimbursement plan for parents whose children attend these nonpublic schools; (c) a tax relief plan for parents who did not qualify for tuition reimbursement.

Although a constant six-man majority of the Court subscribed to Justice Powell's *Nyquist* opinion,[146] the three remaining Justices concurred in some parts and dissented in others. The Court's opinion in "Part II A" dealt with the "maintenance and repairs" provisions;[147] "Part II B" with the "tuition reimbursement" section;[148] and "Part II C" with the "income tax benefit"[149] section of the New York Law. The highly individualistic voting in this case, although among a minority of the Court, would eventually affect a larger number of Justices.[150] This effect becomes evident in *Meek* v. *Pittinger*[151] decided in 1975.

144. Chief Justice Burger and Justices Stewart, White, Blackmun, and Rehnquist joined Powell's opinion for the Court. Justice Brennan dissented and was joined by Justices Douglas and Marshall.

145. 413 U.S. 756 (1973).

146. Justice Powell's opinion of the Court was joined by Justices Douglas, Brennan, Stewart, Marshall, and Blackmun.

147. 413 U.S. 756, at 774–80.

148. Ibid., at 780–89.

149. Ibid., at 789–94.

150. "Powell, J., delivered the opinion of the Court, in which Douglas, Brennan, Stewart, Marshall, and Blackmun, JJ., joined. Burger, C.J., filed an opinion concurring in Part II-A of the Court's opinion, in which Rehnquist, J., joined, and dissenting from Parts II-B and II-C, in which White and Rehnquist, JJ., joined, *post*, p. 798. Rehnquist, J., filed an opinion dissenting in part, in which Burger, C.J., and White, J., joined, *post*, p. 805. White, J., filed a dissenting opinion, in those portions of which relating to Parts II-B and II-C of the Court's opinion Burger, C.J., and Rehnquist, J., joined, *post*, p. 813." 413 U.S. 756, at 758–59.

151. 421 U.S. 349 (1975).

In *Meek*, whereas one Pennsylvania Statute (Act 195) that allowed public funds to be used to acquire and to loan nonpublic school children textbooks that are "acceptable for use in the public schools" was upheld as constitutional through the use of the "Child-Benefit" theory,[152] another Pennsylvania Law (Act 194) that would allow the State to provide "auxiliary services" (such as counseling, testing, psychological services, speech and hearing therapy, teaching and related services for exceptional children, for remedial students, and for the educationally disadvantaged, among others) to nonpublic schools was held in violation of the Establishment Clause because the constant state supervision of these services, necessary to see that they "remain strictly neutral and nonideological," would require significant "political entanglement together with administrative entanglement."[153] A section of Act 195, which would have allowed direct loan of instructional materials and equipment to parochial schools, was also held unconstitutional by the Court's opinion in that it was seen as primarily having the effect of advancing the religious character of the schools.[154]

The voting alignment in *Meek* allowed for an opinion of the Court declaring the provision for the "auxiliary services" and the equipment as unconstitutional aid, but only a plurality opinion by Justices Stewart, Blackmun, and Powell sustained the textbook loan provision.[155] The concurrence of Chief Justice Burger and Justices White and Rehnquist allowed the textbook provision of the Pennsylvania Law to be saved. These three members of the Court disagreed with most of the Court's opinion and would have also upheld as constitutional the providing of "auxiliary services" for nonpublic schools.

Justices Brennan, Douglas, and Marshall, who had been part of the six-man majority opinion of the Court, broke ranks and dissented from "the judgment upholding the constitutionality of the textbook provisions of Act 195."[156] For Justices allegedly using the same criteria for evaluating the constitutionality of an act challenged under the same constitutional passage, the conclusion—judging from the voting as recorded—that value judgments abounded is hard to avoid.[157]

152. Ibid., at 359–60.
153. Ibid., at 372.
154. Ibid., at 362.
155. Ibid.
156. Ibid., at 373.
157. "Stewart, J., announced the judgment of the Court and delivered an opinion of the Court, in which Blackmun and Powell, JJ., joined, and in all but Part III of which Douglas, Brennan, and Marshall, JJ., joined.

Brennan, J., filed an opinion concurring in part and dissenting in part, in which Douglas and Marshall, JJ., joined, *post*, p. 373. Burger, C.J., filed an opinion concurring in the judgment in part and dissenting in part, *post*, p. 385. Rehnquist, J., filed an opinion concurring in the judgment in part and dissenting in part, in which White, J., joined, *post*, p. 387." 421 U.S. 349, at 350.

Making matters even more difficult, Justice Brennan in his dissenting statement in *Meek* introduced a new "fourth factor" by which public aid to religion challenged under the Establishment Clause ought to be judged. After a listing of the "three-factor test by which to determine the compatibility with the Establishment Clause of state subsidies of sectarian educational institutions,"[158] Brennan added:

> ... four years ago, the Court, albeit without express recognition of the fact, added a significant *fourth factor* to the test: "A broader base of entanglement of yet a different character is presented by the divisive political potential of these state programs." Lemon v. Kurtzman, 403 U.S. 602, 622 (1971).[159]

Brennan's separate dissent then added that the textbooks and other instructional aids to sectarian schools would depend on "continuing annual appropriations" involving massive sums and creating "a serious potential for divisive conflict over the issue of aid to religion."[160] For Brennan, as well as Douglas and Marshall who joined his opinion, the "politically divisive factor" would now be a significant criterion in future cases involving aid to sectarian educational institutions.

While Justice Brennan was adding another "fourth factor" to evaluate the constitutionality of public aid to sectarian schools in these Establishment Clause cases in 1975, Justices White and Rehnquist in 1976 challenged the need for the "threefold test" of *Lemon v. Kurtzman.*[161]

In *Roemer* v. *Board of Public Works of Maryland*[162] a plurality opinion written by Justice Blackmun, concurred in by Chief Justice Burger and Justice Powell, found that a Maryland Statute which provided "annual noncategorical grants to private colleges, among them religiously affiliated institutions, subject only to restrictions that the funds not be used for 'sectarian purposes' " passed the "threefold" *Lemon I* test and was not therefore in conflict with the Establishment Clause.

Justice White's concurring opinion, joined by Justice Rehnquist, clearly indicated that he would have joined the Blackmun plurality opinion, thus making it the opinion of the Court, had it not been for the "superfluous tests" of *Lemon I* used by Blackmun.[163] Attacking the criteria used by the

---

158. See the quote in the text at fn. 134, supra.

159. 421 U.S. 349, at 374. Emphasis added.

160. Ibid., at 381–82.

161. See the "threefold test" at the text of fn. 134, supra.

162. 426 U.S. 736 (1976).

163. Ibid., at 767–68.

Court since *Lemon I*, White virtually challenged his colleagues to clarify what to him seemed to be unclear and redundant standards:

> The threefold test of *Lemon I* imposes unnecessary, and, as I believe today's plurality opinion demonstrates, superfluous tests for establishing "when the State's involvement with religion passes the peril point" for First Amendment purposes. *Nyquist, supra.*
>
> "It is enough for me that the [State is] financing a separable secular function of overriding importance in order to sustain the legislation here challenged." *Lemon I, supra*, 403 U.S., at 664 (opinion of White, J.). As long as there is a secular legislative purpose, and as long as the primary effect of the legislation is neither to advance nor inhibit religion, I see no reason—particularly in light of the "sparse language of the Establishment Clause," *Committee for Public Education* v. *Nyquist, supra*, 413 U.S., at 820, to take the constitutional inquiry further. See *Lemon I, supra*, 403 U.S., at 661 (opinion of White, J.); *Nyquist, supra*, 413 U.S., at 813 (opinion of White, J.). However, since 1970, the Court has added a third element to the inquiry: whether there is "an excessive government entanglement with religion." *Walz* v. *Tax Comm'n*, 397 U.S. 664. I have never understood the constitutional foundation for this added element; it is at once both insolubly paradoxical, see *Lemon I, supra*, 403 U.S., at 668, and—as the Court has conceded from the outset—a "blurred, indistinct and variable barrier."[164]

The virtual disarray of the present Court, as to which kind of state aid to sectarian educational institutions violates the Establishment Clause and what judicial criteria to use to determine that, is perhaps best seen in *Wolman* v. *Walter*,[165] decided in 1977. The *Wolman* Case dealt with a comprehensive Ohio Statute that authorized "the State to provide *non-public* school pupils with books, instructional materials and equipment, standardized testing and scoring, diagnostic services, therapeutic services, and field transportation."[166] The major opinion of the Case by Justice Blackmun has eight parts identified by Roman numerals that deal with specific substantive aids in the Ohio Law, together with a summary statement identified as Roman numeral IX. An opinion of the Court, written by Blackmun, occurs in Parts I, V, VII, and VIII, and a plurality opinion by Blackmun occurs in Parts II, III, and IV in which he is joined by Chief Justice Burger and Justices Stewart and Powell.

---

164. Ibid., at 768–69.
165. 433 U.S. 229 (1977).

166. Ibid., at 233.

Part I of the opinion deals largely with the content of the Ohio Statute and a statement about the facts of the case.[167] This part of Blackmun's opinion is joined by Chief Justice Burger and Justices Brennan, Stewart, Marshall, Powell, and Stevens.

Part II of the Blackmun opinion is a restatement of the traditional "three-part" test of *Lemon I* which—in this case in 1977—did not command a majority of the Court.[168] Chief Justice Burger and Justices Stewart and Powell joined Blackmun in the use of the "three-part" test. The Court's report is silent about Justices White and Rehnquist on Part II, but the cases cited indicate that both White and Rehnquist apparently abstained from the "three-part" test for the reasons mentioned above in the *Roemer* Case.[169] Justices Brennan and Marshall dissented because the "test" did not include the "fourth factor"—the potential of political divisiveness, developed in Brennan's dissent in *Meek*.[170] Justice Stevens dissented in a separate opinion indicating that he preferred Black's *Everson* test to any other. "Under that test," Stevens wrote, "a state subsidy of sectarian schools is invalid regardless of the form it takes."[171]

Textbooks for loan to nonpublic schools was the subject of Part III of the Blackmun opinion.[172] As indicated above, Chief Justice Burger and Justices Stewart and Powell joined Blackmun in upholding the constitutionality of this program. Justices White and Rehnquist joined in the judgment only.[173] Marshall dissented indicating that he would now have overruled the *Allen* "New York Textbook" Case, thus recanting his vote in that case.[174] Justice Brennan, who also voted with the majority in *Allen*, also dissented on the textbook aspect of the Ohio Law.[175] Justice Stevens—who was not on the Court in 1968 when *Allen* was decided—dissented on the textbook loan provision of the Ohio Law in his own separate opinion.[176] In all there were five different statements made by the nine Justices on the issue of textbook lending under the Statute.

In Part IV of the Blackmun opinion, the constitutionality of the Ohio Statute section that authorized public funds to be spent to supply nonpublic schools with "such standardized tests and scoring services as are in use in

---

167. Ibid., at 233–35.
168. Ibid., at 235–36.
169. See the quote in the text at fn. 164, supra.
170. Brennan, 433 U.S. 229, at 256; and Marshall, id., at 258–59.

171. Ibid., at 265–66.
172. Ibid., at 236–38.
173. Ibid., at 255.
174. Ibid., at 257.
175. Ibid., at 256.
176. Ibid., at 265–66.

the public schools of the state" was considered.[177] The vote was identical to that on Part III. Blackmun, Burger, Stewart, and Powell voted together to uphold the "testing and scoring" section of the Ohio Act; White and Rehnquist concurring together joined them; and Brennan, Marshall, and Stevens dissented separately.

The Diagnostic Services for speech, hearing and psychological problems were discussed in Part V of the Blackmun opinion. Because Justices Marshall and Stevens joined Blackmun, Burger, Stewart, and Powell, this section too became part of the opinion by the Court.[178] Again Justices White and Rehnquist together concurred in the disposition of this section of the case only. Justice Brennan was the sole dissenter in a separate statement.

When the section of the Ohio Statute, which provided for the "expenditure of funds for certain therapeutic, guidance, and remedial services for nonpublic school students who have been identified as having a need for specialized attention,"[179] was considered in Part VI, Justice Stevens joined the Blackmun opinion along with Burger, Stewart, and Powell making that section also part of the opinion of the Court. Justices White and Rehnquist together continued to concur in the judgment of the Court while Justice Marshall reverted to his dissenting stance. Justice Brennan also dissented in Part VI.

Instructional materials and equipment, discussed in Part VII, brought together the votes of Brennan, Stewart, Marshall, Stevens, and Blackmun, who declared in the opinion of the Court, that these sections of the Ohio Law[180] were unconstitutional because they "inescapably had the primary effect of providing a direct and substantial advancement of the sectarian enterprise" of the parochial schools.[181] Now Chief Justice Burger dissented,[182] as did Justices White and Rehnquist. Justice Powell in a separate opinion concurred in the judgment of the majority in Part VII.[183] Once more the voting alignments had changed.

Part VIII dealt with "Field Trips." Justice Blackmun, joined again by Justices Brennan, Stewart, Marshall, and Stevens, also held this section of

---

177. Ibid., at 238–39.

178. When all of the nine justices take part in a case, the agreement of at least five not only on the disposition of the case but also the *rationale* of one opinion is necessary to make it an "opinion of the Court." Such an opinion has the clout of "settled law" where a "plurality opinion" does not.

179. 433 U.S. 229, at 244.

180. Ohio Revised Code Annotated, Section 3317.06 (B) and (C). (Supp. 1976).

181. 433 U.S. 229, at 250.

182. Ibid., at 255.

183. Ibid., at 263.

the Ohio Law unconstitutional.[184] Five Justices voting together on one opinion made this rejection of the Statute part of the opinion of the Court. Chief Justice Burger, and Justices White, Rehnquist, and Powell dissented.

In the summary statement, Part IX, Justice Blackmun sensing the need for a modicum of clarity provided it: ". . . we hold constitutional those portions of the Ohio statute authorizing the State to provide nonpublic school pupils with books, standardized testing and scoring, diagnostic services, and therapeutic and remedial services. We hold unconstitutional those portions relating to instructional materials and equipment and field trip services."[185]

The *Wolman* Case illustrates how accurate Chief Justice Burger was when in the *Walz* Case he wrote that "[i]n attempting to articulate the scope of the two Religious Clauses [of the First Amendment], the Court's opinion reflects the limitations inherent in formulating general principles on a case-by-case basis."[186] The "case-by-case" analysis clearly reflects a U.S. Supreme Court greatly divided, not only on the criteria to be used in examining a statute purportedly unconstitutional because it provided some public funding for nonpublic sectarian school children, but also in the most part as to which specific aids may be constitutionally provided and which may not. One finds it difficult—after surveying most of the Establishment Clause cases of both the Warren and Burger Courts—to disagree with Justice Steven's apt quote in *Wolman* concerning the inadequacy of the Court's decisions in providing guidelines for other courts to follow in Church and State cases: " 'Corrosive precedents' have left us without firm principles on which to decide these cases. As this case demonstrates the States have been encouraged to search for new ways of achieving forbidden ends . . . . What should be a 'high and impregnable' wall between church and state has been reduced to a 'blurred, indistinct, and variable barrier,'. . . "[187]

Within three years after the *Wolman* decision, an opinion of the Court openly admitted the need for, and the lack of, a single and more encompassing interpretation of the Establishment Clause. In *Committee For Public Education and Religious Liberty* v. *Regan*,[188] Justice White re-embraced the "threefold" test of *Lemon I*,[189] which he had attacked in

---

184. Section 3317.06(L); ibid., at 255.
185. 433 U.S. 229, at 255.
186. 397 U.S. 664 (1970), at 668.
187. 433 U.S. 229, at 266.

188. 444 U.S. 646 (1980).
189. See the quote in the text at fn. 134, supra.

the *Roemer* Case,[190] and wrote the opinion for a deeply divided (5–4) Supreme Court. Chief Justice Burger and Justices Stewart, Powell, and Rehnquist joined White in holding that "a New York State statute authorizing the use of public funds to reimburse church-sponsored and secular nonpublic schools for performing various testing and reporting services mandated by state law" did not constitute the kind of public aid to sectarian schools that violates the Establishment Clause.[191]

Deciding that the *Wolman* Case established the controlling principles to be applied in *Regan*,[192] White's opinion held that although the New York tests were not wholly administered, graded, and reported by the State or its agents—as was the situation under the Ohio Statute upheld in *Wolman*—the differences between the two statutes were "not of [a] constitutional dimension."[193] In conformity with the "threefold" test, the Court held: that the New York Statute's purpose was clearly secular;[194] that the Statute had "primarily a secular effect;"[195] that as written "the New York plan suggest[ed] no excessive [government] entanglement."[196]

With Justice Blackmun—who had written the complex *Wolman* decision constantly invoked by White's opinion for the Court in *Regan*—dissenting,[197] there should be no amazement with Justice White's candid conclusion of his opinion for the Court:

---

190. See the quote in the text at fn. 164, supra.

191. 444 U.S. 646, at 648.

192. Ibid., at 654.

193. Ibid.

194. Ibid., at 654–55.

195. Ibid., at 657.

196. Ibid., at 660. The Court's opinion also noted that there was "no merit" to the "future political divisiveness" argument urged as an appropriate criterion to be used in Establishment Clause cases. Id., at 660–61, fn. 8.

197. Justice Blackmun differentiated the New York testing plan, from the Ohio one he upheld in *Wolman*, as giving direct financial assistance to sectarian schools. Under the Ohio Statute, the State provided the tests itself with the grading and reporting to be done by persons outside of the sectarian schools. No direct financial aid of any type was, consequently, authorized for religious schools. 444 U.S. 646, at 662. The New York Act provided direct reimbursement costs to the religious schools for expenses resulting from the testing, grading, and reporting requirements of the Act performed by personnel at the sectarian schools. Id., at 663–64. Blackmun's dissent was joined by Justices Brennan and Marshall, both of whom dissented from the section of the *Wolman* Case which upheld the Ohio testing procedures. Id., at 662.

Justice Stevens dissented separately—as he had in *Wolman*—invoking the *Everson* "Bus Transportation" Case of 1947. "I would resurrect the 'high and impregnable' wall between church and state constructed by the Framers of the First Amendment." Id., at 671. Apparently in both *Wolman* and *Regan*, the Supreme Court's decision in *Everson*, to reimburse parents for transportation costs incurred by sending their children to Catholic parochial schools, evaded Justice Stevens reading of that 1947 Court opinion.

Establishment Clause cases are not easy; they stir deep feelings; and we are divided among ourselves, perhaps reflecting the different views on this subject of the people of this country. What is certain is that our decisions have tended to avoid categorical imperatives and absolutist approaches at either end of the range of possible outcomes. *This course sacrifices clarity and predictability for flexibilty*, but this promises to be the case until the continuing interaction between the courts and the States—the former charged with interpreting and upholding the Constitution and the latter seeking to provide education for their youth—produces a single, more encompassing construction of the Establishment Clause.[198]

From my point of view, not only are the Court's failures to provide clear precedent cases in this constitutional area regretable for an appellate court system, but the consumption of all the Court's time in this area of legislating public funds for sectarian school children was, and continues to be, necessary only because the *Everson* Case and other precedent cases have not been decided in harmony with a more historically accurate interpretation of what the Establishment Clause was intended to prohibit. Inasmuch as none of these "sectarian school children aid" laws establish a federal or state church nor provide aid for only the students attending particular church-affiliated schools—thus discriminating against the students of other church-affiliated schools and thereby elevating the religion practiced by the aided church-affiliated school children into a preferred legal status—they are not violations of the Establishment Clause. In addition, it seems that the appropriate test of constitutionality—which the U.S. Supreme Court and every other court should apply when legislation providing aid to nonpublic school children or even nonpublic schools themselves is constitutionally challenged—is the one developed by Chief Justice John Marshall in *McCulloch* v. *Maryland*.[199]

Discussing the scope of Congress's legislative power in 1819, Marshall wrote: "Let the end be legitimate, let it be within the scope of the Constitution, and all means which are appropriate, which are plainly adapted to that end, which are not prohibited, but consistent with the letter and spirit of the Constitution, are constitutional."[200] For the more than eight-score years since Marshall wrote those words, the U.S. Supreme Court has in general used them as a standard against which to measure state as well as national legislation. Applying this test of constitutionality to the state legislation that aids sectarian or nonpublic school children would not be difficult.

198. 444 U.S. 646, at 662. Emphasis added.

199. 4 Wheat. 316 (1819).
200. Ibid., at 421.

It is certainly not contested by students of the American *Constitution* that under their Tenth Amendment residual powers the States of the Union possess the "police power." It is equally accepted that pursuant to that "police power" the States may pass laws constitutionally requiring a compulsory minimum education. This compulsory education of children is a legitimate end that a State may seek. The means being used by the State is what is frequently questioned in Establishment Clause education cases.

If the State laws regarding education provide means that embrace sectarian or other nonpublic schools, as long as those means do not place any religion and/or religious sect or tradition in a preferred legal position, neither the letter nor the spirit of the Establishment Clause, when correctly viewed historically, is violated. It is axiomatic that schools are appropriate means that are plainly adapted to meet the constitutionally legitimate end of the state—the education of its children and sometimes its adult population.

If Thomas Jefferson was able to use sectarian means to achieve secular ends, as the treaty with the Kaskaskia Indians of 1803 clearly indicates, and if the United States Government could use church schools to aid in the secular goal of "civilizing the Indians" as American historical documents substantiate, in my judgment, it is not unconstitutional for the States of the Union to do likewise. All of the "aid to sectarian school" cases are merely contemporary examples of the States using sectarian institutions to reach the secular end of educating its students. Can anyone seriously pretend that the Catholic Church built by Jefferson's treaty of 1803 dispensed less ideology than a parochial school or a national university affiliated with the Catholic Church such as Notre Dame? Perhaps Justice White struck closer to the current error prevalent on the Court when he recently wrote: ". . . the Court continues to misconstrue the First Amendment in a manner that discriminates against religion and is contrary to the fundamental educational needs of the country, . . ."[201]

Thomas Jefferson, not blind to the fundamental needs of his native Virginians, made sure that the facilities of the public university that he founded would be available where needed to the sectarian institutions "adjacent to its precincts" and especially to their students. Perhaps Jefferson had a conviction that where education is truly available, one need not worry about the flourishing of blind dogma.

The examination of the Warren and Burger Courts' Establishment Clause cases in this chapter points to several conclusions. First, only in the

201. *New York* v. *Cathedral Academy*, 434 U.S. 125, at 134–35 (1977).

"Anti-Evolution" Case, *Epperson* v. *Arkansas*, and the *Walz* "Tax-Exemption" Case did the Court correctly employ the historical concept of separation of Church and State that the Framers of the First Amendment embraced. Second, the Supreme Court's decisions in the "Sunday Closing Laws" cases have allowed a single religious tradition's "day of rest," in a religiously pluralistic society, to be legally prescribed, contrary to the Establishment Clause's prohibition of elevating any religion or religious tradition into an exclusively preferred position. Third, *contrary* to the practice of every early national administration that was closest to the addition of the Establishment Clause to our *Constitution*, including those of Madison and Jefferson, both the Warren and Burger Courts have held that sectarian methods may not be used as constitutional means toward achieving secular constitutional ends. This practice by the Court is especially evident in the state cases in which aid to education of students in church-affiliated schools has incidentally aided those schools. Fourth, the number of Establishment Clause cases needlessly consuming the U.S. Supreme Court's time is due in part to the apparent failure of the present Court to settle on a clear test as to what the Clause precludes, a test which faithfully commands a *constant majority* of the Court's personnel as they continue, in the main, to misapply the American constitutional doctrine of separation of Church and State.

Chapter Eight

Judicial Pre-emption Vs. Democratic Decision Making

This study has established from primary historical sources that the American constitutional doctrine of separation of Church and State has been misconstrued at least since the *Everson* Case of 1947, when the U.S. Supreme Court first comprehensively, through Justice Black, defined the prohibitions of the Establishment Clause. These documents clearly show that the excessively broad interpretation of the First Amendment requiring a virtual absolute separation of Church and State (advocated by Justice Rutledge in the *"Everson* Bus Transportation" Case and associated with some long-standing authorities in this field of American Constitutional Law) is both historically unsupportable and erroneous.

In the light of the historical documentation presented in earlier chapters, the constitutional prohibitions in the First Amendment, that "Congress shall make no law respecting an establishment of religion or prohibiting the free exercise thereof," lead inescapably to the conclusion that the Framers of the Bill of Rights *were not* subscribers to any all-encompassing concept of *absolute* separation of Church and State. To be sure, they believed in separation of Church and State, but the separation between government and religion to which they subscribed, according to their public actions and statements, does not support the broad concept of separation advanced by the U.S. Supreme Court and some scholars such as Professor Leo Pfeffer who may embrace an even broader separation. While some historical documents may be interpreted differently, this study shows conclusively that the "Rutledge-Pfeffer" thesis of virtually absolute separation of Church and State was not contemplated by the First Congress, which framed the Establishment Clause, nor by those who shared governmental power after them in the early successive Congresses.

The significant documents presented in previous chapters are best, albeit not totally, reconciled with the First Amendment through a much narrower interpretation of the Establishment of Religion Clause. Few major historical contradictions arise when the Framers of the First Amendment are seen as providing for a separation of government and religion that would achieve only the following objectives: First, the national legislature or Congress was denied the power to establish a national religion or church; Second, the Congress was forbidden to give any religion or religious sect a legally preferred status which characterized governmentally established religion in Europe; and Third, the issue of the establishment or disestablishment of state churches in the States of the new Federal Union was to be decided by the governments of the individual States.

Since the last state established church was disestablished in Massachusetts in 1833, and the Fourteenth Amendment has been interpreted to apply the prohibitions of the Establishment Clause to the State governments in 1947, today neither the State governments nor the Federal Government may establish a religion or church. Further, inasmuch as the full weight of the Establishment Clause now limits the powers of the individual States of the Union, they can no longer exercise any greater degree of freedom in regard to religion in any way than could the Federal Government after the Establishment Clause was added to the *Constitution* in 1791. Consequently, today, federal or state governmental actions most likely to violate an historically correct understanding of the Establishment of Religion Clause are only those public acts that in some way elevate a single religion, religious sect, or religious tradition into a legally preferred status.

If this analysis of the limitations which the Establishment Clause was intended to place on government correctly reflects the original intentions of the Framers, we must ask why the decisions of the United States Supreme Court have been at such a variance with these conclusions? One answer is that the U.S. Supreme Court has never fully examined the historical facts concerning the origin and history of the Establishment Clause. In addition, the High Court has failed to consider carefully the relevant actions of the First Congress, the actions of our early Presidents, and the other early Congresses, thus using their public behavior and statements to gauge the meaning of the constitutional prohibition against combining Church and State.

In perhaps no other classification of Constitutional Law cases does the U.S. Supreme Court rely so much on American history for its textual interpretation as to what the U.S. *Constitution* forbids as it does in Establishment Clause cases. Chapter five's examination of the early precedent-setting cases interpreting the Establishment Clause shows conclusively that the Court has embraced what might be called "history by omission." Illustrative of this approach to history are the major written opinions in the important and often cited precedent case, the *Everson* "Bus Transportation" Case in which the Supreme Court rendered its first and most definitive interpretation of the prohibitions of the Establishment Clause.[1]

Justice Black's opinion of the Court reviewing the struggle in Virginia for religious freedom and against the established church indicates that Virginians and others had "reached the conviction that individual religious liberty could be achieved best under a government which was stripped of all power to tax, to support, or *otherwise to assist any or all religions*, or to interfere with the beliefs of any religious individual or group."[2] Black is careful to point out that this movement to remove governmental involvement with religion reached "*its dramatic climax in Virginia in 1785–1786*" with Thomas Jefferson and James Madison leading the fight against a renewal of a "tax levy for the support of the established church."[3] The reader is informed by Justice Black that "Madison wrote his great 'Memorial and Remonstrance' against the law"[4] and in 1786 the Virginia Assembly enacted "the famous 'Virginia Bill for Religious Liberty' originally written by Thomas Jefferson."[5] The dissenters, Justices Rutledge, Frankfurter, Jackson, and Burton, also rely heavily on the "Memorial" of 1785 and the "Bill for Establishing Religious Freedom" of 1786 to trace the meaning and history of religious disestablishment in Virginia in 1785–1786,[6] so much so that the "Memorial and Remonstrance" is appended to the *Everson* opinions.[7] In *Everson* and in the many other Establishment Clause cases in which *Everson* and the "Memorial and Remonstrance" are cited by the U.S. Supreme Court, no mention is made of any other legislation voted by the Virginia Assembly in 1785–1786 as they revised the laws of that Commonwealth.

The historical picture of Madison and Jefferson working to stop any "assistance to any or all religions" painted by both Justices Black and Rutledge is flawed and inaccurate because omitted from their historical review of the "climactic years of disestablishment in Virginia in 1785 and 1786" are at least two pieces of legislation introduced by Madison that run counter to the now accepted traditional view of Madison and Jefferson. Some brief historical background would be useful here.

---

1. The *Everson* Case is discussed in depth in chap. five.

2. *Everson v. Board of Education*, 330 U.S. 1, at 11. Emphasis added.

3. Ibid., at 11–12. Emphasis added.

4. Ibid., at 12.

5. Ibid.

6. Ibid., at 34–40.

7. Ibid., starting at 63.

After declaring independence from Great Britain, Jefferson and several other politically prominent Virginians were appointed to a committee to recommend revision of their Commonwealth's laws.[8] The "Committee of Revisors" began their work in the autumn of 1776 and although some of the proposed revisions were treated selectively, it was not until the October 1785 session of the Virginia Assembly that the proposed revision as a whole was considered.[9] With Jefferson out of the country as U.S. minister in France in 1785, "the sponsorship of the reform rested upon James Madison."[10] Nevertheless, according to a Madison letter of November 4, 1826, Jefferson was nominally and actually the leading figure in the revisal.[11]

In all the "Committee for the Revision of the Laws" prepared 126 bills for adoption.[12] Among the bills contained in the *Revisal* was Bill No. 82, "A Bill for Establishing Religious Freedom," passed in 1786,[13] invariably invoked by U.S. Supreme Court Justices and "complete separationist" scholars as evidence that Jefferson and Madison believed in absolute or nearly absolute separation of Church and State.

The two bills omitted from the Black and Rutledge opinions in *Everson*, referred to above, were both presented by James Madison. On October 31, 1785, Madison introduced Bill No. 84 of the *Revisal* entitled: "A Bill for Punishing Disturbers of Religious Worship and *Sabbath Breakers*."[14] It was postponed to the next session and passed after a few amendments in 1786, the same year as the "Bill for Establishing Religious Freedom."[15] It is reproduced here as introduced by Madison.

---

8. The "Committee of Revisors" was appointed by resolution of the General Assembly, printed under the date 15 October 1776 and included in addition to Jefferson, George Mason (who declined to serve), Thomas Ludwell (who died before the Committee began its work), Edmund Pendleton, and George Wythe. Jefferson, Pendleton, and Wythe did the actual Revision. Julian P. Boyd, ed., *The Papers of Thomas Jefferson* (Princeton, N.J.: Princeton University Press, 1950), Vol. 2, 1777 to 18 June 1779, Including the Revisal of the Laws, 1776–1786, p. 312.

9. Boyd, *The Papers of Thomas Jefferson*, pp. 305–7.

10. Ibid., p. 307.

11. Ibid., p. 313.

12. Ibid., pp. 329–33.

13. Ibid., pp. 545–47.

14. Ibid., pp. 555–56. Emphasis added. Although the Boyd-edited *Papers of Thomas Jefferson* cited here did not appear until 1950, three years after the *Everson* opinions were written, the text of the act "Punishing . . . Sabbath Breakers" as adopted was published earlier and available to the Court in William Waller Hening, *The Statutes at Large; Being a Collection of All the Laws of Virginia* (Richmond: Printed for the Editor by George Cochran, 1823), pp. 336–37.

15. Ibid., see the notes, pp. 555 and 556.

84. A Bill for Punishing Disturbers of Religious Worship
and Sabbath Breakers

Be it enacted by the General Assembly, that no officer, for any civil cause, shall arrest any minister of the gospel, licensed according to the rules of his sect, and who shall have taken the oath of fidelity to the commonwealth, while such minister shall be publicly preaching or performing religious worship in any church, chapel, or meeting-house, on pain of imprisonment and amercement, at the discretion of a jury, and of making satisfaction to the party so arrested.

And if any person shall of purpose, maliciously, or contemptuously, disquiet or disturb any congregation assembled in any church, chapel, or meeting-house, or misuse any such minister being there, he may be put under restraint during religious worship, by any Justice present, which Justice, if present, or if none be present, then any Justice before whom proof of the offence shall be made, may cause the offender to find two sureties to be bound by recognizance in a sufficient penalty for his good behavior, and in default thereof shall commit him to prison, there to remain till the next court to be held for the same county; and upon conviction of the said offence before the said court, he shall be further punished by imprisonment and amercement at the discretion of a jury.

If any person on Sunday shall himself be found labouring at his own or any other trade or calling, or shall employ his apprentices, servants or slaves in labour, or other business, except it be in the ordinary houshold [sic] *offices of daily necessity, or other work of necessity or charity, he shall forfeit the sum of ten shillings for every such offence, deeming every apprentice, servant, or slave so employed, and every day he shall be so employed as constituting a distinct offence.*[16]

Although Madison introduced Bill No. 84, the most accepted theory seems to be that Jefferson was responsible for revising it and it was one of some fifty-one bills that Jefferson drew up.[17] In brief, the relevant historical documents show that in 1785 James Madison sponsored a Bill punishing "Sabbath Breakers," which was probably drawn up by Thomas Jefferson. Even though the Bill was slightly amended, the important part for our consideration—the third paragraph—had only one change involving the word "Sunday." The same Virginia Assembly that passed the "Bill for Establishing Religious Freedom" changed the fifth word from "Sunday" to "Sabbath Day."[18]

16. Ibid., p. 555. Emphasis added.

17. Ibid., "Editorial Note," Revisal of the Laws, 1776–1786, pp. 318–20.

18. Although this amendment is not noted in Boyd, *The Papers of Thomas Jef-* *ferson*, pp. 555–56, the Act as adopted and reported in Hening, *The Statutes at Large*, p. 337, has the words "Sabbath day" where "Sunday" appears in Bill 84.

Why does this Madison-Jefferson legislative effort go unnoticed in *Everson*? Why is Madison's effort of 1785 in regard to the "Memorial and Remonstrance" mentioned over and over again in the U.S. Supreme Court decisions (and why moreover is it reproduced as an appendix) but no notice is given in the early precedent-setting decisions to this joint Madison-Jefferson venture regarding the state punishing "Sabbath Breakers"?[19] This is

19. Chief Justice Warren specifically mentions this Madison-Jefferson Bill in *McGowan* v. *Maryland* but confines his argument to the issue of Sunday Closing Laws instead of seeing the larger conflict between the Jefferson-Madison proposal about "Sabbath Breakers" and the beliefs attributed to them supporting absolute or nearly absolute separation of Church and State. Below is the relevant portion of Warren's opinion in *McGowan*:

This Court has considered the happenings surrounding the Virginia General Assembly's enactment of "An act for establishing religious freedom," 12 Hening's Statutes of Virginia 84, written by Thomas Jefferson and sponsored by James Madison, as best reflecting the long and intensive struggle for religious freedom in America, as particularly relevant in the search for the First Amendment's meaning. See the opinions in Everson v. Board of Education (US) supra. In 1776, nine years before the bill's passage, Madison co-authored Virginia's Declaration of Rights which provided, inter alia, that "all men are equally entitled to the free exercise of religion, according to the dictates of conscience...." 9 Hening's Statutes of Virginia 109, 111–112. Virginia had had Sunday legislation since early in the seventeenth century; in 1776, the laws penalizing "maintaining any opinions in matters of religion, *forbearing to repair to church*, or the exercising any mode of worship whatsoever" (emphasis added), were repealed, and all dissenters were freed from the taxes levied for the support of the established church. Id., at 164. *The Sunday labor prohibitions remained; apparently, they were not believed to be inconsistent with the newly enacted Declaration of Rights*. Madison had sought also to have the Declaration expressly con-

demn the existing Virginia establishment. This hope was finally realized when "A Bill for Establishing Religious Freedom" was passed in 1785. In this same year, Madison presented to Virginia legislators "A Bill for Punishing... Sabbath Breakers" which provided, in part:

"If any person on Sunday shall himself be found laboring at his own or any other trade or calling, or shall employ his apprentices, servants or slaves in labour, or other business, except it be in the ordinary household offices of daily necessity, or other work of necessity or charity, he shall forfeit the sum of ten shillings for every such offence, deeming every apprentice, servant, or slave so employed, and every day he shall be so employed as constituting a distinct offence."

This became law the following year and remained during the time that Madison fought for the First Amendment in the Congress. It was the law of Virginia, and similar laws were in force in other States, when Madison stated at the Virginia ratification convention:

"Happily for the states, they enjoy the utmost freedom of religion.... Fortunately for this commonwealth, a majority of the people are decidedly against any exclusive establishment. I believe it to be so in the other states.... I can appeal to my uniform conduct on this subject, that I have warmly supported religious freedom."

In 1799, Virginia pronounced "An act for establishing religious freedom" as "a true exposition of the principles of the bill of rights and constitution," and repealed all subsequently enacted legislation deemed inconsistent with it. 2 Shepherd, Statutes at Large of Virginia, 149. *Virginia's statute banning Sunday labor stood*. 366 U.S. 420, at 437–39. Emphasis added.

merely one example of the Court's "history by omission." Bill No. 84 of the *Revisal* of Virginia's Laws deserves some further consideration.

Unlike Chief Justice Warren's defense of "Sunday Closing Laws" as manifestations of social legislation reflecting government's protection of working people from exploiting entrepreneurs enticed by the principles of "laissez-faire" economics and "Social Darwinism," Bill No. 84 predates those concerns by more than 100 years. The title straightforwardly indicates that this legislation was designed to punish those who worked on the "Sabbath," which was originally identified in the third paragraph of the proposed law as "Sunday." The religious intent of this Bill was clearly reflected in the word "Sabbath" in the title and later, after amendment, in the text of the Act itself. This Bill became law in 1786 partly through the efforts of James Madison. It was not the outcome of political battles to lessen the burdens of the exploited worker as was social legislation limiting the number of working hours during the "Progressive Era" and afterward. This Madison-Jefferson Bill was state legislation to keep the "Sabbath" free of work.

The fact that this evidence as to what Madison and Jefferson in part thought about separation of Church and State does not appear in a U.S. Supreme Court decision until fourteen years after *Everson*[20]—and even then is not used to reappraise the Court's alleged subscription to an absolute, or nearly absolute, separation of Church and State—does not speak well for the U.S. Supreme Court's examination of American history at the time of *Everson* in 1947, an examination which it supposedly undertook to determine the prohibitions of the Establishment of Religion Clause. Nor does the Court's knowledge of this document, but failure to use it to reassess its views on Madison and Jefferson, speak well for its willingness to examine their questionable past judgments.

Perhaps an even more glaring act of historical omission in *Everson* involves Bill No. 85 of the *Revisal* and the subject of "Thanksgiving Day" proclamations. Justice Black footnotes Madison's "Detached Memorandum [sic]"[21] which had been published only a year before the *Everson* opinion.[22] As discussed in chapter two, in the "Memoranda", Madison indicated late in life that he thought "Religious proclamations by the Executive recommending Thanksgiving and fasts" were unconstitutional.[23] While the opinion of the Court in *Everson* notes research published only one year before its decision, no mention is made of Bill No. 85 of the *Revisal* pub-

---

20. Ibid.

21. 330 U.S. 1 (1947), at 12, fn. 12.

22. Elizabeth Fleet, "Madison's Detached Memoranda," 3 *William and Mary Quarterly*, 534 (1946). See the discussion about the "Detached Memoranda" in chap. two.

23. Fleet, "Madison's Detached Memoranda," p. 560.

lished more than one hundred and sixty years before the Supreme Court so broadly construed the Establishment Clause in the names of Madison, Jefferson, and its "Framers."

The *Revisal*'s Bill No. 85, "A Bill for Appointing Days of Public Fasting and Thanksgiving" was also presented in the Virginia Assembly by James Madison on October 31, 1785:

85. A Bill for Appointing Days of Public Fasting and Thanksgiving

Be it enacted by the General Assembly, that the power of appointing days of public fasting and humiliation, or thanksgiving, throughout this commonwealth, may in the recess of the General Assembly, be exercised by the Governor, or Chief Magistrate, with the advice of the Council; and such appointment shall be notified to the public, by a proclamation, in which the occasion of the fasting or thanksgiving shall be particularly set forth. Every minister of the gospel shall on each day so to be appointed, attend and perform divine service and preach a sermon, or discourse, suited to the occasion, in his church, *on pain of forfeiting fifty pounds for every failure, not having a reasonable excuse.*[24]

Bill No. 85 apparently did not become law but it was introduced by Madison; one manuscript copy indicates in the "Clerk's hand, endorsed by T.J.: 'A Bill Concerning Public Fasts.' "[25] Whether or not the Virginia Assembly adopted Bill No. 85 has no bearing on the Madison-Jefferson position on separation of Church and State. What is of significance is that James Madison sponsored Bill No. 85 and that the proposal may have had the endorsement of Thomas Jefferson, the *Revisal*'s chief architect.[26] Both the "Bill for . . . Punishing Sabbath Breakers" and the "Bill for . . . Public Fasting and Thanksgiving" were introduced by James Madison in the same year, 1785, and in the same forum as was his "Memorial and Remonstrance." It seems more than irony and evasion that those who argue that Madison and Jefferson stood for absolute or nearly absolute separation of Church and State based largely on little more than Madison's "Memorial"

---

24. Inasmuch as Bill No. 85 did not become law, it does not appear in Hening, *The Statutes at Large.* However, the text of the bill as presented here was available to the U.S. Supreme Court in 1947 (before the publication of Boyd, *The Papers of Thomas Jefferson*) at pp. 59–60 of the *Report of the Committee of Revisors Appointed by the*

General Assembly of Virginia in 1776 (Richmond: Printed by Dixon and Holt, 1784). Emphasis added.

25. Boyd, *The Papers of Thomas Jefferson*, p. 556.

26. *Journal of the House of Delegates of Virginia*, October 17, 1785–January 21, 1786 (Richmond: 1786), p. 11.

and Jefferson's "Bill for Religious Freedom," in the *Everson* opinions or independent scholarly works, do not explain or even note the glaring contradiction that stems from the historical evidence that James Madison— sponsoring what appear to be Jefferson's bills—introduced in the Virginia Assembly on October 31, 1785 not only Bill No. 82, "A Bill for Establishing Religious Freedom"[27] but also Bill No. 84, "A Bill for Punishing Disturbers of Religious Worship and Sabbath Breakers" and Bill No. 85, "A Bill for Appointing Days of Public Fasting and Thanksgiving."

Taken together these three bills of the Virginia *Revisal* and Madison's "Memorial" give a much clearer picture of what Madison and Jefferson believed about the relationship of Church and State in Virginia in 1785– 1786. They opposed a state church. They opposed financing the teachers of one religious tradition with tax dollars. They subscribed to no tradition of absolute separation of Church and State, unless using state authority to punish "Sabbath breakers" and proclaiming "Thanksgiving days" do not violate that concept. The thesis advanced throughout this book has no difficulty with any of Mr. Madison's behavior in the Virginia Assembly in October 1785 or 1786. Justice Black's *Everson* opinion and all the U.S. Supreme Court decisions that invoke it, or the more absolute Rutledge-Pfeffer thesis cannot be easily reconciled with the *totality* of Madison's actions in 1785 concerning the relationship between religion and the state's power. As for Madison's inconsistency in the "Detached Memoranda," that document is given the insignificant historical note it deserves by Justice Brennan, who, oddly enough, comes as close to being a subscriber to the Rutledge-Pfeffer thesis as anyone on the present U.S. Supreme Court.[28]

The selective history used by the Court in almost all Establishment Clause cases rarely includes any mention or explanation of most of the documents discussed in chapters one, two, three, five and six. Occasionally the Supreme Court makes minor reference to some of these documents but there is little attempt to deal systematically with as much of the historical picture as a scholarly examination of the Establishment Clause should. Perhaps realizing that American history carefully explored would not support the Court's position, Justice Jackson in 1948, one year after *Everson*, expressed the thought that even the search for the meaning of the Establishment Clause in the *Constitution* or "other legal source[s]" was futile.

In his concurring opinion in the "*McCollum* Released Time" Case,[29]

---

27. Ibid.
28. For Justice Brennan's comment about Madison's "Detached Memoranda,"

see chap. seven, fn. 97.
29. 333 U.S. 203 (1948).

Justice Jackson observed: "It is idle to pretend that this task is one for which we can find in the Constitution one word to help us as judges to decide where the secular ends and the sectarian begins in education. *Nor can we find guidance in any other legal source.* It is a matter on which *we can find no law* but our own prepossessions."[30]

I strongly disagree with Justice Jackson's assessment. The U.S. Supreme Court in *McCollum* had, and still has, legal sources available to it that could have been used in 1948 or that can be used today as guidelines for permissible governmental involvement in sectarian-affiliated educational institutions under the Establishment Clause. These legal guidelines are available not only in the field of education but in many other areas of Church-State relations under the First and Fourteenth Amendment. Now, as in 1948, all that the U.S. Supreme Court needs to do is to embrace these legal guidelines in interpreting the prohibitions of the Establishment Clause in the same manner used by the Court to ascertain the prohibitions of the "Free Speech Guarantee" Clause which is also in the First Amendment and like the Establishment Clause is equally binding on the States through the Fourteenth Amendment.

Legal scholarship defining the First Amendment admonition that "Congress shall make no law . . . abridging the freedom of speech" has long recognized that the speech protected by that Amendment does not encompass "verbal crimes." In short, not all verbal communication is constitutionally protected speech.[31] Reflecting this concept, the U.S. Supreme Court has used the historical "common law" and some of the existing written laws, which defined certain verbal crimes at the time the First Amendment speech protections were drawn up and added to the *Constitution*, as legal guidelines as to what was not constitutionally protected speech. In a 1942 case, *Chaplinsky* v. *New Hampshire*,[32] Justice Jackson was a member of the U.S. Supreme Court that unanimously took careful judicial note of the nonabsolute nature of the First Amendment prohibition that "Congress shall make no law . . . abridging the freedom of speech. . . ." Speaking for the Court, Justice Murphy wrote:

> Allowing the broadest scope to the language and purpose of the Fourteenth Amendment, it is well understood that the right of free speech is not absolute at all times and under all circumstances. *There are certain well-defined and narrowly limited classes of speech, the prevention and*

---

30. Ibid., at 237–38. Emphasis added.

31. See "The Normal Criminal Law of Words" in Zechariah Chafee, Jr., *Free Speech in the United States* (New York: Atheneum, 1969), p. 149 (originally published by Harvard University Press in 1941).

32. 315 U.S. 568 (1942).

punishment of which have never been thought to raise any Constitutional problem. These include the lewd and obscene, the profane, the libelous, and the insulting or "fighting" words—those which by their very utterance inflict injury or tend to incite an immediate breach of the peace. . . .[33]

If historical analysis can yield certain classifications of speech not intended to be protected by the First Amendment, why cannot a similar historical search cast light on the kinds of Church-State relationships that were not "thought to raise any Constitutional problem"? Instead of following its "own prepossessions" in declaring what kind of governmental behavior is precluded by the Establishment Clause, the Court, as with the "Speech" Clause, could ascertain the Establishment Clause's prohibitions from the ample historical public behavior and the opinion of the Framers of the First Amendment and the early Presidents and Congresses that were guided by it.

Historical documents and the public record lend little support to most of Justice Black's interpretation of the Establishment Clause in the *Everson* Case and virtually none to the Rutledge-Pfeffer thesis of absolute separation of Church and State. Indeed most justices on the Court have followed their "own preposessions" in interpreting the Establishment Clause, but not because of the paucity of "legal sources," as Justice Jackson declared. They have ignored the historical legal sources, with the exception of a few select documents, so that they can continue to decide Establishment Clause cases in harmony with the *Everson* decision and the many cases which follow it. All of the Establishment Clause cases ought to be examined anew by a U.S. Supreme Court willing to scrutinize for the first time, the full history of that Clause's prohibitions. It is time for the Supreme Court to discontinue promulgating a distorted version of American history brought into being, and carefully maintained, by the selection and omission of primary historical sources.

Now a more responsible U.S. Supreme Court needs to specify by more than mere repeated affirmation what historical traditions and policies dictate its Establishment Clause decisions. It should not be enough for fairminded constitutional scholars on the Court or in different capacities as they peruse the historical documents relevant to the American constitutional doctrine of separation of Church and State to be told by the Chief Justice of the United States speaking for the Court that "[w]e have no long history of state aid to church-related educational institutions. . . . "[34] If

33. Ibid., at 571–72. Emphasis added.
34. *Lemon* v. *Kurtzman*, 403 U.S. 622, at 626 (1971).

Chief Justice Burger and other members of the U.S. Supreme Court believe that, then let them explain the land grant trusts by the Federal Government during the Washington, Adams, and Jefferson Administrations to a religious society dedicated to propagating the Gospel among the Indians.[35] Let the Supreme Court explain the hundreds of thousands of dollars provided by the U.S. Government to civilize the Indians by direct aid to church schools during the early administrations of the Federal Republic.[36] Public acceptance of Chief Justice Burger's statement and the Court's constitutional invalidation of public aid by the several States in the form of tuition tax credits or tuition reimbursement to parents who send their children to private sectarian or parochial schools would be served,[37] if the Court would explain why all of the above aids to religious education and schools were not considered Establishment Clause violations to those who framed the First Amendment, but are considered unconstitutional today. Let the Supreme Court also explain why millions of dollars—technically belonging to the Indians but *in fact* controlled by the laws of the United States and U.S. officials certainly under the control of the First Amendment—could be constitutionally spent for Indian education at religious schools until a congressional decision, *not* a constitutional command, changed that policy in the last decade of the nineteenth century.[38]

In fact, there has not only been a long historical tradition of state aid to religious education as a method of reaching constitutional secular goals—the pacification of the Indians and the formal education of the public—but other sectarian means have also been used to reach constitutionally valid state ends. Building churches by treaty commitments to enlarge the property of the United States is an additional example, as is the issuance of Thanksgiving religious proclamations, even by President James Madison, to unify a troubled people. Subsidy to religious organizations, which may work for the common good, through tax exemption is not uncommon in the United States and was legislated by Congress in 1802 and even signed into law by President Thomas Jefferson.[39]

---

35. See chap. two, "The Quest for Mr. Jefferson."

36. See chap. three, "Direct Federal Support of Religion by Treaties" and "Civilization of the Indians: Federal Money to Support Religious Schools and Religious Teaching."

37. *Committee for Public Education* v. *Nyquist*, 413 U.S. 756 (1973); *Sloan* v. *Lemon*, 413 U.S. 825 (1973); and *Byrne* v. *Public Funds for Public Schools of New Jersey*, 590 F2d 514, Affirmed 61 L. Ed 2d 1 (1979).

38. See the text in chap. five at fns. 118–26.

39. "An Act additional to, and amendatory of, an act, intituted [sic] 'An Act Concerning the District of Columbia'," 2 *Statutes at Large* 194, Seventh Congress, Sess. 1, Chap. 52.

Sectarian means were definitely used to reach constitutional secular ends. There is little historical support for the theory that all sectarian means to reach a constitutional end were prohibited by the First Amendment. What can be historically established is that those who framed the First Amendment did not want the use of *unconstitutional* sectarian means to reach valid secular ends. Unconstitutional sectarian means today would be means which would put one particular religion, religious sect, or religious tradition into a constitutionally forbidden preferred legal position.[40]

In sum, as to the various interpretations that the U.S. Supreme Court—and the lower courts that have followed its decisions—has given to the Establishment Clause since the precedent case of *Everson* in 1947, I must conclude that the Court has never logically, carefully, or fully considered all the available historical evidence and consequently has, for the most part, erred in its definition and application of the American constitutional doctrine of separation of Church and State.

Another inquiry ought to be raised about my interpretation of the Establishment Clause. If the Establishment Clause was historically intended to prohibit constitutionally what I declare, then why haven't many constitutional scholars embraced the interpretation of it as put forth here? As indicated in chapter one, in the nineteenth century the distinguished constitutional scholars Justice Joseph Story[41] and Thomas Cooley[42] did support the narrow interpretation of the Establishment Clause defended here. In the twentieth century some scholarly writings on this issue have also supported the narrow thesis endorsed here,[43] but more have followed the lead of Leo Pfeffer and have subscribed to a nearly absolute interpretation of the constitutional separation of Church and State. Part of the reason why the Rutledge-Pfeffer thesis is more universally accepted is that the U.S. Supreme Court has at times invoked Rutledge's *Everson* opinion and has cited Pfeffer's scholarship. Probably a more important reason for the accep-

---

40. An example of using *unconstitutional sectarian* means to reach a valid public end is evident in the public school "Bible Reading" Cases. It would probably be generally agreed that societal morality may be encouraged or taught by the States in schools as a valid public end, but this study of the Establishment Clause leads me to the conclusion that this secular goal may not be constitutionally accomplished in such a way as to officially sanction the use of the sectarian writings of only one religious tradition in a highly heterogeneous religious society. See chapter six, "The 'Lord's Prayer' and Bible Reading Cases."

41. See the text in chap. one at fn. 41.

42. Ibid., fn. 42.

43. Edward S. Corwin, "The Supreme Court as a National School Board," 14 *Law and Contemporary Problems* 3 (1949), and James M. O'Neill, *Religion and Education Under the Constitution* (New York: Harper, 1949). O'Neill's book was reprinted without change in 1972 by Da Capo Press.

tance of the Rutledge-Pfeffer thesis is that scholars frequently consult each others' secondary source books instead of examining the primary sources. Thus, once a reputation for scholarship in a given area is earned or acknowledged—as is Pfeffer's in the constitutional area of Church and State—others writing major secondary sources involving an enormous range of topics frequently rely on the secondary source works of such scholars and thus perpetuate their interpretation of the primary sources. A recent example perpetuating the "accepted scholarly interpretation" of the Establishment Clause appears in the *Congressional Quarterly's Guide to the U.S. Supreme Court*.[44]

Published in 1979 and given excellent reviews by many distinguished lawyers and constitutional scholars, the *Guide* presents in its opening discussion of "Establishment of Religion"[45] the following paragraph:

> The two men most responsible for its [the Establishment Clause] inclusion in the Bill of Rights construed the clause *absolutely*. Thomas Jefferson and James Madison thought that the prohibition of establishment meant that a presidential proclamation of Thanksgiving Day was just as improper as a tax exemption for churches.[51,46]

Inasmuch as I assume that whoever wrote this paragraph did not intend to deceive, I must conclude that the author did not check primary sources and did not know that President James Madison issued at least four Thanksgiving Day Proclamations.[47] This error raises at least two important questions: First, what would someone who knew nothing about Madison or his proclamations believe about President Madison's view of the Establishment Clause on Thanksgiving Proclamations from merely reading this overall valuable secondary source book? Second, how could anyone represent President Thomas Jefferson as believing that church tax exemptions were unconstitutional under the First Amendment when he signed the Congressional Act of 1802 providing tax exemption for churches in Alexandria County?[48] Justice Brennan's concurring opinion in the *Walz* "Tax Exemption" Case, with historical accuracy, clearly shows this assertion about Jefferson's and Madison's view of church tax-exemption in the *Guide to the U.S. Supreme Court* statement to be incorrect.[49] Never-

---

44. *Congressional Quarterly's Guide to the U.S. Supreme Court* (Washington, D.C.: Congressional Quarterly, Inc., 1979).

45. Ibid., p. 461.

46. Ibid., fn. included. Emphasis added.

47. See chap. two for Madison's 1815 Thanksgiving Day Proclamation in the text at fn. 63.

48. See fn. 39, supra.

49. See the Brennan statement at the text of fn. 95 in chap. seven.

theless many will continue to consult this paragraph and no doubt will consider it to be both authoritative and correct.

The authors of the *Congressional Quarterly Guide* relied on an established and distinguished constitutional expert in writing the paragraph, quoted above, about Jefferson and Madison. Footnote 51 on page 470 of the *Guide* refers to C. Herman Pritchett's, *The American Constitution*, third edition, published in 1977.[50] In this most recent edition of *The American Constitution*, Pritchett wrote the following about Madison's and Jefferson's tenure as President:

> During their terms as President, moreover, both Jefferson and Madison took very strict positions on establishment. Both believed that presidential proclamations of Thanksgiving Day were contrary to the Constitution. They also regarded as unconstitutional tax exemptions for churches, payment from government funds to chaplains in Congress and the armed services and nonpreferential land grants for the support of churches. . . .[51]

This statement not only reflects the historical errors commented on in the *Guide to the U.S. Supreme Court*, but it also fails to explain why Jefferson would allow U.S. land grants, in trust, to the United Brethren dedicated to propagating the Gospel among the Indians if he considered all land grants for the support of churches to be unconstitutional.[52]

Inasmuch as Pritchett's statement does not inform the reader that Madison was a member of the Committee that recommended the establishment of the chaplain system in Congress when he was in the First House of Representatives, which framed the First Amendment, the reader probably will assume that Madison opposed chaplains in the Congress. Of course, that is not true. Further, Pritchett cites no validating sources for this paragraph and consequently the reader cannot examine the supportive evidence for his statement about Madison's views on chaplains when he was President. While it has already been indicated here that Jefferson did not

---

50. Pritchett's *The American Constitution*, 3rd ed. (New York: McGraw-Hill, 1977) was first published in 1959 when he was Professor of Political Science at the University of Chicago. Pritchett's published works in the field of American Constitutional Law are many and highly respected. Among his books are *Civil Liberties and the Vinson Court* (Chicago: University of Chicago Press, 1954); *The Political Offender and the Warren Court* (Boston: Boston University Press, 1958); *The Roosevelt Court: A Study in Judicial Politics and Values, 1937–1947* (New York: The Macmillan Company, 1948); and *Congress versus the Supreme Court: 1957–1960* (Minneapolis: The University of Minnesota Press, 1961).

51. Pritchett, *The American Constitution*, pp. 401–2.

52. See the text in chap. two at fns. 87–108.

think Thanksgiving Day Proclamations were constitutional when he was President—and he declined to issue them—Pritchett says nothing about the States' Rights issue that Jefferson raised about those proclamations.[53]

Thus, without citing one primary historical source, Pritchett has perpetuated the most currently accepted views attributed to Presidents Jefferson and Madison, some of which are clearly inaccurate as shown by several of the primary historical documents presented in this study. While Madison may have embraced many of the views that Pritchett mentions, most of them are attributed to Madison clearly because of the content of the "Detached Memorandum [sic]" written *after Madison left the Presidency and public life*. As already argued in this study,[54] and even by Justice Brennan,[55] the "Detached Memoranda" is certainly not a valid basis on which to judge what Madison believed, either when he was President or in his earlier active public life.

As with the U.S. Supreme Court, some scholars of the *Constitution* have also relied on too few and often quoted selected historical documents to attribute to Jefferson, Madison, and the Establishment Clause an absolute concept of separation of Church and State. Consider the following statement in *The American Constitution*:

> Jefferson and Madison were the dominant figures in developing the constitutional policy on establishment, and *they both espoused strict separation of church and state*. A bill providing for tax support of religion had been presented to the Virginia Legislature in 1784. Those who professed no religion were permitted by the bill to direct that their tax be used for general educational purposes. Madison attacked the bill in his famous "Memorial and Remonstrance against Religious Assessments," which was so persuasive that the bill was not even presented in the 1785 session. Instead, Jefferson's Act for Establishing Religious Freedom was passed by the Virginia Legislature.[56]

How can Jefferson and Madison have espoused "strict separation of church and state" when, in 1785, Madison, acting largely as a surrogate for Jefferson, introduced the "Sabbath Breaking Bill" and the "Bill for Appointing Days of Public Fasting and Thanksgiving" discussed above? It seems certain that while both men believed in separation of Church and State, they could not have honestly and consistently subscribed to the abso-

---

53. See the text in chap. two at fns. 83–85.

54. See the discussion of Madison's "Detached Memoranda" in chap. two.

55. See chap. seven, fn. 97.

56. Pritchett, *The American Constitution*, p. 401. Emphasis added.

lute separation commonly attributed to them today in most U.S. Supreme Court decisions and in many secondary source books of competent and respected American constitutional scholars.

This study of the Establishment Clause will more than justify the labors that produced it, if because of academic values and scholarly fairness it generates a more complete and accurate dialogue concerning the meaning of the American constitutional doctrine of separation of Church and State. Scholarship may inadvertently contain errors, but errors discovered cannot be properly clothed with the mantle of integrity endemic to a true scholarly dialogue. The contradictions that exist between what prevailing American constitutional scholars have attributed to Madison, the Framers of the First Amendment, Thomas Jefferson, and those who took part in making the Establishment Clause part of the U.S. *Constitution* on the one hand, and the contrary interpretations—which are supported by primary historical sources—presented here on the other hand, should be carefully and fully scrutinized. This study, it is hoped, will be part of that process.

The arguments, primary historical documents, undisputed historical facts and the interpretations here clearly show that an *absolute* separation of Church and State was not contemplated or intended either by the Framers of the First Amendment, or by those who were responsible for its addition to the *Constitution*. Nor does the early history of the Republic under the Federal *Constitution* even support the theory that the First Amendment mandated a "strict" separation of Church and State or the complete independence of religion and the state. Not until 1947 did the U.S. Supreme Court advance an opinion even approaching such an interpretation of the prohibitions of the Establishment Clause. As Justice Douglas has written, "we are a religious people" and moral values frequently expressed in religious terms have permeated United States documents as unique as the Declaration of Independence or as commonplace as "In God We Trust" on the one dollar bill. Nevertheless, those who built the foundations of the American constitutional system did subscribe to the separation of Church and State, so much so that they placed the twofold religious guarantees into the *Constitution* "with all deliberate speed."

Historically it is clear that the Framers of our constitutional system did not subscribe to the doctrine of separation of Church and State as most of the U.S. Supreme Court—and other like-minded federal and state courts—decisions since 1947 have defined it. Even the public actions of such important American statesmen who led the Virginia fight for the disestablishment of religion such as Thomas Jefferson and James Madison in their vital political years cannot be comfortably reconciled with an "absolute" concept of separation of Church and State exemplified by what I have termed here the Rutledge-Pfeffer thesis. While my position concerning the meaning of the Establishment Clause is not entirely free of historical difficulty,[57] when the primary documents are disinterestedly examined, my conviction is that the interpretation detailed here most comfortably fits the historical facts—even to the public actions and public opinions of Thomas Jefferson and James Madison.

Not only is it clear historically that separation of Church and State had a different meaning for the Founding Fathers of the First Amendment than it has had for most justices of the U.S. Supreme Court since 1947, it is also clear that the kind of separation now urged by the Court never existed under the First Amendment because it was never intended. Justice Douglas—a late subscriber to Justice Rutledge's absolute philosophy, which he endorsed in the "*Engel* New York State Regents' Prayer" Case—in 1962 described "[o]ur system [of government] at the federal and state levels" as "honeycombed" with what he considered to be unconstitutional public financed religious exercises.[58] Douglas attributed some of those unconstitutional practices to the "very First Congress which wrote the First Amendment."[59] Apparently, as I have written, those who framed the First Amendment either had a different view of separation of Church and State than did Justices Rutledge or Douglas, or else they sought to enshrine principles concerning a complete independence of religion and government in the *Constitution* one day and violated them another. Inasmuch as a good deal of this study has been largely centered on what the history of the Republic can tell us about the meaning of the First Amendment's prohibition that "Congress shall make no law respecting an establishment of religion. . . . ," the importance of the historical connection should be reviewed once more.

In all the major Establishment Clause cases since 1947, the U.S. Supreme Court has sought to justify its "Church and State" decisions with appeals to American history. "What does the historical intent behind the Establishment Clause require us to rule in this case?" seems to be the unuttered question always to be answered by the Court's opinion. In short, the Court in these cases has invariably indicated either subtlely or blatantly

---

57. For me, the clearest problems of my thesis concern some of James Madison's statements. Specifically, Madison's "Detached Memoranda" runs contrary to my thesis as well as to most of Madison's official documented actions before leaving the Presidency.

A more significant Madison problem is his veto message of February 28, 1811, in the text of chap. two at fn. 62. However, as already mentioned and as noted by Justice Brennan (chap. seven, fn. 97), Madison alone did not add the Establishment Clause to the *Constitution*.

58. *Engel* v. *Vitale*, 370 U.S. 421, at 437.

59. Ibid., fn. 1.

that the command of the Framers of the First Amendment has required its particular decision as it reviewed questions of alleged unconstitutional aids to church or religion. American history and the actions of Jefferson and Madison have been the predominant reasons offered by the Court for its decisions as to what the *Constitution* will abide in the relationship between government and religion. Simply put, the Court has used American history to legitimize its decisions. "Thus saith American history" has been the Court's most common approach. Should American history and the historical reading of the Establishment Clause be other than that which the Court proclaims it to be, however, that judicial tribunal will be making the law, not applying it. If the historical justifications that the Court offers for its decisions in Establishment Clause cases are factually erroneous—as I believe I have shown here—the U.S. Supreme Court decisions contain conclusions but are devoid of any acceptable reasons for them. Even the highest court in the land must face the reality that in a constitutional system, its power, like the power of elected political bodies, must be exercised within the constraints of the constitutional division of authority.

If the modern concept of constitutional government in western political thought means anything, it stands for the principle of government limited by law.[60] Although I am in full accord with Chief Justice John Marshall's admonition in 1803 that: "It is emphatically, the province and duty of the judicial department, to say what the law is," I am equally convinced that in a democratic constitutional system, the judicial department has no legitimate authority to say what the law should be. The step may be seen as a small one but the Court must be careful not to take it. To say what the law should be is emphatically the province and duty of the politically elected branches of government in a constitutional democracy, unless and only unless, they clearly trespass into areas of decision making genuinely denied them. The Supreme Court would do well to rethink the words of Justice James Iredell recorded at the end of the eighteenth century, when our *Constitution* had most recently been established.[61] Concerning the great power that a court exercises in our constitutional system, Iredell, acknowledging that while legislatures, whether national or state, sometimes move beyond the boundaries of their rightful authority, emphasized that the judicial power in its ultimate form must never be exercised lightly. Exhorting the principle of judicial self-restraint, Justice Iredell wrote: "If any act of Congress, or of the legislature of a state violates . . . constitutional provisions, it is unques-

60. Charles H. McIlwain, *Constitutionalism: Ancient and Modern*, rev. ed. (Ithaca, N.Y.: Great Seal Books, 1958), pp. 19–22.

61. *Calder* v. *Bull*, 3 U.S. (Dallas) 386 (1798).

tionably void; though, I admit, the court will never resort to that authority, but in a clear and urgent case. . . ."[62]

In light of the history of the Establishment Clause and its early application at the beginning of the Republic, almost all the laws nullified in the Establishment Clause cases since 1947 can hardly be said to clearly violate any section of the First Amendment. From the historical examination here, there is a paucity of historical evidence to substantiate that most of the laws regarding incidental public aid to religion—invalidated since 1947 as violative of the First and Fourteenth Amendments—have been laws respecting an establishment of religion within the historically accurate constitutional meaning of that term. Consequently, I must conclude, that for want of valid historical reasons and without any other valid reasons offered by the Court for declaring those laws unconstitutional, the constitutionally elected political branches of government—the executive and the legislatures of the nation and its fifty states—have not, by enactment of most of the laws attacked under the Establishment Clause since 1947, ventured into policy-making areas clearly and genuinely denied them by the *Constitution*.

If the narrower interpretation of the Establishment Clause's prohibitions developed here is more easily reconciled with American historical fact than are the currently more accepted absolute or near absolute requirements of separation of Church and State attributed to the First Amendment, other, and more important, ramifications than simply what is "God's" and what is "Caesar's" need to be considered. Also involved in the "separation of Church and State controversy" are the very principles of democratic public decision making in the American constitutional system.

Justice Brennan in his concurring opinion in the "Bible Reading" and "Lord's Prayer" cases[63] suggests another basis for validating the Court's judgments in some Establishment Clause cases. Although in those cases Justice Brennan joined "fully in the opinion and judgment of the Court,"[64] he departs in a section of his opinion from the usual complete reliance on American history that characterizes almost all of the separation of Church and State case opinions. Reminding his reader of Chief Justice John Marshall's famous admonition that "we must never forget, that it is a *Constitution* we are expounding,"[65] Justice Brennan uses this phrase—as it has

---

62. Ibid., at 398.

63. *Murray* v. *Curlett*, 374 U.S. 203 (1963) and *Abington* v. *Schempp*, 374 U.S. 203 (1963). For a discussion of these cases, see chap. six, "The 'Lord's Prayer' and Bible Reading Cases." The facts of these cases are

discussed separately in the text of chap. six at fns. 15–24.

64. Brennan's concurring opinion begins at 374 U.S. 230. Id. at 231.

65. Ibid., at 230. Emphasis in the original.

been occasionally employed for more than a century and a half—to introduce ideas that seem important to contemporary society but that are difficult to support historically as mandated by the *Constitution* or by those who made it the Supreme Law of the Land.

Pursuing his course, Justice Brennan not only seems to stray from the Court's usual "thus saith the history of the First Amendment" approach, but candidly admits that the Framers of that Amendment probably did not even think about whether or not the public school activities, declared unconstitutional under the First Amendment in these cases, would violate it. Consider the following section from Justice Brennan's opinion:

> A too literal quest for the advice of the Founding Fathers upon the issues of these cases seems to me futile and misdirected for several reasons: *First, on our precise problem the historical record is at best ambiguous, and statements can readily be found to support either side of the proposition.* The ambiguity of history is understandable if we recall the nature of the problems uppermost in the thinking of the statesmen who fashioned the religious guarantees; they were concerned with far more flagrant intrusions of government into the realm of religion than any that our century has witnessed. While it is clear to me that the Framers meant the Establishment Clause to prohibit more than the creation of an established federal church such as existed in England, *I have no doubt that, in their preoccupation with the imminent question of established churches, they gave no distinct consideration to the particular question whether the clause also forbade devotional exercises in public institutions.*[66]

On this matter of historical guidance from the Founding Fathers, the Brennan opinion turns out to be somewhat contradictory. In the last analysis the history of the Establishment Clause loses its ambiguity for Brennan when he later writes in this same opinion that the actions of the Court in these cases—and further the general principles which the Court has followed in all the Establishment Clause cases—are in faithful accordance with the intentions of the "Founding Fathers." Here is Justice Brennan returning to the "historical fold":

66. Ibid., at 237–38. Emphasis added. Although the Founding Fathers may not have considered the precise religious practices in these cases, unlike Justice Brennan, I am of the opinion that the principles embodied in the Establishment Clause are not so ambiguous historically as to preclude their application to the facts of the *Abington* and *Murray* cases when I conclude above that the particular religious exercises challenged in those cases violate the First and Fourteenth Amendment. See fn. 63, supra.

Specifically, I believe that the line we must draw between the permissible and the impermissible *is one which accords with history and faithfully reflects the understanding of the Founding Fathers*. It is a line which the Court has consistently sought to mark in its decisions expounding the religious guarantees of the First Amendment. *What the Framers meant to foreclose*, and what our decisions under the Establishment Clause have forbidden, are those involvements of religious with secular institutions which (a) serve the essentially religious activities of religious institutions; (b) employ the organs of government for essentially religious purposes; or (c) use essentially religious means to serve governmental ends, where secular means would suffice. When the secular and religious institutions become involved in such a manner, there inhere in the relationship precisely those dangers—as much to church as to state—*which the Framers feared would subvert religious liberty and the strength of a system of secular government* . . . .[67]

Whether Justice Brennan saw the history of the Establishment Clause clearly or not is of less significance here than what appears to be his candid willingness in at least some portions of his opinion to indicate that the Court must be free to improvise what is best for present-day American society if the historical picture is unclear or irrelevant to our contemporary societal needs as a majority of the Supreme Court sees them. But therein lies the danger for decision making in a democratic society.

In another day, Justice Frankfurter spoke to this same concern with an entirely different view of judicial obligation. "As a member of this Court," wrote Frankfurter, "I am not justified in writing my private notions of policy into the Constitution, no matter how deeply I may cherish them or how mischievous I may deem their disregard. . . . It can never be emphasized too much that one's own opinion about the wisdom or evil or a law should be *excluded altogether* when one is doing one's duty on the bench."[68]

A dozen years later (see chapter seven) in *Meek* v. *Pettinger*,[69] Justice Brennan carried his nonhistorical justification for nullifying alleged aid to sectarian institutions even further by declaring that any program aiding those institutions that had the character of "divisive political potential" would violate the Establishment Clause.[70] As alluded to earlier, this approach by the Court or any member of the Court has grave ramifications for the decision-making process in a democratic constitutional system.

---

67. Ibid., at 294–95. Emphasis added.

68. Frankfurter dissenting, in *West Virginia Board of Education* v. *Barnette*, 319 U.S. 624, at 647 (1943). Emphasis added.

69. 421 U.S. 349 (1975).

70. See the discussion in chap. seven at fns. 158–60.

In the previous chapter, it was established that Justice Brennan, joined by Justices Douglas and Marshall, wanted to make the "potential for political divisiveness in the community" an additional fourth criterion—to be added to the three-criteria test which had been accepted by the Court in *Lemon* I[71]—for determining whether an alleged aid to sectarian schools was constitutional.[72] However much the opinion of the Court by Chief Justice Burger discussed the issue of political divisiveness, it is clear that the test used by the Court to evaluate the alleged sectarian aid statutes in that case did not declare or embrace Brennan's fourth criterion.[73] Nevertheless, Justice Brennan makes good use of a lengthy statement in the Court's opinion in *Lemon* I to justify his political divisiveness criterion.[74] Here is the *obiter dicta* from Burger's opinion in *Lemon* I used as the basis for Justice Brennan's fourth criterion, which Brennan developed in his concurring opinion in *Meek*:

A broader base of entanglement of yet a different character is presented by the divisive political potential of these state programs. In a community where such a large number of pupils are served by church-related schools, it can be assumed that state assistance will entail considerable political activity. Partisans of parochial schools, understandably concerned with rising costs and sincerely dedicated to both the religious and secular educational missions of their schools, will inevitably champion this cause and promote political action to achieve their goals. Those who oppose state aid, whether for constitutional, religious, or fiscal reasons, will inevitably respond and employ all of the usual political campaign techniques to prevail. Candidates will be forced to declare and voters to choose. It would be unrealistic to ignore the fact that many people confronted with issues of this kind will find their votes aligned with their faith.

Ordinarily political debate and division, however vigorous or even partisan, are normal and healthy manifestations of our democratic system of government, but political division along religious lines was one of the principal evils against which the First Amendment was intended to protect. Freund, Comment: Public Aid to Parochial Schools, 82 Harv. L. Rev. 1680, 1692 (1969). The potential divisiveness of such conflict is a threat to the normal political process . . . . To have States or communities divide on the issues presented by state aid to parochial schools would tend to confuse and obscure other issues of great urgency. We have an expanding array of vexing issues, local and national, domestic

---

71. See the text in chap. seven at fn. 134.
72. See fn. 70, supra.
73. The test used by the Court is explained and noted at 403 U.S. 602, at 612–13.
74. 421 U.S. 349, at 374–75.

and international, to debate and divide on. It conflicts with our whole history and tradition to permit questions of the Religion Clauses to assume such importance in our legislatures and in our elections that they could divert attention from the myriad issues and problems which confront every level of government. . . .[75]

What is of enormous importance about Brennan's additional criterion and the Burger *obiter dicta* in *Lemon* I is that members of the Court are advancing the notion that their assessment of the political climate in a community will play a part—perhaps a decisive part—in determining whether a law is constitutional or not. Do the prohibitions of the Establishment of Religion Clause expand and contract to coincide with the Court's reading of the political mood of a community?

In a democratic society *value judgments* regarding the welfare of the community rest with the popularly elected branches of government. Difficult as it may be to confine them, an axiom of constitutional government is that courts, too, are under the law.[76] A judgment by the courts that a certain policy is "politically divisive" or, still more removed, has "divisive political *potential*" is not within the area of judicial competence. If there is no clear constitutional barrier for the enactment of any given legislative program, fear of unhealthy societal ramifications resulting from that program is not a proper basis for a judicial veto. "The Judicial cannot prescribe to the Legislative Departments of the Government limitations upon the exercise of its acknowledged powers."[77] While Chief Justice Marshall did recognize that some flexibility had to reside with the judiciary when they were "expounding" a constitution, he also recognized that where discretionary political power is constitutionally vested in a political branch of government, the accountability for the acts taken are in the political not the judicial process.[78]

At issue here is more than a nonhistorical criterion advanced by some of the members of the U.S. Supreme Court to justify invoking the ban of the Establishment Clause against alleged aid to religion. What is involved is the very bedrock issue of how important policy questions are raised and resolved in a democratic constitutional society. Where are politically divi-

---

75. 403 U.S. 602, at 622–23.

76. Raoul Berger, "Constitutionalism and the Rule of Law," *Government By Judiciary* (Cambridge, Mass.: Harvard University Press, 1977), pp. 288–99.

77. Justice Holmes approvingly quoting from *Veazie Bank* v. *Fenno*, 8 Wall. 533 (1869), in his dissent in *Hammer* v. *Dagenhart*, 247 U.S. 251 (1918).

78. *Marbury* v. *Madison*, 5 U.S. (1 Cranch) 137, at 165–66 (1803).

sive issues to be addressed more effectively than in the political forum? Can anyone pretend that a Supreme Court decision will truly preempt the right of the people to debate the most heated societal issues? Have U.S. Supreme Court decisions settled the divisive issues of sexual equality, racial equality, what constitutes pornography, and whether abortion should be a woman's prerogative or the State's concern for "unborn children"? And even if Supreme Court decisions could save American Society from the vigorous exchange of passions and ideas on these perplexing questions, is that or should that be the way major socio-political problems get decided in a democracy?

If Jefferson and Madison had been preempted from the issue of Church and State in their day, we might not have Madison's eloquent "Memorial and Remonstrance" against a *discriminatory* religious assessment. And perhaps a court would have disestablished the Anglican-Episcopal Church relieving Thomas Jefferson and his compatriots of the decade-long fight to disestablish the Virginia Church through the political process risking the divisiveness that important issues tend to cause decision makers and those who live in an "open society" free of fear about ideas and strongly held differences.

Whatever else may be said about judicial preemption of potentially divisive societal issues, there is certainly little evidence that that approach to problem solving has dissipated serious national problems. The decisions of the U.S. Supreme Court have not stopped the political dialogue and divisiveness about federal and/or state tax credits for parents who send their children to parochial schools. Nor have those decisions made it more likely that public school budgets will be passed in school districts where many children go to sectarian schools. Instead the "absolute separationist" position has caused a casualty in the union movement when the United States Circuit Court of Appeals for the Seventh Federal Circuit declared that lay teachers in church schools could not organize under the National Labor Relations Act. If the Act was construed to reach sectarian schools, the Court held, it would violate the Religion Clauses of the First Amendment.[79]

Further, even if judicial preemption of potentially divisive political issues could be reconciled with the decision-making process of a politically

---

79. *National Labor Relations Board* v. *The Catholic Bishop of Chicago*, 559 F2d 1112 (1977). Subsequently the U.S. Supreme Court in a 5–4 opinion written by Chief Justice Burger sustained the U.S. Circuit Court's decision on statutory grounds. Burger's opinion for the Court held that Congress had not intended that teachers in religious schools be included in the unionization coverage of the National Labor Relations Act. 440 U.S. 490; 59 L. Ed. 2d. 533, at 545 (1979).

"open society," there is little evidence that such preemption will diffuse the potential divisiveness inherent in sensitive societal problems. Indeed, the last decade in the United States seems to illustrate the converse in the area of race relations, pornography, abortion, and aid to children who attend church-affiliated schools. In a democratic constitutional system courts are at best the decison makers of last resort. But that can be the case only if they are not perceived as political bodies prematurely involved in day-to-day decisions that the *Constitution* has vested with the political branches of government. To be sure, when basic rights guaranteed in the *Constitution* are clearly violated and redress cannot be secured in the political process, as with legalized racial segregation before 1954, a judicial remedy should be fashioned and available but, as Justice Iredell counselled us, only "in a *clear* and urgent case."

A nation that takes pride in having an open political decision-making process must risk the consequences of debating issues that have the potential of political divisiveness. To do otherwise—to have politically divisive problems defined as judicial or constitutional ones because they are potentially dangerous in a heterogeneous society—is tantamount to proclaiming that our national political and societal dialogue must be limited to only insignificant and politically sterile public matters. If the U.S. Supreme Court cannot legitimize its Establishment Clause decisions on the basis of accurate, impressive, and satisfying appeals to history, it certainly cannot do so, to my satisfaction, with the argument that it is saving us from ourselves.

On an earlier day, addressing a different issue—the forced saluting of the flag and recitation of the pledge of allegiance, required by an intolerant law, of children who believed it against their religion—Justice Frankfurter spoke eloquently to the issue of courts saving us from ourselves:

> Of course patriotism can not be enforced by the flag salute. *But neither can the liberal spirit be enforced by judicial invalidation of illiberal legislation.* Our constant preoccupation with the constitutionality of legislation rather than with its wisdom tends to preoccupation of the American mind with a false value. The tendency of focussing attention on constitutionality is to make constitutionality synonymous with wisdom, to regard a law as all right if it is constitutional. Such an attitude is a great enemy of liberalism. Particularly in legislation affecting freedom of thought and freedom of speech much which should offend a free-spirited society is constitutional. *Reliance for the most precious interests of civilization, therefore, must be found outside of their vindication in courts of law. Only a persistent positive translation of the faith of a free society into the*

convictions and habits and actions of a community is the ultimate reliance against unabated temptations to fetter the human spirit.[80]

Perhaps the final consideration here should reach back, once more, to the Supreme Court's historical arguments. In a highly pluralistic society, clear and valid justification for judicial decisions invalidating legislative acts—rendered in the name of the *Constitution*—especially involving extremely sensitive political and social issues, *must* be provided by the Supreme Court as a basis for popular acceptance. The proper separation between Church and State in the United States constitutes such an issue. The U.S. Supreme Court has appealed almost solely to U.S. history to legitimize its Establishment Clause decisions. As shown in this study, U.S. history does no such thing. In most instances, the Court's decisions involving separation of Church and State are not in accord with American historical fact. Since this is the case, the Court has failed to provide adequate reasons as to why nondiscriminatory aid to religion or religiously-affiliated institutions, in pursuit of a constitutionally valid public goal, violates the *Constitution* of the United States. Inasmuch as the Court has failed, in most instances, to show an historically sound violation of the Establishment Clause, in the last analysis what is involved in these cases *is not* a valid question of constitutionality, but rather one of whether or not these legislative activities are wise or foolish public policy. The answer to that question is a political one, to be determined by the political not the judicial process.

Democratic constitutional government in the Western political tradition does not embrace the concept that value judgments on political issues or public policy should be made by nonelected jurists, who often serve for life, no matter how good their intentions or how great their wisdom. That kind of decision-making is alien to the intrinsic nature of democracy. In an "open society" public policy should be made by the elected representatives of the sovereign people, after a free, open, and robust political dialogue, which should hopefully include much input from what Justice Frankfurter once called "an informed, civically militant electorate." That kind of public policy decision-making is the very essence of democratic government itself.

80. Frankfurter dissenting, *West Virginia Board of Education* v. *Barnette*, 319 U.S. 624, at 670. Emphasis added.

Addenda

1. "A Bill Establishing A Provision For Teachers of the Christian Religion."

2. "Memorial and Remonstrance Against Religious Assessments, 1785." James Madison.

3. Bill No. 82 of the Revisal of the Laws of Virginia: "A Bill for Establishing Religious Freedom." Thomas Jefferson.

4. Presidential Thanksgiving Proclamations:*

George Washington,	1789;
George Washington,	1795;
John Adams,	1798;
John Adams,	1799;
James Madison,	1812;
James Madison,	1813;
James Madison,	1814.

5. Jefferson's Letter of Submission of the Kaskaskia Indian Treaty to the U.S. Senate, 1st Session, 8th Congress, 1803;

and

The Treaty with the Kaskaskia Indians and the Other Tribes, 1803.

*President James Madison's Thanksgiving Proclamation of 1815 is provided in chapter two, at pp. 34–35.

6. Laws of the United States providing Land Grant Trusts for the "Society of the United Brethren for the propagating the Gospel among the Heathen:"**

   - Act of March 2, 1799, signed by President John Adams;

   - Act of March 1, 1800, signed by President John Adams;

   - Act of April 26, 1802, signed by President Thomas Jefferson;

   - Act of March 3, 1803, signed by President Thomas Jefferson.

7. *Everson* v. *Board of Education of the Township of Ewing et al.*, 330 U.S. 1 (1947).

**The Land Grant Trust Laws for the United Brethren passed in 1796 and 1804 and signed by Presidents Washington and Jefferson are provided in chapter two, at pp. 42–43 and pp. 44–45 respectively.

A BILL ESTABLISHING A PROVISION FOR TEACHERS OF THE CHRISTIAN RELIGION

Whereas the general diffusion of Christian knowledge hath a natural tendency to correct the morals of men, restrain their vices, and preserve the peace of society; which cannot be effected without a competent provision for learned teachers, who may be thereby enabled to devote their time and attention to the duty of instructing such citizens, as from their circumstances and want of education, cannot otherwise attain such knowledge; and it is judged that such provision may be made by the Legislature, without counteracting the liberal principle heretofore adopted and intended to be preserved by abolishing all distinctions of pre-eminence amongst the different societies or communities of Christians;

Be it therefore enacted by the General Assembly, That for the support of Christian teachers,   per centum on the amount, or   in the pound on the sum payable for tax on the property within this Commonwealth, is hereby assessed, and shall be paid by every person chargeable with the said tax at the time the same shall become due; and the Sheriffs of the several Counties shall have power to levy and collect the same in the same manner and under the like restrictions and limitations, as are or may be prescribed by the laws for raising the Revenues of this State.

And be it enacted, That for every sum so paid, the Sheriff or Collector shall give a receipt, expressing therein to what society of Christians the person from whom he may receive the same shall direct the money to be paid, keeping a distinct account thereof in his books. The Sheriff of every County, shall, on or before the   day of   in every year, return to the Court, upon oath, two alphabetical lists of the payments to him made, distinguishing in columns opposite to the names of the persons who shall have paid the same, the society to which the money so paid was by them appropriated; and one column for the names where no appropriation shall be made. One of which lists, after being recorded in a book to be kept for that purpose, shall be filed by the Clerk in his office; the other shall by the Sheriff be fixed up in the Court-house, there to remain for the inspection of all concerned. And the Sheriff, after deducting five per centum for the collection, shall forthwith pay to such person or persons as shall be appointed to receive the same by the Vestry, Elders, or Directors, however denominated of each such society, the sum so stated to be due to that society; or in default thereof, upon the motion of such person or persons to the next or any succeeding Court, execution shall be awarded for the same against the Sheriff and his security, his and their executors or administrators; provided that ten days previous notice be give of such motion. And upon every such execution, the Officer serving the same shall proceed to immediate sale of the estate taken, and shall not accept of security for payment at the end of three months, nor to have the goods forthcoming at the day of sale; for his better direction wherein, the Clerk shall endorse upon every such execution that no security of any kind shall be taken.

And be it further enacted, That the money to be raised by virtue of this Act, shall be by the Vestries, Elders, or Directors of each religious society, appropriated to a provision for a Minister or Teacher of the Gospel of their denomination, or the providing places of divine worship, and to none other use whatsoever; except in the denominations of Quakers and Menonists, who may receive what is collected from their members, and place it in their general fund, to be disposed of in a manner which they shall think best calculated to promote their particular mode of worship.

And be it enacted, That all sums which at the time of payment to the Sheriff or Collector may not be appropriated by the person paying the same, shall be accounted for with the Court in manner as by this Act is directed; and after deducting for his collection, the Sheriff shall pay the amount thereof (upon account certified by the Court to the Auditors of Public Accounts, and by them to the treasurer) into the public Treasury, to be disposed of under the direction of the General Assembly, for the encouragement of seminaries of learning within the Counties whence such sums shall arise, and to no other use or purpose whatsoever.

THIS Act shall commence, and be in force, from and after the   day of in the year

A Copy from the Engrossed Bill.

JOHN BECKLEY, C.H.D.

Source: *Washington Mss. (Papers of George Washington, Vol. 231); Library of Congress.*

---

*This copy of the assessment Bill is from one of the handbills which on December 24, 1784, when the third reading of the bill was postponed, were ordered distributed to the Virginia counties by the House of Delegates. See Journal of the Virginia House of Delegates, December 24, 1784; Eckenrode, 102–103. The bill is therefore in its final form, for it never again reached the floor of the House. Eckenrode, 113.

MEMORIAL AND REMONSTRANCE AGAINST RELIGIOUS ASSESSMENTS, 1785[1]

To the Honorable the General Assembly of the Commonwealth of Virginia

A Memorial and Remonstrance

We, the subscribers, citizens of the said Commonwealth, having taken into serious consideration, "a Bill establishing a provision for Teachers of the Christian Religion," and conceiving that the same, if finally armed with the sanctions of a law, will be a dangerous abuse of power, are bound as faithful members of a free State, to remonstrate against it, and to declare the reasons by which we are determined. We remonstrate against the said Bill,

1. Because we hold it for a fundamental and undeniable truth, "that Religion or the duty which we owe to our Creator and the conviction, not by force or violence." The Religion then of every man must be left to the conviction and conscience of every man; and it is the right of every man to exercise it as these may dictate. This right is in its nature an unalienable right. It is unalienable; because the opinions of men, depending only on the evidence contemplated by their own minds, cannot follow the dictates of other men: It is unalienable also; because what is here a right towards men, is a duty towards the Creator. It is the duty of every man to render to the Creator such homage, and such only, as he believes to be acceptable to him. This

---

1. *To George Mason, July 14, 1826.*

I have received, sir, your letter of the 6th instant, requesting such information as I may be able to give as to the origin of the document [Memorial and Remonstrance against Religious Establishments], a copy of which was inclosed in it.

The motive and manner of the request would entitle it to respect, if less easily complied with than by the following statement:

During the session of the General Assembly, 1784–5, a bill was introduced into the House of Delegates providing for the legal support of the teachers of the Christian religion, and being patronized by the most popular talents in the House, it seemed likely to obtain a majority of votes. In order to arrest its progress, it was insisted, with success, that the bill should be postponed till the ensuing session, and in the mean time

printed for public consideration, that the sense of the people might be the better called forth. Your highly-distinguished ancestor, Col. Geo. Mason, Col Geo. Nicholas also possessing much weight, and some others, thought it advisable that a remonstrance against the bill should be prepared for general circulation and signature, and imposed on me the task of drawing up such a paper. This draught having received their sanction, a large number of printed copies were distributed, and so extensively signed by the people of every religious denomination, that at the ensuing session the projected measure was entirely frustrated; and under the influence of the public sentiment thus manifested, the celebrated bill "establishing religious freedom" enacted into [?] a permanent barrier against future attempts on the rights of conscience, as declared in the great charter prefixed to the Constitution of the State.

duty is precedent both in order of time and degree of obligation, to the claims of Civil Society. Before any man can be considered as a member of Civil Society, he must be considered as a subject of the Governor of the Universe: And if a member of Civil Society, who enters into any subordinate Association, must always do it with a reservation of his duty to the general authority; much more must every man who becomes a member of any particular Civil Society, do it with a saving of his allegiance to the Universal Sovereign. We maintain therefore that in matters of Religion, no man's right is abridged by the institution of Civil Society, and that Religion is wholly exempt from its cognizance. True it is, that no other rule exists, by which any question which may divide a Society, can be ultimately determined, but the will of the majority; but it is also true, that the majority may trespass on the rights of the minority.

2. Because if religion be exempt from the authority of the Society at large, still less can it be subject to that of the Legislative Body. The latter are but the creatures and vicegerents of the former. Their jurisdiction is both derivative and limited: it is limited with regard to the co-ordinate departments, more necessarily is it limited with regard to the constituents. The preservation of a free government requires not merely, that the metes and bounds which separate each department of power may be invariably maintained; but more especially, that neither of them be suffered to overleap the great Barrier which defends the rights of the people. The Rulers who are guilty of such an encroachment, exceed the commission from which they derive their authority, and are Tyrants. The People who submit to it are governed by laws made neither by themselves, nor by an authority derived from them, and are slaves.

3. Because, it is proper to take alarm at the first experiment on our liberties. We hold this prudent jealousy to be the first duty of citizens, and one of [the] noblest characteristics of the late Revolution. The freemen of America did not wait till usurped power had strengthened itself by exercise, and entangled the question in precedents. They saw all the consequences in the principle, and they avoided the consequences by denying the principle. We revere this lesson too much, soon to forget it. Who does not see that the same authority which can establish Christianity, in exclusion of all other Religions, may establish with the same ease any particular sect of Christians, in exclusion of all other Sects? That the same authority which can force a citizen to contribute three pence only of his property for the support of any one establishment, may force him to conform to any other establishment in all cases whatsoever?

4. Because, the bill violates that equality which ought to be the basis of every law, and which is more indispensable, in proportion as the validity or expediency of any law is more liable to be impeached. If "all men are by nature equally free and independent,"[2] all men are to be considered as entering into Society on equal conditions; as relinquishing no more, and therefore retaining no less, one than another, of their natural rights. Above all are they to be considered as retaining an "*equal* title to the free exercise of Religion according to the dictates of conscience."[3]

2. Declaration of Rights, Art. I (note in the original).

3. *Ibid.,* Art. 16 (note in the original).

Whilst we assert for ourselves a freedom to embrace, to profess and to observe the Religion which we believe to be of divine origin, we cannot deny an equal freedom to those whose minds have not yet yielded to the evidence which has convinced us. If this freedom be abused, it is an offence against God, not against man: To God, therefore, not to men, must an account of it be rendered. As the Bill violates equality by subjecting some to peculiar burdens; so it violates the same principle, by granting to others peculiar exemptions. Are the Quakers and Menonists the only sects who think a compulsive support of their religions unnecessary and unwarantable? Can their piety alone be intrusted with the care of public worship? Ought their Religions to be endowed above all others, with extraordinary privileges, by which proselytes may be enticed from all others. We think too favorably of the justice and good sense of these denominations, to believe that they either covet pre-eminences over their fellow citizens, or that they will be seduced by them, from the common opposition to the measure.

5. Because the bill implies either that the Civil Magistrate is a competent Judge of Religious truth; or that he may employ Religion as an engine of Civil policy. The first is an arrogant pretension falsified by the contradictory opinions of Rulers in all ages, and throughout the world: The second an unhallowed perversion of the means of salvation.

6. Because the establishment proposed by the Bill is not requisite for the support of the Christian Religion. To say that it is, is a contradiction to the Christian Religion itself; for every page of it disavows a dependence on the powers of this world: it is a contradiction to fact; for it is known that this Religion both existed and flourished, not only without the support of human laws, but in spite of every opposition from them; and not only during the period of miraculous aid, but long after it had been left to its own evidence, and the ordinary care of Providence: Nay, it is a contradiction in terms; for a Religion not invented by human policy, must have pre-existed and been supported, before it was established by human policy. It is moreover to weaken in those who profess this Religion a pious confidence in its innate excellence, and the patronage of its Author; and to foster in those who still reject it, a suspicion that its friends are too conscious of its fallacies, to trust it to its own merits.

7. Because experience witnesseth that ecclesiastical establishments, instead of maintaining the purity and efficacy of Religion, have had a contrary operation. During almost fifteen centuries, has the legal establishment of Christianity been on trial. What have been its fruits? More or less in all places, pride and indolence in the Clergy; ignorance and servility in the laity; in both, superstition, bigotry and persecution. Enquire of the Teachers of Christianity for the ages in which it appeared in it greatest lustre; those of every sect, point to the ages prior to its incorporation with Civil policy. Propose a restoration of this primitive state in which its Teachers depended on the voluntary rewards of their flocks; many of them predict its downfall. On which side ought their testimony to have greatest weight, when for or when against their interest?

8. Because the establishment in question is not necessary for the support of Civil Government. If it be urged as necessary for the support of Civil Government only as it is a means of supporting Religion, and it be not necessary for the latter purpose, it cannot be necessary for the former. If Religion be not within [the] cognizance of Civil Government, how can its legal establishment be said to be necessary to civil Government? What influence in fact have ecclesiastical establishments had on Civil Society? In some instances they have been seen to erect a spiritual tyranny on the ruins of Civil authority; in many instances they have been seen upholding the thrones of political tyranny; in no instance have they been seen the guardians of the liberties of the people. Rulers who wished to subvert the public liberty, may have found an established clergy convenient auxiliaries. A just government, instituted to secure & perpetuate it, needs them not. Such a government will be best supported by protecting every citizen in the enjoyment of his Religion with the same equal hand which protects his person and his property; by neither invading the equal rights of any Sect, nor suffering any Sect to invade those of another.

9. Because the proposed establishment is a departure from that generous policy, which, offering an asylum to the persecuted and oppressed of every Nation and Religion, promised a lustre to our country, and an accession to the number of its citizens. What a melancholy mark is the Bill of sudden degeneracy? Instead of holding forth an asylum to the persecuted, it is itself a signal of persecution. It degrades from the equal rank of Citizens all those whose opinions in Religion do not bend to those of the Legislative authority. Distant as it may be, in its present form, from the Inquisition it differs from it only in degree. The one is the first step, the other the last in the career of intolerance. The magnanimous sufferer under this cruel scourge in foreign Regions, must view the Bill as a Beacon on our Coast, warning him to seek some other haven, where liberty and philanthrophy in their due extent may offer a more certain repose from his troubles.

10. Because, it will have a like tendency to banish our Citizens. The allurements presented by other situations are every day thinning their number. To superadd a fresh motive to emigration, by revoking the liberty which they now enjoy, would be the same species of folly which has dishonoured and depopulated flourishing kingdoms.

11. Because, it will destroy that moderation and harmony which the forbearance of our laws to intermeddle with Religion, has produced amongst its several sects. Torrents of blood have been spilt in the old world, by vain attempts of the secular arm to extinguish Religious discord, by proscribing all difference in Religious opinions. Time has at length revealed the true remedy. Every relaxation of narrow and rigorous policy, wherever it has been tried, has been found to assuage the disease. The American Theatre has exhibited proofs, that equal and compleat liberty, if it does not wholly eradicate it, sufficiently destroys its malignant influence on the health and prosperity of the State. If with the salutary effects of this system under our own eyes, we begin to contract the bonds of Religious freedom, we know

no name that will too severely reproach our folly. At least let warning be taken at the first fruits of the threatened innovation. The very appearance of the Bill has transformed that "Christian forbearance,[4] love and charity," which of late mutually prevailed, into animosities and jealousies, which may not soon be appeased. What mischiefs may not be dreaded should this enemy to the public quiet be armed with the force of a law?

12. Because, the policy of the bill is adverse to the diffusion of the light of Christianity. The first wish of those who enjoy this precious gift, ought to be that it may be imparted to the whole race of mankind. Compare the number of those who have as yet received it with the number still remaining under the dominion of false Religions; and how small is the former! Does the policy of the Bill tend to lessen the disproportion? No; it at once discourages those who are strangers to the light of [revelation] from coming into the Region of it; and countenances, by example the nations who continue in darkness, in shutting out those who might convey it to them. Instead of levelling as far as possible, every obstacle to the victorious progess of truth, the Bill with an ignoble and unchristian timidity would circumscribe it, with a wall of defence, against the encroachments of error.

13. Because attempts to enforce by legal sanctions, acts obnoxious to so great a proportion of Citizens, tend to enervate the laws in general, and to slacken the bands of Society. If it be difficult to execute any law which is not generally deemed necessary or salutary, what must be the case where it is deemed invalid and dangerous? And what may be the effect of so striking an example of impotency in the Government, on its general authority.

14. Because a measure of such singular magnitude and delicacy ought not to be imposed, without the clearest evidence that it is called for by a majority of citizens: and no satisfactory method is yet proposed by which the voice of the majority in this case may be determined, or its influence secured. "The people of the respective counties are indeed requested to signify their opinion respecting the adoption of the Bill to the next Session of Assembly." But the representation must be made equal, before the voice either of the Representatives or of the Counties, will be that of the people. Our hope is that neither of the former will, after due consideration, espouse the dangerous principle of the Bill. Should the event disappoint us, it will still leave us in full confidence, that a fair appeal to the latter will reverse the sentence against our liberties.

15. Because, finally, "the equal right of every citizen to the free exercise of his Religion according to the dictates of conscience" is held by the same tenure with all our other rights. If we recur to its origin, it is equally the gift of nature; if we weigh its importance, it cannot be less dear to us; if we consult the Declaration of those rights which pertain to the good people of Virginia, as the "basis and foundation of Government,"[5] it is enumerated with equal solemnity, or rather studied emphasis. Either then, we must say, that the will of the Legislature is the only measure of their authority; and that in the plenitude of this authority, they may sweep away all our

---

4. *Ibid.*, Art. 16 (note in the original).   5. *Ibid.*, title (note in the original).

fundamental rights; or, that they are bound to leave this particular right untouched and sacred: Either we must say, that they may controul the freedom of the press, may abolish the trial by jury, may swallow up the Executive and Judiciary Powers of the State; nay that they may despoil us of our very right of suffrage, and erect themselves into an independent and hereditary assembly: or we must say, that they have no authority to enact into law the Bill under consideration. We the subscribers say, that the General Assembly of this Commonwealth have no such authority: And that no effort may be omitted on our part against so dangerous an usurpation, we oppose to it, this remonstrance; earnestly praying, as we are in duty bound, that the Supreme Lawgiver of the Universe, by illuminating those to whom it is addressed, may on the one hand, turn their councils from every act which would affront his holy prerogative, or violate the trust committed to them: and on the other, guide them into every measure which may be worthy of his [blessing, may re] dound to their own praise, and may establish more firmly the liberties, the prosperity, and the Happiness of the Commonwealth.

Source: Saul K. Padover, *The Complete Madison* (New York: Harper & Brothers; 1953).

---

82. A Bill for Establishing Religious Freedom

Well aware that the opinions and belief of men depend not on their own will, but follow involuntarily the evidence proposed to their minds; that Almighty God hath created the mind free, *and manifested his supreme will that free it shall remain by making it altogether insusceptible of restraint;* that all attempts to influence it by temporal punishments, or burthens, or by civil incapacitations, tend only to beget habits of hypocrisy and meanness, and are a departure from the plan of the holy author of our religion, who being lord both of body and mind, yet chose not to propagate it by coercions on either, as was in his Almighty power to do, *but to extend it by its influence on reason alone;* that the impious presumption of legislators and rulers, civil as well as ecclesiastical, who, being themselves but fallible and uninspired men, have assumed dominion over the faith of others, setting up their own opinions and modes of thinking as the only true and infallible, and as such endeavoring to impose them on others, hath established and maintained false religions over the greatest part of the world and through all time: That to compel a man to furnish contributions of money for the propagation of opinions which he disbelieves *and abhors,* is sinful and tyrannical; that even the forcing him to support this or that teacher of his own religious persuasion, is depriving him of the comfortable liberty of giving his contributions to the particular pastor whose morals he would make his pattern, and whose powers he feels most persuasive to righteousness; and is withdrawing from the ministry those temporary rewards, which proceeding from an approbation of their personal conduct, are an additional incitement to earnest and unremitting labours for the instruction of mankind; that our civil rights have no dependance on our religious opinions, any more than our opinions in physics or geometry; that therefore the proscribing any citizen as unworthy the public confidence by laying upon him an incapacity of being called to offices of trust and emolument, unless he profess or renounce this or that religious opinion, is depriving him injuriously of those privileges and advantages to which, in common with his fellow citizens, he has a natural right; that it tends also to corrupt the principles of that *very* religion it is meant to encourage, by bribing, with a monopoly of worldly honours and emoluments those who will externally profess and conform to it; that though indeed these are criminal who do not withstand such temptation, yet neither are those innocent who lay the bait in their way; *that the opinions of men are not the object of civil government, nor under its jurisdiction* that to suffer the civil magistrate to intrude his powers into the field of opinion and to restrain the profession or propagation of principles on supposition of their ill tendency is a dangerous falacy, which at one destroys all religious liberty, because he being of course judge of that tendency will make his opinions the rule of judgment, and approve or condemn the sentiments of others only as they shall square with or differ from his own; that it is time enough for the rightful purposes of civil government for its officers to interfere when principles break out into overt acts against peace and good order; and finally, that truth is great and will prevail if left to herself; that she is the proper and sufficient antagonist to error, and has nothing to fear from the conflict unless by human interposition disarmed of her natural weapons, free argument and debate; errors ceasing to be dangerous when it is permitted freely to contradict them.

We the General Assembly of Virginia do enact that no man shall be compelled to frequent or support any religious worship, place, or ministry whatsoever, nor shall be enforced, restrained, molested, or burthened in his body or goods, nor shall otherwise suffer, on account of his religious opinions or belief; but that all men shall be free to profess, and by argument to maintain, their opinions in matters of religion, and that the same shall in no wise diminish, enlarge, or affect their civil capacities.

And though we well know that this Assembly, elected by the people for the ordinary purposes of legislation only, have no power to restrain the acts of succeeding Assemblies, constituted with powers equal to our own, and that therefore to declare this act irrevocable would be of no effect in law; yet we are free to declare and do declare, that the rights hereby asserted are of the natural rights of mankind, and that if any act shall be hereafter passed to repeal the present or to narrow its operation, such act will be an infringement of natural right.

Source: Julian P. Boyd, Ed., *The Papers of Thomas Jefferson* (Princeton, NJ: Princeton University Press, 1950), Vol. 2, 1777 to 18 June 1779, Including the Revisal of the Laws, 1776–1786. Bill 82 of the Revisal of the Laws.

PROCLAMATION.

A NATIONAL THANKSGIVING.

[From Spark's Washington, Vol. XII, p. 119.]

Whereas it is the duty of all nations to acknowledge the providence of Almighty God, to obey His will, to be grateful for His benefits, and humbly to implore His protection and favor; and

Whereas both Houses of Congress have, by their joint committee, requested me "to recommend to the people of the United States a day of public thanksgiving and prayer, to be observed by acknowledging with grateful hearts the many and signal favors of Almighty God especially by affording them an opportunity peaceably to establish a form of government for their safety and happiness:"

Now, therefore, I do recommend and assign Thursday, the 26th day of November next, to be devoted by the people of these States to the service of that great and glorious Being who is the beneficent author of all the good that was, that is, or that will be; that we may then all unite in rendering unto Him our sincere and humble thanks for His kind care and protection of the people of this country previous to their becoming a nation; for the signal and manifold mercies and the favorable interpositions of His providence in the course and conclusion of the late war; for the great degree of tranquillity, union, and plenty which we have since enjoyed; for the peaceable and rational manner in which we have been enabled to establish constitutions of government for our safety and happiness, and particularly the national one now lately instituted; for the civil and religious liberty with which we are blessed, and the means we have of acquiring and diffusing useful knowledge; and, in general, for all the great and various favors which He has been pleased to confer upon us.

And also that we may then unite in most humbly offering our prayers and supplications to the great Lord and Ruler of Nations, and beseech Him to pardon our national and other trangressions; to enable us all whether in public or private stations, to perform our several and relative duties properly and punctually; to render our National Government a blessing to all the people by constantly being a Government of wise, just, and constitutional laws, discreetly and faithfully executed and obeyed; to protect and guide all sovereigns and nations (especially such as have shown kindness to us), and to bless them with good governments, peace, and concord; to promote the knowledge and practice of true religion and virtue, and the increase of science among them and us; and, generally, to grant unto all mankind such a degree of temporal prosperity as He alone knows to be best.

Given under my hand, at the city of New York, the 3d day of October, A.D. 1789.

G⁰. WASHINGTON.

Source: James D. Richardson, *A Compilation of the Messages and Papers of the Presidents, 1789–1897*, Vol. I (Washington, D.C.: Bureau of National Literature and Art, 1901).

PROCLAMATIONS.

BY THE PRESIDENT OF THE UNITED STATES OF AMERICA.

A PROCLAMATION.

When we review the calamities which afflict so many other nations, the present condition of the United States affords much matter of consolation and satisfaction. Our exemption hitherto from foreign war, an increasing prospect of the continuance of the exemption, the great degree of internal tranquillity we have enjoyed, the recent confirmation of that tranquillity by the suppression of an insurrection which so wantonly threatened it, the happy course of our public affairs in general, the unexampled prosperity of all classes of our citizens, are circumstances which peculiarly mark our situation with indications of the Divine beneficence toward us. In such a state of things it is in an especial manner our duty as a people, with devout reverence and affectionate gratitude, to acknowledge our many and great obligations to Almighty God and to implore Him to continue and confirm the blessings we experience.

Deeply penetrated with this sentiment, I, George Washington, President of the United States, do recommend to all religious societies and denominations, and to all persons whomsoever, within the United States to set apart and observe Thursday, the 19th day of February next, as a day of public thanksgiving and prayer, and on that day to meet together and render their sincere and hearty thanks to the Great Ruler of Nations for the manifold and signal mercies which distinguish our lot as a nation, particularly for the possession of constitutions of government which unite and by their union establish liberty with order; for the preservation of our peace, foreign and domestic; for the seasonable control which has been given to a spirit of disorder in the suppression of the late insurrection, and generally, for the prosperous course of our affairs, public and private; and at the same time humbly and fervently to beseech the kind Author of these blessings graciously to prolong them to us; to imprint on our hearts a deep and solemn sense of our obligations to Him for them; to teach us rightly to estimate their immense value; to preserve us from the arrogance of prosperity, and from hazarding the advantages we enjoy by delusive pursuits; to dispose us to merit the continuance of His favors by not abusing them; by our gratitude for them, and by a correspondent conduct as citizens and men; to render this country more and more a safe and propitious asylum for the unfortunate of other countries; to extend among us true and useful knowledge; to diffuse and establish habits of sobriety, order, morality, and piety, and finally, to impart all the blessings we possess, or ask for ourselves to the whole family of mankind.

In testimony whereof I have caused the seal of the United States of America to be affixed to these presents, and signed the same with my hand.

[SEAL.]   Done at the city of Philadelphia, the 1st day of January, 1795, and of the Independence of the United States of America the nineteenth.

G°. WASHINGTON.

By the President:
EDM: RANDOLPH.

Source: James D. Richardson, *A Compilation of the Messages and Papers of the Presidents, 1789–1897*, Vol. I (Washington, D.C.: Bureau of National Literature and Art, 1901).

PROCLAMATIONS.

BY THE PRESIDENT OF THE UNITED STATES OF AMERICA.

A PROCLAMATION.

As the safety and prosperity of nations ultimately and essentially depend on the protection and the blessing of Almighty God, and the national acknowledgement of this truth is not only an indispensable duty which the people owe to Him, but a duty whose natural influence is favorable to the promotion of that morality and piety without which social happiness can not exist nor the blessings of a free government be enjoyed; and as this duty, at all times incumbent, is so especially in seasons of difficulty or of danger, when existing or threatening calamities, the just judgments of God against prevalent iniquity, are a loud call to repentance and reformation; and as the United States of America are at present placed in a hazardous and afflictive situation by the unfriendly disposition, conduct, and demands of a foreign power, evinced by repeated refusals to receive our messengers of reconciliation and peace, by depredations on our commerce, and the infliction of injuries on very many of our fellow-citizens while engaged in their lawful business on the seas—under these considerations it has appeared to me that the duty of imploring the mercy and benediction of Heaven on our country demands at this time a special attention from its inhabitants.

I have therefore thought fit to recommend, and I do hereby recommend, that Wednesday, the 9th of May next, be observed throughout the United States as a day of solemn humiliation, fasting, and prayer; that the citizens of these States, abstaining on that day from their customary worldly occupations, offer their devout addresses to the Father of Mercies agreeably to those forms or methods which they have severally adopted as the most suitable and becoming; that all religious congregations do, with the deepest humility, acknowledge before God the manifold sins and transgressions with which we are justly chargeable as individuals and as a nation, beseeching Him at the same time, of His infinite grace, through the Redeemer of the World, freely to remit all our offenses, and to incline us by His Holy Spirit to that sincere repentance and reformation which may afford us reason to hope for his inestimable favor and heavenly benediction; that it be made the subject of particular and earnest supplication that our country may be protected from all the dangers which threaten it; that our civil and religious privileges may be preserved inviolate and perpetuated to the latest generations; that our public councils and magistrates may be especially enlightened and directed at this critical period; that the American people may be united in those bonds of amity and mutual confidence and inspired with that vigor and fortitude by which they have in times past been so highly distinguished and by which they have obtained such invaluable advantages; that the health of the inhabitants of our land may be preserved, and their agriculture, commerce, fisheries, arts, and manufactures be blessed and prospered; that the principles of genuine piety and sound morality may influence the minds and govern the lives of every description of our citizens, and that the blessings of peace, freedom, and pure religion may be speedily extended to all the nations of the earth.

And finally, I recommend that on the said day the duties of humiliation and prayer be accompanied by fervent thanksgiving to the Bestower of Every Good Gift, not only for His having hitherto protected and preserved the people of these United States in the independent enjoyment of their religious and civil freedom, but also for having prospered them in a wonderful progress of population, and for conferring on them many and great favors conducive to the happiness and prosperity of a nation.

Given under my hand and the seal of the United States of America, at [SEAL.] Philadelphia, this 23d day of March, A.D. 1798, and of the Independence of the said States the twenty-second.

JOHN ADAMS

By the President:
    TIMOTHY PICKERING,
        Secretary of State.

Source: James D. Richardson, *A Compilation of the Messages and Papers of the Presidents, 1789–1897*, Vol. I (Washington, D.C.: Bureau of National Literature and Art, 1901).

PROCLAMATIONS.

[From C.F. Adams's Works of John Adams, Vol. IX, p. 172.]

PROCLAMATION.

MARCH 6, 1799.

As no truth is more clearly taught in the Volume of Inspiration, nor any more fully demonstrated by the experience of all ages, than that a deep sense and a due acknowledgement of the governing providence of a Supreme Being and of the accountableness of men to Him as the searcher of hearts and righteous distributer of rewards and punishments are conducive equally to the happiness and rectitude of individuals and to the well-being of communities; as it is also most reasonable in itself that men who are made capable of social acts and relations, who owe their improvements to the social state, and who derive their enjoyments from it, should, as a society, make their acknowledgments of dependence and obligation to Him who hath endowed them with these capacities and elevated them in the scale of existence by these distinctions; as it is likewise a plain dictate of duty and a strong sentiment of nature that in circumstances of great urgency and seasons of imminent danger earnest and particular supplications should be made to Him who is able to defend or to destroy; as, moreover, the most precious interests of the people of the United States are still held in jeopardy by the hostile designs and insidious acts of a foreign nation, as well as by the dissemination among them of those principles, subversive of the foundations of all religious, moral, and social obligations, that have produced incalculable mischief and misery in other countries; and as, in fine, the observance of special seasons for public religious solemnities is happily calculated to avert the evils which we ought to deprecate and to excite to the performance of the duties which we ought to discharge by calling and fixing the attention of the people at large to the momentous truths already recited, by affording opportunity to teach and inculcate them by animating devotion and giving to it the character of a national act.

For these reasons I have thought proper to recommend, and I do hereby recommend accordingly, that Thursday, the 25th day of April next, be observed throughout the United States of America as a day of solemn humiliation, fasting, and prayer; that the citizens on that day abstain as far as may be from their secular occupations, devote the time to the sacred duties of religion in public and in private; that they call to mind our numerous offenses against the Most High God, confess them before Him with the sincerest penitence, implore His pardoning mercy, through the Great Mediator and Redeemer, for our past transgressions, and that through the grace of His Holy Spirit we may be disposed and enabled to yield a more suitable obedience to His righteous requisitions in time to come; that He would interpose to arrest the progress of the impiety and licentiousness in principle and practice so offensive to Himself and so ruinous to mankind; that He would make us deeply sensible that "righteousness exalteth a nation, but sin is a reproach to any people;" that He would turn us from our transgressions and turn His displeasure from us; that He would withhold us from unreasonable discontent, from disunion, faction, sedition, and insurrection; that He would preserve our country from the desolating sword; that He would save our cities and towns from a repetition of those awful pestilential visitations under which they have lately suffered so severly, and that the health of our inhabitants generally may be precious in His sight; that He would favor us with fruitful seasons and so bless the labors of the husbandman as that there may be food in abundance for man and beast; that He would prosper our commerce, manufactures, and fisheries, and give success to the people in all their lawful industry and enterprise; that He would smile on our colleges, academies, schools, and seminaries of learning, and make them nurseries of sound science, morals, and religion; that He would bless all magistrates, from the highest to the lowest, give them the true spirit of their station, make them a terror to evil doers and a praise to them that do well; that he would preside over the councils of the nation at this critical period, enlighten them to a just discernment of the public interest, and save them from mistake, division, and discord; that He would make succeed our preparations for defense and bless our armaments by land and by sea; that He would put an end to the effusion of human blood and the accumulation of human misery among the contending nations of the earth by disposing them to justice, to equity, to benevolence, and to peace; and that he would extend the blessing of knowledge, of true liberty, and of pure and undefiled religion throughout the world.

And I do also recommend that with these acts of humiliation, penitence, and prayer fervent thanksgiving to the Author of All Good be united for the countless favors which He is still continuing to the people of the United States, and which render their condition as a nation eminently happy when compared with the lot of others.

Given, etc.

JOHN ADAMS.

Source: James D. Richardson, *A Compilation of the Messages and Papers of the Presidents, 1789–1897*, Vol. I (Washington, D.C.: Bureau of National Literature and Art, 1901).

[From Annals of Congress, Twelfth Congress, part 2, 2224.]

BY THE PRESIDENT OF THE UNITED STATES OF AMERICA.

A PROCLAMATION

Whereas the Congress of the United States, by a joint resolution of the two Houses, have signified a request that a day may be recommended to be observed by the people of the United States with religious solemnity as a day of public humiliation and prayer; and

Whereas such a recommendation will enable the several religious denominations and societies so disposed to offer at one and the same time their common vows and adorations to Almighty God on the solemn occasion produced by the war in which He has been pleased to permit the injustice of a foreign power to involve these United States:

I do therefore recommend the third Thursday in August next as a convenient day to be set apart for the devout purposes of rendering the Sovereign of the Universe and the Benefactor of Mankind the public homage due to His holy attributes; of acknowledging the transgressions which might justly provoke the manifestations of His divine displeasure; of seeking His merciful forgiveness and His assistance in the great duties of repentance and amendment, and especially of offering fervent supplications that in the present season of calamity and war He would take the American people under His peculiar care and protection; that He would guide their public councils, animate their patriotism, and bestow His blessing on their arms; that He would inspire all nations with a love of justice and of concord and with a reverence for the unerring precept of our holy religion to do to others as they would require that others should do to them; and finally, that, turning the hearts of our enemies from the violence and injustice which sway their councils against us, He would hasten a restoration of the blessings of peace.

Given at Washington, the 9th day of July, A.D. 1812.

[SEAL.]   JAMES MADISON.

By the President:
    JAMES MONROE,
       Secretary of State.

Source: James D. Richardson, *A Compilation of the Messages and Papers of the Presidents, 1789–1897*, Vol. I (Washington, D.C.: Bureau of National Literature and Art, 1901).

PROCLAMATION.

[From Niles's Weekly Register, vol. 4, p. 345.]

A PROCLAMATION.

Whereas the Congress of the United States, by a joint resolution of the two Houses, have signified a request that a day may be recommended to be observed by the people of the United States with religious solemnity as a day of public humiliation and prayer; and

Whereas in times of public calamity such as that of the war brought on the United States by the injustice of a foreign government it is especially becoming that the hearts of all should be touched with the same and the eyes of all be turned to that Almighty Power in whose hand are the welfare and the destiny of nations:

I do therefore issue this my proclamation, recommending to all who shall be piously disposed to unite their hearts and voices in addressing at one and the same time their vows and adorations to the Great Parent and Sovereign of the Universe that they assemble on the second Thursday of September next in their respective religious congregations to render Him thanks for the many blessings he has bestowed on the people of the United States; that He has blessed them with a land capable of yielding all the necessaries and requisites of human life, with ample means for convenient exchanges with foreign countries; that he has blessed the labors employed in its cultivation and improvement; that He is now blessing the exertions to extend and establish the arts and manufactures which will secure within ourselves supplies too important to remain dependent on the precarious policy or the peaceable dispositions of other nations, and particularly that He has blessed the United States with a political Constitution founded on the will and authority of the whole people and guaranteeing to each individual security, not only of his person and his property, but of those sacred rights of conscience so essential to his present happiness and so dear to his future hopes; that with those expressions of devout thankfulness be joined supplications to the same Almighty Power that He would look down with compassion on our infirmities; that He would pardon our manifold transgressions and awaken and strengthen in all the wholesome purposes of repentance and amendment; that in this season of trial and calamity he would preside in a particular manner over our public councils and inspire all citizens with a love of their country and with those fraternal affections and that mutual confidence which have so happy a tendency to make us safe at home and respected abroad; and that as He was graciously pleased heretofore to smile on our struggles against the attempts of the Government of the Empire of which these States then made a part to wrest from them the rights and privileges to which they were entitled in common with every other part and to raise them to the station of an independent and sovereign people, so He would now be pleased in like manner to bestow His blessing on our arms in resisting the hostile and persevering efforts of the same power to degrade us on the ocean, the common inheritance of all, from rights and immunities belonging and essential to the American people as a coequal member of the great community of independent nations; and that, inspiring our enemies with moderation, with justice, and with that spirit of reasonable accommodation which our country has continued to manifest, we may be enabled to beat our swords into plowshares and to enjoy in peace every man the fruits of his honest industry and the rewards of his lawful enterprise.

If the public homage of a people can ever be worthy the favorable regard of the Holy and Omniscient Being to whom it is addressed, it must be that in which those who join in it are guided only by their free choice, by the impulse of their hearts and the dictates of their consciences; and such a spectacle must be interesting to all Christian nations as proving that religion, that gift of Heaven for the good of man, freed from all coercive edicts, from that unhallowed connection with the powers of this world which corrupts religion into an instrument or an usurper of the policy of the state, and making no appeal but to reason, to the heart, and to the conscience, can spread its benign influence everywhere and can attract to the divine altar those freewill offerings of humble supplication, thanksgiving, and praise which alone can be acceptable to Him whom no hypocrisy can deceive and no forced sacrifices propitiate.

Upon these principles and with these views the good people of the United States are invited, in conformity with the resolution aforesaid, to dedicate the day above named to the religious solemnities therein recommended.

Given at Washington, this 23d day of July, A.D. 1813.

[SEAL.]   JAMES MADISON.

Source: James D. Richardson, *A Compilation of the Messages and Papers of the Presidents, 1789–1897*, Vol. I (Washington, D.C.: Bureau of National Literature and Art, 1901).

PROCLAMATIONS.

BY THE PRESIDENT OF THE UNITED STATES

A PROCLAMATION.

The two Houses of the National Legislature having by a joint resolution expressed their desire that in the present time of public calamity and war a day may be recommended to be observed by the people of the United States as a day of public humiliation and fasting and prayer to Almighty God for the safety and welfare of these States, His blessing on their arms, and a speedy restoration of peace, I have deemed it proper by this proclamation to recommend that Thursday, the 12th of January next, be set apart as a day on which all may have an opportunity of voluntarily offering at the same time in their respective religious assemblies their humble adoration to the Great Sovereign of the Universe, of confessing their sins and transgressions, and of strengthening their vows of repentance and amendment. They will be invited by the same solemn occasion to call to mind the distinguished favors conferred on the American people in the general health which has been enjoyed, in the abundant fruits of the season, in the progess of the arts instrumental to their comfort, their prosperity, and their security, and in the victories which have so powerfully contributed to the defense and protection of our country, a devout thankfulness for all which ought to be mingled with their supplications to the Beneficent Parent of the Human Race that He would be graciously pleased to pardon all their offenses against Him; to support and animate them in the discharge of their respective duties; to continue to them the precious advantages flowing from political institutions so auspicious to their safety against dangers from abroad, to their tranquillity at home, and to their liberties, civil and religious; and that He would in a special manner preside over the nation in its public councils and constituted authorities, giving wisdom to its measures and success to its arms in maintaining its rights and in overcoming all hostile designs and attempts against it; and, finally, that by inspiring the enemy with dispositions favorable to a just and reasonable peace its blessings may be speedily and happily restored.

Given at the city of Washington, the 16th day of November, 1814, and of the Independence of the United States the thirty-eighth.

[SEAL.]   JAMES MADISON.

Source: James D. Richardson, *A Compilation of the Messages and Papers of the Presidents, 1789–1897*, Vol. I (Washington, D.C.: Bureau of National Literature and Art, 1901).

THE KASKASKIA AND OTHER TRIBES.

8th CONGRESS.   No. 104.   1st SESSION.

THE KASKASKIA AND OTHER TRIBES.

COMMUNICATED TO THE SENATE, OCTOBER, 31, 1803.

To the Senate of the United States of America:

I now lay before you the treaty, mentioned in my general message at the opening of the sessions, as having been concluded with the Kaskaskia Indians, for the transfer of their country to us, under certain reservations and conditions.

Progress having been made in the demarcation of Indian boundaries, I am now able to communicate to you, a treaty with the Delawares, Shawanese, Pattawatamies, Miamies, Eel Rivers, Weas, Kickapoos, Piankeshaws, and Kaskaskias, establishing the boundaries of the territory around St. Vincennes.

Also, a supplementary treaty with the Eel rivers, Wyandots, Piankeshaws, Kaskaskias, and Kickapoos, in confirmation of the fourth article of the preceding treaty.

Also, a treaty with the Choctaws, describing and establishing our demarcation of boundaries with them.

Which several treaties are accompanied by the papers relating to them, and are now submitted to the Senate for consideration whether they will advise and consent to their ratification.

TH. JEFFERSON.

October 31, 1803.

Articles of a Treaty made at Vincennes, in the Indiana territory, between William Henry Harrison, Governor of the said territory, Superintendent of Indian Affairs, and commissioner plenipotentiary of the United States for concluding any treaty or treaties which may be found necessary, with any of the Indian tribes northwest of the river Ohio, of the one part; and the head chiefs and warriors of the Kaskaskia tribe of Indians, so called, (but which tribe is the remains and rightfully represent all the tribes of the Illinois Indians, originally called the Kaskaskia, Mitchigamia, Cahokia, and Tamoria,) of the other part.

ARTICLE. 1. Whereas, from a variety of unfortunate circumstances, the several tribes of Illinois Indians are reduced to a very small number, the remains of which have been long consolidated and known by the name Kaskaskia tribe, and finding themselves unable to occupy the extensive tract of country, which of right belongs to them, and which was possessed by their ancestors for many generations: the chiefs and warriors of the said tribe being also desirous of procuring the means of improvement in the arts of civilized life, and a more certain and effectual support for their women and children, have, for the considerations hereinafter mentioned, relinquished, and, by these presents, do relinquish, and cede to the United States, all the lands in the Illinois country, which the said tribe has heretofore possessed, or which they may rightfully claim; reserving to themselves, however, the tract of about three hundred and fifty acres, near the town of Kaskaskia, which they have always held, and which was secured to them by the act of Congress of the third day of March, one thousand seven hundred and ninety one; and also the right of locating one other tract of twelve hundred and eighty acres, within the bounds of that now ceded; which two tracts of land shall remain to them for ever.

ART. 2. The United States will take the Kaskaskia tribe under their immediate care and patronage, and will afford them a protection as effectual, against the other Indian tribes, and against all other persons whatever, as is enjoyed by their own citizens. And the said Kaskaskia tribe do hereby engage to refrain from making war, or giving any insult or offence, to any other Indian tribe, or to any foreign nation, without having first obtained the approbation and consent of the United States.

ART. 3. The annuity heretofore given by the United States to the said tribe, shall be increased to one thousand dollars, which is to be paid to them, either in money, merchandise, provisions, or domestic animals, at the option of the said tribe; and when the said annuity, or any part thereof, is paid in merchandise, it is to be delivered to them either at Vincennes, Fort Massac, or Kaskaskia, and the first cost of the goods in the sea port where they may be procured, is alone to be charged to the said tribe, free from the cost of transportation, or any other contingent expense. Whenever the said tribe may choose to receive money, provisions, or domestic animals, for the whole or in part of the said annuity, the same shall be delivered at the town of Kaskaskia. The United States will also cause to be built, a house suitable for the accommodation of the chief of the said tribe, and will enclose for their use a field, not exceeding one hundred acres, with a good and sufficient fence. *And whereas* the greater part of the said tribe have been baptised and received into the Catholic church, to which they are much attached, the United States will give, annually, for seven years, one hundred dollars towards the support of a priest of that religion, who will engage to perform for said tribe the duties of his office, and also to instruct as many of their children as possible, in the rudiments of literature. And the United States will further give the sum of three hundred dollars, to assist the said tribe in the erection of a church. The stipulations made in this and the preceding article, together with the sum of five hundred and eighty dollars, which is now paid, or assured to be paid, for the said tribe, for the purpose of procuring some necessary articles, and to relieve them from debts which they have heretofore contracted, is considered as a full an ample compensation for the relinquishment made to the United States, in the first article.

ART. 4. The United States reserve to themselves the right, at any future period, of dividing the annuity now promised to the said tribe, amongst the several families thereof, reserving always a suitable sum for the great chief and his family.

ART. 5. And to the end that the United States may be enabled to fix, with the other Indian tribes a boundary between their respective claims, the chiefs and head warriors of the said Kaskaskia tribe do hereby declare that their rightful claim is as follows, viz: Beginning at the confluence of the Ohio and the Mississippi; thence up the Ohio to the mouth of the Saline creek, about twelve miles below the mouth of the Wabash; thence along the dividing ridge, between the said creek and the Wabash, until it comes to the general dividing ridge, between the waters which fall into the Wabash, and those which fall into the Kaskaskia river; and thence along the said ridge until it reaches the waters which fall into the Illinois river; thence in a direct course to the mouth of the Illinois river; and thence down the Mississippi to the beginning.

ART. 6. As long as the lands which have been ceded by this treaty shall continue to be the property of the United States, the said tribe shall have the privilege of living and hunting upon them, in the same manner that they have hitherto done.

ART. 7. This treaty is to be in force, and binding upon the said parties, so soon as it shall be ratified by the President and Senate of the United States.

In witness whereof, the said commissioner plenipotentiary, and the head chiefs and warriors of the said Kaskaskia tribe of Indians, have hereunto set their hands, and affixed their seals, the thirteenth day of August, in the year of our Lord one thousand eight hundred and three, and of the independence of the United States the twenty-eighth.

WM. HENRY HARRISON.

[Signed, also, by certain chiefs and warriors.]

Source: *American State Papers,* Class II, *Indian Affairs,* Vol. IV, *Documents, Legislative and Executive, of the Congress of the United States,* Selected and Edited, Under the Authority of Congress, by Walter Lowrie, *Secretary of the Senate,* and Matthew St. Clair Clarke, *Clerk of the House of Representatives* (Washington: Published by Gales and Seaton, 1832).

CHAP. XXIX.—*An Act to amend the act intituled "An act regulating the grants of land appropriated for military services, and for the Society of the United Brethren, for propagating the Gospel among the Heathen."*

March 2, 1799

1796, ch. 46.

SECTION 1. *Be it enacted by the Senate and House of Representatives of the United States of America in Congress assembled,* That the fourth section of an act, intituled "An act regulating the grants of land appropriated for military services, and for the society of the United Brethren, for propagating the gospel among the Heathen," be, and the same is hereby repealed.

SEC. 2. *And it be further enacted,* That all the lands set apart by the first section of the above mentioned act, which shall remain unlocated on the first day of January, in the year one thousand eight hundred and two, shall be released from the said reservation, and shall be at the free disposition of the United States, in like manner as any other vacant territory of the United States. And that all warrants or claims for lands on account of military services, which shall not, before the day aforesaid, be registered and located, shall be for ever barred.

APPROVED, March 2, 1799.

Source: *The Public Statutes at Large of the United States of America*, Edited by Richard Peters, Esq., Volume I (Boston: Charles C. Little and James Brown, 1845), "Acts of the Fifth Congress," Session 3, Chapter 29.

March 1, 1800.

CHAP. XIII.—*An Act in addition to an act intituled "An act regulating the grants of land appropriated for Military services, and for the Society of the United Brethren for propagating the Gospel among the Heathen." (a)*

Points of intersection of the lines actually run are to be considered as the corners of townships.

Vol. i. 490.

SECTION 1. *Be it enacted by the Senate and House of Representatives of the United States of America in Congress assembled*, That the respective points of intersection of the lines actually run, as the boundaries of the several townships surveyed by virtue of the act intituled "An act regulating the grants of land appropriated for military services and for the society of the United Brethren for propagating the Gospel among the Heathen," accordingly as the said lines have been marked and ascertained at the time when the same were run, notwithstanding the same are not in conformity to the act aforesaid, or shall not appear to correspond with the plat of the survey which has been returned by the Surveyor General, shall be considered, and they are hereby declared to be the corners of the said townships: That in regard to every such township as by the plat and survey returned by the Surveyor General is stated to contain four thousand acres in each quarter thereof, the points on each of the boundary lines of such township, which are at an equal distance from those two corners of the same township, which stand on the same boundary line, shall be considered and they are hereby declared to be corners of the respective quarters of such township; that the other boundary lines of the said quarter townships shall be straight lines run from each of the last mentioned corners of quarter townships to the same corner of quarter townships on the opposite boundary line of the same township; and that in regard to every such township as by the said return is stated to contain in any of the quarters thereof more or less than the quantity of four thousand

Boundaries of quarter townships, where they are stated to contain four thousand acres.

Boundaries of quarter townships, where they are stated to contain more or less than four thousand acres.

(a) Act of June 1, 1796, chap. 46; act of March 2, 1799, chap. 29; act of April 26, 1802, chap. 30.

acres, the corners marked in the boundary lines of such township to designate the quarters thereof, shall be considered and they are hereby declared to be the corners of the quarter townships thereof, although the same may be found at unequal distances from the respective corners of such townships: And such townships shall be divided by running lines through the same from the corners of the quarter townships actually marked, whether the interior lines thus extended shall be parallel to the exterior lines of the said township or not; and that each of the said quarter townships thus bounded, shall, in every proceeding to be had under the above-mentioned or this act, be considered as containing the exact quantity expressed in the plat and survey thereof returned by the Surveyor General. Method of running lines.

SEC. 2. *And be it further enacted,* That it shall be lawful for the proprietors or holders of warrants for military services, which have been, or shall be registered at the treasury in pursuance of the act intituled "An act regulating the grants of land appropriated for military services, and for the Society of the United Brethren, for propagating the Gospel among the Heathen," during the time, in the manner, and according to the rights of priority, which may be acquired in pursuance of said act, to locate the quantities of land mentioned in the warrants by them respectively registered, as aforesaid, on any quarter township or fractional part of a quarter township, in the general tract mentioned and described in said act: *Provided always,* that the fractional quarter townships upon the river Sciota, and those upon the river Muskingum adjoining the grant made to Ebenezer Zane, or the towns Salem, Gnadenhutten or Shoenbrun, or the Indian boundary line, shall in every case be accepted and taken in full satisfaction for four thousand acres. Locations may be made on the general tract by the holders of warrants for military services. Certain fractional quarter townships to be taken for four thousand acres. Vol. i. 491.

SEC. 3. *And be it further enacted,* That whenever locations shall be made on any quarter township, which, according to the actual survey and plat thereof, returned by the Surveyor General, is stated to contain less than the quantity of four thousand acres, except in the case of fractions provided for in the preceding section, it shall be lawful for the Secretary of the Treasury to issue, or cause to be issued, certificates expressing the number of acres remaining unsatisfied of any registry of warrants for the quantity of four thousand acres, made in pursuance of the act before recited, which certificates shall have the same validity and effect, and be liable to be barred in like manner as warrants granted for military services, but no certificate shall be granted, nor any claim allowed for less than fifty acres, nor for the navigable water contained within the limits of any quarter township or fractional quarter township. When locations are made on quarter townships stated to contain less than four thousand acres, the Secretary of Treasury shall cause certificates to be issued for the deficiency.

SEC. 4. *And be it further enacted,* That whenever a location shall be made on any quarter township, which, according to the actual survey and plat thereof, returned by the Surveyor General, is stated to exceed the quantity of four thousand acres, no patent shall What is to be done when they are made on quarter town-

ships stated to contain more than four thousand acres.

be issued in pursuance thereof, until the person making such location, shall deposit at the treasury, warrants for military services or certificates issued by virtue of the preceding section, equal to the excess above four thousand acres, contained in such quarter township, or shall pay into the treasury of the United States two dollars per acre, in the certificates of the six per cent. funded debt of the United States, or money, for each acre of the excess above four thousand acres as aforesaid.

Land at two dollars per acre.

Reservations for satisfying warrants granted to individuals for their services.

SEC. 5. *And be it further enacted,* That after the priority of location shall have been determined, and after the proprietors or holders of warrants for military services shall have designated the tracts by them respectively elected; it shall be the duty of the Secretary of the Treasury to designate by lot, in the presence of the Secretary of War, fifty quarter townships, of the lands remaining unlocated, which quarter townships, together with the fractional parts of townships remaining unlocated, shall be reserved for satisfying warrants granted to individuals for their military services, in the manner hereafter provided.

Reservations to be divided into lots of one hundred acres.

SEC. 6. *And be it further enacted,* That the land in each of the quarter townships designated as aforesaid, and in such of the fractional parts of quarter townships, as may then remain unlocated, shall be divided by the Secretary of the Treasury, upon the respective plats thereof, as returned by the Surveyor General, into as many lots, of one hundred acres each, as shall be equal, as nearly as may be, to the quantity such quarter township or fraction is stated to contain; each of which lots shall be included, where practicable, between parallel lines, one hundred and sixty perches in length, and one hundred perches in width, and shall be designated by progressive numbers upon the plat, or survey of every such quarter township and fraction respectively.

Manner in which they shall be surveyed.

Holders of such warrants may make locations on those lots, and receive patents to their own use only, after 16th March, 1800, and before Jan. 1st, 1802.

Post 155.

Vol. i. 464
Vol. i. 491.

SEC. 7. *And be it further enacted,* That from and after the sixteenth day of March next, it shall be lawful for the holder of any warrant granted for military services, to locate, at any time before the first day of January, one thousand eight hundred and two, the number of hundred acres expressed in such warrant, on any lot or lots, from time to time, remaining unlocated within the tracts reserved as aforesaid, and upon surrendering such warrant to the treasury, the holder thereof shall be entitled to receive a patent in the manner, and upon the conditions heretofore prescribed by law; which patent shall in every case express the range, township, quarter township or fraction, and number of the lot located as aforesaid. But no location shall be allowed, nor shall any patent be issued for any lot or lots of one hundred acres, except in the name of the person originally entitled to such warrant, or the heir or heirs of the person so entitled; nor shall any land, so located and patented, to a person originally entitled to such warrant, be considered as in trust for any purchaser, or be subject to any contract made before the date of such patent, and the title to lands acquired, in consequence of patents issued as aforesaid, shall and may be alienated in pursuance of the laws, which have been, or shall be passed in the territory of the United States, northwest of the river Ohio, for regulating the transfer of real property, and not otherwise. Upon surrender of warrant shall receive patent.

SEC. 8. *And be it further enacted,* That in all cases after the sixteenth of March next, where more than one application is made for the same tract, at the same time, under this act, or under the act to which this is in addition, the Secretary of the Treasury shall determine the priority of location by lot. Where locations are made on the same tract, priority to be determined by lot.

SEC. 9. *And be it further enacted,* That it shall be the duty of the Secretary of the Treasury to advertise the tracts which may be reserved for location, in lots of one hundred acres, in one newspaper in each of the states, and in the territory aforesaid, for and during the term of three months. Public notice to be given of the reservations by the Secretary of the Treasury.

SEC. 10. *And be it further enacted,* That the actual plat and survey returned by the Surveyor General, of quarter townships and fractional parts of quarter townships, contained in the tract mentioned and described in the act to which this is a supplement, shall be considered as final and conclusive, so far as relates to the quantity of land supposed to be contained in the quarter townships, and fractions, so that no claim shall hereafter be set up against the United States, by any proprietor, or holder of warrants for military services, on account of any deficiency in the quantity of land contained in the quarter township or fractional part of a quarter township, which shall have been located by such proprietor or holder, nor shall any claim be hereafter set up by the United States, against such proprietor or holder, on account of any excess in the quantity of land contained therein. The plat returned by the Surveyor General to be conclusive as to quantity.

APPROVED, March 1, 1800.

Source: *The Public Statutes at Large of the United States of America,* Edited by Richard Peters, Esq., Volume II (Boston: Charles C. Little and James Brown, 1845) "Acts of the Sixth Congress," Session I, Chapter 13.

CHAP. XXX.—*An Act in addition to an act, intituled "An act, in addition to an act regulating the grants of land appropriated for military services, and for the society of the United Brethren, for propagating the gospel among the Heathen."* April 26, 1802.

Act of March 1, 1800, ch. 13. Act of March 3, 1803, ch. 30.

Be it enacted by the Senate and House of Representatives of the United States of America in Congress assembled, That from and after the passing of this act, and until the first day of January next, it shall be lawful for the holders or proprietors of warrants heretofore granted in consideration of military services, or register's certificates of fifty acres, or more, granted, or hereafter to be granted How the holders of certain warrants for military services, or regis-

ter's certificates, may register or locate the same.

agreeable to the third section of an act intituled "An act in addition to an act, intituled An act regulating the grants of land appropriated for military services; and for the society of the United Brethren for propagating the gospel among the Heathen," approved the first day of March one thousand eight hundred, to register and locate the same, in the same manner, and under the same restrictions, as might have been done before the first day of January last: *Provided*, that persons holding register's certificates for a less quantity than one hundred acres, may locate the same on such parts of fractional townships, as shall, for that purpose, be divided by the Secretary of the Treasury into lots of fifty acres each.

Provision with respect to certain register's certificates.

Secretary of War to receive claims to lands, and for duplicates of warrants, suggested to have been lost.

SEC. 2. *And be it further enacted,* That it shall be the duty of the Secretary of War to receive claims to lands for military services, and claims for duplicates of warrants issued from his office, or from the land office of Virginia, or of plats and certificates of surveys founded on such warrants, suggested to have been lost or destroyed, until the first day of January next, and no longer; and immediately thereafter, to report the same to Congress, designating the numbers of claims of each description, with his opinion thereon.

To report the same to Congress, with his opinion.

APPROVED, April 26, 1802.

Source: *The Public Statutes at Large of the United States of America,* Edited by Richard Peters, Esq., Volume II (Boston: Charles C. Little and James Brown, 1845), "Acts of the Seventh Congress," Session I, Chapter 30.

March 3, 1803.

CHAP. XXX.—*An Act to revive and continue in force, an act in addition to an act intituled "An act in addition to an act regulating the grants of land appropriated for Military Services and for the Society of the United Brethren for propagating the Gospel among the Heathen," and for other purposes.*

Act of April 26, 1802, ch. 30, revived and continued in force four weeks.

Be it enacted by the Senate and House of Representatives of the United States of America in Congress assembled, That the first section of an act in addition to an act intituled "An act in addition to an act regulating the grants of land appropriated for military services, and for the society of the United Brethren for propagating the gospel among the heathen," approved the twenty-sixth of April, eighteen hundred and two, be, and the same is hereby revived and continued in force until the first day of April next.

Act of March 19, 1804, ch. 26. Act of March 27, 1804, ch. 61.

Secretary of War to issue land warrants; when and to whom.

SEC. 2. *And be it further enacted,* That the Secretary of War be, and he hereby is authorized, from and after the first day of April next, to issue warrants for military bounty lands to the two hundred and fifty-four persons who have exhibited their claims, and produced satisfactory evidence to substantiate the same to the Secretary of War, in pursuance of the act of the twenty-sixth of April, eighteen hundred and two, intituled "An act in addition to an

1802, ch. 30.

act, intituled An act in addition to an act regulating the grants of land appropriated for military services, and for the society of the United Brethren for propagating the gospel among the heathen."

SEC. 3. *And be it further enacted,* That the holders or proprietors of the land warrants issued by virtue of the preceding section, shall and may locate their respective warrants only, on any unlocated parts of the fifty quarter townships and the fractional quarter townships which had been reserved for original holders, by virtue of the fifth section of an act intituled "An act in addition to an act intituled An act regulating the grants of land appropriated for military services, and for the society of the United Brethren for propagating the gospel among the heathen." *Where to be located.*

1800, ch. 13.

SEC. 4. *And be it further enacted,* That the Secretary of War be, and he is hereby authorized to issue land warrants to Major General La Fayette, for eleven thousand five hundred twenty acres, which shall, at his option, be located, surveyed and patented, in conformity with the provisions of an act intituled "An act regulating the grants of land appropriated for military services, and for the society of the United Brethren for propagating the gospel among the heathen," or which may be received acre for acre, in payment for any lands of the United States north of the river Ohio, and above the mouth of Kentucky river. *Land warrants to General La Fayette.*

1804, ch. 61, sec. 14.

SEC. 5. *And be it further enacted,* That all the unappropriated lands within the military tract, shall be surveyed into half sections, in the manner directed by the act intituled "An act to amend the act intituled An act providing for the sale of the lands of the United States in the territory northwest of the Ohio, and above the mouth of Kentucky river," and that so much of the said lands as lie west of the eleventh range within the said tract, shall be attached to, and made a part of the district of Chilicothe, and be offered for sale at that place, under the same regulations that other lands are within the said district. *Unappropriated lands within the military tract; how to be surveyed.*
Part to be attached to the district of Chilicothe; and for sale.

SEC. 6. *And be it further enacted,* That the lands within the said eleventh range, and east of it, within the said military tract, and all the lands north of the Ohio company's purchase, west of the seven first ranges, and east of the district of Chilicothe, shall be offered for sale at Zanesville, under the direction of a register of the land-office and receiver of public monies to be appointed for that purpose, who shall reside at that place, and shall perform the same duties and be allowed the same emoluments as are prescribed for and allowed to registers and receivers of the land-offices by law. *Certain tracts for sale.*
Where to be offered.
Register and receiver appointed.
Duties and compensation.

SEC. 7. *And be it further enacted,* That all persons who have obtained certificates for the right of pre-emption to lands by virtue of two acts, the one intituled "An act giving a right of pre-emption to certain persons who have contracted with John Cleves Symmes, or his associates for lands lying between the Miami rivers in the *Possessors of rights of pre-emption under*

John Cleves Symmes and others allowed further time of payment.

territory of the United States northwest of the Ohio," and the other "An act to extend and continue the provisions of the said act, passed on the first day of May, eighteen hundred and two," and who have not made the first payment therefor, before the first day of January last, shall be allowed until the tenth day of April next to complete the same; and that all persons who have become purchasers of land by virtue of the aforesaid acts, be, and they are hereby allowed until the first day of January, eighteen hundred and five, to make the second instalment; until the first day of January eighteen hundred and six, to make their third instalment; and until the first day of January, eighteen hundred and seven, to make their fourth and last instalment; any thing in the acts aforesaid, to the contrary notwithstanding.

1801, ch. 23.
1802, ch. 44.

Land patents how to be obtained when the military warrants are lost or destroyed.

SEC. 8. *And be it further enacted,* That where any warrants granted by the state of Virginia, for military services, have been surveyed on the northwest side of the river Ohio, between the Sciota and the little Miami rivers, and the said warrants, or the plats and certificates of survey made thereon, have been lost or destroyed, the persons entitled to the said land may obtain a patent therefor, by producing a certified duplicate of the warrant from the land-office of Virginia, or of the plat and certificate of survey from the office of the surveyor in which the same is recorded, and giving satisfactory proof to the Secretary of War, by his affidavit or otherwise, of the loss or destruction of said warrant, or plat and certificate of survey.

APPROVED, March 3, 1803.

Source: *The Public Statutes at Large of the United States of America*, Edited by Richard Peters, Esq., Volume II (Boston: Charles C. Little and James Brown, 1845), "Acts of the Seventh Congress," Session II, Chapter 30.

EVERSON *v.* BOARD OF EDUCATION OF THE TOWNSHIP OF EWING ET AL.

330 U.S. 1 (1947)

MR. JUSTICE BLACK delivered the opinion of the Court.

A New Jersey statute authorizes its local school districts to make rules and contracts for the transportation of children to and from schools.[1] The appellee, a township board of education, acting pursuant to this statute, authorized reimbursement to parents of money expended by them for the bus transportation of their children on regular busses operated by the public transportation system. Part of this money was for the payment of transportation of some children in the community to Catholic parochial schools. These church schools give their students, in addition to secular education, regular religious instruction conforming to the religious tenets and modes of worship of the Catholic Faith. The superintendent of these schools is a Catholic priest.

The appellant, in his capacity as a district taxpayer, filed suit in a state court challenging the right of the Board to reimburse parents of parochial school students. He contended that the statute and the resolution passed pursuant to it violated both the State and the Federal Constitutions. That court held that the legislature was without power to authorize such payment under the state constitution. 132 N.J.L. 98, 39 A. 2d 75. The New Jersey Court of Errors and Appeals reversed, holding that neither the statute nor the resolution passed pursuant to it was in conflict with the State constitution or the provisions of the Federal Constitution in issue. 133 N.J.L. 350, 44 A. 2d 333. The case is here on appeal under 28 U.S.C. § 344 (a).

Since there has been no attack on the statute on the ground that a part of its language excludes children attending private schools operated for profit from enjoying State payment for their transportation, we need not consider this exclusionary language; it has no relevancy to any constitutional question here

---

1. "Whenever in any district there are children living remote from any schoolhouse, the board of education of the district may make rules and contracts for the transportation of such children to and from school, including the transportation of school children to and from school other than a public school, except such school as is operated for profit in whole or in part.

"When any school district provides any transportation for public school children to and from school, transportation from any point in such established school route to any other point in such established school route shall be supplied to school children residing in such school district in going to and from school other than a public school, except such school as is operated for profit in whole or in part." New Jersey Laws, 1941, c. 191, p. 581; N.J.R.S. Cum. Supp., tit. 18, c. 14, § 8.

presented.[2] Furthermore, if the exclusion clause had been properly challenged, we do not know whether New Jersey's highest court would construe its statutes as precluding payment of the school transportation of any group of pupils, even those of a private school run for profit.[3] Consequently, we put to one side the question as to the validity of the statute against the claim that it does not authorize payment for the transportation generally of school children in New Jersey.

The only contention here is that the state statute and the resolution, insofar as they authorized reimbursement to parents of children attending parochial schools, violate the Federal Constitution in these two respects, which to some extent overlap. *First.* They authorize the State to take by taxation the private property of some and bestow it upon others, to be used for their own private purposes. This, it is alleged, violates the due process clause of the Fourteenth Amendment. *Second.* The statute and the resolution forced inhabitants to pay taxes to help support and maintain schools which are dedicated to, and which regularly teach, the Catholic Faith. This is alleged to be a use of state power to support church schools contrary to the prohibition of the First Amendment which the Fourteenth Amendment made applicable to the states.

First. The due process argument that the state law taxes some people to help others carry out their private purposes is framed in two phases. The first phase is that a state cannot tax A to reimburse B for the cost of transporting his children to church

---

2. Appellant does not challenge the new Jersey statute or the resolution on the ground that either violates the equal protection clause of the Fourteenth Amendment by excluding payment for the transportation of any pupil who attends a "private school run for profit." Although the township resolution authorized reimbursement only for parents of public and Catholic school pupils, appellant does not allege, nor is there anything in the record which would offer the slightest support to an allegation, that there were any children in the township who attended or would have attended, but for want of transportation, any but public and Catholic schools. It will be appropriate to consider the exclusion of students of private schools operated for profit when and if it is proved to have occurred, is made the basis of a suit by one in a position to challenge it, and New Jersey's highest court has ruled adversely to the challenger. Striking down a state law is not a matter of such light moment that it should be done by a federal court *ex mero motu* on a postulate neither charged nor

proved but which rests on nothing but a possibility. *Cf. Liverpool, N.Y. & P.S.S. Co.* v. *Comm'rs of Emigration,* 113 U.S. 33, 39.

3. It might hold the excepting clause to be invalid, and sustain the statute with that clause excised. N.J.R.S., tit. 1, c. 1, § 10, provides with regard to any statute that if "any provision thereof, shall be declared to be unconstitutional . . . in whole or in part, by a court of competent jurisdiction, such . . . article . . . shall, to the extent that it is not unconstitutional, . . . be enforced . . . ." The opinion of the Court of Errors and Appeals in this very case suggests that state law now authorizes transportation of *all* pupils. Its opinion stated: "Since we hold that the legislature may appropriate general state funds or authorize the use of local funds for the transportation of pupils to *any* school, we conclude that such authorization of the use of local funds is likewise authorized by *Pamph. L.* 1941, *ch.* 191, and *R.S.* 18:7–78." 133 N.J.L. 350, 354, 44 A. 2d 333, 337. (Italics supplied.)

schools. This is said to violate the due process clause because the children are sent to these church schools to satisfy the personal desires of their parents, rather than the public's interest in the general education of all children. This argument, if valid, would apply equally to prohibit state payment for the transportation of children to any non-public school, whether operated by a church or any other non-government individual or group. But, the New Jersey legislature has decided that a public purpose will be served by using tax-raised funds to pay the bus fares of all school children, including those who attend parochial schools. The New Jersey Court of Errors and Appeals has reached the same conclusion. The fact that a state law, passed to satisfy a public need, coincides with the personal desires of the individuals most directly affected is certainly an inadequate reason for us to say that a legislature has erroneously appraised the public need.

It is true that this Court has, in rare instances, struck down state statutes on the ground that the purpose for which tax-raised funds were to be expended was not a public one, *Loan Association* v. *Topeka*, 20 Wall. 655; *Parkersburg* v. *Brown*, 106 U.S. 487; *Thompson* v. *Consolidated Gas Utilities Corp.*, 300 U.S. 55. But the Court has also pointed out that this far-reaching authority must be exercised with the most extreme caution. *Green* v. *Frazier*, 253 U.S. 233, 240. Otherwise, a state's power to legislate for the public welfare might be seriously curtailed, a power which is a primary reason for the existence of states. Changing local conditions create new local problems which may lead a state's people and its local authorities to believe that laws authorizing new types of public services are necessary to promote the general well-being of the people. The Fourteenth Amendment did not strip the states of their power to meet problems previously left for individual solution. *Davidson* v. *New Orleans*, 96 U.S. 97, 103–104; *Barbier* v. *Connolly*, 113 U.S. 27, 31–32; *Fallbrook Irrigation District* v. *Bradley,* 164 U.S. 112, 157–158. . . . .

*　　*　　*　　*　　*

Insofar as the second phase of the due process argument may differ from the first, it is by suggesting that taxation for transportation of children to church schools constitutes support of a religion by the State. But if the law is invalid for this reason, it is because it violates the First Amendment's prohibition against the establishment of religion by law. This is the exact question raised by appellant's second contention, to consideration of which we now turn.

Second. The New Jersey statute is challenged as a "law respecting an establishment of religion." The First Amendment, as made applicable to the states by the Fourteenth, *Murdock* v. *Pennsylvania,* 319 U.S. 105, commands that a state "shall make no law respecting an establishment of religion, or prohibiting the free exercise thereof . . . ." These words of the First Amendment reflected in the minds of early Americans a vivid mental picture of conditions and practices which they fervently wished to stamp out in order to preserve liberty for themselves and for their posterity. Doubtless their goal has not been entirely reached; but so far has the Nation moved toward it that the expression "law respecting an establishment of religion," probably does not so vividly remind present-day Americans of the evils, fears, and political problems that caused that expression to be written into our Bill of Rights. Whether this New Jersey law is one respecting an "establishment of religion" requires an understanding of the meaning of that language, particularly with respect to the imposition of taxes. Once again,[4] therefore, it is not inappropriate briefly to review the background and environment of the period in which that constitutional language was fashioned and adopted.

A large proportion of the early settlers of this country came here from Europe to escape the bondage of laws which compelled them to support and attend government-favored churches. The centuries immediately before and contemporaneous with the colonization of America had been filled with turmoil, civil strife, and persecutions, generated in large part by established sects determined to maintain their absolute political and religious supremacy. With the power of government supporting them, at various times and places, Catholics had persecuted Protestants, Protestants had persecuted Catholics, Protestant sects had persecuted other Protestant sects, Catholics of one shade of belief had persecuted Catholics of another shade of belief, and all of these had from time to time persecuted Jews. In efforts to force loyalty to whatever religious group happened to be on top and in league with the government of a particular time and place, men and women had been fined, cast in jail, cruelly tortured, and killed. Among the offenses for which these punishments had been inflicted were such things as speaking disrespectfully of the views of ministers of government-established churches, non-attendance at those churches, expressions of non-belief in their doctrines, and failure to pay taxes and tithes to support them.[5]

These practices of the old world were transplanted to and began to thrive in the soil of the new America. The very charters granted by the English Crown to the individuals and companies designated to make the laws which would control the destinies of the colonials authorized these individuals and companies to erect religious establishments which all, whether believers or non-believers, would be required to support and attend.[6] An exercise of this authority was accompanied by a

4. See *Reynolds* v. *United States*, 98 U.S. 145, 162; *cf. Knowlton* v. *Moore*, 178 U.S. 41, 89, 106.

5. See *e. g.* Macaulay, History of England (1849) I, cc. 2, 4; The Cambridge Modern History (1908) V, cc. V, IX, XI; Beard, Rise of American Civilization (1933) I, 60; Cobb, Rise of Religious Liberty in America (1902) c. II; Sweet, The Story of Religion in America (1939) c. II; Sweet, Religion in Colonial America (1942) 320–322.

6. See *e. g.* the charter of the colony of Carolina which gave the grantees the right of "patronage and advowsons of all the churches and chapels . . . together with licence and power to build and found churches, chapels and oratories . . . and to cause them to be dedicated and consecrated, according to the ecclesiastical laws of our kingdom of England." Poore, Constitutions (1878) II, 1390, 1391. That of Maryland gave to the grantee Lord Baltimore "the Patronages, and Advowsons of all Churches which . . . shall happen to be built, together with Licence and Faculty of erecting and founding Churches, Chapels, and Places of Worship . . . and of causing the same to be dedicated and consecrated according to the Ecclesiastical Laws of our Kingdom of *England*, with all, and singular such,

repetition of many of the old-world practices and persecutions. Catholics found themselves hounded and proscribed because of their faith; Quakers who followed their conscience went to jail; Baptists were peculiarly obnoxious to certain dominant Protestant sects; men and women of varied faiths who happened to be in a minority in a particular locality were persecuted because they steadfastly persisted in worshipping God only as their own consciences dictated.[7] And all of these dissenters were compelled to pay tithes and taxes[8] to support government-sponsored churches whose ministers preached inflammatory sermons designed to strengthen and consolidate the established faith by generating a burning hatred against dissenters.

These practices became so commonplace as to shock the freedom-loving colonials into a feeling of abhorrence.[9] The imposition of taxes to pay ministers' salaries and to build and maintain churches and church property aroused their indignation.[10] It was these feelings which found expression in the First Amendment. No one locality and no one group throughout the Colonies can rightly be given credit for having aroused the sentiment that culminated in adoption of the Bill of Rights' provisions embracing religious liberty. But Virginia, where the established church had achieved a dominant influence in political affairs and where many excesses attracted wide public attention, provided a great stimulus and able leadership for the movement. The people there, as elsewhere, reached the conviction that individual

and as ample Rights, Jurisdictions, Privileges, . . . as any Bishop . . . in our Kingdom of *England*, ever . . . hath had . . . ." MacDonald, Documentary Source Book of American History (1934) 31, 33. The Commission of New Hampshire of 1680, Poore, *supra*, II, 1277, stated: "And above all things We do by these presents will, require and command our said Councill to take all possible care for ye discountenancing of vice and encouraging of virtue and good living; and that by such examples ye infidel may be invited and desire to partake of ye Christian Religion, and for ye greater ease and satisfaction of ye sd loving subjects in matters of religion, We do hereby require and command yt liberty of conscience shall be allowed unto all protestants; yt such especially as shall be conformable to ye rites of ye Church of Engd shall be particularly countenanced and encouraged." See also *Pawlet* v. *Clark*, 9 Cranch 292.

7. See *e. g.* Semple, Baptists in Virginia (1894); Sweet, Religion in Colonial America, *supra* at 131–152, 322–339.

8. Almost every colony exacted some

kind of tax for church support. See *e. g.* Cobb, *op. cit. supra*, note 5, 110 (Virginia); 131 (North Carolina); 169 (Massachusetts); 270 (Connecticut); 304, 310, 339 (New York); 386 (Maryland); 295 (New Hampshire).

9. Madison wrote to a friend in 1774: "That diabolical, hell-conceived principle of persecution rages among some . . . This vexes me the worst of anything whatever. There are at this time in the adjacent country not less than five or six well-meaning men in close jail for publishing their religious sentiments, which in the main are very orthodox. I have neither patience to hear, talk, or think of anything relative to this matter; for I have squabbled and scolded, abused and ridiculed, so long about it to little purpose, that I am without common patience. So I must beg you to pity me, and pray for liberty of conscience to all." I Writings of James Madison (1900) 18, 21.

10. Virginia's resistance to taxation for church support was crystalized in the famous "Parsons' Cause" argued by Patrick Henry in 1763. For an account see Cobb, *op. cit., supra*, note 5, 108–111.

religious liberty could be achieved best under a government which was stripped of all power to tax, to support, or otherwise to assist any or all religions, or to interfere with the beliefs of any religious individual or group.

The movement toward this end reached its dramatic climax in Virginia in 1785–86 when the Virginia legislative body was about to renew Virginia's tax levy for the support of the established church. Thomas Jefferson and James Madison led the fight against this tax. Madison wrote his great Memorial and Remonstrance against the law.[11] In it, he eloquently argued that a true religion did not need the support of law; that no person, either believer or non-believer, should be taxed to support a religious institution of any kind; that the best interest of a society required that the minds of men always be wholly free; and that cruel persecutions were the inevitable result of government-established religions. Madison's Remonstrance received strong support throughout Virginia,[12] and the Assembly postponed consideration of the proposed tax measure until its next session. When the proposal came up for consideration at that session, it not only died in committee, but the Assembly enacted the famous "Virginia Bill for Religious Liberty" originally written by Thomas Jefferson.[13] The preamble to that Bill stated among other things that

> "Almighty God hath created the mind free; that all attempts to influence it by temporal punishments or burthens, or by civil incapacitations, tend only to beget habits of hypocrisy and meanness, and are a departure from the plan of the Holy author of our religion, who being Lord both of body and mind, yet chose not to propagate it by coercions on either . . .; that to compel a man to furnish contributions of money for the propagation of opinions which he disbelieves, is sinful and tyrannical; that even the forcing him to support this or that teacher of his own religious persuasion, is depriving him of the comfortable liberty of giving his contributions to the particular pastor, whose morals he would make his pattern . . . ."

And the statute itself enacted

> "That no man shall be compelled to frequent or support any religious worship, place, or ministry whatsoever, nor shall be enforced, restrained,

11. II Writings of James Madison, 183.

12. In a recently discovered collection of Madison's papers, Madison recollected that his Remonstrance "met with the approbation of the Baptists, the Presbyterians, the Quakers, and the few Roman Catholics, universally; of the Methodists in part; and even of not a few of the Sect formerly established by law." Madison, *Monopolies, Perpetuities, Corporations, Ecclesiastical Endowments*, in Fleet, *Madison's "Detached Memorandum."* 3 William and Mary Q. (1946) 534, 551, 555.

13. For accounts of background and evolution of the Virginia Bill for Religious Liberty see *e.g.* James, The Struggle for Religious Liberty in Virginia: The Baptists (1900); Cobb, *op. cit., supra,* note 5, 74–115; Madison, *Monopolies, Perpetuities, Corporations, Ecclesiastical Endowments, op. cit., supra,* note 12, 554, 556.

molested, or burthened in his body or goods, nor shall otherwise suffer on account of his religious opinions or belief . . . ."[14]

This Court has previously recognized that the provisions of the First Amendment, in the drafting and adoption of which Madison and Jefferson played such leading roles, had the same objective and were intended to provide the same protection against governmental intrusion on religious liberty as the Virginia statute. *Reynolds* v. *United States, supra* at 164; *Watson* v. *Jones,* 13 Wall. 679; *Davis* v. *Beason,* 133 U.S. 333, 342. Prior to the adoption of the Fourteenth Amendment, the First Amendment did not apply as a restraint against the states.[15] Most of them did soon provide similar constitutional protections for religious liberty.[16] But some states persisted for about half a century in imposing restraints upon the free exercise of religion and in discriminating against particular religious groups.[17] In recent years, so far as the provision against the establishment of a religion is concerned, the question has most frequently arisen in connection with proposed state aid to church schools and efforts to carry on religious teachings in the public schools in accordance with the tenets of a particular sect.[18] Some churches have either sought or accepted state financial support for their schools. Here again the efforts to obtain state aid or acceptance of it have not been limited to any one particular faith.[19] The state courts, in the main, have remained faithful to the language of their own constitutional provisions designed to protect religious freedom and to separate religions and governments. Their decisions, however, show the difficulty in drawing the line between tax legislation which provides funds for the welfare of the general public and that which is designed to support institutions which teach religion.[20]

The meaning and scope of the First Amendment, preventing establishment of religion or prohibiting the free exercise thereof, in the light of its history and the evils it was designed forever to suppress, have been several times elaborated by the decisions of this Court prior to the application of the First Amendment to the states by the Fourteenth.[21] The broad meaning given the Amendment by these earlier

14. 12 Hening, Statutes of Virginia (1823) 84; Commager, Documents of American History (1944) 125.

15. *Permoli* v. *New Orleans,* 3, How. 589. *Cf. Barron* v. *Baltimore,* 7 Pet. 243.

16. For a collection of state constitutional provisions on freedom of religion see Gabel, Public Funds for Church and Private Schools (1937) 148–149. See also 2 Cooley, Constitutional Limitations (1927) 960–985.

17. Test provisions forbade officeholders to "deny . . . the truth of the Protestant religion," *e. g.* Constitution of North Carolina (1776) § XXXII, II Poore, *supra,* 1413. Maryland permitted taxation for support of

the Christian religion and limited civil office to Christians until 1818, *id.,* I, 819, 820, 832.

18. See Note 50 Yale L.J. (1941) 917; see also cases collected 14 L.R.A. 418; 5 A.L.R. 879; 141 A.L.R. 1148.

19. See cases collected 14 L.R.A. 418; 5 A.L.R. 879; 141 A.L.R. 1148.

20. *Ibid.* See also Cooley, *op. cit., supra,* note 16.

21. *Terrett* v. *Taylor,* 9 Cranch 43; *Watson* v. *Jones,* 13 Wall. 679; *Davis* v. *Beason,* 133 U.S. 333; *Cf. Reynolds* v. *United States, supra,* 162; *Reuben Quick Bear* v. *Leupp,* 210 U.S. 50.

cases has been accepted by this Court in its decisions concerning an individual's religious freedom rendered since the Fourteenth Amendment was interpreted to make the prohibitions of the First applicable to state action abridging religious freedom.[22] There is every reason to give the same application and broad interpretation to the "establishment of religion" clause. The interrelation of these complementary clauses was well summarized in a statement of the Court of Appeals of South Carolina,[23] quoted with approval by this Court in *Watson* v. *Jones*, 13 Wall. 679, 730: "The structure of our government has, for the preservation of civil liberty, rescued the temporal institutions from religious interference. On the other hand, it has secured religious liberty from the invasion of the civil authority."

The "establishment of religion" clause of the First Amendment means at least this: Neither a state nor the Federal Government can set up a church. Neither can pass laws which aid one religion, aid all religions, or prefer one religion over another. Neither can force nor influence a person to go to or to remain away from church against his will or force him to profess a belief or disbelief in any religion. No person can be punished for entertaining or professing religious beliefs or disbeliefs, for church attendance or non-attendance. No tax in any amount, large or small, can be levied to support any religious activities or institutions, whatever they may be called, or whatever form they may adopt to teach or practice religion. Neither a state nor the Federal Government can, openly or secretly, participate in the affairs of any religious organizations or groups and *vice versa*. In the words of Jefferson, the clause against establishment of religion by law was intended to erect "a wall of separation between church and State." *Reynolds* v. *United States, supra* at 164.

We must consider the New Jersey statute in accordance with the foregoing limitations imposed by the First Amendment. But we must not strike that state statute down if it is within the State's constitutional power even though it approaches the verge of that power. See *Interstate Ry.* v. *Massachusetts*, Holmes, J., *supra* at 85, 88. New Jersey cannot consistently with the "establishment of religion" clause of the First Amendment contribute tax-raised funds to the support of an institution which teaches the tenets and faith of any church. On the other hand, other language of the amendment commands that New Jersey cannot hamper its citizens in the free exercise of their religion. Consequently, it cannot exclude individual Catholics, Lutherans, Mohammedans, Baptists, Jews, Methodists, Non-believers, Presbyterians, or the members of any other faith, *because of their faith, or lack of it,* from receiving the benefits of public welfare legislation. While we do not mean to intimate that a state could not provide transportation only to children attending public schools, we must be careful, in protecting the citizens of New Jersey against state-

22. *Cantwell* v. *Connecticut* 310 U.S. 296; *Jamison* v. *Texas*, 318 U.S. 413; *Largent* v. *Texas*, 318 U.S. 418; *Murdock* v. *Pennsylvania, supra; West Virginia State Board of Education* v. *Barnette*, 319 U.S. 624; *Follett* v. *McCormick*, 321 U.S. 573; *Marsh* v. *Alabama*, 326 U.S. 501. *Cf. Bradfield* v. *Roberts*, U.S. 291.

23. *Harmon* v. *Dreher*, Speer's Equity Reports (S.C., 1843), 87, 120.

established churches, to be sure that we do not inadvertently prohibit New Jersey from extending its general state law benefits to all its citizens without regard to their religious belief.

Measured by these standards, we cannot say that the First Amendment prohibits New Jersey from spending tax-raised funds to pay the bus fares of parochial school pupils as a part of a general program under which it pays the fares of pupils attending public and other schools. It is undoubtedly true that children are helped to get to church schools. There is even a possibility that some of the children might not be sent to the church schools if the parents were compelled to pay their children's bus fares out of their own pockets when transportation to a public school would have been paid for by the State. The same possibility exists where the state requires a local transit company to provide reduced fares to school children including those attending parochial schools,[24] or where a municipally owned transportation system undertakes to carry all school children free of charge. Moreover, state-paid policemen, detailed to protect children going to and from church schools from the very real hazards of traffic, would serve much the same purpose and accomplish much the same result as state provisions intended to guarantee free transportation of a kind which the state deems to be best for the school children's welfare. And parents might refuse to risk their children to the serious danger of traffic accidents going to and from parochial schools, the approaches to which were not protected by policemen. Similarly, parents might be reluctant to permit their children to attend schools which the state had cut off from such general government services as ordinary police and fire protection, connections for sewage disposal, public highways and sidewalks. Of course, cutting off church schools from these services, so separate and so indisputably marked off from the religious function, would make it far more difficult for the schools to operate. But such is obviously not the purpose of the First Amendment. That Amendment requires the state to be a neutral in its relations with groups of religious believers and non-believers; it does not require the state to be their adversary. State power is no more to be used so as to handicap religions than it is to favor them.

This Court has said that parents may, in the discharge of their duty under state compulsory education laws, send their children to a religious rather than a public school if the school meets the secular educational requirements which the state has power to impose. See *Pierce* v. *Society of Sisters,* 268 U.S. 510. It appears that these parochial schools meet New Jersey's requirements. The State contributes no

---

24. New Jersey long ago permitted public utilities to charge school children reduced rates. See *Public S.R. Co.* v. *Public Utility Comm'rs*, 81 N.J.L. 363, 80 A. 27 (1911); see also *Interstate Ry.* v. *Massachusetts, supra*. The District of Columbia Code requires that the new charter of the District public transportation company provide a three-cent fare "for school children . . . going to and from public, parochial, or like schools . . . " 47 Stat. 752, 759.

money to the schools. It does not support them. Its legislation, as applied, does no more than provide a general program to help parents get their children, regardless of their religion, safely and expeditiously to and from accredited schools.

The First Amendment has erected a wall between church and state. That wall must be kept high and impregnable. We could not approve the slightest breach. New Jersey has not breached it here.

Affirmed.

JUSTICE JACKSON'S CONCURRING OPINION OMITTED.

MR. JUSTICE RUTLEDGE, with whom MR. JUSTICE FRANKFURTER, MR. JUSTICE JACKSON and MR. JUSTICE BURTON agree, dissenting.

"Congress shall make no law respecting an establishment of religion, or prohibiting the free exercise thereof . . . ." U.S. Const., Amend. I.

"Well aware that Almighty God hath created the mind free; . . . that to compel a man to furnish contributions of money for the propagation of opinions which he disbelieves, is sinful and tyrannical; . . . .

"*We, the General Assembly, do enact,* That no man shall be compelled to frequent or support any religious worship, place, or ministry whatsoever, nor shall be enforced, restrained, molested, or burthened in his body or goods, nor shall otherwise suffer, on account of his religious opinions or belief . . . ."[1]

I cannot believe that the great author of those words, or the men who made them law, could have joined in this decision. Neither so high nor so impregnable today as yesterday is the wall raised between church and state by Virginia's great statute of religious freedom and the First Amendment, now made applicable to all the states by the Fourteenth.[2] New Jersey's statute sustained is the first, if indeed it is not the second breach to be made by this Court's action. That a third, and a fourth, and still others will be attempted, we may be sure. For just as *Cochran* v. *Board of*

---

1. "A Bill for Establishing Religious Freedom," enacted by the General Assembly of Virginia, January 19, 1786. See 1 Randall, The Life of Thomas Jefferson (1858) 219–220; XII Hening's Statutes of Virginia (1823) 84.

2. *Schneider* v. *State*, 308 U.S. 147; *Cantwell* v. *Connecticut*, 310 U.S. 296; *Murdock* v. *Pennsylvania*, 319 U.S. 516, 530.

Education, 281 U.S. 370, has opened the way by oblique ruling[3] for this decision, so will the two make wider the breach for a third. Thus with time the most solid freedom steadily gives way before continuing corrosive decision.

This case forces us to determine squarely for the first time[4] what was "an establishment of religion" in the First Amendment's conception; and by that measure to decide whether New Jersey's action violates its command. The facts may be stated shortly, to give setting and color to the constitutional problem.

By statute New Jersey has authorized local boards of education to provide for the transportation of children "to and from school other than a public school" except one operated for profit wholly or in part, over established public school routes, or by other means when the child lives "remote from any school."[5] The school board of Ewing Township has provided by resolution for "the transportation of pupils of Ewing to the Trenton and Pennington High Schools and Catholic Schools by way of public carrier...."[6]

Named parents have paid the cost of public conveyance of their children from their homes in Ewing to three public high schools and four parochial schools outside the district.[7] Semiannually the Board has reimbursed the parents from public school

---

3. The briefs did not raise the First Amendment issue. The only one presented was whether the state's action involved a public or an exclusively private function under the due process clause of the Fourteenth Amendment. See Part IV *infra*. On the facts, the cost of transportation here is inseparable from both religious and secular teaching at the religious school. In the *Cochran* case the state furnished secular textbooks only. But see text *infra* at note 40 *et seq.,* and Part IV.

4. Cf. note 3 and text Part IV; see also note 35.

5. The statute reads: "Whenever in any district there are children living remote from any schoolhouse, the board of education of the district may make rules and contracts for the transportation of such children to and from school ... other than a public school, except such school as is operated for profit in whole or in part.

"When any school district provides any transportation for public school children to and from school, transportation from any point in such established school route to any other point in such established school route shall be supplied to school children residing

in such school district in going to and from school other than a public school, except such school as is operated for profit in whole or in part." Laws of New Jersey (1941) c. 191.

6. The full text of the resolution is given in note 59 *infra*.

7. The public schools attended were the Trenton Senior High School, the Trenton Junior High School and the Pennington High School. Ewing Township itself provides no public high schools, affording only elementary public schools which stop with the eighth grade. The Ewing school board pays for both transportation and tuitions of pupils attending the public high schools. The only private schools, all Catholic, covered in application of the resolution are St. Mary's Cathedral High School, Trenton Catholic Boys High School, and two elementary parochial schools, St. Hedwig's Parochial School and St. Francis School. The Ewing board pays only for transportation to these schools, not for tuitions. So far as the record discloses, the board does not pay for or provide transportation to any other elementary school, public or private. See notes 58, 59 and text *infra*.

funds raised by general taxation. Religion is taught as part of the curriculum in each of the four private schools, as appears affirmatively by the testimony of the superintendent of parochial schools in the Diocese of Trenton.

The Court of Errors and Appeal of New Jersey, reversing the Supreme Court's decision, 132 N.J.L. 98, 39 A. 2d 75, has held the Ewing board's action not in contravention of the state constitution or statutes or of the Federal Constitution. 133 N.J.L. 350, 44 A. 2d 333. We have to consider only whether this ruling accords with the prohibition of the First Amendment implied in the due process of the Fourteenth.

I.

Not simply an established church, but any law respecting an establishment of religion is forbidden. The Amendment was broadly but not loosely phrased. It is the compact and exact summation of its author's views formed during his long struggle for religious freedom. In Madison's own words characterizing Jefferson's Bill for Establishing Religious Freedom, the guaranty he put in our national charter, like the bill he piloted through the Virginia Assembly, was "a Model of technical precision, and perspicuous brevity."[8] Madison could not have confused "church" and "religion," or "an established church" and "an establishment of religion."

The Amendment's purpose was not to strike merely at the official establishment of a single sect, creed or religion, outlawing only a formal relation such as had prevailed in England and some of the colonies. Necessarily it was to uproot all such relationships. But the object was broader than separating church and state in this narrow sense. It was to create a complete and permanent separation of the spheres of religious activity and civil authority by comprehensively forbidding every form of public aid or support for religion. In proof the Amendment's wording and history unite with this Court's consistent utterances whenever attention has been fixed directly upon the question.

"Religion" appears only once in the Amendment. But the word governs two prohibitions and governs them alike. It does not have two meanings, one narrow to forbid "an establishment" and another, much broader, for securing "the free exercise thereof." "Thereof" brings down "religion" with its entire and exact content, no more and no less, from the first into the second guaranty, so that Congress and now the states are as broadly restricted concerning the one as they are regarding the other.

8. IX Writings of James Madison (ed. by Hunt, 1910) 288; Padover, Jefferson (1942) 74. Madison's characterization related to Jefferson's entire revision of the Virginia Code, of which the Bill for Establishing Religious Freedom was part. See note 15.

No one would claim today that the Amendment is constricted, in "prohibiting the free exercise" of religion, to securing the free exercise of some formal or creedal observance, of one sect or of many. It secures all forms of religious expression, creedal, sectarian or nonsectarian, wherever and however taking place, except conduct which trenches upon the like freedoms of others or clearly and presently endangers the community's good order and security.[9] For the protective purposes of this phase of the basic freedom, street preaching, oral or by distribution of literature, has been given "the same high estate under the First Amendment as . . . worship in the churches and preaching from the pulpits."[10] And on this basis parents have been held entitled to send their children to private, religious schools. *Pierce* v. *Society of Sisters,* 268 U.S. 510. Accordingly, daily religious education commingled with secular is "religion" within the guaranty's comprehensive scope. So are religious training and teaching in whatever form. The word connotes the broadest content, determined not by the form or formality of the teaching or where it occurs, but by its essential nature regardless of those details.

"Religion" has the same broad significance in the twin prohibition concerning "an establishment." The Amendment was not duplicitous. "Religion" and "establishment" were not used in any formal or technical sense. The prohibition broadly forbids state support, financial or other, of religion in any guise, form or degree. It outlaws all use of public funds for religious purposes.

II.

No provision of the Constitution is more closely tied to or given content by its generating history than the religious clause of the First Amendment. It is at once the refined product and the terse summation of that history. The history includes not only Madison's authorship and the proceedings before the First Congress, but also the long and intensive struggle for religious freedom in America, more especially in

---

9. See *Reynolds* v. *United States,* 98 U.S. 145; *Davis* v. *Beason,* 133 U.S. 333; *Mormon Church* v. *United States,* 136 U.S. 1; *Jacobson* v. *Massachusetts,* 197 U.S. 11; *Prince* v. *Massachusetts,* 321 U.S. 158; also *Cleveland* v. *United States,* 329 U.S. 14.

Possibly the first official declaration of the "clear and present danger" doctrine was Jefferson's declaration in the Virginia Statute for Establishing Religious Freedom: "That it is time enough for the rightful purposes of

civil government for its officers to interfere when principles break out into overt acts against peace and good order." 1 Randall, The Life of Thomas Jefferson (1858) 220; Padover, Jefferson (1942) 81. For Madison's view to the same effect, see note 28 *infra.*

10. *Murdock* v. *Pennsylvania,* 319 U.S. 105, 109; *Martin* v. *Struthers,* 319 U.S. 141; *Jamison* v. *Texas,* 318 U.S. 413; *Marsh* v. *Alabama 326 U.S. 501; Tucker* v. *Texas,* 326 U.S. 517.

Virginia,[11] of which the Amendment was the direct culmination.[12] In the documents of the time, particularly of Madison, who was leader in the Virginia struggle before he became the Amendment's sponsor, but also in the writings of Jefferson and others and in the issues which engendered them is to be found irrefutable confirmation of the Amendment's sweeping content.

For Madision, as also for Jefferson, religious freedom was the crux of the struggle for freedom in general. Remonstrance, Par. 15, Appendix hereto. Madison was coauthor with George Mason of the religious clause in Virginia's great Declaration of Rights of 1776. He is credited with changing it from a mere statement of the principle of tolerance to the first official legislative pronouncement that freedom of conscience and religion are inherent rights of the individual.[13] He sought also to have the Declaration expressly condemn the existing Virginia establishment.[14] But the forces supporting it were then too strong.

Accordingly Madison yielded on this phase but not for long. At once he resumed the fight, continuing it before succeeding legislative sessions. As a member of the General Assembly in 1779 he threw his full weight behind Jefferson's historic Bill for Establishing Religious Freedom. That bill was a prime phase of Jefferson's broad program of democratic reform undertaken on his return from the Continental Congress in 1776 and submitted for the General Assembly's consideration in 1779

11. Conflicts in other states, and earlier in the colonies, contributed much to generation of the Amendment, but none so directly as that in Virginia or with such formative influence on the Amendment's content and wording. See Cobb, Rise of Religious Liberty in America (1902); Sweet, The Story of Religion in America (1939). The Charter of Rhode Island of 1663, II Poore, Constitutions (1878) 1595, was the first colonial charter to provide for religious freedom.

The climactic period of the Virginia struggle covers the decade 1776–1786, from adoption of the Declaration of Rights to enactment of the Statute for Religious Freedom. For short accounts see Padover, Jefferson (1942) c. V; Brant, James Madison, The Virginia Revolutionist (1941) cc. XII, XV; James, The Struggle for Religious Liberty in Virginia (1900) cc. X, XI; Eckenrode, Separation of Church and State in Virginia (1910). These works and Randall, see note 1, will be cited in this opinion by the names of their authors. Citations to "Jefferson" refer to The Works of Thomas Jefferson (ed. by Ford, 1904–1905); to "Madison," to The Writings of James Madison (ed. by Hunt, 1901–1910).

12. Brant, cc. XII, XV; James, cc. X, XI; Eckenrode.

13. See Brant, c. XII, particularly at 243. Cf. Madison's Remonstrance, Appendix to this opinion. Jefferson of course held the same view. See note 15.

"Madison looked upon . . . religious freedom, to judge from the concentrated attention he gave it, as the fundamental freedom." Brant, 243; and see Remonstrance, Par. 1, 4, 15, Appendix.

14. See Brant, 245–246. Madison quoted liberally from the Declaration in his Remonstrance and the use made of the quotations indicates that he considered the Declaration to have outlawed the prevailing establishment in principle, if not technically.

as his proposed revised Virginia code.[15] With Jefferson's departure for Europe in 1784, Madison became the Bill's prime sponsor.[16] Enactment failed in successive legislatures from its introduction in June, 1779, until its adoption in January, 1786. But during all this time the fight for religious freedom moved forward in Virginia on various fronts with growing intensity. Madison led throughout, against Patrick Henry's powerful opposing leadership until Henry was elected governor in November, 1784.

The climax came in the legislative struggle of 1784–1785 over the Assessment Bill. See Supplemental Appendix hereto. This was nothing more nor less than a taxing measure for the support of religion, designed to revive the payment of tithes suspended since 1777. So long as it singled out a particular sect for preference it incurred the active and general hostility of dissentient groups. It was broadened to include them, with the result that some subsided temporarily in their opposition.[17] As altered, the bill gave to each taxpayer the privilege of designating which church should receive his share of the tax. In default of designation the legislature applied it

15. Jefferson was chairman of the revising committee and chief draftsman. Corevisers were Wythe, Pendleton, Mason and Lee. The first enacted portion of the revision, which became known as Jefferson's Code, was the statute barring entailments. Primogeniture soon followed. Much longer the author was to wait for enactment of the Bill for Religious Freedom; and not until after his death was the corollary bill to be accepted in principle which he considered most important of all, namely, to provide for common education at public expense. See V Jefferson, 153. However, he linked this with disestablishment as corollary prime parts in a system of basic freedoms. I Jefferson, 78.

Jefferson, and Madison by his sponsorship, sought to give the Bill for Establishing Religious Freedom as nearly constitutional status as they could at the time. Acknowledging that one legislature could not "restrain the acts of succeeding Assemblies . . . and that therefore to declare this act irrevocable would be of no effect in law," the Bill's concluding provision as enacted nevertheless asserted: "Yet we are free to declare, and do declare, that the rights hereby asserted are of

the natural rights of mankind, and that if any act shall be hereafter passed to repeal the present or to narrow its operation, such act will be an infringement of natural right." 1 Randall, 220.

16. See I Jefferson, 70–71; XII Jefferson, 447; Padover, 80.

17. Madison regarded this action as desertion. See his letter to Monroe of April 12, 1785; II Madison, 129, 131–132; James, cc. X, XI. But see Eckenrode, 91, suggesting it was surrender to the inevitable.

The bill provided: "That for every sum so paid, the Sheriff or Collector shall give a receipt, expressing therein to what society of Christians the person from whom he may receive the same shall direct the money to be paid . . . ." See also notes 19, 43 *infra*.

A copy of the Assessment Bill is to be found among the Washington manuscripts in the Library of Congress. Papers of George Washington, Vol. 231. Because of its crucial role in the Virginia struggle and bearing upon the First Amendment's meaning, the text of the Bill is set forth in the Supplemental Appendix to this opinion.

to pious uses.[18] But what is of the utmost significance here, "in its final form the bill left the taxpayer the option of giving his tax to education."[19]

Madison was unyielding at all times, opposing with all his vigor the general and nondiscriminatory assessments proposed. The modified Assessment Bill passed second reading in December, 1784, and was all but enacted. Madison and his followers, however, maneuvered deferment of final consideration until November, 1785. And before the Assembly reconvened in the fall he issued his historic Memorial and Remonstrance.[20]

This is Madison's complete, though not his only, interpretation of religious liberty.[21] It is a broadside attack upon all forms of "establishment" of religion, both general and particular, nondiscriminatory or selective. Reflecting not only the many legislative conflicts over the assessment Bill and the Bill for Establishing Religious Freedom but also, for example, the struggles for religious incorporations and the continued maintenance of the glebes, the Remonstrance is at once the most concise and the most accurate statement of the views of the First Amendment's author concerning what is "an establishment of religion." Because it behooves us in the dimming distance of time not to lose sight of what he and his coworkers had in mind when, by a single sweeping stroke of the pen, they forbade an establishment of religion and secured its free exercise, the text of the Remonstrance is appended at the end of this opinion for its wider current reference, together with a copy of the bill against which it was directed.

The Remonstrance, stirring up a storm of popular protest, killed the Assessment Bill.[22] It collapsed in committee shortly before Christmas, 1785. With this, the way was cleared at last for enactment of Jefferson's Bill for Establishing Religious Freedom. Madison promptly drove it through in January of 1786, seven years from the time it was first introduced. This dual victory substantially ended the fight over establishments, settling the issue against them. See note 33.

18. Eckenrode, 99, 100.

19. Id., 100; II Madison, 113. The bill directed the sheriff to pay "all sums which . . . may not be appropriated by the person paying the same . . . into the public Treasury, to be disposed of under the direction of the General Assembly, for the encouragement of seminaries of learning within the Counties whence such sums shall arise, and to no other use or purpose whatsoever." Supplemental Appendix.

20. See generally Eckenrode, c.V; Brant, James, and other authorities cited in note 11 above.

21. II Madison, 183; and the Appendix to this opinion. Eckenrode, 100 ff. See also Fleet, Madison's "Detached Memoranda"

(1946) III William & Mary Q. (3d Series) 534, 554–562.

22. The major causes assigned for its defeat include the elevation of Patrick Henry to the governorship in November of 1784; the blunder of the proponents in allowing the Bill for Incorporations to come to the floor and incur defeat before the Assessment Bill was acted on; Madison's astute leadership, taking advantage of every "break" to convert his initial minority into a majority, including the deferment of action on the third reading to the fall; the Remonstrance, bringing a flood of protesting petitions; and the general poverty of the time. See Eckenrode, c. V, for an excellent short, detailed account.

The next year Madison became a member of the Constitutional Convention. Its work done, he fought valiantly to secure the ratification of its great product in Virginia as elsewhere, and nowhere else more effectively.[23] Madison was certain in his own mind that under the Constitution "there is not a shadow of right in the general government to intermeddle with religion"[24] and that "this subject is, for the honor of America, perfectly free and unshackled. The government has no jurisdiction over it . . . ."[25] Nevertheless, he pledged that he would work for a Bill of Rights, including a specific guaranty of religious freedom, and Virginia, with other states, ratified the Constitution on this assurance.[26]

Ratification thus accomplished, Madison was sent to the first Congress. There he went at once about performing his pledge to establish freedom for the nation as he had done in Virginia. Within a little more than three years from his legislative victory at home he had proposed and secured the submission and ratification of the First Amendment as the first article of our Bill or Rights.[27]

All the great instruments of the Virginia struggle for religious liberty thus became warp and woof of our constitutional tradition, not simply by the course of history, but by the common unifying force of Madison's life, thought and sponsorship. He epitomized the whole of that tradition in the Amendment's compact, but nonetheless comprehensive, phrasing.

As the Remonstrance discloses throughout, Madison opposed every form and degree of official relation between religion and civil authority. For him religion was a wholly private matter beyond the scope of civil power either to restrain or to support.[28] Denial or abridgment of religious freedom was a violation of rights both of conscience and of natural equality. State aid was no less obnoxious or destructive to freedom and to religion itself than other forms of state interference. "Establishment" and "free exercise" were correlative and coextensive ideas, representing

23. See James, Brant, *op. cit. supra* note 11.

24. V Madison, 176. Cf. notes 33,37.

25. V Madison, 132.

26. Brant, 250. The assurance made first to his constituents was responsible for Madison's becoming a member of the Virginia Convention which ratified the Constitution. See James, 154–158.

27. The amendment with respect to religious liberties read, as Madison introduced it: "The civil rights of none shall be abridged on account of religious belief or worship, nor shall any national religion be established, nor shall the full and equal rights of conscience be in any manner, or on any pretext, infringed." 1 Annals of Congress 434. In the process of debate this was modified to its present form.

See especially 1 Annals of Congress 729–731, 765; also note 34.

28. See text of the Remonstrance, Appendix; also notes 13, 15, 24, 25 *supra* and text.

Madison's one exception concerning restraint was for "preserving public order." Thus he declared in a private letter, IX Madison, 484, 487, written after the First Amendment was adopted: "The tendency to a usurpation on one side or the other, or to a corrupting coalition or alliance between them, will be best guarded agst. by an entire abstinance of the Govt. from interference in any way whatever, beyond the necessity of preserving public order, & protecting each sect agst. trespasses on its legal rights by others." Cf. note 9.

only different facets of the single great and fundamental freedom. The Remonstrance, following the Virginia statute's example, referred to the history of religious conflicts and the effects of all sorts of establishments, current and historical, to suppress religion's free exercise. With Jefferson, Madison believed that to tolerate any fragment of establishment would be by so much to perpetuate restraint upon that freedom. Hence he sought to tear out the institution not partially but root and branch, and to bar its return forever.

In no phase was he more unrelentingly absolute than in opposing state support or aid by taxation. Not even "three pence" contribution was thus to be exacted from any citizen for such a purpose. Remonstrance, Par. 3.[29] Tithes had been the lifeblood of establishment before and after other compulsions disappeared. Madison and his coworkers made no exceptions or abridgments to the complete separation they created. Their objection was not to small tithes. It was to any tithes whatsoever. "If it were lawful to impose a small tax for religion, the admission would pave the way for oppressive levies."[30] Not the amount but "the principle of assessment was wrong." And the principle was as much to prevent "the interference of law in religion" as to restrain religious intervention in political matters.[31] In this field the authors of our freedom would not tolerate "the first experiment on our liberties" or "wait till usurped power had strengthened itself by exercise, and entangled the question in precedents." Remonstrance, Par. 3. Nor should we.

In view of this history no further proof is needed that the Amendment forbids any appropriation, large or small, from public funds to aid or support any and all religious exercises. But if more were called for, the debates in the First Congress and this Court's consistent expressions, whenever it has touched on the matter directly,[32] supply it.

---

29. The third ground of remonstrance, see the Appendix, bears repetition for emphasis here: "Because, it is proper to take alarm at the first experiement on our liberties . . . The freemen of America did not wait till usurped power had strengthened itself by exercise, and entangled the question in precedents. They saw all the consequences in the principle, and they avoided the consequences by denying the principle. We revere this lesson too much, soon to forget it. Who does not see that . . . the same authority which can force a citizen to *contribute three pence* only of his property for the support of any one establishment, may force him to conform to any other establishment in all cases whatsoever?" (Emphasis added.) II

Madison 183, 185–186.

30. Eckenrode, 105, in summary of the Remonstrance.

31. "Because the bill implies either that the Civil Magistrate is a competent Judge of Religious truth; or that he may employ Religion as an engine of Civil policy. The first is an arrogant pretention falsified by the contradictory opinions of Rulers in all ages, and throughout the world: The second an unhallowed perversion of the means of salvation." Remonstrance, Appendix, Par. 5; II Madison 183, 187.

32. As is pointed out above, note 3, and in Part IV *infra, Cochran* v. *Board of Education,* 281 U.S. 370, was not such a case.

By contrast with the Virginia history, the congressional debates on consideration of the Amendment reveal only sparse discussion, reflecting the fact that the essential issues had been settled.[33] Indeed the matter had become so well understood as to have been taken for granted in all but formal phrasing. Hence, the only enlightening reference shows concern, not to preserve any power to use public funds in aid of religion, but to prevent the Amendment from outlawing private gifts inadvertently by virtue of the breadth of its wording.[34] In the margin are noted also the principal

33. See text *supra* at notes 24, 25. Madison, of course, was but one of many holding such views, but nevertheless agreeing to the common understanding for adoption of a Bill of Rights in order to remove all doubt engendered by the absence of explicit guaranties in the original Constitution.

By 1791 the great fight over establishments had ended, although some vestiges remained then and later, even in Virginia. The glebes, for example, were not sold there until 1802. Cf. Eckenrode, 147. Fixing an exact date for "disestablishment" is almost impossible, since the process was piecemeal. Although Madison failed in having the Virginia Bill of Rights declare explicitly against establishment in 1776, cf. note 14 and text *supra*, in 1777 the levy for support of the Anglican clergy was suspended. It was never resumed. Eckenrode states: "This act, in effect, destroyed the establishment. Many dates have been given for its end, but it really came on January 1, 1777, when the act suspending the payment of tithes became effective. This was not seen at the time. . . . But in freeing almost half of the taxpayers from the burden of the state religion, the state religion was at an end. Nobody could be forced to support it, and an attempt to levy tithes upon Anglicans alone would be to recruit the ranks of dissent." P. 53. See also pp. 61, 64. The question of assessment however was revived "with far more strength than ever, in the summer of 1784." *Id.,* 64. It would seem more factual therefore to fix the time of disestablishment as of December, 1785–January, 1786, when the issue in large

was finally settled.

34. At one point the wording proposed: "No religion shall be established by law, nor shall the equal rights of conscience be infringed." 1 Annals of Congress 729. Cf. note 27. Representative Huntington of Connecticut feared this might be construed to prevent judicial enforcement of private pledges. He stated "that he feared . . . that the words might be taken in such latitude as to be extremely hurtful to the cause of religion. He understood the amendment to mean what had been expressed by the gentleman from Virginia; but others might find it convenient to put another construction upon it. The ministers of their congregations to the Eastward were maintained by the contributions of those who belonged to their society; the expense of building meeting-houses was contributed in the same manner. These things were regulated by by-laws. If an action was brought before a Federal Court on any of these cases, the person who had neglected to perform his engagements could not be compelled to do it; for a support of ministers or building of places of worship might be construed into a religious establishment." 1 Annals of Congress 730.

To avoid any such possibility, Madison suggested inserting the word "national" before "religion," thereby not only again disclaiming intent to bring about the result Huntington feared but also showing unmistakably that "establishment" meant public "support" of religion in the financial sense. 1 Annals of Congress 731. See also IX Madison, 484–487.

decisions in which expressions of the Court confirm the Amendment's broad prohibition.[35]

III.

Compulsory attendance upon religious exercises went out early in the process of separating church and state, together with forced observance of religious forms and ceremonies.[36] Test oaths and religious qualification for office followed later.[37] These things none devoted to our great tradition of religious liberty would think of bringing back. Hence today, apart from efforts to inject religious training or exercises and sectarian issues into the public schools, the only serious surviving threat to maintaining that complete and permanent separation of religion and civil power which the First Amendment commands is through use of the taxing power to support religion, religious establishments, or establishments having a religious foundation whatever their form or special religious function.

Does New Jersey's action furnish support for religion by use of the taxing power? Certainly it does, if the test remains undiluted as Jefferson and Madison made it, that money taken by taxation from one is not to be used or given to support another's religious training or belief, or indeed one's own.[38] Today as then the

---

35. The decision most closely touching the question, where it was squarely raised, is *Quick Bear* v. *Leupp*, 210 U.S. 50. The Court distinguished sharply between appropriations from public funds for the support of religious education and appropriations from funds held in trust by the Government essentially as trustee for private individuals, Indian wards, as beneficial owners. The ruling was that the latter could be disbursed to private, religious schools at the designation of those patrons for paying the cost of their education. But it was stated also that such a use of public moneys would violate both the First Amendment and the specific statutory declaration involved, namely, that "it is hereby declared to be the settled policy of the Government to hereafter make no appropriation whatever for education in any sectarian school." 210 U.S. at 79. Cf. *Ponce* v. *Roman Catholic Apostolic Church*, 210 U.S. 296, 322. And see *Bradfield* v. *Roberts*, 175 U.S. 291, an instance of highly artificial grounding to support a decision sustaining an appropriation for the care of indigent patients pursuant to a contract with a private hospital. Cf. also the authorities cited in note 9.

36. See text at note 1.

37. ". . . but no religious Test shall ever be required as a Qualification to any Office or public Trust under the United States." Const., Art. VI, § 3. See also the two forms prescribed for the President's Oath or Affirmation. Const., Art II, § 1. Cf. *Ex parte Garland*, 4 Wall. 333; *Cummings* v. *Missouri*, 4 Wall. 277; *United States* v. *Lovett*, 328 U.S. 303.

38. In the words of the Virginia statute, following the portion of the preamble quoted at the beginning of this opinion: ". . . even the forcing him to support this or that teacher of his own religious persuasion, is depriving him of the comfortable liberty of giving his contributions to the particular pastor, whose morals he would make his pattern, and whose powers he feels most persuasive to righteousness, and is withdrawing from the ministry those temporary rewards, which proceeding from an approbation of their personal conduct, are an additional incitement to earnest and unremitting labours for the instruction of mankind . . . ." Cf. notes 29, 30, 31 and text *supra*.

furnishing of "contributions of money for the propagation of opinions which he disbelieves" is the forbidden exaction; and the prohibition is absolute for whatever measure brings that consequence and whatever amount may be sought or given to that end.

The funds used here were raised by taxation. The Court does not dispute, nor could it, that their use does in fact give aid and encouragement to religious instruction. It only concludes that this aid is not "support" in law. But Madison and Jefferson were concerned with aid and support in fact, not as a legal conclusion "entangled in precedents." Remonstrance, Par. 3. Here parents pay money to send their children to parochial schools and funds raised by taxation are used to reimburse them. This not only helps the children to get to school and the parents to send them. It aids them in a substantial way to get the very thing which they are sent to the particular school to secure, namely religious training and teaching.

Believers of all faiths, and others who do not express their feeling toward ultimate issues of existence in any creedal form, pay the New Jersey tax. When the money so raised is used to pay for transportation to religious schools, the Catholic taxpayer to the extent of his proportionate share pays for the transportation to religious schools, of Lutheran, Jewish and otherwise religiously affiliated children to receive their non-Catholic religious instruction. Their parents likewise pay proportionately for the transportation of Catholic children to receive Catholic instruction. Each thus contributes to "the propagation of opinions which he disbelieves" in so far as their religions differ, as do others who accept no creed without regard to those differences. Each thus pays taxes also to support the teaching of his own religion, an exaction equally forbidden since it denies "the comfortable liberty" of giving one's contribution to the particular agency of instruction he approves.[39]

New Jersey's action therefore exactly fits the type of exaction and the kind of evil at which Madison and Jefferson struck. Under the test they framed it cannot be said that the cost of transportation is no part of the cost of education or of the religious instruction given. That it is a substantial and a necessary element is shown most plainly by the continuing and increasing demand for the state to assume it. Nor is there pretense that it relates only to the secular instruction given in religious schools or that any attempt is or could be made toward allocating proportional shares as between the secular and the religious instruction. It is precisely because the instruction is religious and relates to a particular faith, whether one or another, that parents send their children to religious schools under the *Pierce* doctrine. And the very purpose of the state's contribution is to defray the cost of conveying the pupil to the place where he will receive not simply secular, but also and primarily religious, teaching and guidance.

39. See note 38.

Indeed the view is sincerely avowed by many of various faiths,[40] that the basic purpose of all education is or should be religious, that the secular cannot be and should not be separated from the religious phase and emphasis. Hence, the inadequacy of public or secular education and the necessity for sending the child to a school where religion is taught. But whatever may be the philosophy or its justification, there is undeniably an admixture of religious with secular teaching in all such institutions. That is the very reason for their being. Certainly for purposes of constitutionality we cannot contradict the whole basis of the ethical and educational convictions of people who believe in religious schooling.

Yet this very admixture is what was disestablished when the First Amendment forbade "an establishment of religion." Commingling the religious with the secular teaching does not divest the whole of its religious permeation and emphasis or make them of minor part, if proportion were material. Indeed, on any other view, the constitutional prohibition always could be brought to naught by adding a modicum of the secular.

An appropriation from the public treasury to pay the cost of transportation to Sunday school, to weekday special classes at the church or parish house, or to the meetings of various young people's religious societies, such as the Y.M.C.A., the Y.W.C.A., the Y.M.H.A., the Epworth League, could not withstand the constitutional attack. This would be true, whether or not secular activities were mixed with the religious. If such an appropriation could not stand, then it is hard to see how one becomes valid for the same thing upon the more extended scale of daily instruction. Surely constitutionality does not turn on where or how often the mixed teaching occurs.

Finally, transportation, where it is needed, is as essential to education as any other element. Its cost is as much a part of the total expense, except at times in amount, as the cost of textbooks, of school lunches, of athletic equipment, of writing and other materials; indeed of all other items composing the total burden. Now as always the core of the educational process is the teacher-pupil relationship. Without this the richest equipment and facilities would go for naught. See *Judd* v. *Board of Education*, 278 N.Y. 200, 212, 15 N.E. 2d 576, 582. But the proverbial Mark Hopkins conception no longer suffices for the country's requirements. Without buildings, without equipment, without library, textbooks and other materials, and without transportation to bring teacher and pupil together in such an effective teaching environment, there can be not even the skeleton of what our times require. Hardly can it be maintained that transportation is the least essential of these items, or that it does not in fact aid, encourage, sustain and support, just as they do, the very

---

40. See Bower, Church and State in Education (1944) 58: ". . . the fundamental division of the education of the whole self into the secular and the religious could not be justified on the grounds of either a sound educational philosophy or a modern functional concept of the relation of religion to personal and social experience." See also Vere, The Elementary School, in Essays on Catholic Education in the United States (1942) 110–111; Gabel, Public Funds for Church and Private Schools (1937) 737–739.

process which is its purpose to accomplish. No less essential is it, or the payment of its cost, than the very teaching in the classroom or payment of the teacher's sustenance. Many types of equipment, now considered essential, better could be done without.

For me, therefore, the feat is impossible to select so indispensable an item from the composite of total costs, and characterize it as not aiding, contributing to, promoting or sustaining the propagation of beliefs which it is the very end of all to bring about. Unless this can be maintained, and the Court does not maintain it, the aid thus given is outlawed. Payment of transportation is no more, nor is it any the less essential to education, whether religious or secular, than payment for tuitions, for teachers' salaries, for buildings, equipment and necessary materials. Nor is it any the less directly related, in a school giving religious instruction, to the primary religious objective all those essential items of cost are intended to achieve. No rational line can be drawn between payment for such larger, but not more necessary, items and payment for transportation. The only line that can be so drawn is one between more dollars and less. Certainly in this realm such a line can be no valid constitutional measure. *Murdock* v. *Pennsylvania*, 319 U.S. 105; *Thomas* v. *Collins*, 323 U.S. 516.[41] Now, as in Madison's time, not the amount but the principle of assessment is wrong. Remonstrance, Par. 3.

IV.

But we are told that the New Jersey statute is valid in its present application because the appropriation is for a public, not a private purpose, namely, the promotion of education, and the majority accept this idea in the conclusion that all we have here is "public welfare legislation." If that is true and the Amendment's force can be thus destroyed, what has been said becomes all the more pertinent. For then there could be no possible objection to more extensive support of religious education by New Jersey.

If the fact alone be determinative that religious schools are engaged in education, thus promoting the general and individual welfare, together with the legislature's decision that the payment of public moneys for their aid makes their work a public function, then I can see no possible basis, except one of dubious legislative policy, for the state's refusal to make full appropriation for support of private, religious

---

41. It would seem a strange ruling that a "reasonable," that is, presumably a small, license fee cannot be placed upon the exercise of the right of religious instruction, yet that under the correlative constitutional guaranty against "an establishment" taxes may be levied and used to aid and promote religious instruction, if only the amounts used are small. See notes 30–31 *supra* and text.

Madison's objection to "three pence"

contributions and his stress upon "denying the principle" without waiting until "usurped power had . . . entangled the question in precedents," note 29, were reinforced by his further characterization of the Assessment Bill: "Distant as it may be, in its present form, from the Inquisition it differs from it only in degree. The one is the first step, the other the last in the career of intolerance." Remonstrance, Par. 9; II Madison 183, 188.

schools, just as is done for public instruction. There could not be, on that basis, valid constitutional objection.[42]

Of course paying the cost of transportation promotes the general cause of education and the welfare of the individual. So does paying all other items of educational expense. And obviously, as the majority say, it is much too late to urge that legislation designed to facilitate the opportunities of children to secure a secular education serves no public purpose. Our nation-wide system of public education rests on the contrary view, as do all grants in aid of education, public or private, which is not religious in character.

These things are beside the real question. They have no possible materiality except to obscure the all-pervading, inescapable issue. *Cf. Cochran* v. *Board of Education, supra*. Stripped of its religious phase, the case presents no substantial federal question. *Ibid.* The public function argument, by casting the issue in terms of promoting the general cause of education and the welfare of the individual, ignores the religious factor and its essential connection with the transportation, thereby leaving out the only vital element in the case. So of course do the "public welfare" and "social legislation" ideas, for they come to the same thing.

We have here then one substantial issue, not two. To say that new Jersey's appropriation and her use of the power of taxation for raising the funds appropriated are not for public purposes but are for private ends, is to say that they are for the support of religion and religious teaching. Conversely, to say that they are for public purposes is to say that they are not for religious ones.

This is precisely for the reason that education which includes religious training and teaching, and its support, have been made matters of private right and function, not public, by the very terms of the First Amendment. That is the effect not only in its guaranty of religion's free exercise, but also in the prohibition of establishments. It was on this basis of the private character of the function of religious education that this Court held parents entitled to send their children to private, religious schools. *Pierce* v. *Society of Sisters, supra*. Now it declares in effect that the appropriation of public funds to defray part of the cost of attending those schools is for a public purpose. If so, I do not understand why the state cannot go farther or why this case approaches the verge of its power.

In truth this view contradicts the whole purpose and effect of the First

---

42. If it is part of the state's function to supply to religious schools or their patrons the smaller items of educational expense, because the legislature may say they perform a public function, it is hard to see why the larger ones also may not be paid. Indeed, it would seem even more proper and necessary for the state to do this. For if one class of expenditures is justified on the ground that it supports the general cause of education or benefits the individual, or can be made to do so by legislative declaration, so even more certainly would be the other. To sustain payment for transportation to school, for textbooks, for other essential materials, or perhaps for school lunches, and not for what makes all these things effective for their intended end, would be to make a public function of the smaller items and their cumulative effect, but to make wholly private in character the larger things without which the smaller could have no meaning or use.

Amendment as heretofore conceived. The "public function"—"public welfare"—
"social legislation" argument seeks, in Madison's words, to "employ Religion [that
is, here, religious education] as an engine of Civil policy." Remonstrance, Par. 5. It
is of one piece with the Assessment Bill's preamble, although with the vital
difference that it wholly ignores what that preamble explicitly states.[43]

Our constitutional policy is exactly the opposite. It does not deny the value or the
necessity for religious training, teaching or observance. Rather it secures their free
exercise. But to that end it does deny that the state can undertake or sustain them in
any form or degree. For this reason the sphere of religious activity, as distinguished
from the secular intellectual liberties, has been given the two fold protection and, as
the state cannot forbid, neither can it perform or aid in performing the religious
function. The dual prohibition makes that function altogether private. It cannot be
made a public one by legislative act. This was the very heart of Madison's
Remonstrance, as it is of the Amendment itself.

It is not because religious teaching does not promote the public or the
individual's welfare, but because neither is furthered when the state promotes
religious education, that the Constitution forbids it to do so. Both legislatures and
courts are bound by that distinction. In failure to observe it lies the fallacy of the
"public function"—"social legislation" argument, a fallacy facilitated by easy
transference of the argument's basing from due process unrelated to any religious
aspect to the First Amendment.

By no declaration that a gift of public money to religious uses will promote the
general or individual welfare, or the cause of education generally, can legislative
bodies overcome the Amendment's bar. Nor may the courts sustain their attempts to
do so by finding such consequences for appropriations which in fact give aid to or
promote religious uses. Cf. *Norris* v. *Alabama*, 294 U.S. 587, 590; *Hooven &
Allison Co.* v. *Evatt*, 324 U.S. 652, 659; *Akins* v. *Texas*, 325 U.S. 398, 402.
Legislatures are free to make, and courts to sustain, appropriations only when it can
be found that in fact they do not aid, promote, encourage or sustain religious
teaching or observances, be the amount large or small. No such finding has been or
could be made in this case. The Amendment has removed this form of promoting the
public welfare from legislative and judicial competence to make a public function. It
is exclusively a private affair.

The reasons underlying the Amendment's policy have not vanished with time or
diminished in force. Now as when it was adopted the price of religious freedom is

43. "Whereas the general diffusion of
Christian knowledge hath a natural tendency
to correct the morals of men, restrain their
vices, and preserve the peace of society;
which cannot be effected without a competent provision for learned teachers, who
may be thereby enabled to devote their time
and attention to the duty of instructing such
citizens, as from their circumstances and
want of education, cannot otherwise attain
such knowledge; and it is judged that such
provision may be made by the Legislature,
without counteracting the liberal principle
heretofore adopted and intended to be preserved by abolishing all distinctions of pre-
eminence amongst the different societies of
communities of Christians; . . . ." Supplemental Appendix; Foote, Sketches of Virginia (1850) 340.

double. It is that the church and religion shall live both within and upon that freedom. There cannot be freedom of religion, safeguarded by the state, and intervention by the church or its agencies in the state's domain or dependency on its largesse. Madison's Remonstrance, Par. 6, 8.[44] The great condition of religious liberty is that it be maintained free from sustenance, as also from other interferences, by the state. For when it comes to rest upon that secular foundation it vanishes with the resting. *Id.,* Par. 7, 8.[45] Public money devoted to payment of religious costs, educational or other, brings the quest for more. It brings too the struggle of sect against sect for the larger share or for any. Here one by numbers alone will benefit most, there another. That is precisely the history of societies which have had an established religion and dissident groups. *Id.,* Par. 8, 11. It is the very thing Jefferson and Madison experienced and sought to guard against, whether in its blunt or in its more screened forms. *Ibid.,* The end of such strife cannot be other than to destroy the cherished liberty. The dominating group will achieve the dominant benefit; or all will embroil the state in their dissensions. *Id.,* Par. 11.[46]

Exactly such conflicts have centered of late around providing transportation to religious schools from public funds.[47] The issue and the dissension work typically, in

44. "Because the establishment proposed by the Bill is not requisite for the support of the Christian Religion. To say that it is, is a contradiction to the Christian Religion itself; for every page of it disavows a dependence on the powers of this world . . . . Because the establishment in question is not necessary for the support of Civil Government. . . . What influence in fact have ecclesiastical establishments had on Civil Society? . . . in no instance have they been seen the guardians of the liberties of the people." II Madison 183, 187, 188.

45. "Because experience witnesseth that ecclesiastical establishments, instead of maintaining the purity and efficacy of Religion, have had a contrary operation." II Madison 183, 187.

46. "At least let warning be taken at the first fruits of the threatened innovation. The very appearance of the Bill has transformed that 'Christian forbearance, love and charity,' which of late mutually prevailed, into animosities and jealousies, which may not soon be appeased." II Madison 183, 189.

47. In this case briefs *amici curiae* have been filed on behalf of various organizations representing three religious sects, one labor union, the American Civil Liberties Union, and the states of Illinois, Indiana, Louisiana, Massachusetts, Michigan and New York. All these states have laws similar to New Jersey's and all of them, with one religious sect, support the constitutionality of New Jersey's action. The others oppose it. Maryland and Mississippi have sustained similar legislation. Note 49 *infra.* No state without legislation of this sort has filed an opposing brief. But at least six states have held such action invalid, namely Delaware, Oklahoma, New York, South Dakota, Washington and Wisconsin. Note 49 *infra.* The New York ruling was overturned by amendment to the state constitution in 1938. Constitution of New York, Art. XI, 4.

Furthermore, in this case the New Jersey courts divided, the Supreme Court holding the statute and resolution invalid, 132 N.J.L. 98, 39 A. 2d 75, the Court of Errors and Appeals reversing that decision, 133 N.J.L. 350, 44 A. 2d 333. In both courts, as here, the judges split, one of three dissenting in the Supreme Court, three of nine in the Court of Errors and Appeals. The division is typical. See the cases cited in note 49.

Madison's phrase, to "destroy that moderation and harmony which the forbearance of our laws to intermeddle with Religion, has produced amongst its several sects." *Id.,* Par. 11. This occurs, as he well knew, over measures at the very threshold of departure from the principle. *Id.,* Par. 3, 9, 11.

In these conflicts wherever success has been obtained it has been upon the contention that by providing the transportation the general cause of education, the general welfare, and the welfare of the individual will be forwarded; hence that the matter lies within the realm of public function, for legislative determination.[48] A few have recognized that this dicotomy is false, that both in fact are aided.[50]

The majority here does not accept in terms any of those views. But neither does it deny that the individual or the school, or indeed both, are benefited directly and substantially.[51] To do so would cut the ground from under the public function—social legislation thesis. On the contrary, the opinion concedes that the children are aided by being helped to get to the religious schooling. By converse necessary implication as well as by the absence of express denial, it must be taken to concede also that the school is helped to reach the child with its religious teaching. The religious enterprise is common to both, as is the interest in having transportation for its religious purposes provided.

48. See the authorities cited in note 49; and see note 54.

49. Some state courts have sustained statutes granting free transportation or free school books to children attending denominational schools on the theory that the aid was a benefit to the child rather than to the school. See *Nichols* v. *Henry,* 301 Ky. 434, 191 S.W. 2d 930, with which compare *Sherrard* v. *Jefferson County Board of Education,* 294 Ky. 496, 171 S.W. 2d 963; *Cochran* v. *Board of Education,* 168 La. 1030, 123 So. 664, aff'd, 281 U.S. 370; *Borden* v. *Board of Education,* 168 La. 1005, 123 Ao. 655; *Board of Education* v. *Wheat,* 174 Md. 314, 199 A. 628; *Adams* v. *St. Mary;s County,* 180 Md. 550, 26 A. 2d 377; *Chance* v. *State Textbook R. & P. Board,* 190 Miss. 453, 200 So. 706. See also *Bowker* v. *Baker,* 73 Cal. App. 2d 653, 167 P. 2d 256. Other courts have held such statutes unconstitutional under state constitutions as aid to the schools. *Judd* v. *Board of Education,* 278 N.Y. 200, 15 N.E. 2d 576, but see note 47 *supra; Smith* v. *Donahue,* 202 App. Div. 656, 195 N.Y.S. 715; *State ex rel. Traub* v. *Brown,* 36 Del. 181, 172 A. 835; *Gurney* v. *Ferguson,* 190 Okla. 254,

122 P. 2d 1002; *Mitchell* v. *Consolidated School District,* 17 Wash. 2d 61, 135 P. 2d 79; *Van Strated* v. *Milquet,* 180 Wis. 109, 192 N.W. 392. And cf. *Hlebanja* v. *Brewe,* 58 S.D. 351, 236 N.W. 296. And since many state constitutions have provisions forbidding the appropriation of public funds for private purposes, in these and other cases the issue whether the statute was for a "public" or "private" purpose has been present. See Note (1941) 50 Yale L.J. 917, 925.

50. *E.g., Gurney* v. *Ferguson,* 190 Okla. 254, 255, 122 P. 2d 1002, 1003; *Mitchell* v. *Consolidated School District,* 17 Wash. 2d 61, 68 135 P. 2d 79, 82; *Smith* v. *Donahue,* App. Div. 656, 664, 195 N.Y.S. 715, 722; *Board of Education* v. *Wheat,* 174 Md. 314, dissenting opinion at 340, 199 A. 628 at 639. This is true whether the appropriation and payment are in form to the individual or to the institution. *Ibid.* Questions of this gravity turn upon the purpose and effect of the state's expenditure to accomplish the forbidden object, not upon who receives the amount and applies it to that end or the form and manner of the payment.

51. The payments here averaged roughly $40.00 a year per child.

Notwithstanding the recognition that this two-way aid is given and the absence of any denial that religious teaching is thus furthered, the Court concludes that the aid so given is not "support" of religion. It is rather only support of education as such, without reference to its religious content, and thus becomes public welfare legislation. To this elision of the religious element from the case is added gloss in two respects, one that the aid extended partakes of the nature of a safety measure, the other that failure to provide it would make the state unneutral in religious matters, discriminating against or hampering such children concerning public benefits all others receive.

As will be noted, the one gloss is contradicted by the facts of record and the other is of whole cloth with the "public function" argument's excision of the religious factor.[52] But most important is that this approach, if valid, supplies a ready method for nullifying the Amendment's guaranty, not only for this case and others involving small grants in aid for religious education, but equally for larger ones. The only thing needed will be for the Court again to transplant the "public welfare—public function" view from its proper nonreligious due process bearing to First Amendment application, holding that religious education is not "supported" though it may be aided by the appropriation, and that the cause of education generally is furthered by helping the pupil to secure that type of training.

This is not therefore just a little case over bus fares. In paraphrase of Madison, distant as it may be in its present form from a complete establishment of religion, it differs from it only in degree; and is the first step in that direction. *Id.*, Par. 9.[53] Today as in his time "the same authority which can force a citizen to contribute three pence only . . . for the support of any one [religious] establishment, may force him" to pay more; or "to conform to any other establishment in all cases whatsoever." And now, as then, "either . . . we must say, that the will of the Legislature is the only measure of their authority; and that in the plenitude of this authority, they may sweep away all our fundamental rights; or, that they are bound to leave this particular right untouched and sacred." Remonstrance, Par. 15.

The realm of religious training and belief remains, as the Amendment made it, the kingdom of the individual man and his God. It should be kept inviolately private, not "entangled . . . in precedents"[54] or confounded with what legislatures legitimately may take over into the public domain.

V.

No one conscious of religious values can be unsympathetic toward the burden which our constitutional separation puts on parents who desire religious instruction mixed with secular for their children. They pay taxes for others' children's

52. See Part V.

53. See also note 46 *supra* and Remonstrance, Par. 3.

54. Thus each brief filed here by the supporters of New Jersey's action, see note 47, not only relies strongly on *Cochran* v. *Board of Education*, 281 U.S. 370, but either explicitly or in effect maintains that it is controlling in the present case.

education, at the same time the added cost of instruction for their own. Nor can one happily see benefits denied to children which others receive, because in conscience they or their parents for them desire a different kind of training others do not demand.

But if those feelings should prevail, there would be an end to our historic constitutional policy and command. No more unjust or discriminatory in fact is it to deny attendants at religious schools the cost of their transportation than it is to deny them tuitions, sustenance for their teachers, or any other educational expense which others receive at public cost. Hardship in fact there is which none can blink. But, for assuring to those who undergo it the greater, the most comprehensive freedom, it is one written by design and firm intent into our basic law.

Of course discrimination in the legal sense does not exist. The child attending the religious school has the same right as any other to attend the public school. But he foregoes exercising it because the same guaranty which assures this freedom forbids the public school or any agency of the state to give or aid him in securing the religious instruction he seeks.

Were he to accept the common school, he would be the first to protest the teaching there of any creed or faith not his own. And it is precisely for the reason that their atmosphere is wholly secular that children are not sent to public schools under the *Pierce* doctrine. But that is a constitutional necessity, because we have staked the very existence of our country on the faith that complete separation between the state and religion is best for the state and best for religion. Remonstrance, Par. 8, 12.

That policy necessarily entails hardship upon persons who forego the right to educational advantages the state can supply in order to secure others it is precluded from giving. Indeed this may hamper the parent and the child forced by conscience to that choice. But it does not make the state unneutral to withhold what the Constitution forbids it to give. On the contrary it is only by observing the prohibition rigidly that the state can maintain its neutrality and avoid partisanship in the dissensions inevitable when sect opposes sect over demands for public moneys to further religious education, teaching or training in any form or degree, directly or indirectly. Like St. Paul's freedom, religious liberty with a great price must be bought. And for those who exercise it most fully, by insisting upon religious education for their children mixed with secular, by the terms of our Constitution the price is greater than for others.

The problem then cannot be cast in terms of legal discrimination or its absence. This would be true, even though the state in giving aid should treat all religious instruction alike. Thus, if the present statute and its application were shown to apply equally to all religious schools of whatever faith,[55] yet in the light of our tradition it

---

55. See text at notes 17–19 *supra* and authorities cited; also Foote, Sketches of Virginia (1850) c. XV. Madison's entire thesis, as reflected throughout the Remonstrance and in his other writings, as well as in his opposition to the final form of the Assessment Bill, see note 43, was altogether incompatible with acceptance of general and "non-discriminatory" support. See Brant, c. XII.

could not stand. For then the adherent of one creed still would pay for the support of another, the childless taxpayer with others more fortunate. Then too there would seem to be no bar to making appropriations for transportation and other expense of children attending public or other secular schools, after hours in separate places and classes for their exclusively religious instruction. The person who embraces no creed also would be forced to pay for teaching what he does not believe. Again, it was the furnishing of "contributions of money for the propagation of opinions which he disbelieves" that the fathers outlawed. That consequence and effect are not removed by multiplying to all-inclusiveness the sects for which support is exacted. The Constitution requires, not comprehensive identification of state with religion, but complete separation.

VI.

Short treatment will dispose of what remains. Whatever might be said of some other application of New Jersey's statute, the one made here has no semblance of bearing as a safety measure or, indeed, for securing expeditious conveyance. The transportation supplied is by public conveyance, subject to all the hazards and delays of the highway and the streets incurred by the public generally in going about its multifarious business.

Nor is the case comparable to one of furnishing fire or police protection, or access to public highways. These things are matters of common right, part of the general need for safety.[56] Certainly the fire department must not stand idly by while the church burns. Nor is this reason why the state should pay the expense of transportation or other items of the cost of religious education.[57]

---

56. The protections are of a nature which does not require appropriations specially made from the public treasury and earmarked, as is New Jersey's here, particularly for religious property or activities from protection against disorder or the ordinary accidental incidents of community life. It forbids support, not protection from interference or destruction.

It is a matter not frequently recalled that President Grant opposed tax exemption of religious property as leading to a violation of the principle of separation of church and state. See President Grant's Seventh Annual Message to Congress, December 7, 1875, in IX Messages and Papers of the Presidents (1897) 4288–4289. Garfield, in a letter accepting the nomination for the presidency said: ". . . it would be unjust to our people, and dangerous to our institutions, to apply

any portion of the revenues of the nation, or of the States, to the support of sectarian schools. The separation of the Church and the State in everything relating to taxation should be absolute." II The Works of James Abram Garfield (ed. by Hinsdale, 1883) 783.

57. Neither do we have here a case of rate-making by which a public utility extends reduced fares to all school children, including patrons of religious schools. Whether or not legislative compulsion upon a private utility to extend such an advantage would be valid, or its extension by a municipally owned system, we are not required to consider. In the former instance, at any rate, and generally if not always in the latter, the vice of using the taxing power to raise funds for the support of religion would not be present.

Needless to add, we have no such case as *Green* v. *Frazier*, 253 U.S. 233, or *Carmichael* v. *Southern Coal Co.*, 301 U.S. 495, which dealt with matters wholly unrelated to the First Amendment, involving only situations where the "public function" issue was determinative.

I have chosen to place my dissent upon the broad ground I think decisive, though strictly speaking the case might be decided on narrower issues. The New Jersey statute might be held invalid on its face for the exclusion of children who attend private, profit-making schools.[58] I cannot assume, as does the majority, that the New Jersey courts would write off this explicit limitation from the statute. Moreover, the resolution by which the statute was applied expressly limits its benefits to students of public and Catholic schools.[59] There is no showing that there are no other private or religious schools in this populous district.[60] I do not think it can be assumed that there were none.[61] But in the view I have taken, it is unnecessary to limit grounding to these matters.

Two great drives are constantly in motion to abridge, in the name of education, the complete division of religion and civil authority which our forefathers made. One is to introduce religious education and observances into the public schools. The other, to obtain public funds for the aid and support of various private religious

---

58. It would seem at least a doubtfully sufficient basis for reasonable classification that some children should be excluded simply because the only school feasible for them to attend, in view of geographic or other situation, might be one conducted in whole *or in part* for profit. Cf. note 5.

59. See note 7 *supra*. The resolution was as follows, according to the school board's minutes read in proof: "The transportation committee recommended the transportation of pupils of Ewing to the Trenton and Pennington High Schools *and Catholic Schools* by way of public carrier as in recent years. On Motion of Mr. Ralph Ryan and Mr. M. French the same was adopted." (Emphasis added.) The New Jersey courts holding that the resolution was within the authority conferred by the state statute is binding on us. *Reinman* v. *Little Rock*, 237 U.S. 171, 176; *Hadacheck* v. *Sebastian*, 239 U.S. 394, 414.

60. The population of Ewing Township, located near the City of Trenton, was 10,146 according to the census of 1940. Sixteenth Census of the United States, Population, Vol. 1, 674.

61. In *Thomas* v. *Collins*, 323 U.S. 516, 530, it was said that the preferred place given in our scheme to the great democratic freedoms secured by the First Amendment gives them "a sanctity and a sanction not permitting dubious intrusions." Cf. Remonstrance, Par. 3, 9. And in other cases it has been held that the usual presumption of constitutionality will not work to save such legislative excursions in this field. *United States* v. *Carolene Products Co.*, 304 U.S. 144, 152, note 4; see Wechsler, Stone and the Constitution (1946). 46 Col. L. Rev. 764, 795 *et seq.*

Apart from the Court's admission that New Jersey's present action approaches the verge of her power, it would seem that a statute, ordinance or resolution which on its face singles out one sect only by name for enjoyment of the same advantages as public schools or their students, should be held discriminatory on its face by virtue of that fact alone, unless it were positively shown that no other sects sought or were available to receive the same advantages.

schools. See Johnson, The Legal Status of Church-State Relationships in the United States (1934); Thayer, Religion in Public Education (1947); Note (1941) 50 Yale L.J. 917. In my opinion both avenues were closed by the Constitution. Neither should be opened by this Court. The matter is not one of quantity, to be measured by the amount of money expended. Now as in Madison's day it is one of principle, to keep separate the separate spheres as the First Amendment drew them; to prevent the first experiment upon our liberties; and to keep the question from becoming entangled in corrosive precedents. We should not be less strict to keep strong and untarnished the one side of the shield of religious freedom than we have been of the other.

The judgment should be reversed.

Index